WRITE LIKE A MAN

Write like a Man

JEWISH MASCULINITY AND THE NEW YORK INTELLECTUALS

——◆——

Ronnie A. Grinberg

PRINCETON UNIVERSITY PRESS

PRINCETON & OXFORD

Published by Princeton University Press
41 William Street, Princeton, New Jersey 08540
99 Banbury Road, Oxford OX2 6JX

press.princeton.edu

Library of Congress Cataloging-in-Publication Data

Names: Grinberg, Ronnie A., author.
Title: Write like a man : Jewish masculinity and the New York intellectuals / Ronnie A. Grinberg.
Other titles: Jewish masculinity and the New York intellectuals
Description: Princeton : Princeton University Press, [2024] | Includes bibliographical references and index.
Identifiers: LCCN 2023024894 (print) | LCCN 2023024895 (ebook) | ISBN 9780691193090 (hardback) | ISBN 9780691255620 (ebook)
Subjects: LCSH: Jews—New York (State)—New York—Intellectual life. | Intellectuals—New York (State)—New York—History—20th century. | Critics—New York (State)—New York—History—20th century. | Authors—New York (State)—New York—History—20th century. | Jews—Cultural assimilation—New York (State)—New York—History—20th century. | New York (N.Y.)—Intellectual life—20th century. | United States—Intellectual life—20th century. | Masculinity—Religious aspects—Judaism. | Machismo in literature, | BISAC: SOCIAL SCIENCE / Jewish Studies | SOCIAL SCIENCE / Gender Studies
Classification: LCC F128.9.J5 G678 2024 (print) | LCC F128.9.J5 (ebook) | DDC 974.7/1004924—dc23/eng/20230523
LC record available at https://lccn.loc.gov/2023024894
LC ebook record available at https://lccn.loc.gov/2023024895

British Library Cataloging-in-Publication Data is available

Editorial: Fred Appel & James Collier
Production Editorial: Ali Parrington
Jacket Design: Katie Osborne
Production: Erin Suydam
Publicity: Kate Hensley
Copyeditor: Dawn Hall
Jacket illustration by Ken Krimstein

This book has been composed in Miller

Printed in the United States of America

10 9 8 7 6 5 4 3 2 1

For Marc, Paloma, and Reuben

In Memory of David Shneer (1972–2020)

CONTENTS

ILLUSTRATIONS

ACKNOWLEDGMENTS

THERE ARE MANY PEOPLE to thank over the years it took for this book to come to fruition. I almost don't know where to begin. First, thank you to my undergraduate advisors at Barnard College—Kathryn Jay and Bruce Lenthall. Both encouraged and supported my dream of becoming a historian while aptly warning of the risks involved in pursuing a doctorate in a dwindling academic market. At Barnard, I wrote a senior thesis under the direction of Bruce Lenthall, which bears some links to what eventually became this book. At Barnard and Columbia University, I was also lucky to take courses with many eminent historians who inspired my love of American history, among them Alan Brinkley, Eric Foner, and Rosalind Rosenberg.

A kernel of what became *Write Like a Man* began as a dissertation at Northwestern University. I wish to thank my stellar committee: Nancy MacLean, Mark Bradley, Tony Michels, Kirsten Fermaglich, and especially my advisor, Michael Sherry, who taught me so much about the craft of history and the art of writing. With unceasing patience and humor, he put up with my many "one last" questions, often outside of his office hours. A model scholar and intellectual, Sherry is also caring and kind, and I am so grateful to have had him as a mentor. I also wish to thank Henry Binford, John Bushnell, and Alexandra Owen for believing in me as a very tentative graduate student. Thank you to Lane Fenrich, the first person I ever TAed for. An amazing and dynamic lecturer, I learned so much watching Lane in action and also found a kindred yoga spirit. The yoga community Lane helped foster in Chicago kept me sane in graduate school. Thank you to all of them, too.

At Northwestern, a cohort of friends and fellow students made graduate school bearable: Demetra Kasimis (a dear friend and holdover from college), Andreana Prichard, Erin-Marie Legacey, Mary Grace Tyrell, David Sellers Smith, Guy Ortolano, Jenny Mann, and Neil Kodesh and Shanee Ellison. Neil and Shanee moved to Madison shortly after I arrived but opened their home to me whenever I needed to escape Evanston. Special thanks to Stephen Mak and Zachary Jacobson. Stephen was my confidant and dear friend from day one. We did graduate school together. Zach, meanwhile, showed up just when I needed him.

I asked Kirsten Fermaglich and Tony Michels to serve as outside members of my dissertation committee when it became clear how much my project had veered into the field of American Jewish history. Both have served as role models ever since. Tony has an encyclopedic knowledge of the intricacies of radicalism and has become a sounding board for all things related to Jewish and intellectual history. Kirsten welcomed me into her home in East Lansing, Michigan when I was still a graduate student so I could take a summer course with her on American Jewish history. Over the course of that summer, as I commuted from Chicago to East Lansing, she became a true friend and rock of support. I had first met Kirsten at a conference at New York University on "The Jewish Feminine Mystique," where I also met Shira Kohn and Rachel Kranson. Both have since become cherished colleagues. Special thank you to Shira, who took me under her wing and helped me navigate the world of Jewish Studies. Shira became a good friend who I still turn to for professional advice, as well as tasty dinners in Manhattan. Through them I met David Weinfeld, now a go to collaborator when it comes to conference panels. It was Weinfeld who first convinced me to attend the Society for U.S. Intellectual History's annual conference, which has since become an academic home of sorts. Two stalwarts of that group, Andrew Hartman and Kevin Schultz, have been especially supportive of my work. I actually first met Kevin at a conference in Israel. Kevin read and commented on my first article and encouraged me to think big. It's a message that has stayed with me. Both Andrew and Kevin graciously shared my book proposal with editors at various presses. After I settled with Princeton, Josh Lambert read my entire manuscript and offered invaluable critiques. I wish to also thank the other anonymous reviewer who provided incisive feedback, which greatly improved this book. Thank you also to Stacie Taranto, who I met at a graduate school conference many years ago, and Brian Rosenwald for more recently helping sharpen some of the arguments in this book as editors of the *Washington Post*, Made By History blog.

After Northwestern, I spent two years as a postdoctoral fellow at the University of Colorado at Boulder. That position was made possible by the inestimable David Shneer (z"l), may his memory be a blessing. There are not enough words to thank David, a brilliant scholar and true mensch, from whom I learned so much about how to be an effective teacher and public-facing intellectual. I know I am just one of the many people David touched over the course of his life. I am grateful to have known him and called him a friend. Thank you also to the extraordinary community at CU's Jewish Studies Program during these years, especially Caryn Aviv, Jamie Polliard, Gregg Drinkwater, and Nick Underwood.

When I moved to Oklahoma, initially for my partner's job, I threw a fit. Little did I know how good Oklahoma would be to me and my own career. A special thank you to Noam Stillman, director emeritus of the Schusterman Center for Judaic and Israel Studies, and Alan Levenson, its current director. Alan saw me give a talk at the Association for Jewish Studies (AJS) conference and arranged for me to give a talk at the Schusterman Center's monthly JuSt Lunch Brown Bag Series. Rob Griswold, then chair of the History Department, attended the talk and thereafter arranged a lectureship for me in the department. Academia is a field that requires a lot of luck; I was very lucky to land in a place where so many people came together to support me.

At the University of Oklahoma I have found a collegial community of scholars in the History Department and beyond. Special thanks to James Hart, our former chair, who always believed that I could write this book, and our current chair, Elyssa Faison, who steadfastly helped me navigate these last few years on the tenure clock, which included a global pandemic. Thank you to the Schusterman Center for Judaic and Israel Studies, especially to Alan Levenson, who has been a fierce advocate and mentor since I got here, and to Tryce Hyman, who holds our program together. Thank you to Committee G, especially Jennifer Davis, who served as my department mentor and has offered much wise advice over the years. Thanks to Christa Seedorf, Janie Adkins, and Danni McCuthchen for all you do. When I first came to OU, I found a supportive writing group in Erica Robb Larkins, Kim Marshall, Dan Emery, Ellen Rubenstein, Sarah Ellis, and Andreana Prichard. Andreana was a good friend from graduate school who welcomed my husband and I to this strange new land in Oklahoma. Thanks, also, to Raphael Folsom, who led a grant-writing workshop for several of us in that group, which generated what turned into a strong book proposal and sharpened my arguments. I'm also grateful for the many good friends I have made at OU: Jennifer Holland, Kathryn Schumaker, Rhona Seidelman, Adam Malka, Rachel Shelden, Jane Wickersham, Sarah Hines, Elyse Singer, and Lauren Duval. I'd also like to thank Sarah Griswold for her steadfast friendship and counsel throughout these years.

Jennifer Holland, Katy Schumaker, Sarah Griswold, and Jennifer Davis provided crucial feedback and editing as I neared completion of the manuscript. Katy read multiple chapters, even while far away in Australia. Jennifer Davis stepped in with key advice on a final chapter and again during the copyediting stage. She and Jennifer Holland read chapters out loud with me to help catch mistakes, a technique we use as editors at the *Journal of Women's History*. Sarah Griswold and Lauren Duval read and edited *multiple* chapters using this technique. I am beyond grateful to them and look forward to returning the favor. Finally, thank you to David Chappell. When I was in grad school, I read and admired David's work, never imagining I would one day call him a colleague and friend. David introduced me to numerous editors, including Fred Appel, at Princeton. Moreover, he read *every* page of this manuscript. He could see what I was trying to say and argue even when the prose was clunky, and I had lost faith in my own abilities to tell the story. A consummate editor with deep knowledge of American intellectual history, David always believed in this project and helped me reach the finish line.

Several institutions, libraries, and archives also deserve special thanks. Through the American Association for Jewish Studies Women's Caucus and its Paula Hyman Mentorship Program, I met Pamela Nadell, who became a mentor in Jewish Studies. Over the years, she has read and commented on draft articles, book proposals, grants, and even my dissertation. Thank you also to Lila Corwin Berman and Steve Weitzman for spearheading an American Academy for Jewish Research Early Career Faculty Workshop. Fellowships from Northwestern University, the Jacob Rader Marcus Center of the American Jewish Archives, the University of Oklahoma, and the Harry Ransom Center at the University of Texas at Austin made archival research possible. Archivists at the Harry Ransom Center and the Columbia University Rare Books and Manuscript Library merit special thanks. Thank you also to Elisheva Urbas, editor extraordinaire, who helped get me past the mental hurdles to complete this book. Thank you to Laura Clark, who did a wonderful job cleaning up the footnotes and to Sam Gainsburg for securing permissions for photos.

Some of my closest and dearest friends allowed me to crash on their couches in New York City and other locales in the early years of this project: Jared Shepard, Sarah Holtze Treadway, Noa Beck, Anna Haykin, and Mirka Feinstein. Lily Pollans and Thacher Tiffany deserve a special thank you, continuing to provide a home away from home when I'm on the East Coast. I also want to thank Faith, Madison, and Mercedes for taking such wonderful care of my children while I worked on this book. With no family in Oklahoma, we had to create our own village to raise our children. Faith, our first nanny, made going back to work seamless. From the moment my daughter smiled big and essentially picked Faith, I knew she was in capable and loving hands. That Faith went on to pursue her own career fills me with joy. Through Faith, we eventually met Mercedes. Mercy spent six wonderful years with our family, including moving with us to Puebla, Mexico with her husband (and assistant "manny") Aaron. Mercy helped raise both my children; her warmth is forever etched in both of them. She is better than Mary Poppins, and there are not enough words to describe how much she means to our family.

Over the course of writing this book, I was able to interview several individuals tied to the New York intellectuals. Midge Decter spoke to me at length in 2011. I am so appreciative that she shared her experiences and answered my probing questions. Thank you to Susan Ferber of Oxford University Press, who encouraged me to reach out to historian David A. Bell. David has graciously shared memories of his parents, read and commented on drafts of the manuscript, as well as kindly contributed family photographs for this book. I was honored when he recommended I appear on a panel with him on the New York intellectuals at the Center for Jewish History, alongside the filmmaker Joseph Dorman, director of *Arguing the World* (2000), a terrific documentary about this group of intellectuals and a film I have long admired. David also encouraged me to reach out to his cousin, historian Michael Kazin. I had spoken with Michael about his father at an AHA meeting, and he later read and commented on my chapter on Howe and *Dissent*, as well as the epilogue. I still pinch myself when I think about having the support of these two renowned historians. Thank you to Eric Alterman, who read and commented on my Norman Podhoretz chapter and to Jo-Ann Mort who spoke to me at length about writing for *Dissent* and her friendship with Irving Howe. Thank you to Joanne Barkan, who also shared her memories of Howe and *Dissent* when we met in person and over many email conversations. Barkan's incisive comments and editing very much strengthened that chapter. Thank you to Maxine Phillips, who answered questions about Howe over email. Finally, thank you to Judith and Michael Walzer. Here is where I pinch myself once again. Michael and Judy invited me into their home and graciously shared memories of Howe and *Dissent*. They also read and commented on parts of the manuscript. All mistakes are my own. Undoubtedly, however, this network enriched my book immeasurably.

It was my editor at Princeton University Press, Fred Appel, who encouraged me to reach out to Michael Walzer. Since reading the proposal for this book, Fred has been a steadfast supporter of this project. I could not ask for a more kind, thoughtful, and experienced editor. We have talked about this project over many drinks and meals, and I am so thankful he has been in my corner, always offering sound advice and encouragement. The whole team at PUP has also been terrific. Special thanks to editorial associate James Collier and managing editor Ali Parrington, who so patiently worked with me and shepherded the book through production. As I write this, the PUP design team is working on what I know will be an amazing cover. The artist Ken Krimstein kindly agreed to design a cover image for my book. I've long admired his work and I am ecstatic he took on this project. The stunning image he created for the cover is nothing short of perfect.

Finally, thank you to my family. My brother Itai and sister Anat warrant special thanks. Both of you inspire me. I know I'm not always easy. Thank you for putting up with me and for supporting me. More practically, thank you for entertaining my children as I raced to the finish line to complete this book. That goes to their spouses, too, Eran and Jessamyn. A special thank you to my sister-in-law, Jessamyn, who edited a chapter at the eleventh hour. Thank you to my in-laws Carolyn and Michael Levine, who have long championed my work, and to Eliana and Dina. Big *toda* to my Israeli family. Thank you also to my stepdad, Yosi, who in his zen-like way has supported me and my family, and who has brought so much joy and happiness to my mom in the second half of her life. I love our big, blended family. Thank you also to Eyal, Jen, Hye-Jeong, Joe, and Maya. Most of all, thank you to my ima—my mom, Rivka. No words can do justice to all she has done for me during the many years it took to complete this book. I am so grateful for her unconditional love, her empathy, her faith in my abilities, and her joy at being a savta. To Paloma and Reuben: Paloma has lived with this book her entire life and is, without a doubt, my biggest cheerleader. At four years old she was drawing pictures of "intellectuals" and in the last couple years she has left so many notes in my office saying, "you can do it" and "I love you, ima." Reuben was supposed to be child number three, the book being child number two. But when age started to creep up on me, priorities shifted. Reuben entered the world with a bang at the height of the Covid pandemic. With his red hair, infectious smile, and hilarious sense of humor, he completed our family. Finally, to Marc, my partner in life: this book would not have been possible without your love, unceasing support, and yes, your wicked sense of humor. You are my greatest advocate—always reminding me that the tortoise wins the race. There is not a day that goes by that I don't feel so lucky to have found you. This book is for you.

Introduction

"UNLESS A MAN, in the intellectual community, was bent on sexual conquest he was never interested in women," Diana Trilling recalled of the New York intellectuals, a renowned group of writers and critics at midcentury. "He wanted to be with the men. They always wanted to huddle in a corner to talk. Their shop talk did not include women, even the women whom they had regard for professionally." Trilling was one of the few women in this group. She entered their ranks when she married literary critic Lionel Trilling. Others echoed her comments. Jason Epstein, for example, who cofounded the *New York Review of Books* (*NYRB*) in 1963, said: "With women in that crowd, the first thing you thought about was whether they were good-looking and if you could sleep with them. But if a woman could write like a man, that was enough. You wanted a piece, a piece of writing—you'd forget everything else for a good piece." Epstein, of course, left a certain ambiguity as to whether he meant a piece of writing or a piece of ass. But his remarks, along with Trilling's, underscore the importance of virility in this testosterone-driven literary circle. What did masculinity mean to these intellectuals? Epstein's directive to "write like a man" indicated that the act of writing itself constituted a form of masculine performance. But what did "writing like a man" entail?[1]

Literary critic Irving Howe, another member of the group, hinted at an answer in 1968 when he chronicled its shared history. Writing in *Commentary*, Howe used pugilistic terms to describe the group. Its members saw "intellectual life as a form of combat," he said. They developed that attitude when they were anti-Stalinist radicals in the 1930s. Debates within the group constituted a "*tournament*, the writer as gymnast with one eye on other rings, or as a skilled infighter juggling knives of dialectic." These intellectuals embodied a "style of brilliance," Howe said, that at its best "reflected a certain view of the intellectual life: free-lance dash, peacock strut, daring hypothesis, knockabout synthesis." In summarizing what bound the group together, Howe wrote:

> They appear to have a common history, prolonged now for more than thirty years; a common political outlook, even if marked by ceaseless internecine quarrels; a common style of thought and perhaps composition; a common focus on intellectual interests; and once you get past politeness—which becomes, these days, easier and easier—a common ethnic origin. They are, or until recently have been, anti-Communists; they are, or until some time ago were, radicals; they have a fondness for ideological speculation; they write literary criticism with a strong social emphasis; they revel in polemic; they strive self-consciously to be "brilliant"; and by birth or osmosis they are Jews.[2]

Howe was not alone in juxtaposing Jewishness and masculinity when describing these writers and critics. A year earlier, in his 1967 memoir *Making It*, Norman Podhoretz characterized them as a "Jewish family."[3] He, too, emphasized their pugilism. "The family's prose had verve, vitality, wit, texture, and above all brilliance," he wrote. "Here the physical analogy would be with an all-round athlete." There was also a Jewish analogy, to "Talmudic scholars," which is to say to men who "not only regard books as holy objects but, haunted by what was perhaps the most ferociously tyrannical tradition of scholarship the world has ever seen, they seem to believe that one must have mastered everything before one is entitled to the temerity of saying anything on paper."[4] Women were not traditionally allowed to study Talmud.[5] Podhoretz suggested that the New York intellectuals were the modern descendants of this masculine tradition. But they were also virile in the way that athletes were in American culture.

Daniel Bell, another prominent New York intellectual, described them as one of the few intelligentsias ever in the United States. A term of Russian origin, intelligentsia initially "was meant to apply to a generation," Bell said, "who were becoming critical of society—and it received its definitive stamp in the novel of [Ivan] Turgenev, *Fathers and Sons*" (1862). Thereafter, intelligentsia came to mean a "collectivity" of intellectuals, a "curia" of thinkers who "come from some common milieu and seek common meanings." Though Bell did not say so explicitly, he imagined these collectivities as a male space. Curia comes from the Latin word *coviria*, meaning "a gathering of men." And when he spoke in specifics he referred to the New York Jewish intellectuals as men: "the background of all these men was largely immigrant, their parents themselves working-class or petty bourgeoisie," he wrote. Like Howe and Podhoretz, Bell highlighted how they combined "political radicalism and cultural modernism," and the ways in which "ideas were passionately and fiercely debated."[6]

Speaking at Hebrew Union College in 1976, Bell lamented that little had been written on the New York intellectuals. "There are almost no memoirs, no biographical accounts, no reflections which try to explain their lives."[7] Bell's observation now seems quaint. In the 1980s and '90s a slew of memoirs by members of the group appeared in print.[8] Countless scholarly monographs followed.[9] Yet despite the many books published on the New York intellectuals, few scholars have focused on either gender or Jewishness and the ways in which they intersected in the lives and careers of these figures.[10]

Write Like a Man argues that masculinity and Jewishness were linked in the minds of the New York intellectuals. Men and women, Jews and non-Jews in the group all came to espouse a secular Jewish machismo. This evolved into an ideology of secular Jewish masculinity. Those who developed and embraced this ideology prized verbal combativeness, polemical aggression, and an unflinching style of argumentation. Hard-hitting and impassioned arguments, especially in print, undergirded their understanding of a new kind of masculinity.

The ideology of secular Jewish masculinity that they developed was not all-encompassing. I use the term "ideology," in part, to distinguish from other constructions of Jewish masculinity in twentieth-century America.[11] By ideology, I mean the often unstated, even unconscious assumptions, habits, and maxims that inform how people understand and experience the world.[12] Yet ideologies by nature mean different things to differently situated people. The New York intellectuals wrestled over the meaning and consequences of their newly created secular Jewish masculinity, which contributed to political divisions among them. The term "ideology" is also apt because their new construction of secular Jewish masculinity was deeply informed by other prominent ideologies in the twentieth century, especially Marxism and Freudianism, and it in turn helped shape political ideologies like Cold War liberalism and neoconservatism.

The New York intellectuals' conception and performance of secular Jewish masculinity was thus hardly binary. It was a deeply anxious project of both self-definition and political significance. Could Jews "make it," as Norman Podhoretz put it, if they didn't prove that they were "real" men? But what did being a "real" man entail? For Podhoretz, and a few others, that question led to neoconservatism, a political persuasion or ideology that came to signify a muscular and preemptive approach to foreign affairs.[13] In domestic life, it often involved an embrace of "family values," a catchall phrase for sexual morality in the culture wars of the late twentieth century.[14] Most New York intellectuals rejected the politics of neoconservatism, remaining tied to liberalism, like most American Jews.[15] Yet they were still just as engaged in a project of defining and proving Jewish masculinity.

Write Like a Man shows how the tether of masculinity, so crucial to the lives and works of the New York intellectuals, shaped broader political, intellectual, and cultural debates in American life in the last quarter of the twentieth and early twenty-first centuries.[16] In the postwar years, these intellectuals became well-known. They were read by readers and writers from coast to coast.[17] Their combative, masculinized style and politicized work became fashionable. Hollywood even took note, referring to them or creating characters based on them on screen.[18] Accordingly, their intellectual culture, with its redefinitions of what it meant to be a man, demands special attention. As intellectuals, they wrestled with modern alienation. As Americans, they came of age with the triumphalism of "the American Century." As Ashkenazi Jews, they had fresh, intimate experience with the specter of their own annihilation. Their struggles in fact illuminate modern American intellectual life more broadly.

———

To the nineteenth century, writing was feminine—though never simplistically so. Ladies were the main audience of literature, as Jane Austen, the Brontës, Elizabeth Barrett Browning, Harriet Beecher Stowe, Emily Dickinson, George Eliot, and Edith Wharton were recognized as masters of the verse and prose—though George Eliot was well advised to change her name from Mary Anne Evans, and to have an affair with an influential man. Moreover, male writers obviously had great authority and made unimpeachable contributions to what women read. That said, women also took over the teaching profession and shaped everybody's sense of literature and, to an extent, controlled their very access to it. Half a century ago, Ann Douglas argued that writers, like ministers, painters, and professional actors, were considered "sissies" in the golden age of the novel. If not always implicitly homosexual, they were sexual outlaws, like the pioneering New Yorker Walt Whitman.[19] The Manhattanite Teddy Roosevelt was not the first to try to reclaim writing—and high culture in general—as masculine.[20] But, according to Douglas, nobody succeeded in remasculinizing literary culture until Hemingway's generation. That "lost" generation's urban culture was shaped not only by Black migrants moving north from the rural South but also post–Civil War immigrants from Eastern and Southern Europe.[21] That a distinctly "Jewish intelligentsia" contributed to this process of masculinization is significant, especially given stereotypes that had long cast Jews as unmanly.[22]

The Jewish New York intellectuals were one of only a handful of "intelligentsias" in the United States. According to Bell, the first distinct intelligentsia to emerge on this side of the Atlantic were the Greenwich Village intellectuals of the 1910s.[23] Figures like Walter Lippmann, Van Wyck Brooks, John Reed, Waldo Frank, Sinclair Lewis, and Edmund Wilson were united by "the protest against the genteel tradition, the domination of America by the small town, and the crabbed respectability which the small town enforced." The second intelligentsia was the "lost generation" of the Jazz Age. Disenchanted with American life in the wake of World War I, these "literary expatriates" looked abroad to Paris, and included "the Hemingways and Fitzgeralds." Third were the Southern Agrarians that gathered at Vanderbilt University in the 1920s and '30s. They included Allen Tate, Robert Penn Warren, and John Crowe Ransom. "What they were defending," Bell wrote, "was an agrarian way of life, the rhythms of a gentler time and quieter place—and with it a model of aristocratic learning which would take the word as the text and ignore the mundane biographical [and] sociological."[24]

The New York intellectuals differed from these other American intelligentsias in several ways, most significantly, because of their Jewishness. "They had no *yichus*," a Yiddish word meaning "eminent pedigree," Bell said. They did not "flee" the United States but rather "inherited the cultural establishment of America in ways that they, and certainly their fathers," poor Jews who had fled the shtetls of the Pale of Settlement for the ghettos of the Lower East Side, Brooklyn, and the Bronx, "could never have dreamed of."[25]

In the years after World War I, New York started becoming the Western world's cultural capital, rivaled only by Paris. Before the passage of immigration restriction, the city's population grew on average over a million a decade from the 1890s through the 1920s. New York Jews were heirs to the unique new polyglot melting pot that had been celebrated in the prewar years, along with Vaudeville and early motion pictures. In the Roaring Twenties—the Jazz Age—New York had the unprecedented reach of radio and the uncontrollable festivity of the speakeasy belt, along with the "uptown" clubs and theaters where the Harlem Renaissance was flourishing.[26] In the 1930s came a numerically small wave of refugees that included many famous writers, scientists, and orchestra conductors. They filled the city with highbrow culture, even though the anti-immigration laws of 1921 and 1924 allowed only the tiniest trickle from those parts of Europe (the Pale of Settlement) to enter. The New York intellectuals had grown up in that city in those years.[27] It was their turf.

The New York intellectuals' understanding of masculinity emerged among this nascent group of thinkers in the 1920s and 1930s in immigrant enclaves in New York City. These sons of immigrants sought to forge their own vision of masculinity that contrasted with their working-class, immigrant-born fathers, some of whom were unlearned, who struggled to earn a living—and were, in their own sons' eyes, emasculated. Their sons yearned to be American men. But these were also years when American nativist tendencies climaxed. After immigration halted with the outbreak of war in Europe in 1914, nativists succeeded in urging Congress to prevent the resumption of immigration (especially from Asia, Southern Europe, and heavily Jewish parts of Eastern Europe), in two radical National Origins Acts (1921 and 1924).[28] In reaction to mass immigration, Anglo-American ideals of masculinity had grown more extreme and discriminatory around the turn of the twentieth century, emphasizing physical strength, honor, individualism, and athleticism (which professionalized and became part of college culture in those years) that nonwhite non-Protestants allegedly lacked. Excluded from this construction, Jewish masculinity evolved alongside mainstream American gender ideals.[29]

The New York intellectuals' ideology of secular Jewish masculinity was not assimilationist, however—at least not wholly. In the wider culture in those years, intellectual prowess was often seen as a sign of effeminacy—the scholar was the opposite of the virile male athlete. But it also was not merely bound by traditional Jewish gender ideals as embodied in the Talmudic scholar.[30] Rather, secular American Jewish masculinity, as the New York intellectuals came to define it, was an amalgam of Jewish and Anglo-American ideals that formed something new: the combative secular intellectual.

After World War II, the New York intellectuals became some of the most renowned critics and writers in the country—bringing their fractious masculinity with them. "The real contribution of the New York writers," Howe said, "was toward creating a new, and for this country almost exotic, style of work."[31] In the postwar years, they found "respected places in universities, publishing houses, and magazines" and became "some of the brightest stars in American culture itself," Bell wrote.[32] *Write Like a Man*, then, is in part a story of how this important construction of Jewish masculinity helped propel American Jews from outsiders to insiders in postwar America.[33]

Some scholars of American Jewish history have described the fifteen years following World War II as a golden era for American Jews, a period marked by prosperity, consensus, and affluence. In these years Jews became "insiders" in American society in religious, ethnic, political, and socioeconomic terms.[34] The defeat of Nazism discredited scientific racism and its corollary, prevalent on both sides of the Atlantic, that Jews constituted an inferior and unassimilable "race."[35] In the postwar years, discriminatory barriers against Jews crumbled significantly, and many Jews moved from the working to the middling classes, joining other white ethnic groups in the suburbs.[36] Meanwhile, during World War II a tri-faith America replaced an older view that America was an Anglo-Saxon Protestant nation. Thereafter a Judeo-Christian tradition was held up as a bulwark against godless Communism.[37] Second-generation American Jews by and large abandoned the leftist-radicalism of the immigrant generation and embraced the Cold War liberal consensus, a liberalism that the New York intellectuals worked hard to define.[38] Thus the New York intellectuals in many ways exemplified this golden age. By the 1960s they were some of the best-known and most respected critics and writers in the country.[39]

But on the terrain of gender, the process of acculturation was arduous and complex, belying notions of easy accommodation.[40] The New York intellectuals clashed over the meaning of Jewish masculinity in the postwar years. Should intellectuals remain critics of society—outsiders when it came to both the intellectual vocation and masculinity? If not, what did assimilation into norms of American masculinity entail? How did the early years of the Cold War, which saw heightened fears over political and sexual subversion, shape how the New York intellectuals understood Jewish masculinity?[41] In the 1960s and '70s, when a younger generation of radicals rejected the New York intellectuals' model of intellectual masculinity, how did figures in the group respond? Second-wave feminists, whose leaders and theorists were also disproportionately secular Jews, challenged the ways in which the New York intellectuals had engendered the intellectual vocation masculine.[42] What did Jewish masculinity look like in the wake of feminist critiques? How did Jewish masculinity shape their political trajectories? *Write Like a Man* seeks to answer these questions, tracing how the New York intellectuals' ideology of secular Jewish masculinity evolved from the 1920s and '30s through the 1970s, how it interacted with and responded to other constructions of masculinity—Jewish and normative—in the second half of the twentieth century, and how it affected American politics more broadly.

In 1977 Woody Allen satirized the fame of the New York intellectuals in his Academy Award-winning film *Annie Hall*. The film's protagonist, Alvy Singer, played by Allen, joked that he heard the magazines "*Commentary* and *Dissent* had merged to form '*Dysentery*.'" Allen's quip spoke to the prominence of the New York intellectuals and to the many magazines they founded in the postwar years, as well as to "their ceaseless internecine quarrels," as Howe put it.[43] But Allen's focus on *Commentary* and *Dissent* was acute. The two journals staked out two ends of a spectrum of secular Jewish masculinity in postwar America. Norman Podhoretz, the editor of *Commentary* between 1960 and 1995, forged what came to be known as neoconservatism—a rightward politics centered on a greater assertiveness in anti-Soviet and pro-Israel policies and an embrace of "family values." Howe, the longtime editor of *Dissent*, a magazine he founded with Lewis Coser in 1954, remained tied to a scholarly ideal of Jewish masculinity that emphasized independence and the intellectual as vigilant outsider and critic of society.

Historians, literary critics, and journalists alike have long been drawn to these figures because they left such a vivid mark on American intellectual life. Yet aside from discussing their immigrant roots, they have largely ignored the Jewishness of these intellectuals. This is in part because Howe himself de-emphasized it in his 1968 article: "It was precisely the idea of discarding the past, breaking away from families, traditions, and memories which excited intellectuals," he wrote.[44] Even scholars of American Jewish history, as historian Tony Michels has observed, "have paid minimal attention to these celebrated figures, despite the fact that most were Jews either by birth, or as Howe once wrote, by 'osmosis.'"[45] In reality, the New York intellectuals did not evade their Jewish identities, even when they were young. Rather, they refashioned the meaning of American Jewishness through their definition and embodiment of a secular masculine ideal.

Gender has also been conspicuously absent from most studies of the New York intellectuals despite the almost axiomatic recognition that this was a decidedly male and sexist milieu. Alexander Bloom's comprehensive history of the group, revealingly titled *Prodigal Sons: The New York Intellectuals and Their World*, is indicative. Bloom's title acknowledges the overwhelming maleness of this group while the book itself ignores gender almost completely.[46] Bloom's book was published in 1986, but most books on the New York intellectuals have followed suit. Those scholars who do examine the ways gender operated among the New York intellectuals tend to focus on the group's female members.[47] *Write Like a Man* looks at masculinity as a lens to understand both its male and female members, as well as mid-century American intellectual life more broadly. The New York intellectuals assessed each other, and indeed everyone, through their standard of secular Jewish masculine toughness.[48]

"New York intellectual" was an imagined community, not an affixed category. One scholar titled a book, *The Other Jewish New York Intellectuals*, to make the fair point that there were numerous important Jewish thinkers not considered part of this group.[49] Lucy S. Dawidowicz is a case in point. "Like the immigrant Jewish men of her generation who came of age in the politically intense 1930s, Dawidowicz relished a political argument, was verbally adroit, and did not shy away from a strongly worded rebuff," historian Nancy Sinkoff writes. She identified as a neoconservative and was closely tied to *Commentary* in the 1970s and '80s. But she was not considered a New York intellectual. Dawidowicz differed from them, Sinkoff argues, in that she associated with Jewish causes and organizations and wrote explicitly about Jewish issues, most notably the Holocaust. This is also why American Jewish historians have shied away from the New York intellectuals. They have tended to "[neglect] or [ignore] Jews who felt alienated, indifferent, or ambivalent towards Jewishness or were simply uninvolved in Jewish communal life," as Michels has pointed out. *Write Like a Man* employs what the historian David Hollinger has called a "dispersionist" approach to examining American Jewish history, meaning paying attention "to the role in history of persons of Jewish ancestry regardless of their degree of affiliation with communal Jewry." As to why Dawidowicz was not considered a New York intellectual, Sinkoff argues that she differed from them "by her choice to become deeply rooted in the culture and history of Eastern European Jewry and to defend tirelessly its particularism" in contrast to the New York intellectuals' "cosmopolitanism" and "universalism." But the sexist underpinnings of this milieu also had something to do with it.[50]

So how did one become a New York intellectual? What made someone be considered part of this group? Bell tallied "some fifty within the inner group" and perhaps "several hundred others" on the periphery. Not all were Jewish, nor did all reside in New York. Saul Bellow, for example, lived in Chicago. Leslie Fiedler taught at the University of Montana. "These New

York Jewish intellectuals came together as a self-conscious group, knowing each other, writing primarily for each other, discussing ideas they held in common, differing widely and sometimes savagely, and yet having that sense of kinship which made each of them aware that they were part of a distinctive sociohistorical phenomenon," Bell wrote.[51]

Thus, writing for their magazines was an indisputable qualification. Before they were known as the New York intellectuals—a term Howe coined in his essay—they were referred to as the *Partisan Review* group, or sometimes as the "boys" by its scant women members, known as the "*PR* girls."[52] The genesis of the group is often dated to the relaunching of *Partisan Review* in 1937 by William Phillips and Philip Rahv as independent from the Communist Party's John Reed Club.[53] *Partisan Review*'s anti-Stalinism, combined with its embrace of modernism, provided a "political-literary position," Podhoretz wrote, that "developed an intellectual style which for a long while was almost unique to *Partisan Review*, and which eventually came of its own force to be identified in the eyes of many with the quality of intellectuality itself."[54]

But the group's roots ran deeper. In the 1920s, its oldest members wrote for the *Menorah Journal* when Elliot E. Cohen served as its managing editor between 1925 and 1931. Cohen was a demanding and combative editor. "To write a piece for Cohen was an ordeal which not everyone was willing to suffer," Podhoretz said. "But it was also, and especially for novices, an education in the impossibly difficult art of effective exposition." Under Cohen's leadership, the *Menorah Journal* created the first space where this ideology of secular Jewish masculinity flourished.[55]

Cohen would become the inaugural editor of *Commentary*, a magazine funded by the American Jewish Committee in 1945. Born with the dawn of the Cold War, *Commentary* sought to demonstrate the Americanness and anti-communist credentials of American Jewry.[56] That the New York intellectuals played a central role in delineating Cold War liberalism is well-known.[57] Less recognized is that by defining anti-communist liberalism in more masculine terms, the New York intellectuals helped render American Jews, a group long associated with left-wing radicalism, as not only properly anti-communist but properly masculine in Cold War America. Other magazines founded by members of the group included Dwight Macdonald's short-lived journal *politics*, published between 1944 and 1949; *Encounter*, founded by the Congress for Cultural Freedom (CCF) in 1952 and initially edited by Irving Kristol and the British poet Stephen Spender; the *New York Review of Books*, founded by Jason Epstein, Barbara Epstein, and Robert Silvers in 1963; and the *Public Interest*, a journal that came to be closely associated with neoconservatism after its founding in 1965 by Irving Kristol and Daniel Bell, later also edited by Nathan Glazer.[58] To be a New York intellectual one had to write for these magazines. But there were numerous intellectuals who wrote for these journals. There was more to it.

The second major characteristic was anti-communism. In the 1930s, the anti-Stalinism of the nascent New York intellectuals made them outsiders. As young radicals they dissented from the Popular Front (1935–39), when communists around the world—following the dictates of the Communist International (Comintern) in Moscow—worked with other leftists and liberals to defeat fascism.[59] This minority position within the decade's radicalism was central to their ideology of secular Jewish masculinity, as we will see in chapter 1. "The radicalism of the 1930s gave the New York intellectuals their distinctive style: a flair for polemic, a taste for grand generalization, an impatience with what they regarded (often parochially) as parochial scholarship," Howe wrote. Though many had abandoned radicalism in the postwar years, "brief and superficial as their engagement with Marxism may have been, it gave [these] intellectuals the advantage of dialectic." According to Podhoretz, the "combination of a commitment to left-wing anti-Stalinism and a commitment to avant-gardism became the distinguishing family trait."[60]

Finally, Jewishness. There were non-Jews in the group. "Nevertheless, the term 'Jewish' can be allowed to stand by clear majority rule and by various peculiarities of temper," Podhoretz wrote.[61] Bell referred to them as the "New York Jewish Intelligentsia," while Howe quipped that non-Jewish members became Jews by "osmosis." Dwight Macdonald seemed to corroborate this view. "I have spent my whole adult life in radical-intellectual circles," he told an interviewer, and "have long proclaimed myself an 'Honorary Jew.'"[62] In 1950 one writer joked in *Commentary* that to be accepted in the world of letters one had to adopt "the wise style of the Jewish intellectual," which included using "Jewish inflections and expressions" like saying "'*nu*?' instead of '*so*?'"[63]

Podhoretz and Bell divided these intellectuals into three generations, more or less. Podhoretz referred to the oldest among them as the "Founding Fathers." They were born around 1905 and included *Partisan Review* editors Philip Rahv and William Phillips, literary critics Lionel Trilling and Lionel Abel, art critics Meyer Schapiro, Harold Rosenberg, and Clement Greenberg, and critics Sidney Hook, Paul Goodman, Fred Dupee, and Dwight Macdonald. Its second generation was made up of "Mary McCarthy (who possibly even belongs among the first)," Podhoretz wrote,

"Delmore Schwartz, William Barrett, Isaac Rosenfeld, Richard Chase, and Alfred Kazin." They were joined by "those members of the second generation who came to visibility a little later, toward the end of the war and right after it": Leslie Fiedler, Elizabeth Hardwick, Daniel Bell, James Baldwin, David Bazelon, Robert Warshow, Nathan Glazer, and Irving Howe. Many of them had been Trotskyists. But they were more "Freudian" than Marxist. "It was truly a second generation in that the Founding Fathers had exerted a formative influence upon its members, helping to shape their ideas, their tastes, their prose, and in general their conception of the nature of true intellectuality and of the intellectual life itself," Podhoretz wrote. Podhoretz was part of its third and last generation. He also named Susan Sontag as one of its youngest members.[64]

Bell sketched out a genealogy, a family tree of sorts, complete with a cladogram (see box 1). "The Elders" came of age in the 1920s and '30s. They included Elliot Cohen, Sidney Hook, Philip Rahv, Lionel Trilling, Meyer Schapiro, William Phillips, Hannah Arendt, and Diana Trilling. Their "younger brothers," came of age a little later "in the mid to late 1930s": Alfred Kazin, Richard Hofstadter, Saul Bellow, Delmore Schwartz, Bernard Malamud, Harold Rosenberg, Clement Greenberg, Lionel Abel, Paul Goodman, and Isaac Rosenfeld. Its second generation emerged in the late 1930s and early 1940s and included Daniel Bell, Irving Howe, Leslie Fiedler, Robert Warshow, Gertrude Himmelfarb, Irving Kristol, Melvin Lasky, Nathan Glazer, Seymour Martin Lipset, and David Bazelon. Their "younger brothers" joined in the late 1940s and early 1950s and included Norman Podhoretz, Steven Marcus, Robert Brustein, Midge Decter, Jason Epstein, Robert Silvers, Susan Sontag, Theodore Solotaroff, Norman Mailer, and Philip Roth. Bell also listed "gentile cousins," figures like Fred Dupee, Dwight Macdonald, Mary McCarthy, Elizabeth Hardwick, William Barrett, and C. Wright Mills, and "European relatives," like Nicola Chiaramonte.[65]

Bell and Podhoretz generally agreed about who were members of the group, despite minor discrepancies. Significantly, both chose male categories to describe them: "founding fathers" and "younger brothers." Both named only a of handful women. Podhoretz mentioned Mary McCarthy, Elizabeth Hardwick, Hannah Arendt, and Susan Sontag. Bell added Diana Trilling, Gertrude Himmelfarb, and Midge Decter. Diana Trilling was offended that Podhoretz did not mention her as part of the "family" in *Making It*. "For reasons I do not know and can only surmise," she told Norman Mailer, "he never mentions me as a member. The several times

Box 1. *The New York Jewish Intellectuals* c. 1935–c. 1965

The Elders: coming of age in the late 1920s and early 1930s

Elliot Cohen	Lionel Trilling	Hannah Arendt*
Sidney Hook	Meyer Schapiro	Diana Trilling
Philip Rahv	William Phillips	
Gentile Cousins:	Max Eastman	Fred Dupee
	Edmund Wilson	Dwight Macdonald
	Reinhold Niebuhr	James T. Farrell
The "Other Synagogue":	Michael Gold	Joseph Freeman

Magazines: *Menorah Journal, The New Masses, Partisan Review*

The Younger Brothers: coming of age in the mid and late 1930s

Alfred Kazin	Harold Rosenberg	
Richard Hofstadter	Clement Greenberg	
Saul Bellow**	Lionel Abel	
Delmore Schwartz	Paul Goodman	
Bernard Malamud	Isaac Rosenfeld	
European Relatives:	Nicola Chiaramonte	George Lichtheim
Gentile Cousins:	Mary McCarthy	William Barrett
	Elizabeth Hardwick	Richard Chase
	James Baldwin	Ralph Ellison
	Arthur Schlesinger Jr.	

Magazines: *The Nation, The New Republic, Partisan Review, Commentary, Politics*

The Second Generation: coming of age in the late 1930s and early 1940s

Daniel Bell	Irving Kristol	
Irving Howe	Melvin Lasky	
Leslie Fiedler**	Nathan Glazer	
Robert Warshow	S. M. Lipset**	
Gertrude Himmelfarb	David Bazelon	
Gentile Cousins:	Murray Kempton	C. Wright Mills

Magazines: *Commentary, Partisan Review, Encounter, ** The New Leader, Dissent, The Public Interest*

Continued on next page

Box 1. (*continued*)

The Younger Brothers: coming of age in the late 1940s and early 1950s

Norman Podhoretz	Robert Silvers
Steven Marcus	Susan Sontag
Robert Brustein	Theodore Solotaroff
Midge Decter	Norman Mailer
Jason Epstein	Philip Roth
Gentile Cousins:	Michael Harrington "The Paris Review"†

Magazines: *Commentary, Partisan Review, New York Review of Books*

The European Intelligentsia

Raymond Aron	David Rousset
Arthur Koestler	Jean-Paul Sartre
Ignazio Silone	Albert Camus
George Orwell	Simone de Beauvoir
Manes Sperber	

The English Intelligentsia

Isaiah Berlin	Noel Annan
Stuart Hampshire	John Gross
Stephen Spender	Jonathan Miller

Institutional Attachments

Columbia University
Congress for Cultural Freedom

Influentials—at a distance

T. S. Eliot	Robert Lowell	Edward Shils
W. H. Auden	James Agee	

The New York Jewish Intellectuals (by field of interest)

Art: Meyer Schapiro, Clement Greenberg, Harold Rosenberg

Philosophy: Sidney Hook, Hannah Arendt (Ernest Nagel)

Literary Criticism: Lionel Trilling, Philip Rahv, Alfred Kazin, Irving Howe, Leslie Fiedler, Paul Goodman, Lionel Abel, Steven

Marcus, Robert Warshow, Robert Brustein, Susan Sontag,
Diana Trilling

Intellectual Journalism: Elliot Cohen, William Phillips, Irving Kristol,
Melvin Lasky, Robert Silvers, Norman Podhoretz, Jason Epstein,
Theodore Solotaroff, Midge Decter

Poetry: Delmore Schwartz

Fiction: Saul Bellow, Bernard Malamud, Norman Mailer,
Isaac Rosenfeld, Philip Roth (Harvey Swados)

Theology: (Will Herberg) (Emil Fackenheim) (Jacob Taubes)
(Arthur Cohen)

Sociology: Daniel Bell, Nathan Glazer, S. M. Lipset (Philip Selznick)
(Edward Shils) (Lewis Coser)

History: Richard Hofstadter, Gertrude Himmelfarb

Economics: (Robert Heilbroner) (Robert Lekachman)

* Arrived later, yet became one of the elders.
** Outside New York but had status as members.
† The social and intellectual coterie that included George Plimpton and William Styron.

Note: Parentheses indicate individuals who were close enough at times to be regarded as
"cousins."

I am mentioned in the book I appear as Lionel's on-the-scene wife, not as a
writer."[66] While Diana Trilling had a reputation for being easily offended—
she was a "pot of resentment," one person who knew her told me—she was
nonetheless perceptive about the treatment of women in this milieu.[67]

A total of seven women were considered full-fledged New York intel-
lectuals. Five of the seven were romantically linked to men in the group.
McCarthy had been involved with Philip Rahv when he relaunched *Partisan
Review* in 1937. Hardwick, too, was rumored to have had an affair with
Rahv. She went on to marry the poet Robert Lowell in 1949. Diana Trilling, Gertrude Himmelfarb, and Midge Decter were married to men in the
group. Diana married Lionel Trilling in 1929; Himmelfarb married Irving
Kristol in 1942; and Podhoretz and Decter wed in 1956. Arendt and Sontag
were the exceptions. Neither were romantically linked with any New York
intellectual. But both were viewed as attractive and alluring, qualifications
Jason Epstein suggested were essential for its women members.

All of these women were brilliant. Yet they were not always treated as intellectual equals. Moreover, to be part of this milieu, they too performed secular Jewish masculinity.[68] They wrote like men. They would not have put it this way. They thought of themselves as just writers. But they were often scorned and seen as more acerbic than their male counterparts in the public realm *because* they had to perform the combative masculine identity that was "Jewish intellectual."

Indeed, nothing was more insulting to these women than to be dismissed as mere "lady" writers. That term connoted superficiality and frivolity. Yet that is exactly the term Podhoretz used when he discussed women in the group. Susan Sontag became the group's "Dark Lady of American Letters" in the 1960s, Podhoretz wrote, "a position that had originally been carved out by Mary McCarthy in the thirties and forties." McCarthy, Podhoretz said, had "been promoted to the more dignified status of *Grande Dame* as a reward for her long years of brilliant service."[69] But the moniker "lady," as Podhoretz knew, was a backhanded compliment. And "dark" suggested something sinister and dangerous. These women were "dark" because they seemingly embodied an intellectual masculinity. The notion that only one woman could shine at a time also betrayed the group's sexism. No such standard existed for its men.

Midge Decter took issue with Diana Trilling's suggestion that the New York intellectuals did not take women seriously. Decter argued that its women were "members in absolutely good, powerful standing . . . What? Hannah Arendt? Are you kidding? She was all but worshipped. And Mary [McCarthy] was held to be infinitely more brilliant than she was, in fact. I mean—the women were part of the crowd." But she also acknowledged that women needed to behave differently. They needed to "be pleasant. If possible—amusing. If possible—flirtatious. If possible—earnest," and not be like Diana Trilling by going "in there with fists pumping."[70] Decter was a neoconservative, and her views on gender roles reflected a social conservatism that she had embraced. But Decter's own career suggests that she was just as combative as any New York intellectual. One's fists had to pump; one had to "write like a man" to be considered an intellectual among this group.

But there were in fact two types of women in this milieu: those who got credit for being intellectuals and those who did not. Other women married to figures in this group were writers but were not recognized as such. Instead, they were viewed as mere wives. Ann Birstein, Alfred Kazin's wife from 1952 until their divorce in 1982 (Kazin had four wives in total), is a case in point. A novelist and essayist who published six books while married to Kazin, Birstein was not included in this group.[71] In her 2003 memoir,

What I Saw at the Fair, she chronicled her difficult marriage to Kazin, including charges of emotional and physical abuse. She said that among the Jewish "West Side" intellectuals, "wives didn't figure at all, neither did any women in terms of thinkers on their own." Men in the group, she wrote, "feared losing their manhood to literary women." That is why so many often divorced or ended up with "dim wives" who would support them financially.[72]

Alfred Kazin's younger sister, Pearl Kazin Bell, is another example. She was married to Daniel Bell and was thus related to not one but two titans in this group. In the 1940s and '50s she worked at various magazines—as a researcher at *Time*, as a literary editor at *Harper's Bazaar*, and as a copyeditor at the *New Yorker*. She was also a gifted writer. She "really plunged into the literary world on her own," her son, historian David A. Bell, told me. In 1955 she published her first story in the *New Yorker*. After being hired as a copyeditor, she wrote for the magazine's then unsigned "Talk of the Town" section. Her more established brother, Alfred Kazin, had little to do with her career. "He would introduce her to people, and she appreciated that," David Bell said, "but he was certainly not interested in promoting her career really in any sense or helping her. She made her own way."[73]

Pearl Kazin and Daniel Bell traveled in the same literary circles and likely met in the late 1940s or early 1950s. But both were then involved with other people. Pearl had a passionate affair with the Welsh writer Dylan Thomas in 1950–51. In 1952 she married the photographer Victor Kraft. The marriage lasted only a few months, since he "was also gay so it wasn't the best match."[74] Bell, meanwhile, was married twice before he settled down with Kazin.[75] He was quite a "womanizer" in the six years between his divorce and his marriage to Pearl. The two casually dated in 1955–56 but broke things off when Bell departed for Europe to work for the Congress for Cultural Freedom (CCF). They got back together in late 1959 or early 1960 and married in December 1960. Their only son was born the following year, when Pearl was thirty-nine years old. Bell also had a daughter from a previous marriage.[76]

Pearl quit working as a copyeditor at the *New Yorker* after she married Daniel Bell. In 1960 he published *The End of Ideology*, his magisterial work of social theory that predicted the end of political ideologies like Marxist socialism. In 1995 the *Times Literary Supplement* called it one of the "100 most influential non-fiction books published since World War II."[77] Over the next fifteen years, Daniel's public profile exploded. In addition to numerous articles, he published *The Coming of Post-Industrial Society* in 1973 and *The Cultural Contradictions of Capitalism* in 1976. In

1965 he cofounded the magazine the *Public Interest*, with Irving Kristol. In these years Pearl focused on raising their son. "I'm sure my father never changed a diaper," David Bell said. That made him little different from most men of his generation. But "I can't recall [a lot] of times when she was working that he was taking care of me."[78]

In 1970 Pearl started writing regular reviews of fiction for the *New Leader*. She was one of two contributors to its monthly "Writers on Writing" column. She left the *New Leader* in 1977 after Podhoretz asked her to review fiction regularly for *Commentary*.[79] Both were publications, David Bell told me, where "my father and uncle, Alfred Kazin, had long-standing connections." But even in these later years her husband's career came first. Daniel Bell struggled with various ailments, including "leg trouble" and "an annual siege of back trouble." He was in and out of the hospital and in bed for weeks. "It is impossible for me to read without interruption, much less write," she told *New Leader* editor Myron "Mike" Kolatch, in the summer of 1976.[80] A few months later she confided to the poet Stanley Burnshaw that, "through all of this, I went on with my reviewing, but Dan was all but helpless so much of the time that I could only work late at night, when he had finally been able to fall asleep." Pearl wrote that she "was more exhausted than I ever can remember being."[81]

Pearl also labored for years over a novel that she never published. In 1982 she told Burnshaw she was "in the final stretch" of her novel and hoped to "have the first few chapters rewritten" to send to an agent. But her husband came first. "Dan's eye problems are not as severe as they were a year ago," she told Burnshaw. "But when things go wrong—as did yesterday, when he discovered that both lenses were cracked and unusable—I have to drop everything to help Dan through the day." Daniel would also get depressed when he could not write.[82] The physical and mental ailments blurred.[83] Daniel was always supportive of Pearl's writing career, but his needs came first.

Pearl also struggled to find her voice as a writer. Being Daniel Bell's wife but also Alfred Kazin's sister likely had something to do with her difficulties writing. She was seven years younger than Alfred. "By the time she went to college, he was already a very well-established figure, so she was always under his shadow," David Bell told me. "Clearly, she resented that, and she resented, I think, that he got all the attention, and that he was really not very interested in her."[84]

Daniel Bell did not include his own wife in his genealogy of New York intellectuals. Perhaps she did not consider herself part of the group since she struggled as a writer. Alfred Kazin, meanwhile, scarcely mentioned

FIGURE 1. Pearl and Alfred Kazin. Courtesy of David A. Bell.

his sister in any of his three famous memoirs: *A Walker in the City* (1951); *Starting Out in the Thirties* (1965); and *New York Jew* (1978). It was as if she didn't exist—not as a sister or as a writer who traveled in the same literary circles.[85]

Diana Trilling and Pearl Bell were friends, and Trilling noticed her absence in discussions of the New York intellectuals. In the late 1970s Trilling conducted a series of interviews with figures in the group because she wanted to record their history for posterity and future use by historians. Speaking to Irving Howe, she wondered about "the fate of people like Pearl Bell." She told Howe she had been talking to Dwight Macdonald, who asked her if she ever read Pearl's essays. "'I said yes, with pleasure, she was a very good reviewer'" Macdonald then inquired, "'Why isn't she being celebrated the way you were when you started to review?' This is very important," Trilling told Howe. But the conversation shifted gears and the subject was dropped.[86]

Scholars have also conjectured that some of these women played crucial but unrecognized roles editing their husbands' work. Historian Lila Corwin Berman has written about how the historian Oscar Handlin, who circled this milieu, was aided by his wife, Mary Flugin Handlin, a "trained social scientist with a master's degree from Columbia." One of Handlin's early doctoral students recalled "noticing her sitting in the back at Handlin's lectures feverishly taking notes. He later learned that she used those notes to help write some of her husband's books, filling in and revising where necessary. Occasionally listed as a coauthor," writes Berman, "Mary Handlin never received the public recognition or respect her husband did. This was not the least unique to their situation."[87] Recently, a debate about mid-century intellectuals' and the role of their wives in their work took place on the Society for U.S. Intellectual History blog. In a post about Richard Hofstadter and his wife, Beatrice Hofstadter, scholars wondered whether Beatrice edited her husband's writings. One emeritus historian who knew the couple argued that Beatrice was "a highly skilled editor" who undoubtedly read and commented on her husband's work. But "so did a lot of other people, including especially his colleagues and grad students." He argued that "there is a major difference between author and editor." Others felt her contributions were rendered invisible, aside for a brief mention in the acknowledgments of one of his books.[88] Perhaps the archives could resolve the issue. But this sort of research might prove inconclusive. Diana Trilling claimed that her contributions to Lionel's writings were destroyed. After he died, she was furious to see he had thrown away the drafts she wrote on. She was sure he wanted to block future scholars from knowing how much she helped him. It is possible other intellectuals did the same.[89]

———

This book is about the men and the women New York intellectuals and their interaction with and performance of secular Jewish masculinity. *Write Like a Man* explores this history using two different methodological approaches. Chapters 1, 3, and 5 are chronological and thematic. They focus on particularly important eras in the evolution of the group's ideology of secular Jewish masculinity. Chapters 2, 4, 6, and 7 focus on individuals—two men and two women—as case studies for how secular

Jewish masculinity molded those on the left and right of the political spectrum. Diana Trilling, the subject of chapter 2, and Irving Howe, the subject of chapter 4, exemplified those who remained on the left-liberal continuum. Chapters 6 and 7 focus on Midge Decter and Norman Podhoretz, examining their shift rightward and the development of neoconservatism.[90] Other New York intellectuals appear throughout these chapters, as do other writers who engaged with them but fell outside of their purview—Betty Friedan, Kate Millett, and James Baldwin, for example. Chapters also loop back in time and analyze how major events, such as World War II and the Holocaust, shaped the ways in which these intellectuals conceived of Jewish masculinity.

Write Like a Man uncovers the many ways masculinity was a linchpin for mid- to late twentieth-century American Jewish politics. It also reveals the ways in which this this ideology of secular Jewish masculinity extended beyond the confines of this milieu to shape American intellectual and political life more broadly.

CHAPTER ONE

My Weapon Is My Pen

CONSTRUCTING SECULAR JEWISH MASCULINITY

Climb the 137th Street hill east of Broadway, past the Hebrew Orphanage.
Topping it, on your left, are the Gothic buildings of the College of the City
of New York, and on your right, the Greek semicircle of the Lewisohn
Stadium, making for an architectural irony unusual even for an
American college. For the spirit brewing within those walls is no more
Greek or Gothic than the Rand School or Mecca Temple. Within these walls
are gathered more Jewish students than in any college in the world![1]

—A. L. SHANDS

IN A 1981 INTERVIEW, Milton Himmelfarb compared the New York
intellectuals to a celebrated generation of military generals: "There
was a class at West Point that was called the class that the stars fell on,
it produced any number of three-, four- and even five-star generals for
the United States Army. [Dwight David] Eisenhower was in one of those
classes." The Jewish equivalent of West Point, according to Himmelfarb,
was in the heart of Manhattan: "Those years at City College produced an
astonishingly high proportion of really major figures in American intellectual and cultural life, which says something about American Jewish
history as well."[2] For these burgeoning intellectuals, the City College of
New York (CCNY) was not only an elite educational institution, but also a
site of masculine socialization. Like other exclusive single-sex institutions,
CCNY instilled "masculine" ideals. But, unlike West Point, its student
body was predominantly Jewish. Whereas elite Protestants built their
new forms of masculinity on the cultivation of physical strength and athleticism, the future New York intellectuals embraced a Jewish masculinity

[22]

that emphasized intellect and combative debate—the mind over muscle. That formula was the heart of their ideology of secular Jewish masculinity.

Jewish immigrant sons flocked to CCNY because tuition was free, and because quotas limited Jewish enrollment at elite private universities.[3] New York intellectuals who attended CCNY included Sidney Hook (1923), Harold Rosenberg (attended 1923–24), William Phillips (1928), Paul Goodman (1931), Alfred Kazin (1935), Bernard Malamud (1936), Milton Himmelfarb (1938), Melvin Lasky (1939), Daniel Bell (1939), Seymour Melman (1939), Irving Kristol (1940), Irving Howe (1940), Seymour Martin Lipset (1943), and Nathan Glazer (1944). At CCNY, these nascent intellectuals absorbed a masculinity that was neither assimilationist nor bound by Jewish tradition. Rather, it centered on a new construct: the combative thinker who argued for a living and as a pastime.[4]

Other fertile breeding grounds for this ideology of secular Jewish masculinity were the offices of the *Menorah Journal* in the 1920s and early 1930s, and the *Partisan Review* in the late 1930s. Scholars usually cite the relaunching of *Partisan Review* in 1937 as marking the beginning of this milieu. But the group's roots go back further. Its oldest members wrote for the *Menorah Journal* when Elliot E. Cohen served as its managing editor between 1924 and 1931. Cohen would become the inaugural editor of *Commentary* in 1945, a magazine that joined *Partisan Review* (*PR*), edited by William Phillips and Philip Rahv, as a New York intellectual mainstay in the postwar years.

Significantly, what became the New York intellectuals' ideology of secular Jewish masculinity was by no means the dominant model of masculinity available to young Jews in the first half of the twentieth century. "There was a tremendous pull of Americanism at that time," Lionel Abel recalled. His contemporaries equated American manhood with strength, athleticism, resolve, and independence.[5] Jewish masculine norms were also always fluid, even in the late nineteenth and early twentieth centuries, when a new aggressive nativism combined with a racialized and gendered anti-Semitism to cast Jewish masculinity as "other." Jewish men, like other modern men in this period, had multiple models of masculinity.[6]

The restrictive quotas of the early twentieth century that prevented Jews from attending Ivy League universities were a product of nativism, itself a response to the Industrial Revolution and the accompanying processes of mass immigration and urbanization, and growing anti-Semitism. Between 1880 and World War I, over twenty million immigrants came to the United States. Most settled in American cities. Those "second-wave" immigrants came from the poorest areas of Eastern and Southern Europe, where the highest concentrations of Catholics and Jews were, along with others from Asia who landed in the American West. While industrial capitalists were overthrowing a once rural, agrarian society, immigrant workers, who tended to settle in the rapidly expanding industrial and commercial cities, appeared to change the character of a once overwhelmingly Protestant population.[7]

Nativists claimed—drawing on persistent Jeffersonian ideals—that true freedom required a means of widespread personal autonomy in an overwhelmingly agricultural, individualistic, physically vigorous rural population. According to the nativists' popular mythology, America had such a population prior to mass immigration. It was the Old World that had overcrowded cities full of pitifully dependent poor people—now immigrating to the United States. That "American exceptionalist" ethos had particularly been associated with the expanding Western frontier, until the Census Bureau suddenly announced the frontier was dead in 1890. That announcement spawned a whole new literature (among whose most influential figures was Teddy Roosevelt) dedicated to finding replacement sources of invigorating self-reliance and armed strength, including a more robust masculinity.[8]

In reaction to mass immigration and unease about shifting racial categories, Victorian ideals of masculinity became more virile and discriminating.[9] Fears of the growing power and influence of the urban masses and the decline of white Protestant male dominance led to the inculcation of what one historian calls an "imperial masculinity." The Protestant elite undertook this project mainly in exclusive, all-male institutions: boarding schools, Ivy League universities, and secret fraternal societies, like Yale University's Skull and Bones. By the 1920s, these institutions had devised ways to screen out students deemed "socially undesirable," a euphemism for Jews of Eastern European background. Administrators invented a new system of admissions that made "character" central to the admissions process, a quality distinct from academic performance and "thought to be in short supply among Jews but present in abundance among high-status Protestants," as sociologist Jerome Karabel argues. Sturdy character implied proper class origin and social rearing and a genteel masculinity that encompassed physical strength, honor, and athleticism, particularly on the new American football fields—a sport invented at Yale in the 1870s to breed martial virtues. Excluded from that world, American Jewish masculinity evolved beside and in reaction to mainstream American gender ideals.[10]

American Jewish masculinity was also shaped in response to European stereotypes, which had long cast Jewish men as weak, passive, and effeminate

in body and character. Western Christians had for centuries viewed cir-
cumcision as "the most obvious 'sign' of Jewish 'feminization.'" By the late
nineteenth century, such descriptions of Jewish male difference merged
with discourses on racial and sexual inferiority. Non-Jewish commentators characterized Jews and homosexuals as "sexual inverts," alternatively
described as perverted, effeminate, abnormal, mentally diseased, immature, or intellectually gifted. Intellectual prowess, too, was often seen as
a sign of masculine deficiency, since the scholar was the opposite of the
virile male athlete or working-class laborer.[11]

Jews themselves sometimes amplified these stereotypes. Jewish men
differentiated their conception and performance of masculinity from
white Christian constructions of both Jewish and normative masculinity.[12]
Scholar Daniel Boyarin argues that, prior to the twentieth century, the ideal
Ashkenazic Jewish male was the "sissy" Torah scholar, and that this softer,
anti-macho, scholarly man was not the product of anti-Semitism or a mar-
ginalized "other," but of a valorized manifestation of Talmudic culture.[13]

As children of immigrants, the New York intellectuals were not far
removed from older gender stereotypes, whether understood as derogatory or as a secular fulfillment of Talmudic masculinity, even as they tried
to situate themselves in a new culture of masculinity in the industrial
United States. In response to white Protestant constructions of "American" masculinity, the New York intellectuals refashioned aspects of Jewish
manliness that they deemed weak and effeminate. But what became their
ideology of secular Jewish masculinity also did not seek merely to mimic
the new American middle-class rugged individualism. It was new—both
uniquely American and uniquely Jewish.

The few women who became New York intellectuals also performed
secular Jewish masculinity. The first to be taken seriously were the so-
called *PR* girls: Mary McCarthy, Elizabeth Hardwick, and Hannah Arendt.
Hardwick once told an interviewer that as a young writer she aspired to
be a "Jewish New York intellectual." She admired the group's "tradition of
rational skepticism," their "deracination" and "angular vision, love of learning, cosmopolitanism, a word that practically means Jewish in Soviet lexi-
cography."[14] All three women wrote for *PR* in the 1940s and were feared
for their sharp wit and prose.

They were not, however, the first women to write for the group's magazines. Tess Slesinger published short stories in the *Menorah Journal*
under Cohen's editorship. But she left the group in disdain in 1935 and
moved to Hollywood where she became a successful screenwriter. In 1929,
a young Diana Trilling submitted a short story to the *Menorah Journal*.

She never heard back from Cohen. According to Slesinger, Cohen liked the piece. But Diana felt Cohen told Slesinger that "out of mischievousness, in order to make us competitive with each other or simply to undermine [Slesinger's] confidence." The burgeoning group of New York intellectuals had little patience for women writers. Diana Trilling and Slesinger were also both Jewish and married to men in the group; neither was sexually available.[15]

In contrast, McCarthy, Hardwick, and Arendt were perceived as attractive and flirtatious. McCarthy and Hardwick were *shiksas* while Arendt was a striking European émigré who had trained under some of Germany's most revered philosophers. All three women were brilliant, but also *outsiders*, a position that enabled them to be seen as seductive without being reduced entirely to sex objects. The same was not true of the married Jewish women writers who orbited this group.[16]

This chapter begins with an examination of the Jewish immigrant world from which the New York intellectuals emerged before moving to the masculine spaces they created at CCNY, the *Menorah Journal,* and the *Partisan Review*. Immigrant sons looked to the streets, to popular culture, and to sports for models of American masculinity. Few looked backward. They did not venerate rabbis or religious scholars. "The fall of the rabbis and the rise of socialists represented nothing short of a revolution in Jewish culture and politics," notes historian Tony Michels.[17] Immigrant sons, however, also had no desire to replicate the working-class masculinity of their fathers who struggled to earn a living and adapt to American norms. The future New York intellectuals carved out their own vision of cerebral masculinity. But there were many other paths they could have taken.[18]

Poverty

The future New York intellectuals grew up in working-class neighborhoods like the Lower East Side and Harlem, and in Brooklyn and the Bronx. Nearly all came from Eastern European Jewish immigrant families who struggled to earn a living. "We were poor, but then everyone was poor, more or less," Irving Kristol recalled of his childhood in Bensonhurst, Brooklyn. Kristol's father was a "contractor" in the men's clothing trade. He signed contracts with suppliers to cut fabric for boy's clothing that he sent to manufacturers for final finishing. He was in that sense "a small businessman." [19] Irving Howe's family lived in the Bronx. His father owned a grocery store, which went bankrupt in 1930. His parents then became garment workers. His mother "would come home with a paycheck of twelve or fifteen dollars a week, tired and troubled, yet gripping in her hands the life of everyone near her," Howe recalled, while his father accumulated "blisters on his body, the result of hours spent over a steaming press iron."[20] Alfred Kazin grew up in Brownsville, "New York's rawest, remotest, cheapest ghetto."[21] His father was a house painter. His mother was a seamstress who worked at the notorious Triangle Shirtwaist Factory, where 146 workers, mostly young women and girls, died in a fire at the factory in 1911.[22] After she married, she set up shop in the family's apartment. Kazin's father couldn't find work during the Depression and his mother's income kept the family afloat.[23] Nathan Glazer grew up in East Harlem. His father was a garment worker while his mother stayed home to raise seven children. "When there was work, he worked," Glazer recalled of his father. "And when there wasn't, it was 'slack.'"[24] During the Depression, slack periods seemed endless. Glazer's father worked very little. "The steadiest earners" were his older sisters, who worked as secretaries.[25] Sidney Hook also recalled how "slack" shaped his family. "Poverty was at its worst during periods called 'slack.' . . . A slack was a period of seasonal unemployment in the needle trades. It lasted three months or more, during which ordinary income was cut off, and the family had to scrounge around to make ends meet from day to day."[26]

A few New York intellectuals had more middle-class origins. Lionel Abel's father was a reform rabbi who led numerous congregations in various small towns on the East Coast. Born in Brooklyn, Abel moved around as a kid, graduating from Niagara Falls High School.[27] William Phillips's father was "a totally unsuccessful lawyer." Despite constant economic hardships his mother did not work because "it didn't look good for the wife of a professional man to work."[28] Lionel Trilling's mother hailed from England and his father was a tailor who became a factory owner. They regarded themselves as bourgeoisie. "Though vexed by financial worry," Trilling once told a colleague that his family "was firmly and pragmatically middle-class." During the Depression, however, his father's wholesale furrier business went bankrupt. Thus, even those New York intellectuals ostensibly from middle-class backgrounds experienced economic hardship.[29]

Many New York intellectuals recalled the impotency of their fathers, who struggled to provide for their families. Looking back on his childhood, one *Commentary* writer remembered how his "mother did what she could to protect the children from the full impact of our poverty, but we felt it. It reached us in our beds in the low rumble of the nightly discussion. My mother wanted my father to earn more money. My father insisted he was doing his best. 'I can't help it,' he cried. 'There is no work.'"[30]

Such memories were typical. Phillips recalled his father's "failure as a 'provider,'" and how it "was paralleled by a psychological and intellectual decline and a steady removal from the world, from friends, from relatives, and even from those normal activities that took one out of the house."[31] Kristol vividly remembered his "father breaking down and crying" more than once during the Depression, after he "went bankrupt several times" even though "he wasn't the sort of man to do that."[32] Kazin's father was "easily ruled by my mother who was never happier than when he went off at daybreak to paint bridges and subways," which was not often enough.[33] During the 1930s, many American men felt emasculated by their inability to provide for their families. Franklin D. Roosevelt's New Deal and the artwork it promoted was in part meant to remasculinize the American male.[34] But for Jewish men the emasculation ran deep, hitting them from multiple angles.

Jewish emasculation was reflected in the demotion of the religious scholar. In his classic 1902 study of the Lower East Side, *The Spirit of the Ghetto*, journalist Hutchins Hapgood observed this loss of status.[35] Half a century later, a *Commentary* writer remembered how "the old ones, those *zaydehs* with embroidered *yarmelkas* and their white beards worn like orders upon their chests . . . cramped our style." This "Old Guard" disapproved of how young Jewish boys sought to become American men. "But sometimes we couldn't help meeting one of them coming from the synagogue," this writer recalled, "and then we would all have to stand by sheepishly while he asked us questions in Yiddish about our mothers and fathers, how much Talmud we knew, etc., until he left us, shaking his head from side to side." To the young, these religious scholars embodied remnants of a seemingly archaic Jewish past losing its hold. They focused on the Talmud while young Jewish boys sought to play sports. But in the eyes of these elders, young Jews were turning into "hooligans, bums, outcasts, Cossacks!"[36]

The images the New York intellectuals had of their mothers were mixed. On the one hand, their memoirs cast their Jewish mothers as overpowering wives who further emasculated their weak and enervated fathers. Phillips, for example, remembered how as his "father became more withdrawn and less able to 'make a living,'" his mother became resentful, "more demanding, more hysterical, and more hypochondriacal." Unsure what kept his parents' marriage intact, he conjectured that "on my father's side, it seemed to be a kind of nervous, frustrated, abstract devotion. She was part of his fate." As for his mother, "it must have been a combination of hate, fear, father substitution, and a variety of conventional attitudes."

Drawing on psychoanalysis, Williams concluded that "my mother must have cast me in the role of substitute husband. To her last day—she was ninety-six when she died—she was constantly making demands of me that only a neurotic wife could make."[37]

Alfred Kazin had similar recollections of his parents. He remembered "his mother's strength and his father's weakness." In his journals, he wrote about how his "mama talked down" to his father, "an untalented man combined with the superfluous man."[38] Also employing the language of psychoanalysis, Kazin later admitted in his diary "how much of my (unconscious) life has been not competing with my father, Freudian style, but making up for him. Admittedly, I am an 'Oedipal' case."[39] Kazin was always closer to his mother than his reclusive "powerless" father. A "self-admitted 'mama's boy,'" he later concluded, according to Kazin's biographer, Richard Cook, "that she had been too dominant, that their relationship had been too intense, that he had been too dependent, too attentive and responsive to her moods and particularly her fears."[40] Kazin was not alone. In *World of Our Fathers*, Irving Howe's 1976 best-selling book about Jewish immigrant life, Howe described how the Jewish mother "became an object of sentimental veneration. By certain readings, the Oedipal romance was peculiarly Jewish, perhaps even a Jewish invention."[41]

American gender ideals compounded many Jewish men's sense of emasculation by poverty. In Eastern Europe Jewish men and women both worked and made up a "breadwinning partnership." This arrangement was sanctioned by the veneration of the Torah scholar as the ideal Jewish male. "Jews considered it something of a religious obligation for the wife of a Torah scholar to work while her husband devoted most of his time to study and prayer," writes historian Susan Glenn. This reliance on an industrious wife legitimated women who worked outside their own household.[42] "Not all or even most Jewish fathers in Eastern Europe were learned, nor were all wives prepared to take on the burdens of breadwinning. Still, such families did exist and, more importantly, they set a standard honored by even those who could not live up to it," Howe wrote in *World of Our Fathers*. "In the turmoil of the American city, traditional family patterns could not long survive."[43] In the United States men were expected to be the sole breadwinners and providers. "Economic success or failure was the measure of a man," writes historian Beth Wenger.[44] Married women felt pressure not to work outside the home, but Jewish mothers continued to contribute to the economic stability of the family by working from home doing piecework and managing boarders. "Fathers were unable to support their families with their low-paying jobs and were often at a loss for dealing with the outside world," notes one scholar. Jewish women more easily adapted to American gender roles and their new environment.[45]

The labor movement enabled some Jewish immigrants to develop a new kind of masculinity. By joining unions and participating in a series of successful strikes they became "fighters," Howe wrote in *World of Our Fathers*. "To be a fighter, to act in concert with other workers, to bring to one's tongue such inspiring words as 'respect' and 'dignity,'—all this testified to the forging of collective self-hood."[46] According to Howe, unions were not only agents of Americanization but also of masculinization. In *World of Our Fathers*, Howe celebrated a "new social type," "the self-educated worker-intellectual," who bore "the benchmarks of the Talmud Torah." This self-educated worker had to "struggle into his maturity for those elements of learning that his grandsons would accept as their birthrights, yet fired by a vision of universal humanist culture and eager to absorb the words of Marx, Tolstoy, and the other masters of the nineteenth century."[47] For Howe, Jewish masculinity, even in America, encompassed aspects of the traditional Jewish male idea—the scholar—and he sought to cast Jewish immigrant fathers as manly in this way.

Many of the New York intellectuals remembered their fathers differently. Though literate, they often lacked educations. Nathan Glazer noted his "father had certainly not gone to any secular school. Maybe he had gone to a *kheder*," meaning a religious school. But his education was sparse.[48] Kazin recalled in his memoir, *New York Jew*, that "there were always books in the house." In his personal journal, however, he admitted his "contempt for my poor, unlettered parents, still stuck in poor, old Brownsville."[49] According to Milton Himmelfarb, "none of us came from a home where educated or cultivated English was spoken."[50]

Here one of the vexing contradictions of modern ideologies of gender comes into focus. In modern industrial cities, especially in the United States, people increasingly saw the trappings of education as marks of femininity—partially because of the literal feminization of the teaching profession, along with secretarial work in white-collar corporate offices, in the mid- to late nineteenth century. That feminization was inseparable from the feminization of household work and the increasing masculinization and supervision (increasingly called "management") of commerce.[51] At the same time, lack of education deprived the poor, especially recent immigrants who had an uncertain grasp of English, of real opportunities for economic self-determination. Both natives and immigrants saw that deprivation as emasculating. "Personally, they felt trapped," Howe observed of Jewish-American immigrant fathers. "They were trapped in the limitations of their skills, in the skimpiness of their education, in the awkwardness of their speech, in the alienness of their manners. But the sons—*they* would achieve both collective Jewish fulfillment and individual Jewish success." Their fathers wanted their sons to avoid their fate. They projected their own hopes and dreams on to their sons. "It was not for myself alone that I was expected to shine, but for them—to redeem the constant anxiety of their existence," Kazin wrote. "I was the first American child, their offering to the strange new God; I was to be the monument of their liberation from the shame of being—what they were." Though ostensibly directed toward both mother and father, these feelings reflected "the complicated feelings with which sons could look back upon the hopes of their fathers," Howe noted.[52]

In a 1961 essay, "Reflections on Jewish Identity," Daniel Bell wrote that "the basic shaping element of Jewish life in America has been the immigrant experience—an experience with inner tension of anxiety and hope. The anxiety," he continued, "was an inevitable consequence of being uprooted and living in a strange land." Hope lay in the future, in the lives of their children. According to Bell, "the anxiety was translated into the struggle between fathers and sons. Few generational conflicts have had such an exposed nakedness, such depths of strain as this." "The dispossession and shame of many immigrant fathers has been a major subject for fiction about Jewish immigrants, both in English and Yiddish," as Howe wrote in *World of Our Fathers*. But according to Bell, the struggle was particularly acute for "the intelligentsia," especially his own generation of intellectuals who came of age between the Depression and World War II.[53] They rejected their fathers' emasculated past. But "one cannot wholly escape it. One may reject it, but the very mode of rejection is often conditioned by the past itself," Bell observed. "And the sins of the fathers—in the psychological, if not the legal, sense—are apt to be the burdens of the sons as well."[54]

The Jewish Streets

In his celebrated 1951 book, *A Walker in the City*, Alfred Kazin wrote about how Jewish boys growing up in Brownsville, Brooklyn, in the early decades of the twentieth century had two choices as they traversed the path toward manhood: they could be "'good' boys, who proved by our ready compliance and 'manners' that we wanted to get on" by doing well in school and pursuing respectable careers. "The alternative was going bad." "Behind any failure in school," Kazin recalled, "yawned the great abyss of a criminal career." Brownsville, he continued, "grew up how many schoolteachers, city accountants, rabbis, cancer specialists, functionaries of the revolution" but also "strong-arm men for Murder, Inc."[55]

In the American Jewish community crime first emerged as an issue with the influx of Eastern European Jews who crowded urban neighborhoods like the Lower East Side beginning in the 1880s. These immigrants did not bring crime with them from Europe. Rather, gambling, bootlegging, prostitution, and racketeering were a response to grim economic conditions. Crime provided a way to achieve economic mobility. It was "one of the queer ladders of social mobility in American life," Daniel Bell argued in 1953.[56] Writing in the wake of the 1951 Kefauver Committee Hearings on organized crime, Bell noted that "mobsters, like the gamblers, and like the entire gangdom generally, were seeking to become quasi-respectable and establish a place for themselves in American life."[57]

Criminal enterprises also provided access to norms of American masculinity, even as those norms were distorted. "Crime is a Coney Island mirror, caricaturing the morals and manners of society," Bell observed. Cadets, gamblers, and gangsters fashioned themselves as self-made men—similar to the myth of Horatio Alger in these years.[58] Successful cadets became burgeoning entrepreneurs, currying favor from Tammany politicians who turned a blind eye and profited from their illegal activity. The underworld was "'the warp and woof' of America's 'open' society," Bell noted. Upward mobility through organized crime was a path to "such 'normal' goals as independence through a business of one's own, and such 'moral' aspirations as the desire for social advancement and prestige."[59]

Violence and physical aggression, however, were not characteristics associated with Jews at the turn of the century. Both acculturated Jews and non-Jews largely maintained that "Jewish masculinity, even at its criminal moments was not an aggressive, physically dominating masculinity," historian Sarah Imhoff argues. Jewish communal leaders tended to ignore the problem of Jewish gangsters partly because they did not "fit their assumptions about Jewish men." Jewish leaders were more concerned with the significant number of young men who committed petty thefts. That issue gained national attention in 1908 when New York police commissioner Theodore Bingham released a report that declared that half the criminals in New York City were "Hebrews" from Eastern Europe. Non-Jews like Bingham believed that Jewish men had weak and delicate bodies that prevented them from committing violent crimes like murder, assault, and rape. Jews were also thought not to take part in masculine vices like drunkenness. They engaged rather in "soft crimes" like fraud and theft. Anti-immigrant sociologist Edward Alsworth Ross argued in 1910 that, "Jews were 'too cowardly' to engage in violent crimes, they count on shrewdness." Jewish communal leaders sometimes took a similar position. A 1912 issue of the *American Hebrew*, for example, explained "that Jews are less addicted to crimes of violence may be put down to their slighter physique and general tendency to suffer ills without retaliation." Thus, as Imhoff argues, "both those accusing Jews of criminality and those defending Jewish men from these charges agreed on a single line of reasoning: Jewish men were physically small and constitutionally disinclined towards violence, so when they committed crimes, they were unlikely to be physically aggressive and more likely to be crafty."[60]

The existence of Jewish gangsters and their enforcers, however, belied these stereotypes. An aggressive and violent masculinity reverberated in the working-class streets of Jewish immigrant neighborhoods. The founders of Murder Inc.—Louis Lepke Buchalter, "the most dangerous criminal in the United States," according to J. Edgar Hoover, and Jacob "Gurrah" Shapiro—were Jews. Other famed Jewish gangsters included Meyer Lansky, Benjamin "Bugsy" Segal, and Arnold Rothstein, the so-called czar of the underworld.

While most Jewish boys did not become gangsters, they were reared on the same streets as the Jewish underworld. "For the young criminal, hunting in the asphalt jungle of the crowded city," Bell observed, "it was not the businessman with his wily manipulation of numbers but the 'man with the gun' who was the American hero." Bell quoted Teddy Roosevelt, who grew up with a frail, sickly body in a pampered, upper-class household, then became the embodiment of a virile cowboy ethic in the Gilded Age: "'No amount of commercial prosperity,' once wrote Teddy Roosevelt, 'can supply the lack of the heroic virtues.'" According to Bell, "the American was 'the hunter, cowboy, frontiersman, the soldier, the naval hero.' And in the crowded slum, the gangster. He was a man with a gun, acquiring by personal merit what was denied to him by complex orderings of a stratified society."[61]

Howe downplayed this criminal underworld in *World of Our Fathers*. "In the life of the immigrant community as a whole, crime was a marginal phenomenon, a pathology discoloring the process of collective assertion and adjustment." Howe was right. Most Jews were not criminals. "The Lower East Side underworld was a culture of young people," notes one scholar. By middle age, the majority of these Jews had moved onto more respectable work.[62]

But Howe acknowledged the large role the streets played in molding Jewish boys. "Legends of retrospect, woven from wish to make the past seem less rough and abrasive than it actually was, have transformed every Jewish boy into a miniature scholar haunting the Seward Park Library and, before he was even out of knee pants, reading Marx and Tolstoy," he wrote. "The reality was different. Scholarly boys there certainly were; but more numerous by far were the street boys, tough and shrewd if not quite 'bums,' ready to muscle their way past competitors to earn half a dollar, quick to grasp the crude wisdom of the streets."[63] Journalist William Poster argued that "the traditional Jewish passion for higher education as well as many another 'Jewish trait' simply fell apart under the impact of the streets." The boys he knew growing up in Brownsville talked about "'workin', and the maturity and independence it implied." Maturity meant achieving independence by becoming "plumbers, bricklayers, carpenters, or businessmen. A few romantics wanted to be star athletes and a couple of little cynics wanted to be bookies or gangsters."[64] It meant becoming American men.

While most Jewish boys did not become gangsters, many joined the street gangs that proliferated in working-class immigrant neighborhoods in these years. The memoir literature of the New York intellectuals and those in their orbit are filled with recollections of street gangs and the important roles they played in their boyhood. According to one *Commentary* writer, "inclusion in the gang was absolute."[65] Gangs determined whom one socialized with, which blocks in the neighborhood one hung out on, and which sports teams one joined. William Phillips recalled "fighting with sticks and bottles the Italian gangs who came from further East in the Bronx, looking for some soft Jewish victories." Though Phillips was "not very tough, many of [his] blockmates and teammates, who never went beyond high school, and some of whom, I suspected, became gangsters, were tough enough to send the Italian invaders back where they came from."[66] Of his childhood growing up in Williamsburg, Sidney Hook remembered how "armed with the lids of the copper clothes boilers in which the family laundry was done," he and his friends would confront the Irish and Italian boys, "the little toughs to whom we were outsiders— 'Sheenies' they called us," who earlier in the day pelted them with snowballs. These "were not gang wars," Hook explained, because "knives were not in evidence, and the battle was more noisy than bloody." But he and his friends nonetheless traveled in "packs" and "would venture out for combat." For Hook, "the street fights served as a kind of surrogate for organized sports."[67]

Thus gangs provided not merely a conduit to crime but a way to learn about American boyhood. "The gang, willy-nilly, was the average boy's rite of passage to manhood," writes one historian. "It was where he discovered solidarity, purpose, a hierarchy of values, loyalties, duties, a moral authority superior to society's and beyond the reach of his family."[68] Street gangs offered Jewish boys a way to be virile in an era when Jews were largely seen as weak, effeminate, and cowardly. It exposed them to norms of American masculinity. Norman Podhoretz, who like Kazin grew up in Brownsville, proudly recalled in his 1967 memoir, *Making It*, how by age thirteen he had joined a gang known as the Cherokees, S.A.C. He wore the gang's "red satin jacket to school every day," which was his "proudest possession, a badge of manly status."[69] Milton Klonsky, who grew up in Brighton Beach, recalled in an essay in *Commentary* how the Trojan gang that dominated his neighborhood wore "blue flannel jackets with red blazon: TROJANS" on the back. Those who were not members of the gang were ignored, and deemed "*nebichs*, mama's boys, and small fry!"[70]

Sports

Sports were also popular among immigrant boys, as young Jewish men fought against stereotypes of effeminacy as they sought to be American men. Famed Jewish boxers countered "the old stereotype that Jews were meek and cowardly."[71] "More than other sports," notes another scholar, "boxing became the symbol of the immigrants' struggle for status, assimilation, and a path to Americanization."[72] Settlement houses like the New York Educational Alliance and organizations like the Young Men's Hebrew Association (YMHA) also incorporated athletic activities into their programs. "The newfound interest in athletics and physicality," writes Beth Wenger, "reflected an adoption of current American norms of masculinity and became part of a broader program to remake Jewish men in America."[73]

Basketball, a sport invented in 1891, was especially popular. In its early years, basketball "was a Jewish game, not a Black game," Alfred Kazin recalled. First picked up at settlement houses, Jewish boys also played basketball in the streets by "throwing their balls through the bottom hoop of a fire escape."[74] Between 1910 and 1950, CCNY had a championship-winning team. Its mostly Jewish members beat patrician Ivy Leaguers at Yale and Princeton. The sport provided "a subtle yet powerful answer to those who stereotype[d] [Jews] as puny and unmanly," historian Jeffrey Gurock argues. Critics at the time, however, maintained that Jews excelled in basketball because they were shrewd. Paul Gallico, a sports editor for the *Daily News*, argued "that basketball's appeal to the Hebrew, with his Oriental background is that the game places a premium on an alert, scheming mind, flashy trickiness, artful dodging and general smart-aleckness."[75]

Young Jews were also attracted to baseball. They had their first taste of team sports playing a version of it on the streets in immigrant neighborhoods. "Jewish boys became fanatics of baseball, their badge as Americans," Howe wrote in *World of Our Fathers*. But "in the narrow streets baseball was narrowed to stickball: a broomstick used as a bat, a rubber ball pitched on a bounce or sped into the catcher's glove . . . or stoopball, with a rubber ball thrown smartly against the outer steps of a tenement."[76] These games adapted to the necessity of urban life, where few vacant lots or fields were available. "Parks were crowded with mothers wheeling baby carriages, and the schoolyards were taken up by girls playing potsy [*sic*] and skipping rope." Young Jewish boys had no choice but to "take over the streets," creating their own masculine space. In the process, "the brickwork and moldings of buildings, stoops, abutments, cornices, rungs on fire-escape ladders, the squares of sidewalks, even the sewer covers were adapted to some sport which was then given a set of rules and a name."[77] Such street games included slugball, stoopball, boxball, and hit-the-crack, among others. Punchball was the roughest version. Played "right in the gutter outside the house," punchball brought "ball and fist into direct and savage contact," as boys from various gangs competed for dominance.[78] One *Commentary* writer proudly recalled that his powerhouse skills at punchball gained him admission to the notorious Trojan gang of Brighton Beach.[79]

Other street games seemed to be less about strength than speed and agility. In "slug-ball," recalled one *Commentary* writer, "weight and strength are no advantage: only celerity, jump, a shrewd eye, and a quick hand. The kid who knows how to slice the ball and to cut corners with precision can trim anyone bigger and stronger than himself." This writer contrasted this style of "urban" play with "country." "In the country, positions would have been reversed. But that is the difference between the City Character and the Country Character, which is, really, a difference in state of mind and disposition of soul."[80] He implied there was a difference between how Jews and Christians approached sports. For Jews growing up in immigrant neighborhoods, physical strength and size did not dictate victory. Swagger and street smarts were equally important. "Humor and wit," recalled one writer, "were also great values, enhancing one's positions directly by attraction or indirectly when used to degrade someone else. Words were also intoxicants."[81]

Most immigrant parents, however, viewed sports as anathema. In *World of Our Fathers*, Howe wrote of the "suspicion of the physical, fear of hurt, anxiety over the sheer 'pointlessness of play,'" which was the view of many immigrant parents. One concerned parent wrote to Abraham Cahan, the famed editor of the *Jewish Daily Forward*, about his fear that "the children can get crippled," playing sports like baseball. "I want my boy to grow up to be a *mensch*, not a wild American runner," he declared.[82] Indeed, the adult immigrant generation "displayed no interest in sports," writes one scholar. "Not only were they unfamiliar with sports in the Old World, but here in America they regarded athletics as a waste of time that served no useful function and, if anything, was a dangerous force that taught inappropriate social values, drew children away from traditional beliefs and behavior, and led to overexertion and accidents." Sports appealed to their children because sports provided a way to Americanize and because sports countered the stereotype of Jews as weak and cowardly.[83]

The sons of immigrants also learned about American norms of manhood through popular culture. They came of age during the Golden Age of Hollywood in the 1930s and '40s, as films began to mold understandings of American masculinity through popular genres like the western, gangster films, and film noir. Like many working-class immigrant youths, the future New York intellectuals frequented the ornate movie palaces that replaced nickelodeons in these years. Robert Warshow, managing editor at *Commentary* from 1946 until his untimely death in 1955, wrote about movies and the connection they played between "his boyhood and his manhood," as Lionel Trilling observed. Warshow understood that "A man watches a movie and the critic must acknowledge that he is that man," Trilling wrote after Warshow died. By that "he meant, of course, that the man watches the movie with some degree of involvement and pleasure in it, responding to the personal charm of the actors and actresses, finding that the fantasy of the screen suits to some extent, perhaps to a great extent, his own fantasy."[84]

CCNY

The future New York intellectuals carried all of these messages about masculinity—gleaned from the streets, popular culture, and films—as they entered university, where they would shape a new intellectual culture that valued a combative stance shaped by a desire and need to perform a new kind of secular Jewish masculinity. Inspired by the sectarian battles of the 1930s and birthed by the era's radicalism, it was a masculinity severed from their fathers and ultimately more connected to the scholarly ideal of the Jewish past. But it also bore the mark of the streets.

This ideology of secular Jewish masculinity took root at colleges and universities in New York City in the 1920s and '30s: at Columbia University, New York University (NYU), but especially at the City College of New York. "The alternative to City in those days was NYU," Nathan Glazer recalled, "and the feeling was that was where the kids went who were dumber and had more money." Meanwhile, Columbia University, according to Daniel Bell, "was for the genteel."[85]

A *Menorah Journal* series on Jewish campus life in New York City in the early 1930s featured pieces on Columbia, NYU, and CCNY. The *Journal* maintained that all three schools were characteristically Jewish in ways that went beyond numbers. At Columbia, there was a "complete lack of a Gentile atmosphere," according to the *Journal*. At NYU, which was about 40 percent Jewish, there was a sense of "Jewish freedom and quickness seen only when Jews are at home" in "Zion." The most Jewish of the three schools, however, was CCNY, with Jews accounting for an astronomical 80 to 90 percent of its student body. "It has become even more Jewish than perhaps was necessary, because—" the *Journal* argued, "though the Jews do not oust others, the others feel ousted and remain away."[86] With free tuition and no quotas, CCNY was known as the "poor boy's steppingstone to the world."[87]

The *Journal* series produced a composite picture of Jewish students in the 1930s as being both serious and studious. NYU and Columbia, however, tended to attract pre-professional students focused mainly on earning a living. The author of the Columbia article derisively labeled them "vulgar and upstart Jew[s]" as opposed to the type that was "solely interested in his work, a skeptical searching man, absorbed in text or tube." It was this latter type that the *Journal* valorized as the ideal Jewish male. There were "Gentile scholars of such sort, of course; but the type, the 'pure intelligence,' the almost disembodied mind, is something identified with the Jew," the *Journal* reported. This type of student predominated at CCNY, along with radicals.[88] "The composite image of the City College student," one CCNY alumnus later noted, was "an argumentative intellectual, a sometimes brilliant, loquacious, rather truculent young man, who is partial to radical politics, disrespectful of authority" and who, "during the 'golden age' of City College, roughly the 20s and '30s," knew he "was the select of the select." The "City College boy," according to another alumnus, was a "bookworm" and a "serious boy" who "sought learning for its own sake." He was a "curious compound of a scholar, a basketball player, an agitator, a wise guy, a solid citizen, an unsparing critic, a searcher for the truth, a fighter for the good cause, an eager Beaver."[89]

Athletics did not play a large role at any of these three schools, according to the *Journal*. To the chagrin of administrators, Columbia excelled only at chess. NYU students lacked a "rah-rah spirit" and "neither is there much enthusiasm for athletics." But this disinterest in athletics was most conspicuous at CCNY. The school's imposing football stadium was both an "architectural irony" and a farce. CCNY did not have a football team until 1922 because of "a distrust of Jewish prowess in the game," noted the *Journal*. "It was as un-American as that!" When CCNY's football team had a winning season in 1928, the non-Jewish administrators and trustees "were disappointed because the hallowed dogma that Jews could not play the game was exploded." But the author quickly noted that the winning team did not play "what has come to be known, more or less justly, as 'Yale football.'" The team "did little heavy line-plunging. It was light, fast, and cynically deceitful." CCNY football players were devious and cerebral, relying less on strength and athleticism and more on intellect and wit. Moreover, the 1928 season had been a fluke; the football team lost more often than not. The unofficial campus sports cheer was:

Hurray, hurray, we won!
What! We lost?
They cheated!
Ray, City College![90]

Morris Raphael Cohen, a famed CCNY philosophy professor who influenced many New York intellectuals, despised the importance universities placed on football. In a speech to CCNY's popular Social Problems Club, Cohen "disparaged the value of football . . . as a means of bringing out 'college spirit.'" He equated it to a "mob spirit." Cohen argued that students should focus on intellectual rather than athletic activities. "When you found a Social Problems Club or engage in intellectual pursuits, you are really advancing the interests of this College," and "colleges should teach cosmopolitanism, they should inculcate in students respect for all centers of learning" rather than focus on athletics.[91] Cohen did not have much reason to worry. Most observers believed that CCNY students and Jews in general showed little interest or proficiency in sports, aside from basketball, which did not have the same masculine connotation as football in these years.[92]

While other constructions of Jewish masculinity were present at CCNY, rooted, for example, in basketball, the ROTC program, and a street culture that extoled boxing, an ideology of secular Jewish masculinity dominated.[93] The title of the 1930 *Menorah Journal* article on CCNY, "The Cheder on the Hill," encapsulated how CCNY instilled this construction of Jewish masculinity and linked it to an older construction of Talmudic masculinity that idealized the Jewish male scholar. *Cheder* is a Hebrew term for a house of study where boys studied classical Jewish texts. Jewish culture traditionally prohibited women from studying rabbinic texts and also did not make it a priority to educate girls in secular subjects.[94] The allusion to a *cheder* also connoted ambivalence regarding Jewish identity since CCNY was a secular institution. The students had coined the expression "*cheder on the hill*" with a "Hebraic shrug." The phrase betrayed an irreverence many felt toward retaining their Jewish identity, but also a begrudging acknowledgment that they were, and always would be, Jews.[95]

At CCNY, a Talmudic-rooted vision of masculinity merged with the desire to cast off religion to construct a new expression of secular American Jewish masculinity. Morris Cohen embodied this masculine ideal and trained his students to fit it. He was "for the generations of the '20s and '30s, a veritable folk hero," recalled one former student. "He was the Paul Bunyan of Jewish intellectuals, and tales of his gigantic mental prowess were recounted with loving exaggeration, as though anything could be true of him." His reputation for brilliance rested not just on his writings but also on his aggressive classroom style. "You went to a Cohen class in order to be ripped open," recalled Howe. Only "tough spirited boys . . . took his classes—many didn't have the courage." Another student recalled Cohen's "famous probing, combative style—a kind of smiling struggle to the death." When he challenged his pupils, "The room was electrified, we jumped to the defense of our fellow-student, but our teacher took us all on, in a razzle-dazzle of knowledge, of analytic power, of fighting intellect." Howe later recalled that "it was a terrifying, sometimes even a sadistic method of teaching, and only the kinds of students that came to Cohen could have withstood it—Jewish boys with minds honed to dialectic, bearing half-conscious memories of *pilpul*, indifferent to the prescriptions of gentility."[96]

Gentile students abhorred Cohen's teaching style. In the fall of 1938, Harvard Law School extended a teaching invitation to Cohen, who had earned his doctorate from Harvard in 1906. The students there had difficulty adjusting to his style. One alumnus recalled: "In class, Cohen was inclined to be sharp, even tyrannical, and somewhat inconsiderate of the feelings of men, particularly those who were weak and self-doubting." Harvard students cowered in his class, afraid to ask him questions because "his retorts were often sharp and devastating." Though Cohen was renowned for this manner of teaching at CCNY, one former student noted, "It didn't go down well at Harvard. . . . It wasn't quite gentlemanly." Explained another: "I think the approach . . . was not universally welcomed when, on occasion, it was done in a more aggressive manner than they were accustomed to." Cohen's combative teaching style defied Harvard's standards of patrician gentlemanly behavior. "I don't think Cohen's influence upon students at Harvard was anything comparable to the great influence that he had upon students in New York," one Harvard graduate said. "One can only speculate about the reasons. My guess is that Harvard students were too polite to be argumentative and [Cohen] was really at his best when he had hostile students to contend with." Another former Harvard student felt that he and his classmates "had a difficult time adjusting to Morris Cohen's teaching methods" because "it wasn't considered gentlemanly to make a point too hard." When the *Eternal Light* radio show devoted a segment to Cohen in 1949, two years after his death, an interviewer asked the actor portraying Cohen: "What are you doing to make [your students] into gentlemen?" Cohen's reply: "I have been too busy to join a gentleman's club on Fifth Avenue," suggesting that conforming to white Protestant ideals of proper manliness was not a priority.[97]

In contrast, students at CCNY related to Cohen because he had emerged from immigrant roots like them. "Formidable as he seemed on the lecture platform, everything about Cohen testified that he shared with his students' common origins, common experiences, common values," wrote Howe. Cohen epitomized their ideal of secular Jewish masculinity. "Pride in argument, vanity of dialectic, a gleaming readiness for polemic— if these traits sometimes characterized Morris Cohen, so, too, might they be found in the culture from which he emerged and the younger philosophers he helped to shape," Howe observed. Cohen's students looked up to him because he embodied the type of Jewish man they hoped to be. He was "a cultural hero of the City College boys, at least the brighter and tougher ones." For the burgeoning New York intellectuals, Cohen's classes became a "rite of passage." They wore what Sidney Hook labeled "the mark of Cohen," "distinguished by an intensity of ideas" and "by keenness and persistency of logical analysis which often outran social discretion."[98]

It was not just in Cohen's classroom that Jewish students honed their masculinity, but also in the famous CCNY cafeteria alcoves. The alcoves served as a meeting ground for various social groups and clubs. The New York intellectuals congregated in Alcove No. 1, the home of the Trotskyists and anti-Stalinist left, while their Stalinist foes gathered in Alcove

No. 2. "It was between these two alcoves," Kristol recalled, "that the war of the worlds was fought." In the alcoves, Jewish intellectuals perfected the masculine traits they acquired in Cohen's classroom: "You caught your opponent in a fallacy, preferably a logical one, but a historical one would do. You smiled. [Thinking], 'Let him get out of *that* one.'" The arguments in the alcoves were akin to a hypermasculinized intellectual warfare: "A sense of intellectual life as a form of combat" characterized life at CCNY, Howe wrote.[99]

Drawings from the 1936 CCNY yearbook, *The Microcosm*, captured this performance of masculinity in the alcoves. When "at peace," students gathered in the alcoves to eat, study, and play ping-pong (figure 2a). But when animosities exploded between the communists of Alcove No. 1 and the anti-Stalinists of Alcove No. 2, fistfights ensued and the alcoves were "at war" (figure 2b). The ideological standpoint of *The Microcosm* editors is evident in their unflattering depiction of the students who made up Alcove No. 2, whom they pejoratively termed "the Kremlin" (figure 2c). The anti-Stalinist left contingent of Alcove No. 1 despised the communists in Alcove No. 2. "Lord, how dreary a bunch they seemed to be!" Kristol recalled. The truly gifted minds of CCNY, in his view, had emerged out of Alcove No. 1.[100] Julius Rosenberg, he quipped, was a member of Alcove No 1. The drawings of the alcoves also suggest that masculinity was most tangibly on display when the students engaged in intellectual debates. The depictions of the men in the alcove "at peace" are of solitary, unassuming men in suits. Only the ping-pong players exhibit a slightly muscular posturing. But when the alcoves are "at war," Jewish masculinity explodes in a juxtaposition of intellectual and physical strength. The men "at war" are transformed from docile students into hypermasculine warriors—tough, strong, and even violent when debating, turning over tables as they clobber one another in verbal combat. Intellectual battles thus brought out a vision of muscular masculinity for Jewish students at CCNY.[101]

Radicalism also inspired the New York intellectuals at CCNY during the Depression. One scholar argues that radicalism was a way for the New York intellectuals to assert a more virile masculinity.[102] But, importantly, their newfound radicalism merged with intellectualism; it did not supersede it. "The alcoves were classrooms," Seymour Martin Lipset maintained. "The older and more knowledgeable taught the newer recruits. They gave lectures, answered questions, and explained passages in Marx, Lenin, and Trotsky." "There was an academic impulse at work in Alcove No. 1," according to Kristol. It "was the place you went if you wanted to be a radical *and*

ALCOVE: PEACE   ALCOVE: WAR

THE KREMLIN

FIGURE 2. Drawings from the CCNY yearbook, *The Microcosm* (1936): (*above left*) Alcove at Peace, (*above right*) Alcove at War, and (*below*) the Kremlin. From the Archives, The City College of New York, CUNY.

have a theory as to the proper kind of radical you should be."[103] Intellectualism, not radicalism, was always more central to the New York intellectuals' conceptions of masculinity, enduring beyond the 1930s as the central motif of their ideology of Jewish masculinity. As they became renowned writers and critics in the postwar years, they held onto this intellectual construction of masculinity, even as they abandoned their youthful radicalism. Nearly all of them, however, went through a crucial radical stage, beginning with its oldest members at the *Menorah Journal*.

Menorah Journal

Founded in 1915, the *Menorah Journal* was the brainchild of Henry Hurwitz and the Intercollegiate Menorah Association (IMA). The IMA emerged from the Harvard Menorah Society, founded in 1906 by Hurwitz and a small group of undergraduates at Harvard College who wanted to explore Jewish identity within an otherwise exclusionary social scene. The society's emphasis on "the study and promotion of Hebraic ideals" or the "Menorah ideal," a cultural and historical rather than a religious approach to Jewishness, resonated particularly with Eastern European Jewish immigrants, and association chapters soon spread to other colleges. In contrast to the position of many assimilated American Jews of Central European backgrounds who shunned aspects of their Jewishness, the IMA celebrated Jewish culture and history.[104]

Unsurprisingly, Hurwitz encountered opposition to the idea of a specifically Jewish magazine. The sociologist Max Handman declined to contribute to the *Journal* because he believed that Jewish culture equated to "mental attitudes," such as "Talmudism, Chasidism and the Ghetto environment." While individually of "great value and charm," Handman wrote to Hurwitz, "participation in the work of modern civilization invariably means that we divest ourselves . . . of the body of institutions and mental attitudes called Jewish culture." In Handman's view, Jewish culture equated to the "Ghetto with all it entails of separatism, clannishness, and finally decay through lack of adaptation."[105] His characterization of Jewish culture as ghetto-like—feeble, frail, and emasculated—reflected the views of many assimilated Jews. It was also similar to the approach of Zionists of this period, who challenged what they perceived as a weak and effeminate "diaspora" Jewish masculinity. Zionists called for the creation of a Jewish state with "new" and "muscular" Jews with characteristics that would "physically mimic those of the gentiles: tall, virile, close to nature, and physically productive." Though the *Menorah* circle included some Zionists, the vast majority of its members "were inclined to be skeptical about Zionism," according to Lionel Trilling, who worked as an assistant editor at the *Menorah Journal* in 1929.[106] Like the Zionists, however, the *Journal* countered the stereotype of Jewish men as feeble and frail but made the reinvigoration of Jewish culture rather than the remaking of the Jewish body central to its philosophy of masculinity.

Hurwitz founded the *Menorah Journal* as a venue to continue the IMA's exploration of Jewish culture and, perhaps more importantly, to offset notions such as Handman's.[107] "The hope was that the damage to Jewish self-esteem caused by antisemitism might be repaired by accepting one's difference and finding strength in it," Robert Alter wrote in his 1962 epitaph to the magazine. There was an underlying gendered objective in this emphasis on Jewish culture being as robust as Western culture. "What was most important for the *Menorah* writers [was] to be able to talk about Judaism in the same terms, in the same refined accents, that the secular high priests of the polite English world used to discuss their culture and history," Alter observed. The *Journal*'s "aim," Norman Podhoretz later noted, was to prove "to the world that that there really *was* such a thing as respectable (by the genteel standards of Harvard University) Jewish culture."[108]

The *Journal* reached the height of its influence when Elliot Cohen served as managing editor from 1925 to 1931. Born in Iowa in 1899 and raised in Mobile, Alabama, Cohen graduated from Yale at age nineteen and pursued some graduate work there in English literature, then considered a "gentlemanly" pursuit not open to non-Protestants. He abandoned his doctoral studies because he was told that as a Jew, he was unlikely to attain a teaching appointment. Like many Jews of his generation, he encountered discrimination at Yale and gravitated to its Menorah Society, publishing his first story in the *Journal* in 1918.[109]

As editor of the *Journal* beginning in 1924, Cohen attracted a group of young and gifted writers, all unknowns at the time, including Herbert Solow, Clifton Fadiman, Henry Rosenthal, Albert Halper, Felix Morrow, and, most famously, Lionel Trilling. Cohen helped trigger an interest in Jewish culture in these young men that they likely would not have developed otherwise. A disaffected Jew from an Orthodox family, Trilling discovered a new perspective on Jewish life through the *Journal*. Upon seeing the magazine, he "was first struck by its handsomeness: I had never seen a modern Jewish publication that was not shoddy and disgusting. Here I found no touch of clumsiness or vulgarity. . . . This was perhaps the first public Jewish manifestation of which I could say that." Morrow recorded similar thoughts: "The critical intelligence, the broad scholarship and culture we found in its pages, [were] nothing short of amazing to us." Other Jewish journals published in English were uninspiring and insipid, a "hall of fame," Morrow said, "for Jewish pinheads and receptacles for the most disgusting kind of parochial chauvinism." While it is unclear which journals Morrow had in mind—perhaps the Zionists' *The Maccabaean* or

Jewish organizational newsletters—he undoubtedly felt that there was no comparable highbrow, secular, Jewish cultural magazines in America. In the *Journal*, Morrow noted, "We found what I, for one, had never expected to find in contemporary Jewish-American life—prose masters and scholars."[110]

An ideology of secular Jewish masculinity, differentiated from what the *Menorah* writers viewed as a weak and parochial Jewish culture, coalesced under Cohen's tutelage. According to Halper, Cohen was a "literary father" to this group of young men. Trilling similarly observed that he was a "Socratic personality" who "taught the younger men around him that nothing in human life need be alien to their thought, and nothing in American life" was beyond their grasp as Jews.[111] His "genius," Trilling explained, "found its chief and characteristically brilliant expression in a strange and wonderful pedagogy" that he imparted through his skills as an editor.[112]

More to the point, Cohen inspired a renewed interest in all things Jewish among these young writers.[113] He did that by advancing a combatively secular vision of Jewish intellectual life. Under Cohen, the *Journal* criticized the American Jewish establishment—including the leaders of Jewish defense organizations, rabbis, and even the editors of the *New York Times*—as weak, ineffectual, and lacking in sufficient masculinity. Cohen's most famous article, "The Age of Brass," published in 1925, "became the manifesto of the *Menorah Journal* group and inaugurated in its pages a golden age of satire," writes one scholar. [114] According to Cohen, the Jazz Age was not a golden age for American Jewry, but an age of superficiality:

> By Age of Brass we mean simply an age that substitutes rhetoric for knowledge, bold assertions for learning, vainglorious pretensions for soundly based convictions, bluster for strength, and bragging for an inwardly felt insecurity; an era that strives to conceal in "high astounding" terms a low intellectual pressure and weak moral stamina.

In explicitly gendered terms—vainglorious, bluster, strength, insecurity, weak moral stamina—Cohen took aim at the false image of confidence espoused by Jewish leaders, whom he accused of pandering to gentiles. After quoting numerous examples of what he viewed as emasculating discourse among Jewish leaders, Cohen argued, "For the arrogance of the phrasing does not conceal that their inner content is apologetical [*sic*]. Most brags," he wrote, "have a snivel at their core; a strong man simply does not find it necessary to bluster." Sidestepping the anti-Semitism of the era, Cohen argued that the Jewish community had prospered in the 1920s, but that it was spiritually "sterile." He added that cultural and intellectual impotency was akin to Jewish emasculation. "The continuous draining away of our best brains," Cohen warned, "will result in the enfeeblement of Jewish strength." Consequently, American Jews suffered from "pathological character" and "delusions of grandeur and of persecution." "For American Jewry," he wrote, "will continue in its tragically comic impotence, a spectacle of bustling futility, until it has learned to recognize and taken steps utterly to destroy the pretentious, but in essence servile, ideology upon which its life is built." By expending so much energy trying to prove the virtues of Jews to gentiles rather than engaging in the actual study and creation of Jewish culture, Jewish leaders had emasculated American Jewry.[115]

While some scholars have argued that Cohen did not offer a prescription to combat Jewish superficiality in "The Age of Brass," in fact his solution was for Jewish intellectuals to redeem Jewish culture and its scholarly heritage, thereby reclaiming the community's dignity and, ultimately, its masculinity.[116] The metaphors he used in describing his plan for Jewish renewal incorporated traditionally gendered, militarized terminology: "For the single most important fact about Israel's impending battle, both from within and from without, is that it is primarily an intellectual battle and must be fought with the recognized intellectual weapons."[117] Cohen, in turn, launched a project of masculine reinvigoration through culture as editor of the *Menorah Journal*.

The masculine camaraderie fostered at the *Journal* extended outside the office to social engagements as well. In December 1929, Cohen and some *Journal* contributors founded the Samson Gideon Memorial Association, or Lishmoh, a social club that would meet weekly "to engage in an evening of Jewish, that is, high (and loud) conversation on the state of America in the Reign of Hoover and the health of the universe." The name of the society juxtaposed a rebellious secular Jewish figure with the Hebrew word "*lishmoh*," a term for Torah study that means "study for its own sake." Samson Gideon was an eighteenth-century British financier and enthusiast of the arts who resigned from his synagogue and raised his children Christian after the repeal of the Jewish Naturalization Bill in 1753. Upon his death, however, it was discovered that he had contributed to Jewish causes throughout his life under an assumed name. Gideon "appealed to Cohen's waggish and subversive sense of Jewish identity," notes one scholar.[118] But, combined with the word "*lishmoh*," the society's name was purposely ironic, signifying Jewish commitment to learning and, at the same time, rebellion from Jewish identity. Like the magazine, Lishmoh aimed its ire at the Jewish establishment. Its letterhead acerbically listed prominent Jews "in Cherem," a reference to ecclesiastical censure and the highest form of shunning in the Jewish community—something similar to excommunication in the Catholic Church. Those "in Cherem" included figures such as Henry W. Morgenthau Jr., the rabbis Isaac Landman and Abba Hillel Silver, and *New York Times* publisher Adolph S. Ochs. The letterhead also evinced a jocularity that defined the *Menorah* circle. Positions on the board of officers included "Shabbas Goy," "Assistant Shabbas Goy," and a treasurer listed as "When Endowed." In a deliberate attempt to chide the Jewish establishment, the group named as "Gabbai" (assistant to the rabbi) "The Elder of Zion," a pseudonym Cohen used in the *Journal* and a sarcastic reference to the anti-Semitic tract *The Protocols of the Elders of Zion*.[119]

Women were scarce at the *Journal*. One of its few female contributors was Tess Slesinger. Born in 1905 and educated at the progressive Ethical Culture School, Swarthmore College, and the Columbia School of Journalism, Slesinger married Herbert Solow in 1928. Solow was a classmate of Trilling's at Columbia University. A year older than Trilling, he graduated in 1924 and was working as an assistant editor at the *Journal*. Their marriage lasted only a few years; the two divorced in 1933. In 1935 Slesinger moved to Hollywood, where she remarried producer Frank Davis, with whom she had two children, and became a successful screenwriter, working on "such well-received movies as *The Good Earth* and *A Tree Grows in Brooklyn* (the first feature film directed by Elia Kazan)." In 1945 she died of cancer. She was thirty-nine.[120]

Slesinger documented her experience in the *Menorah* group in her 1934 roman à clef, *The Unpossessed*. A scathing satirical indictment of this milieu, the book centered its plot on Bruno, a character based on Cohen, and the magazine he started. It explored the gender dynamics of the group, with Slesinger taking aim at the inability of these male intellectuals to accommodate the ambitions of women.[121] One subplot of the novel was the failing marriage between Margaret and Miles, characters based on Slesinger and Solow. Miles was incapable of sustaining a healthy marriage because he felt insecure about earning less than his wife. Slesinger drew from her own experiences. She and Solow were both writers. But Slesinger's work received more acclaim. Beginning in 1930, her short stories began attracting attention beyond the *Menorah* group. According to Elizabeth Hardwick, she was at "the age of twenty-three, more gifted than any in the group, except [Lionel] Trilling." Trilling later recalled how "in those days, success was not thought to be naturally compatible with purity of intention." Instead, it signified a loss of integrity. The *Menorah* writers nonetheless pined for success, "chiefly in the form of literary achievement. But it was Tess who first had it. This must surely have made a difficult situation for her. It would have been difficult for a man; it was even harder for a woman."[122]

The Unpossessed also dealt with personal issues. When Miles forced Margaret to have an abortion, the plot paralleled Slesinger's own relationship with Solow. Slesinger's yearning to start a family came to fruition only after she divorced Solow and remarried. "Intellectual men thought of children as 'biological traps,'" noted Trilling. But Slesinger refused to put her career over family and, in the novel, she admonished Miles for forcing Margaret to abort her unborn child: "He was not a man; she was not a woman. In each of them the life-stream flowed to a dead-end." In her judgment, these intellectuals lacked virility in their public and private lives and simultaneously stymied women professionally and personally.[123]

The Unpossessed also parodied with some accuracy the turn to Marxism on the part of these young writers. By the 1930s, the Jewish cultural issues that had first excited the *Menorah* writers seemed insignificant in relation to the concerns of Depression-era America. "Against the urgent claims on conscience of the radical movements," Robert Alter noted, "the *Journal's* quest for high culture must have seemed like the most effete *fin-de-siècle* decadence and its insistence on Jewish identity a reactionary gesture of pathetic futility." It was a journal attuned to the 1920s, not the 1930s, and by the 1930s, Marxism seemed a better way to assert a masculine intellectualism.

Radicalized by the Depression, tensions that had long existed at the *Journal* with Hurwitz escalated. While grievances about pay also contributed to the writers' frustration, "the heaviest blow struck by the Depression was ideological rather than financial."[124] The *Menorah* writers charged Hurwitz with turning the magazine into a "cultural-non-controversial" publication and becoming just as weak, spineless, and unmanned as the rest of the Jewish establishment. In a scathing letter, Cohen wrote, "The *Journal* will settle down to be the kept tabby-cat on the hearthstone of the official Jewish community, and purr for a living."[125] Cohen and Solow resigned from the magazine in 1931, and many of its young writers followed suit.[126] *The Unpossessed*, however, suggests that *Menorah Journal* intellectuals were weak, passive, and lacking in masculinity because they spouted radical political rhetoric but failed to act on it. Playing on *The Possessed*, Fyodor Dostoevsky's 1872 novel about radicalism, Slesinger inverted the title to signify that the *Menorah* writers were, unlike Dostoevsky's protagonists, uncommitted to their ideals.[127]

The Depression ushered in an important radical phase among these intellectuals. Marxism provided a way to escape Jewishness and the emasculation of their fathers. It was both cosmopolitan and virile—a fighting faith, which found strength in numbers. Radicalism also provided these intellectuals with "a way of achieving masculinity, activism, and effectiveness rather than passivity and victimhood," writes one scholar. Their knowledge of Marxism, Irving Howe wrote, enabled them to "talk faster than anyone else, they knew their way around better, they were quicker on their feet." While some flirted with communism, they quickly gravitated to Trotskyism.[128]

Yet their commitment to radicalism, as Slesinger's satire showed, was always of an intellectual variety. It "lacked roots in a popular movement which might bring intellectuals into a relationship with the complexities of power and stringencies of organization," according to Howe.[129] Few participated in the strikes of the 1930s, especially after the Communist Party launched the Popular Front in 1935, which called for communists to work with liberals, socialists, and other leftists and moderates to defeat fascism. As early anti-Stalinists, the New York intellectuals opposed the Popular Front. Intellectuality, not activism, ultimately was the crucial feature of their masculine identity. Fighting was better done with brains than with brawn.

Most were also soon disabused of radicalism altogether. "Those of us who left home to seek a new community in Marxism, in the expectation that revolutionary activity could be a vehicle for experience, found themselves caught in a net of abstraction and slogans," according to Daniel Bell. In his view, "they won their intellectual spurs, found places in the academies or the world of publishing, but they were politically betrayed."[130]

They came to that conclusion at *Partisan Review*, a journal that many *Menorah* writers gravitated to after splitting from the *Journal*. A slightly younger cohort at City College in the late 1930s and early 1940s was also drawn to *Partisan Review*. "I would read each article at least twice, in a state of awe and exasperation," Irving Kristol recalled, "depressed at the realization that a commoner like myself could never expect to rise into that intellectual aristocracy."[131] Kristol and his contemporaries did, however, join the ranks of *Partisan Review* after graduating from CCNY. So did the first women considered members of the group.

Partisan Review *and Women Intellectuals*

William Phillips and Philip Rahv initially founded *Partisan Review* in 1934. Phillips, a graduate of CCNY (1928), was working as a journalist and teacher when he became involved in the John Reed Club of artists and writers, a group sponsored by the Communist Party. At one of its meetings,

FIGURE 3. The "new" editorial board of *Partisan Review* in 1937,
minus Mary McCarthy, the only woman in the group.
From Riverside Films.

he met Rahv, a writer for the *New Masses*. Both men were growing disenchanted with "the crude literary positions and the corrupt politics of the Communists who dominated the John Reed Club and the literary left generally." So, they decided to launch a magazine that would combine radical politics and literary modernism. "We were cocky kids, driven by grandiose ideas of launching a new literary movement," Phillips later recalled, "combining older and younger talents, and the best of the new radicalism with the innovative energy of modernism."[132]

Partisan Review was initially sponsored by the John Reed Club. But with the start of the Moscow show trials in 1936, Phillips and Rahv broke with the Communist Party for good. Like many of the burgeoning New York intellectuals, they became Trotskyists, and in 1937 they relaunched *Partisan Review* as independent and anti-Stalinist. Its inaugural editorial board in 1937 included Dwight Macdonald, Fred Dupee, George L. K. Morris, and Mary McCarthy.

McCarthy was the first woman to hold her own among this group of combative men. "There was a lot of bluster, a lot of aggression, a lot of argumentation. We had violent meetings—yelling, screaming, arguing," Phillips recalled. But "Mary was the firmest and most acidic." Elizabeth Hardwick joined her a few years later, first writing for *Partisan Review* in 1945. "Both had broken the gender barrier at *PR* and made the male editors not only publish them but respect and listen to them," writes one scholar.[133] McCarthy and Hardwick did so by learning to embody secular Jewish masculinity.

Both women rejected being described as women writers. "Women writer? A bit of a crunch trying to get those two words together," Elizabeth Hardwick once retorted to an interviewer who asked about the specific challenges women writers faced.[134] Writing about McCarthy, Morris Dickstein has argued, "It would even be a mistake to type her as a woman writer. With brilliance and brio, McCarthy freed herself of the biologism of Lawrence and Freud, with its notions of intrinsic gender difference." She lived by the adage "to play the men's game and beat them at it." It's a description that applies to Hardwick as well.[135]

Yet crucially, both McCarthy and Hardwick were also attractive and perceived as sexually available. McCarthy was "very handsome," according to Phillips. "Her legs weren't good but the upper body was. You couldn't take your eyes off her." Hardwick was equally striking. "Thin, wiry, and flexible as a Calder mobile," wrote Phillips.[136] Lionel Abel described McCarthy as "a real beauty. You don't expect that in someone so bright." [137] Hardwick had "a Betty Boop quality to her. In those days women could still be feminine in that way," Jason Epstein said. She was "the prettiest and sexiest and easiest to have a love affair with."[138] Both women had a relationship with Philip Rahv.

Rahv was one of the most towering, ornery, and enigmatic of the New York intellectuals. He has been described as both repulsive and oddly attractive. He was "swarthy," according to Diana Trilling. "He was not fat but he was big and with his wide face and broad shoulders gave the impression of bulk," she said. "Notwithstanding his expensive clothes, there was something primitive, even animal-like in his appearance—my mother would have called him a mujik, by which she would have meant that he had the stolidity and guile of a Russian peasant."[139] Phillips described him as "aggressive, flamboyantly assertive, and domineering." They never got along as editors at *Partisan Review*.[140] Rahv was "cankerous" and "ruthless," according to Macdonald. "With his equals and with men he could be pretty damn tough." But he was "quite a womanizer."

According to McCarthy, "most of the males of the *PR* circle" were at various times his "enemies." Rahv got along better with younger writers who he mentored—and with women.[141]

In 1936 Rahv and McCarthy began a love affair. McCarthy had arrived in New York City a few years earlier, after graduating from Vassar College in 1933. She had just married the aspiring actor Harold Johnsrud and secured work writing reviews for *The Nation* and *New Republic*. In 1936 *Nation* publisher Pat Covici hired her as a full-time editorial assistant. That year she divorced Johnsrud. At a *New Masses* cocktail party, she met James Farrell. He dragged her to a Defense of Leon Trotsky meeting that changed the course of her life. There she met the "*PR* boys." Rahv was five years her senior. She was drawn to his "shy, soft voice (when he was not shouting), big lustrous eyes, which he rolled with great expression, and the look of a bambino in an Italian sacred painting." They soon moved in together in a small apartment in Greenwich Village.[142] They came from drastically different worlds. But both had difficult childhoods.

McCarthy was born in Seattle in 1912 to upper-middle-class parents. Her father was a patrician though Catholic midwestern lawyer. But both her parents died of the Spanish influenza of 1918 when she was only six years old. Thereafter McCarthy and her two older brothers lived with stern paternal grandparents in Minnesota until McCarthy's maternal Jewish grandmother "rescued" her and took her back to Seattle where McCarthy stayed until she left for Vassar in 1929.[143]

Rahv, meanwhile, was born Fevel (which means wolf in Yiddish) Greenberg in 1908 in Kupyn, Ukraine, then part of the Russian Empire. He was the second of three sons born to Abraham and Schprince Greenberg (she Americanized her name to Sarah, Hebrew name, Aviva).[144] Abraham arrived in Rhode Island in 1913 and peddled goods hoping to earn enough to bring the rest of the family over. But when the Russian Revolution broke out, Sarah along with Rahv and his three brothers escaped to Vienna, where Rahv briefly studied in a gymnasium. Somehow, they made their way to the United States. Rahv went "to grade school" in Providence, "still dressed as an old-fashioned European schoolboy, in long black trousers and black stockings, looking like a somber little man among the American kids," McCarthy later recalled.[145] But Abraham struggled to make a living so the family moved to Palestine. Sarah was an ardent secular Zionist. Rahv's older brother Selig stayed in Rhode Island where he worked as a journalist. Rahv spent some time in Palestine but made his way back to the United States when he was fourteen. He lived for a while with Selig but they did not get along. For the next few years he held odd jobs, eventually crossing the country to Portland, Oregon, where he took courses at Reed College but "found several of his professors intellectually inadequate" and never graduated. "He had no time for college, and got his education alone, in public libraries," according to McCarthy.[146]

When the Depression hit, Rahv made his way to Chicago, where he began to construct a narrative about his past that undergirded his radicalism in the 1930s. "Hemingway once claimed that he had to catch and eat pigeons when starving in Paris; Rahv created a similar myth of his early struggles with poverty," one scholar writes. "In this version, he lost his job during the Depression, had no savings and spent six penniless months in Chicago as he made his way across the country. He educated himself by reading in public libraries, stood in bread lines and slept on park benches before arriving in New York in 1932. He then changed his name to Rahv—which means 'rabbi' in Hebrew—joined the Communist Party and began to publish in their main cultural journal, the *New Masses*."[147] In 1934 he founded *Partisan Review* with Phillips.

When Rahv and Phillips relaunched the magazine in 1937, Rahv asked McCarthy to join its editorial board, the only woman among a group of combative men. She later claimed that Rahv "imposed" her on the board and that the men "were not altogether pleased" to have her join their ranks. She said they made her the magazine's theater critic because they did not trust her "critical skills in other fields." Lionel Abel agreed. "I think it's probably true they gave it to her because Rahv and Phillips didn't think it was important." According to Howe, they had "her writing that criticism because they didn't care about the theater to begin with." But Howe knew "Rahv was a very canny character and he probably thought that this would be a place for Mary to practice." And Mary indeed practiced, honing the polemical skills necessary to be part of the group.[148]

She remained part of the group even after she abruptly left Rahv for the literary critic Edmund "Bunny" Wilson in 1938. Ironically, Rahv had encouraged McCarthy to go out to dinner with Wilson and *Nation* back-of-the-book editor Margret Marshall, because he hoped McCarthy would convince the esteemed literary critic to join *Partisan Review*. When McCarthy slept with Wilson, it was a "crushing blow."[149] Rahv was planning to ask McCarthy to marry him. McCarthy later claimed she was never attracted to nor in love with Wilson. She had been drunk when she slept with him. In her memoir, she wrote that she "could not accept the fact that I slept with this fat, puffing man for no reason," and refused therefore to blame alcohol. "It had to make sense. Marrying him, though against my inclinations, *made* it make sense."[150] Wilson also encouraged McCarthy to write fiction. "If it had been left to Rahv," McCarthy wrote in her memoirs, "I never would have written a single 'creative' word."[151]

Macdonald later claimed McCarthy left Rahv for Wilson because he was a "step up."[152] Wilson was not Jewish but patrician. "The bone of contention" in her relationship with Rahv was "religion—a curious thing to be angry about, since both of us were atheists," McCarthy wrote. Rahv was not religious. But he personified secular Jewish masculinity. The two were deeply in love. But they argued incessantly. Rahv "brought an enormous zest to the exercise. Dispute was his art form." Rahv defined it as "a class war," McCarthy later explained. But Jewishness had much to do with it. "I defended my antecedents, and he his. He boasted of Jewish superiority in every field." When they fought, he would tell her: "Scratch a Gentile and you find an anti-Semite."[153]

Her marriage to Wilson produced one son but did not last. The two divorced by 1945. In 1946 McCarthy married Bowdon Broadwater, an "effete" staff member at the *New Yorker*. Broadwater was "a bright, witty, waspish, sterile intellectual-without-portfolio," who acted as "house husband and sort of personal manager." In 1961, shortly after divorcing Broadwater, McCarthy married the diplomat, James R. West. That marriage lasted nearly thirty years, until McCarthy's death in 1989.[154]

Even as McCarthy married men further removed from the New York intellectuals, she remained a card-carrying member. She performed secular Jewish masculinity through her polemical writings and her fiction, which included biting satires of characters often based on the male intellectuals she knew. She evolved into "essentially a polemical writer" through her association with this group, according to Irving Howe. "Mary didn't write essays for the ages. She wasn't like Thomas Mann positioning herself for posterity. It was always a response to something." McCarthy came to write this way because "that was the sense of the essay that we all did."[155] *Partisan Review* junior editor William Barrett described how "her pen" was "usually dipped in acid." "From the point of view of her possible victims," she carried "a stinging whip—the impeccable syntax with which she might lash out at any time."[156]

In 1941 Rahv married Nathalie Swan, a Vassar classmate of McCarthy's. Some thought the union was revenge for McCarthy's betrayal. He remained married to Swan until 1955. In the late 1940s he was rumored to have had an affair with Hardwick. Hardwick denied it. McCarthy, however, was convinced they had slept together.[157] "Sure Lizzie slept with Rahv," Jason Epstein said. "Everybody slept with everybody in those days."[158]

Born and raised in Lexington, Kentucky, Hardwick came to New York in 1938 after graduating from the University of Kentucky. She started graduate work in English at Columbia University but dropped out because she wanted to be a writer. In 1945 she published her first novel, *The Ghostly Lover*, which caught the attention of Rahv. He had also seen Diana Trilling's critical review of it in *The Nation*. Rahv did not get along with the Trillings. When they met, he asked Hardwick what she thought of Diana's assessment. Hardwick quipped, "not much." Rahv asked her to review for *Partisan Review* on the spot.[159]

In 1949 Hardwick married the poet Robert Lowell, a Boston Brahmin by birth with ties to the Southern New Critics. Norman Podhoretz later described him as a "kissing-cousin" of the Jewish New York intellectuals.[160] Their marriage lasted nearly twenty-five years but was plagued by Lowell's struggles with manic depression and infidelity.[161] They divorced in 1972, following an affair Lowell had with the British writer Caroline Blackwood. It was a public scandal made worse when Lowell published a book of poems, *The Dolphin*, that incorporated private letters he and Hardwick had exchanged.[162]

Hardwick was a New York intellectual while married to Lowell and after their divorce because she too performed secular Jewish masculinity. When she first started at *Partisan Review* it was "touch and go," though, and unclear whether "she might not head back to Kentucky." According to Barrett, she was "plunged now into this intense intellectual milieu," and it took time to adapt.[163] Ultimately, she "became a master of the slashing critical style of the politicized literary intellectuals." She had one of the group's "more cutting minds," said Phillips, "a marvelous talker," who "usually managed—like the English—to be charming even when most devastating or malicious."[164]

Hannah Arendt was the only woman among the oldest generation of New York intellectuals not involved with a man in the group. Born in Hanover, Germany, in 1906, Arendt left Germany for Paris when the Nazis seized power in 1933. There she met and married Heinrich Blücher, also a German émigré. In the spring of 1941, after France fell to Germany, they made their way to the United States. Arendt knew little English, but through connections and with the help of translators, she began writing for the *Menorah Journal*, the *Contemporary Jewish Record*, the precursor of *Commentary*, and in 1944 she published her first essay in *Partisan Review*.[165]

Trained in philosophy in Germany, Arendt already wrote like a man. "She was a tough woman," according to William Barrett, who had grown up in the heady intellectual circles of the Weimar Republic and "had to live by her wits from the time she had fled Germany and Hitler."[166] Barrett also said that Rahv was "thrown off stride by encountering an aggressively intellectual woman who talked back to him."[167] After the publication of *The Origins of Totalitarianism* in 1951, she was nearly worshipped by the men in the group. "Anyone who took her on in debate knew he had taken on a heavyweight and usually found out he was overmatched."[168] But their opinion changed after she applied her theory of totalitarianism to Adolf Eichmann in 1963 (see chapter 7). Thereafter some called her "Hannah Arrogance."[169]

Many men in the group found her sexually alluring. "While far from good looking in any commonplace way," Howe recalled, "Hannah Arendt was a remarkably attractive person, with her razored gestures, imperial eye, dangling cigarette."[170] Alfred Kazin was "enthralled, by no means unerotically," he wrote in his journal after meeting Arendt in 1947. She was "darkly handsome," Kazin wrote, adding that "thinking positively cascades out of her in waves."[171] According to Phillips, Arendt embodied a "very strange and seductive combination: firmness of tone and strength of conviction with a soft, almost caressing manner."[172] According to Barrett, "she was much more womanly" than he had anticipated. He helped translate some of her early articles for *Partisan Review* before she wrote English well. When he told Phillips this, the senior editor at *PR* "pondered it judiciously for a moment and then declared, 'I think of Hannah as a very handsome man.'"[173] Phillips's assessment spoke volumes: To be considered members of this group its women had to perform like men.

Diana Trilling was of the same generation as McCarthy, Hardwick, and Arendt. Yet because she was a Jewish woman in a committed marriage to a man in the group, she was dismissed as a mere wife. "The editors of *Partisan Review* frequently gave parties," Diana wrote in her memoir. "They were torturing affairs for any woman who attended them as a marital appendage rather than in her own literary right; both Edna Phillips and Nathalie Rahv, who had to act as hostesses for their editor husbands, would one day confess to me that in order to get through these evenings they had to fortify themselves with several stiff drinks."[174] Diana, the subject of the next chapter, did not become respected as a writer and critic in the group until the postwar years.

Thus, the masculine culture that the future New York intellectuals created in the 1920s and '30s shaped its women members, too. Moreover, it kept developing in the middle decades of the American century, shaping not just the first generation of New York intellectuals, but later generations of writers as well. It did not—indeed could not—remain wholly the province of Jewish writers, and in the postwar years Jewish masculinity came to have profound political and cultural implications.

CHAPTER TWO

"Crazy" and "Genteel"

DI AND LI TRILLING AND SECULAR
JEWISH MASCULINITY

"UNLESS A MAN in the intellectual community was bent on sexual conquest he was never interested in women," Diana Trilling recalled in a 1993 interview.[1] She spoke from years of experience. She met Lionel Trilling in 1927. They married two years later. They remained stubbornly committed to each other for forty-eight years, until Lionel's death in 1975—an unusual feat among the New York intellectuals. Diana, who died in 1996 at the age of ninety-one, was the only woman present from the birth of the group at the *Menorah Journal* through its dissolution in the 1980s. Yet for many years she was not considered an intellectual in her own right. It was only through her "hard" anti-communism in the 1950s that other New York intellectuals began to see her as a formidable critic and writer, independent of Lionel. The surprise is that they saw her as one who, far more than her husband, embodied secular Jewish masculinity.

For many years, Diana was dismissed as a mere "marital appendage" to her more celebrated husband, the critic Lionel Trilling. After she began writing a book review column in *The Nation* in the early 1940s, her status started to change. "Now at *Partisan Review* parties it was as if I had all at once acquired new powers of mind or a new endowment of personal charm," she wrote in her memoir. But "writing for *Partisan Review* was the union card necessary to being considered a New York intellectual," historian Nancy Sinkoff has observed. "William Phillips once defined an intellectual as anyone who wrote for *Partisan Review* and his fellow travelers. He spoke laughingly but not without seriousness," Diana said.[2] By that standard Diana did not become a card-carrying member of the group until 1950, when she was forty-five years old.

Yet Diana appeared on the scene before Mary McCarthy, Hannah Arendt, and Elizabeth Hardwick. She was a contemporary of Tess Slesinger, who wrote for the *Menorah Journal* when Elliot Cohen was managing editor between 1924 and 1931. Slesinger decamped to Hollywood in 1935. Her roman à clef, *The Unpossessed* (1934), was a blistering commentary on the inability of these male writers to accommodate the ambitions of women, both professional and personal.

McCarthy was the first woman considered a New York intellectual. She served on *Partisan Review*'s editorial board when the magazine was revived with an anti-Stalinist focus in 1937. She became the magazine's theater editor—partly because she had been married to an actor but more because theater was viewed as less important and serious and thus more manageable for a woman. McCarthy seemingly held her own in this male milieu from the beginning. She was a "Valkyrie maiden," according to *Partisan Review*'s junior editor William Barrett, "riding her steed into the circle, amid thunder and lightning, and out again, bearing the body of some dead hero across her saddle—herself unscathed and headed promptly for her typewriter."[3] Hannah Arendt and Elizabeth Hardwick started writing for *PR* in the mid-1940s. Along with McCarthy, they were the "women writers who had their own identities at the magazine and weren't known as literary wives," essayist Darryl Pinckney writes.[4] Diana was not initially among them.

Diana never felt entirely accepted within the group. "My Family membership," she told Norman Mailer in 1968, using Norman Podhoretz's term for the group in his 1967 memoir, *Making It*, "has long been questionable on the score of my deficient or insufficient literariness." Diana also wrote for women's and popular magazines. Perhaps for this reason she felt she was "both of the Family and at the same time outside it, or its not-too-notable—black sheep." Mailer tried to assuage Diana's unease. "You are part of the Family," he told her. "Angel, let's not pretend if one were to choose ten names for the Family, yours by any consensus would have to be one of the ten." Mailer made a sports analogy. "If Norman [Podhoretz] didn't mention you in his list, I know it was one of the characteristic oversights which all of us make when we are listing 10 people essential to a cause or an era, so in a baseball list, Micky Mantle's name might be left out." Diana remained nonplussed. She "was a member of the Family if only because I couldn't get away with saying I am not." Diana could not shake the feeling that she had "gotten in with a false passport." Her passport was Lionel.[5]

The other women in the group, however, also initially gained access to this milieu through relationships with men. McCarthy and Hardwick may have "broken the gender barrier at *PR* and made the male editors not only publish them but respect and listen to them," writer David Laskin notes, but both women were at one time Rahv's girls, meaning they had affairs with *Partisan Review* editor Philip Rahv.[6] Both women were viewed by men in the group as attractive and flirtatious *shiksas*. Both went on to marry prominent writers: McCarthy married literary critic Edmund Wilson in 1938 (they divorced in 1945; McCarthy would go on to marry twice more), and Elizabeth Hardwick married poet Robert Lowell in 1949. Their rocky union lasted until 1972.[7]

Arendt was arguably an exception. She and her husband Heinrich Blücher immigrated to the United States in May 1941 following the Nazi invasion of France. By all accounts, she never strayed from him. "Heinrich was her partner," according to Alfred Kazin. "There was no tension between them over their intellectual standing or accomplishments. They did not compete with each other. It was not like a typical American marriage." Kazin probably should have said typical New York intellectual marriage. But other figures in this group had a more cynical view. Diana told Laskin that, "Arendt kept Blücher 'chained to her bedpost' so he would always be there when she needed him." Lionel Abel said that "Hannah pretended that Blücher was her intellectual equal but he wasn't. . . . He was a nobody." Meanwhile, "William Phillips compared Blücher to the neglected wives of the *PR* editors: he was 'the husband' and not much else." Arendt was the only woman who could have had her partner dismissed as "the husband."[8] Significantly many male New York intellectuals found Arendt alluring, nonetheless.

McCarthy, Hardwick, and Arendt were "power women," according to Diana, who "crossed the line and were accepted among the boys" in ways she never was. All three were viewed as flirtatious, attractive, and in the case of Arendt, exotic as a European émigré. "All of them were very sexually promiscuous," according to Diana. Whether true or not, all three women emanated a sexual radicalism that reflected their bohemianism, cultivated in the prewar years. They "thought life was literature," Diana said. But "they confused the two. Their lives were lived under the aspect of literature in a way my life was not. Mine was lived under the aspect of life."[9]

Diana, in contrast, was a conventional Ashkenazi Jewish woman. She was not viewed as seductive or flirtatious, but was always Lionel's wife. In her 1993 memoir, *The Beginning of the Journey*, Diana wrote at length about her marriage and how it affected her own career. "Lionel felt of my work that it was not enough appreciated and that this was chiefly due to his presence in my life. . . . He was talking about the nature of our marriage, the fact that I not only wrote under my married name but always appeared in public as his wife, never as someone with her own literary identity. He would point out to me—but he never talked about it with anyone else—that there was no other woman writer in our circle who was so unremittingly coupled with a man as I." Diana, however, had a "simpler explanation." People felt she "had enough good fortune in being married to someone as attractive and agreeable and distinguished as Lionel without, in addition, having distinction of my own."[10]

Lionel and Diana had one of the New York intellectuals' most enduring marriages. Their monogamy and general marital disposition stood out. "The Trillings were thoroughly civilized people, and behaved as such: they arrived at parties in time," recalled Barrett, "and they left in time—before the small hours of the morning when too much had been drunk and the gathering that remains becomes loud and bathetic."[11] According to Sidney Hook, "the extraordinary thing about Lionel and Diana is that they were exceedingly proper in their manner."[12] They embodied "the predictability and the cautiousness of what Philip Rahv called 'middleclassicism à la Trilling,'" Laskin writes.[13]

Diana was right, however, to highlight Lionel's public persona. He *was* handsome, outwardly agreeable, and refined. He embodied a genteel masculinity, distinct from the other New York intellectuals.[14] People saw Diana, by contrast, as fiery, loquacious, and combative. It was she, not Lionel, who came to publicly embody secular Jewish masculinity. Lionel "was well-spoken and articulate, but not argumentative," according to Hook.[15] Diana was the more "political" and polemical of the two. In William Phillips's view, "[Lionel] Trilling was able to preserve his working self by dissociating himself from the draining and time-consuming engagements of human relations—a trait, by the way, I admired and envied. Oddly, or maybe naturally, Diana Trilling was just the opposite."[16]

Descriptions of Diana as quarrelsome and sharp were not usually cast as compliments. "She was a dogged woman and looked it," said Alfred Kazin, who was not friendly with either Trilling. Despite his animus, Kazin captured how many in the group viewed Diana. She had "an unforgiving stare that was to last forever," according to Kazin. "Her favorite literary genre seemed to be the letter to the editor. Sometimes she wrote in to criticize an unfavorable review of a book for not being unfavorable enough."[17] According to another writer who circled this milieu, Diana was "an outrageous diva, all temperament, no rationality whatsoever."[18]

Diana was difficult. Yet, most of the men in this group were difficult, too. They were combative, acerbic, callous at times. Their reputations were never reduced to those qualities, however.

The women New York intellectuals had to walk a finer line. They had to write like men to be taken seriously. But when deemed too combative and opinionated, they were denigrated as difficult and bitchy.[19] This was true of McCarthy, Hardwick, and Arendt at various times. But Diana had a reputation as the most annoying and difficult of them all. "Though feared and on occasion revered in her lifetime for her critical intelligence," essayist Daphne Merkin has observed, "she was also regularly snickered at by fellow eminences in the backbiting group around her known as the New York intellectuals." That "snickering continues more than two decades after her death."[20] According to Carolyn G. Heilbrun, who studied under Lionel and was the first woman to receive tenure in the English department at Columbia, "Those who wrote of Diana Trilling, and those who over the years I heard talking of her, found no reason to appreciate or praise her. Almost every reference to her that I had ever read was negative, portraying her as lacking any intellectual power, unimportant, querulous, difficult, flawed."[21]

Diana's combativeness was conspicuous in part because it stood in such contrast with her husband's public image. "Her polemical energies," according to one journalist, ultimately "prompted the sort of hostility her husband largely escaped."[22] She was the aggressive one. "Diana was more downright and direct in her response to people: invariably blunt," writes Morris Dickstein. "She was prone to tell them exactly what she thought," unlike Lionel who "seemed distant, genial, and ironic." "Lionel was much more controlled and abstracted than Diana not only in his writing but in ordinary conversation," according to Phillips. "He did not embroil himself in most of the political controversies of the period."[23]

The New York intellectuals' ideology of secular Jewish masculinity shaped both Lionel and Diana—but with distinct results. Lionel outwardly evaded secular Jewish masculinity to become a professor of English literature. But his reputation for being calm, refined, and aloof depended heavily on being married to the more publicly caustic and acerbic Diana. She made it possible for him to project an image of someone unsullied by the contentious quarrels that busied the New York intellectuals. Examining the couple in tandem reveals much about both the possibilities and limitations of the New York intellectuals' ideology of secular Jewish masculinity in mid-century America.

Daughter of the Middle Class

Diana Rubin was born in 1905 in the East Bronx to Jewish immigrant parents from Poland, the youngest of three children. She had an older sister five years her senior and a brother three years older. Her father, Joseph Rubin, had immigrated to the United States from Warsaw at age eighteen to avoid military conscription by the czar. Her mother, Sadie Helene Forbert, came to New York as a teenager after growing up orphaned in the Polish countryside. According to Diana, she "scarcely knew she was Jewish." Joseph Rubin initially peddled fresh-baked cookies to earn a living. After learning English, he graduated to a braid (ribbon) salesman and then braid manufacturer, opening up his own factory in Bush Terminal in Brooklyn. His business brought the family a degree of economic stability, catapulting the Rubins into the middle class. "We were never wealthy," Diana wrote in her memoir. But "we were what is called 'comfortable.'"[24]

Diana did not grow up in crowded tenements as most other New York intellectuals did. She spent her childhood in Westchester County—in Larchmont and New Rochelle. When she was in high school, her family settled into a large house in the Midwood section of Brooklyn, close to her father's hosiery factory. Diana attended Erasmus High School in Brooklyn, graduating in 1921. Her parents then moved to a large apartment on the Upper West Side. "Most of the intellectuals I have known made their way from what was then accepted as the lower or working class into the middle class by their own efforts," Diana wrote in her memoir. "Lionel and I had our membership in the middle class secured for us by our parents."[25]

In the fall of 1921, Diana headed to Radcliffe. She was sixteen years old. Like many other children of immigrants, she graduated from high school early. The vast majority stayed close to home and enrolled at one of New York City's free public universities: CCNY for men, Hunter College for women, or the co-ed Brooklyn College. Families with more money sent their children to Columbia, Barnard, or NYU. The Rubins were better off than most Eastern European Jews. To send a child to college out of state was the sort of thing that "German" or "uptown" Jews did. They had immigrated a generation earlier and assimilated as they prospered.[26]

Attending Radcliffe did not reflect any extraordinary intellectual acumen on her part, Diana claimed. "For many years, even before it became a part of Harvard, to be accepted by Radcliffe was a badge of uncommon academic distinction. That was not how it was when I went there," she quipped. Rather, she landed on the school somewhat randomly, as if flipping through a "telephone book." She was drawn to the women's college because she wanted to "avoid what I supposed would be the sexual competitiveness of a coeducational college but I also wanted to be near a men's school and near a big city."[27] Women's suffrage, finally ratified in 1920, did not fire Diana's ambitions for public life. Her generation of women, she claimed, went to college to find a husband.

She also longed to get away, if only briefly, from familial obligations. Her father acquiesced despite her mother's protests. "The unspoken but unnegotiable agreement by which I had been permitted to go away to college was that as soon as I graduated I would return home where I belonged." She felt her non-Jewish peers had more autonomy. "Gentiles," she said, "were free of the close ties of Jewish family life." After graduating, they had more freedom to explore before settling down and marrying. Not so for Diana. "I had not been sent to college to prepare for an independent life, either emotional or financial," she wrote in her memoir. "There was no need for me to be financially independent, because my father was there to take care of me." Thereafter the responsibility would fall to her husband. She majored in art history with no plans for a career.[28]

Diana said she encountered little anti-Semitism at Radcliffe, though she matriculated just as elite colleges were beginning to impose quotas to limit Jewish enrollment.[29] But she tended not to associate with the other Jewish students at Radcliffe. Most were commuters from Cambridge and Boston who "huddled together in self-imposed exile." Two exceptions were, like her, assimilated girls who lived in the dorms. They became her closest friends. "Our impulse to join the full life of the college set us apart from the majority of Jewish students." They came from different places but "had basically the same origins: we were all three of us the daughters of immigrant Jews who had not allowed either their foreign birth or their religion to determine the kind of lives they led as Americans. That is to say, we were assimilated Jews—the designation was not yet thought to be pejorative."[30]

After graduating in 1925, she moved back in with her parents on the Upper West Side, as she promised. Her mother was ill and died in the fall of 1926. Diana was only twenty-one. She half-heartedly looked for a job and for a while tried to be an opera singer. But these years were a "bleak and lonely" period. She floundered. "Somewhere between college and the professional world for which we had presumably been trained we women lost our way," Diana observed in her memoir. "We were professionally schooled but not emotionally schooled or properly directed for professional achievement."[31] This was not the only hint of a feminist consciousness in Diana's memoir.

FIGURE 4. Diana Trilling at Radcliffe in the 1920s. From Diana Trilling Papers, Rare Book & Manuscript Library, Columbia University in the City of New York.

Li and Di

In 1927 Diana was introduced to Lionel Trilling by mutual friends. Their first date was at a speakeasy in the West Forties. Lionel was a graduate student at Columbia, teaching part-time at Hunter College. They married two years later. Their marriage lasted until Lionel's death from pancreatic cancer in 1975. They had one son, James, born in 1948, when both were forty-three.[32]

FIGURE 5. Diana Trilling's author photo for *Claremont Essays*
(1964). Photo by: Jim Theologos, photographer,
painter (1940–2021).

Their long-lasting marriage made them atypical. But it was far
from a smooth-sailing union. Diana made those rough patches public
in her 1993 memoir of their marriage, *The Beginning of the Journey*.
All the more remarkable, then, was their self-suppressing feat: the two
remained unflinchingly committed to each other through Lionel's death.
Theirs was a "great marriage," she told her biographer. But "it was not
one of the great love affairs."[33] Their monogamy contrasted with the love
lives of many New York intellectuals, who married serially and who often
strayed.

Lionel's parents were Jewish immigrants from Eastern Europe. His father, David Trilling, arrived in New York from Bialystok at age thirteen. He became a successful tailor, "a skilled workman with an artist's conception of his craft," according to Diana.[34] Lionel's mother, Fannie Cohen, was born and raised in London, like her mother, but her father, Israel Cohen, had immigrated to England from Russia-Poland. The oldest of nine children, Fannie came to the United States at age sixteen. She and David married eight years later in 1889. They were pious and orthodox. But "the Trillings were hardly stereotypical Jewish immigrants from Eastern Europe," according to historian Michael Kimmage. "What separated them from other Eastern European Jews was their Anglophilia."[35]

Fannie shared her love of England with her children: Lionel and his sister Harriet, seven years younger.

Lionel became a professor of English literature. His first book was on the eminent nineteenth-century literary critic Matthew Arnold, who became Trilling's model of literary manhood. Lionel sought to fulfill "Arnold's demand that a critic 'should have the finest tact, the nicest moderation, the most free, flexible, and elastic spirit imaginable,'" Morris Dickstein observed. Lionel "seemed to exemplify the same values. He had an aloof but gracious amiability." In his writings and in his public image, Lionel came to embody masculine Victorian virtues like refinement, civility, stoicism, and self-restraint.[36]

Lionel's genteel masculinity was outwardly at odds with the more verbally aggressive mode of secular Jewish masculinity of the other New York intellectuals. "Lionel was a very mild and good-looking young man," Diana told an interviewer. "He also was not fierce and rude and polemic," like so many of his peers who came of age in the 1930s.[37] William Phillips described Lionel as "jaunty but low-keyed, classically handsome, very much like the aristocratic portraits of the seventeenth century, with soft but defined features, modest but assured in his manner." He was neither combative nor aggressive. William Barrett characterized Lionel as a "graceful man" who "had style in the classic sense—*ars celare artem*—style that seemed to be second nature with the man himself."[38] According to Irving Howe, Lionel had "a grave elegance of style," and a "disinclination toward polemic," which made him both admired in their milieu and "disturbing in one or another way."[39]

Many New York Jewish intellectuals were "uneasy in admiration," according to Howe. Some resented Lionel's Anglo masculine persona, which they believed was a conscious evasion of Jewishness. His "air of unassailability," Diana observed in her memoir, disturbed other Jewish

New York intellectuals.[40] Robert Alter privately characterized Lionel as a Jew "who had succeeded in 'passing' at the country club."[41] Harold Rosenberg "once described Trilling as an Eliotic Cleric of Culture, and mocked his formal demeanor, hedged with irony, as a case of advanced respectability."[42] Rosenberg told Alfred Kazin, "When I first encountered the style of Lionel Trilling, I looked for the joke and discovered there wasn't any."[43]

In his 1978 memoir, *New York Jew*, Kazin provided a famously harsh portrait of Lionel. The two first met in 1942 after Kazin published his groundbreaking study of American literature, *On Native Grounds*, which Lionel warmly reviewed in the *New Republic*.[44] Kazin described Lionel as having a "debonair practiced easiness of manner." Even in the early 1940s, "with the deep sunk colored pouches under his eyes, the cigarette always in hand like an intellectual gesture, an air that combined weariness, vanity, and immense caution, he was already a personage," Kazin wrote. But this was a carefully crafted image, he felt. "I had never encountered a Jewish intellectual so conscious of social position, so full of adopted finery in his conversation." For Lionel, "I would always be too Jewish," Kazin remarked, "too full of my lower-class experience," to ever impress him.[45]

Kazin wrote that Lionel betrayed a "timidity, a self-protectiveness as elegant as a fencer's." Morris Dickstein more charitably determined that, "despite his courtly Anglophile manner, he showed anxieties and strengths that were distinctly Jewish. He weighed his words as though he were an institution, as if one thoughtless remark could make the edifice crumble."[46] Yet when Dickstein taught at Columbia in the mid-1960s, he too felt "inescapably Jewish in a style that" he believed "disturbed" Lionel. In this way he reinforced Kazin's assessment. "I had grown up in the immigrant cauldron of the Lower East Side," Dickstein wrote. "I could be restrained, even stoical, but no one would have mistaken it for" what Lionel praised as "manly reserve."[47]

People assumed that Lionel had changed his name. "That 'Lionel Trilling,' which sounded euphoniously English, was a constructed personality."[48] Many New York intellectuals had changed their names as part of the radical movements of the 1930s: Philip Rahv was born Fevel Greenberg; Irving Howe was born Horowitz; Daniel Bell had been Bolotsky; William Phillips changed his name from Litivinsky. All changed their names to sound less Jewish.[49]

But Lionel had in fact been born Lionel Mordechai Trilling. His first name, Diana claimed, was likely the "Anglicized form of his Hebrew

FIGURE 6. Lionel Trilling photographed by Walker Evans in the 1950s.
© Walker Evans Archive, The Metropolitan Museum of Art.

patronymic, Lev," though she said Lionel never cared for it. "Boy or man, he longed to be a Jack or a John, a Mike or a Bill, anything except a Lionel," Diana wrote. Throughout his life, rumors circulated that he had changed his last name from Cohen (his mother's maiden name) "to pass himself off as an English gentleman, presumably Gentile."[50] Lionel was aware that he benefited from a name that sounded un-Jewish. "'I don't know what the origin of the strangely un-Jewish name is,' Trilling wrote toward the end of his life, 'but that it *was* un-Jewish made, I have no doubt, a significant fact in my life.'"[51]

In this way, it was ironic that Lionel came from a long line of "intellectually distinguished" scholars in Bialystok.[52] His father had "been slated for the rabbinate." But according to family lore, David botched his Bar Mitzvah ceremony so badly that his parents "shipped him off to America in disgrace." His father's humiliation hovered over Lionel's adolescence. If

Lionel "had a part to memorize for a school play or even a lesson to recite," Diana said, "his mother made sure that his father was out of their hearing lest Lionel be infected with his father's boyhood failure."[53]

Lionel's father had failed not only as a scholar but also as a breadwinner. He had decided to go into business for himself as a manufacturer of men's coats because "he did not wish his son to have to say he was a tailor." According to Diana, the elder Trilling was "a good tailor" but "a bad businessman and never again made a reliable living."[54] The family did manage to rise into the lower reaches of the middle class when Lionel was a boy. The Trillings' first apartment on West 108th Street was just blocks from Columbia University.

When the Depression hit, however, his father's business went bankrupt. Like the immigrant fathers of many of these intellectuals, David Trilling was unable to fulfill either Jewish or American norms of manhood. Lionel, then a graduate student, had to support his parents and sister, along with his new young wife, on the salary of "a lowly college instructor dependent on the yearly renewal of his appointment." "Lionel's life," Diana said, "was dangerously dedicated to being as unlike his father as possible."[55]

Lionel would spend nearly the entirety of his adult life in Morningside Heights, the neighborhood that surrounded Columbia University from the south. Harlem bordered from the north. After graduating from DeWitt Clinton High School at sixteen, he entered Columbia College in 1921.[56] He graduated in 1925. He spent the next year at the University of Wisconsin at Madison. But by the fall of 1927, he returned to Columbia and enrolled in the PhD program in English.[57]

Lionel's process of masculine socialization thus differed in so many ways from that of the New York intellectuals who attended City College. But it still shared some similarities. "At Columbia or New York University or the City College of New York," Diana observed, "New York produced young intellectuals with roots in the Jewish European rather than the American past. The Jewish intellectual tradition was a sternly questioning one. The study of Talmud is the disputation of law; there is nothing accepting about it, or genteel, or accommodating," she wrote.[58]

Lionel entered graduate school when Jews were unwelcome in the genteel field of literature. His friend Elliot Cohen, the managing editor of the *Menorah Journal*, had abandoned plans to pursue a doctorate in English at Yale because he was told as a Jew, he would never secure employment. Lionel wrote some of his earliest essays for the *Menorah Journal* when Cohen was its managing editor from 1924 through 1931 and briefly worked as an editor there. But once he settled on the topic of his dissertation, he focused on honing a masculine persona that was not conspicuously Jewish. He had little choice. The English Department at Columbia was "as crowded with three-barreled Anglican names as the House of Bishops," as Kazin observed.[59] "Lionel set himself toward an academic career in English in a period when it was felt to be a betrayal of the Anglo-Saxon tradition to entrust this to anyone other than Anglo-Saxons," Diana later told the writer Francis Steegmuller.[60]

This was not an easy task. "These people would have been very glad to see somebody working on Arnold," Diana told an interviewer, referring to Lionel's colleagues, but "there was no encouragement that Lionel really got from these people." He was the wrong type of person to write on Arnold. They told him it was "too big of a subject," but what they really meant was that "they didn't think he was worthy of it." Because he was Jewish. As his dissertation languished, his teaching appointment was almost not renewed because he was told that, as "a Freudian, Marxist, and a Jew," he would be more comfortable elsewhere. "What they meant," Diana told an interviewer, was "you're not one of us."[61]

Lionel, however, did not accept his termination. He confronted his colleagues in a moment that Diana described as pivotal to his career—and his masculine persona. He told them in no uncertain terms that they "had never had, and never would have, anyone as good as he was." In a display of anger and aggression that startled his colleagues, he cursed and called one of them "a bastard or son of a bitch," Diana later claimed. They "were so astonished" by his words and "actions, so back on their heels that this worm had turned," that they let Lionel keep his job.[62] "Like most people," Diana concluded, "Lionel's senior colleagues preferred the company of the strong."[63]

Prior to that confrontation "he had no confidence in himself," according to Diana. "He was totally unable to assert himself; he wasn't a force as a young man." The "image" he had long "presented to the world was one of powerlessness." Thereafter he exuded the opposite: independence and poise. "For him to change this and impose upon his department an image of determination and deep inner strength was an extraordinary feat of self-renovation." There was a "relationship between the release of aggression and the writing of the dissertation." The confrontation motivated him to finish. The writer's block he long suffered under "was broken."[64] Lionel was writing like a man. His colleagues now respected, maybe even feared him. He was in their eyes, too, a man.

In 1939 the English Department hired him as an assistant professor. In 1944 he became the first Jew to receive tenure in Columbia's English

Department. Columbia president Nicholas Murray Butler intervened to get him both the job and promotion because he was impressed with Lionel's work on Arnold. Lionel's colleagues, however, made sure that he knew that his "appointment would not be used to open the department to other Jews."[65] Attitudes changed after the war. Staying at Columbia until 1975, when he retired, Lionel saw other Jewish colleagues hired. But in those first few decades, he treaded cautiously.[66]

Lionel carefully crafted a public image that while confident and poised, was not too combative or aggressive—not too Jewish. His masculine persona emanated civility, refinement, and an aloofness that allowed him to appear above the fray of politics, in stark contrast to his fellow partisan New York intellectuals. Lionel's "detachment," Dickstein observed, "contributed to his stature. He rarely allowed himself to be sucked into the quarrels of the New York intellectuals or the intense backbiting on the Columbia campus."[67]

Yet "he always felt that *Partisan Review* readers were his readers," Diana recalled. "He had an enormous sense of community there" that grew out of their shared anti-Stalinism. But he never identified with the "avant-gardism" or "fierce polemicism of the magazine."[68] According to Sidney Hook, "none of us close to him recognized Trilling's literary stature—Elliot Cohen, Herbert Solow, and Lionel Trilling's associates at Columbia, Meyer Schapiro and Ernest Nagel." By that Hook meant that there was a disconnect in how Lionel was viewed by his peers and by the broader public. "We liked Lionel," Hook said, "but he never could offer an argument in defense of a position." Hook implied that his genteel masculinity was at odds with the New York intellectuals' ideology of secular Jewish masculinity.[69]

According to Li and Di's son, James Trilling, Lionel's public persona would not have been possible without Diana. "The air of reserve and polite superiority by which he kept the world at a distance" was interpreted as "the emanation of a deeply admirable character," James wrote. "The magic didn't always work, and some people scorned my father for pretending to be English (his mother *was* English). Nevertheless, by the middle of his career his manner was taken widely as a sign of Apollonian detachment and wisdom. . . . He never could have sustained this persona without my mother's help."[70]

In *The Beginning of the Journey*, Diana wrote at length about Lionel's masculinity. Seemingly aware that his masculine persona shaped his career, she wanted to share some of the struggles behind that public image. Diana started with Lionel's childhood. "He had not been allowed a boy's normal life of action," she wrote. His parents treated him like a "princeling," denying him "the usual physical activities of boyhood." Lionel "never had a bicycle" or "roller skates." There was a "constant fuss and nervous attention directed at him," regarding food, clothes, and activities. When he played outside, his parents would not allow him to pack a brown-bag lunch. Lionel's "everlasting dream of manly relaxation," she quipped, "was to eat from a lunch pail."[71]

In Diana's view, Lionel's boyhood deficiencies followed him into adulthood. He was gawky in sports. "There was no doubt a connection between Lionel as a driver and Lionel as a swimmer," Diana wrote. "Even as a pedestrian, Lionel had a deficient sense of direction." He was a "maddening tennis player," "compensating in energy for what he lacked in skill, he raced furiously around the court, never where he should properly have been, yet never refusing a ball." His inferiority allowed many a non-Jewish competitor to take delight in beating their "brainy Jewish" colleague.[72]

Lionel also struggled as a breadwinner. The couple was in chronic debt. Though Lionel eventually became "a steadfast provider," Diana took care of their finances because Lionel "was not to be relied on even in the use of a checkbook."[73] Though this was an inversion of American gender roles, Ashkenazi Jewish women often managed family finances in Eastern Europe and worked alongside their husbands in a "breadwinning partnership." Since Talmudic scholars embodied idealized masculinity, the industrious rabbi's wife legitimated an economic role for Jewish women in Europe. While Diana was never the family's primary breadwinner, she contributed to the family's economic security.[74] As for the New York intellectuals broadly: "Shtetl conditions prevail[ed]," one ex-wife observed. Most had wives who "seemed to support the husbands financially."[75]

Diana's handling of the family's finances also bolstered Lionel's public image as a detached literary professor. "He conveyed the serenity of a man who is free to tackle the big questions because he takes his logistical support for granted," James Trilling wrote. "No one saw my father trying to desperately cope with the responsibilities of daily life, because he never had to. No one saw his life fall apart through inattention, because it never did." His mother, Diana, made that possible.[76]

Diana also edited Lionel's works, especially early in his career. "Many years before I became a literary critic," Diana wrote in an unpublished essay, "I was the diligent in-house critic of my husband's work."[77] Like many other New York intellectuals, Lionel suffered debilitating bouts of writer's block. "There were days and days he sat in front of his typewriter unable to write a word." His dissertation was especially difficult. It took him nearly a decade to complete. Diana helped him finish it and then revise it for publication. "In draft after draft of his *Matthew Arnold*, I removed, added to, or otherwise altered what he had written. What I was trying to bring to his writing was a greater directness and a greater fluidity. I wanted it to have at once more spine and more grace." She edited many of the essays that appeared in his celebrated book, *The Liberal Imagination* (1949). Diana claimed she had an "ease with words" that Lionel lacked. "I helped him to write more attractively, with more clarity and rigor both of thought and expression," she claimed repeatedly in her memoir. But she was careful not to take credit for shaping his "ideas other than as style is inevitably an extension of thought." In her view, "Lionel taught me to think; I taught him to write."[78]

How did Lionel respond to her editing? Early in his career he "welcomed" and even "counted upon" her, which was "good sense on his part," Diana wrote in her memoir. Other male writers they knew were far more defensive. "Over the years, when I have tried to provide similar editorial help to various of our men friends, they have taken it as an assault on their masculinity." Writing equated to masculine performance in this milieu. When Lionel struggled with writing in later years, he often fell into depressions and directed angry "flurries" at Diana.[79]

Diana was not the only wife who edited or otherwise aided the writings of their husbands.[80] In his recent biography of Susan Sontag, Benjamin Moser corroborated long-standing rumors that Sontag wrote most of her husband's, Philip Rieff's 1959 book, *Freud: The Mind of a Moralist*. She also probably ghostwrote many of his essays. Sontag married Rieff in 1950, when she was a seventeen-year-old sophomore at the University of Chicago. Rieff, eleven years her senior, was a lecturer in sociology. The two divorced acrimoniously eight years later. According to Moser, Sontag agreed to relinquish any claims to authorship of the book in exchange for full custody of their young son. In the acknowledgments to the first edition of the book, Rieff "thanked 'my wife, Susan Rieff, who devoted herself unstintingly [*sic*] to this book.'" That Rieff referred to Sontag by a married name that she never adopted was interpreted by many as a not-so-subtle dig at his ex-wife.[81]

After Sontag moved to New York and became one of the junior members of the New York intellectuals, her career outshined Rieff's. According to Moser, four decades after the publication of *Freud: The Mind of a Moralist*, Rieff sent Sontag a copy with the inscription: "Susan, Love of my life, mother of my son, co-author of this book: forgive me. Please. Philip."[82] As for Lionel, he too thanked Diana in the preface to *Matthew Arnold*. "My debt to my wife, Diana Trilling is greatest of all," he wrote. "I cannot calculate its full sum, for it amounted to collaboration; at every stage of the book, she was my conscience, and there was scarcely a paragraph that was not bettered by her unremitting criticism and creative editing."[83]

Diana believed that after Lionel died people would learn just how much she helped him. "I'm afraid it will become public knowledge once his manuscripts [become] available that there was scarcely a sentence he ever wrote that I didn't rewrite," Diana told Midge Decter in February 1976, a few months after Lionel's death.[84] Diana was furious when those manuscripts never materialized. She was convinced Lionel had destroyed the drafts of essays and books she had labored over. She told biographer Natalie Robins that he "left earlier versions on which for one reason or another I hadn't worked [but] wherever there was a really notable amount of my handwriting, he destroyed the manuscripts." Diana concluded that Lionel had consciously rendered her editorial interventions invisible.[85]

Scholars have questioned Diana's claim of coauthorship because of their different public personas. Lionel was known for his civility, while Diana came to be recognized for her sharp tongue. "Lionel was one kind of a writer: elliptical, cerebral, allusive, a teacher who drew the reader forward toward unexpected conclusions precisely because the teacher's words were not the last word. He was a clear-headed virtuoso of ambiguity," Michael Kimmage argues. "This was not Diana's style. She had aspired to be an opera singer in her youth, and she knew how to project her voice, which was direct, intimate, concrete, and opinionated. She was an observer who did not mind weighing in or levying judgement."[86] Indeed, Diana was the more abrasive of the two.

Numerous reviewers have also doubted Diana's characterization of Lionel in her memoir and questioned her motives. It was a "sharp revisionist portrait of Lionel Trilling," according to scholar John Rodden, that revealed "a darker side to Trilling's life, at odds with his public image and well hidden from the view of friends and colleagues."[87] Hers was a "vinegary memoir," in Dickstein's view, "part tribute, part revelation, part declaration of independence by someone who felt she dwelled too long in her husband's shadow."[88] Her characterization of Lionel was jarring because Diana had "previously been a fierce defender of his posthumous reputation," Mark Krupnick observed. "She peels away the image of poise and gentility to reveal a man feckless and inept. . . . The complaint is basically the same from start to finish: Lionel wasn't much of a man."[89]

Midge Decter wrote a review of *The Beginning of the Journey* for *Commentary* magazine. She and her husband, Norman Podhoretz, who studied with Lionel at Columbia as an undergraduate, had been good friends with the couple. But that changed when Podhoretz and Decter became leading neoconservatives. In her review of Diana's memoir, Decter, who established her own reputation as a fierce critic of second-wave feminism, alluded to feminism to disparage Diana's book. "It is impossible not to find lurking in these pages a contemporary feminist subtext," Decter wrote. Diana claimed she did not "[wish] to put herself forward as Lionel's literary superior, or even peer," but the book nonetheless gave "some of her feminist reviewers the impression that Diana was a woman forced to stand in her husband's shadow." Decter charged that this was intentional on Diana's part. But wrong. Anyone who knew Diana and knew the couple knew she was the far more forceful of the two. "Her presence, whether in a room or on the page," Decter said, "was all her own, distinct and, to put it mildly, unignorable."[90]

Attack, Attack, Attack

Decter was referring to Diana's reputation as caustic and "difficult." She was not alone. Writers and critics who looked back on Diana's career remembered her aggressiveness. A *New York Times* reporter in the 1990s, for example, spoke of "her stringent method: 'attack, attack, attack.'"[91] But that method was precisely the method of other New York intellectuals. To be part of this group, one had to attack. The men in the group were combative, polemical, and unyielding in verbal and literary combat. They were not "easy companions," as Diana wrote in her memoir. "They were overbearing and arrogant, excessively competitive; they lacked magnanimity and often they lacked common courtesy."[92] But few were criticized for that publicly. Their personalities were afterthoughts if critics mentioned them at all. Their accomplishments mattered more than their manners. Not so for Diana.

Diana was married to Lionel for twelve years before she began writing professionally. During those years she observed the New York intellectuals' ideology of secular Jewish masculinity. "My career as a critic still lay in the future," she wrote in her memoir, "but unconsciously I may have been preparing for it."[93] Lionel and his friends "were professional intellectuals," she told an interviewer. "I listened to Lionel talk with his friends, and pretty soon their professional idiom became mine."[94] She told a group of Radcliffe students that, "My training in criticism had come wholly from my husband, Lionel Trilling; that is, from my day-by-day association with him and his friends."[95] She in fact "came out of Radcliffe badly underread." It was Lionel who "shared the attitudes and tools of the intellectual trade with me. . . . I learned not only what to read but how to think about what I read. He gave me a literary and critical vocabulary and prepared the path to what eventually became my career. This is not to say," she wrote in her memoir, that "I was an object of his conscious pedagogy. Lionel did not undertake to teach me; I learned from him casually, unconsciously, by association."[96]

In the early years of her marriage, Diana had dabbled in creative writing. She wrote plays and short stories, "only to fill time," she claimed. But in 1929 she sent one of those stories to Elliot Cohen at the *Menorah Journal*. Cohen never responded. Tess Slesinger told Diana that Cohen told her he liked the story. Cohen's silence, however, was deafening. Had Cohen bothered to respond, Diana conjectured she might have begun writing earlier. Perhaps even fiction. "Ours was a society in which there could be few more significant accomplishments than to write a novel." Diana, however, did not publish an original book until after Lionel's death.[97]

Significantly, Lionel also aspired to write fiction. He had published several short stories in the *Menorah Journal* before he turned to his dissertation on Matthew Arnold. In 1947 he published his one and only novel, *The Middle of the Journey*, a fictional account about breaking with the Communist Party. The title of the novel alluded to the various roads the characters took as they came to realize the duplicity of the Communist Party. All were in the middle of their journeys. "The end of the journey will be anti-communist, the novel implies, but it will be reached in separate, conflicting ways by the liberal and the conservative, and possibly never reached at all by the radical," Kimmage writes.[98]

Yet *The Middle of the Journey* received lackluster reviews and sold poorly. The book only gained renown later for foreshadowing one of the biggest trials of the early Cold War era: the Alger Hiss case. About a year after Lionel published the novel, Whittaker Chambers, an editor at *Time* magazine, testified before the House Un-American Activities Committee (HUAC). He admitted that he engaged in espionage in the 1930s and named Alger Hiss, a high-ranking official in the State Department during the Roosevelt administration, as an accomplice. Hiss vehemently denied the charges. Thus began a two-year ordeal that ended in a perjury conviction for Hiss in 1950.[99] "Had *The Middle of the Journey* not been a roman à clef, weirdly prescient of the Hiss case," writes Kimmage, "it would probably have gone from its initial cool reception to outright neglect."[100] Instead, the book was a harbinger of the anti-communist furor to come.

The Middle of the Journey was partly autobiographical. Lionel based one of the characters of the book, Gifford Maxim, on Whittaker Chambers.

Lionel knew Chambers when both were undergraduates at Columbia. They met sometime in 1924–25. "According to Trilling, they had never been friends, but they had friends in common."[101] The novel's hero, John Laskell, bore a striking resemblance to Lionel. Lionel acknowledged as much, telling a student that "I had for a time more or less the political attitudes of John Laskell, whose feelings in general are, I suppose, more or less what mine were likely to be at his age." According to Diana, "Laskell is Lionel's voice in the novel: his political moderation and the quiet humanity which he counters to the fiery emotions of Gifford Maxim or a Nancy Croom closely approximate Lionel's own temperament and approach to politics." Two other characters, Arthur and Nancy Croom, seemed modeled after Alger and Priscilla Hiss. But Trilling wrote the book "before he even heard of the Hisses." Thus, the Crooms were rather "Popular Front archetypes."[102]

While *The Middle of the Journey* received few accolades from critics, the actual process of writing the book made Lionel feel manly. He "felt like Hemingway, whom he always envied and admired for his uninhibited masculinity," notes one scholar. "Trilling associated creativity with masculinity, and to publish a novel made him feel masculine."[103] His "high regard for Hemingway" was a "surprise—a shock" to many, Diana wrote. But "in Freudian terms, Hemingway represented the triumph of the id over superego, with the resultant creative powers." But *The Middle of the Journey* was Lionel's only novel. "The failure to make his career as a novelist," Diana felt, contributed "to the feeling of failure which shadowed Lionel's life even at its most successful."[104] It was emasculating, and Lionel likely did not want Diana to write fiction if he couldn't.

In her memoir, Diana cast Lionel as supportive of her career. But she also concluded that he limited it. "No one could fairly have asked for a more supportive husband than mine," Diana wrote. But "I now see that I regarded any activity other than that of wife and mother as a privilege extended to me by my husband. He gave me the gift of a career, allowed me this enlargement of my life. Because he never proposed that I extend the boundaries of my professional career by writing a book of my own or by trying my hand at another kind of writing than criticism, I took it for granted that things should remain as they were." It was Lionel who got Diana her first job as a reviewer, and she did not pursue writing projects unless Lionel approved of them. "I even interpreted a silence as prohibition," she wrote in an unpublished essay late in her life.[105]

Diana became "a writer by accident" in the fall of 1941. Margaret Marshall, the literary editor of *The Nation*, asked Lionel if he knew anyone who would be interested in writing the magazine's anonymous "brief notes" on fiction. Diana volunteered. With Lionel's endorsement she got the job.[106]

Initially, the anonymity of the reviews emboldened Diana. She had never published before and was terrified to sign her name to a review. "I wished to remain permanently obscure—or so I supposed," she wrote in her memoir. Within a few months, however, Diana realized she wanted her name attached to her work. "My preference for obscurity turned out to be a substantial self-deception."[107] She received her own column but vacillated over whether to write under her maiden or married name. Friends at *Partisan Review* "were united in the advice I write under my maiden name," Diana recalled. "They feared that I was going to be an embarrassment to Lionel." Lionel, however, was "adamant that I write as his wife."[108]

For most of the decade, Diana churned out reviews for *The Nation* on "any new novel with a pretension to seriousness." These reviews began to establish her reputation as a fierce critic. "Apparently, whatever my private timidities, my voice was firm and courageous," Diana wrote in her memoir. She shared the following anecdote to convey the reputation she acquired: "A Viennese novelist, a refugee from Nazi Austria, was said to have remarked that he lost his country, his home, his language, but that he had at least one good fortune: he had not been reviewed by me."[109] In 1948 she began a review by stating: "If anyone has illusions about the happy life of a book reviewer, I suggest he read the three novels I comment on this week."[110]

Diana's sharp prose was directed at highbrow and middlebrow novelists alike. Ayn Rand's first major literary success, *The Fountainhead*, was "the curiosity of the year," Diana wrote in 1943. It was a "754-page orgy of glorification" and "anyone who is taken in by it deserves a stern lecture on paper-rationing." John Hersey's Pulitzer Prize–winning 1944 novel, *A Bell for Adano*, was made up of no more than "Hollywood-naïve prose." Of the writers in her orbit, she was equally harsh. Saul Bellow was "talented and clever and he writes with control and precision," but his 1944 debut novel, *A Dangling Man*, was one of those "small novels of sterility." The gendered undertones of Diana's critique stung. "My book is probably not great," Bellow supposedly grumbled to his editor, "but it is not 'small.'"[111]

Diana could be especially harsh toward women writers. "Even more than our men writers, our women writers, especially when they deal with their sexual emotions, have a way of filling the world with themselves alone and of exploiting fiction to promote their own follies and grievances," Diana wrote in 1944. "They produce almost without exception one-character books in which the one character is the author and the book is more case history than fiction."[112] Here she likely had in mind, among other genres, the roman à clef, which brought success to Tess Slesinger (*The Unpossessed*, 1934) and Mary McCarthy, whose 1942 novella, *The Oasis*, satirized the *Partisan Review* crowd. Its plot revolved around a group of liberal intellectuals who try to form a utopian community in the countryside but fracture along ideological lines. Diana was not a fan. After reading the book, she supposedly said of McCarthy: "that woman is a thug."[113]

In Diana's view, women writers generally lacked "courage," or a point of view. "This lack reveals itself in a style which creates no overtones of the author's own comment on her narrative but many overtones of *New Yorker* chic."[114] That is, they wrote differently from men, which meant they did not write well.

That criticism extended to women in New York intellectual circles, too. Elizabeth Hardwick engaged in "a kind of romantic literary mediocrity," Diana wrote of Hardwick's debut novel in 1945. Though Hardwick would soon become known for her acerbic prose, Diana dismissed her as essentially a "lady" writer, a pejorative often used by the New York intellectuals to describe women writers. "For by any of the usual tests *The Ghost Lover* earns a poor score: it lacks drama or even a coherent story, few of the characters are given their narrative due, there is no unity of rhythm in the prose, and much of the book is dull reading," Diana wrote. While Hardwick had "promise," Diana doubted she could bring "her talent to fulfillment." To do so, "Miss Hardwick has a tremendous task ahead of her: she must learn to make her prose her servant rather than her mistress."[115]

Diana felt little kinship or sense of "sisterhood" with other women writers, and she gave little indication in these years that she was sympathetic to feminism. She accused Virginia Woolf, who passed away in 1941, of engaging in "sexual chauvinism." In a review of Woolf's posthumous collection of essays, *The Moment* (1948), and the republication of *The Common Reader* (the first volume originally published in 1928; the second volume in 1932), Diana argued that male critics had given Woolf "preferential treatment" because she was a woman who wrote about women. They "handled" her "carefully" as a result, lest they be accused of cruelty. Yet "this delicate lady," as Diana called her, "insisted upon equal consideration in the male world." But Woolf "always took her ultimate refuge in female sensibility." Thus, "despite her pride of intellect and her open feministic protest," Woolf "made it almost impossible to meet her head-on like a man."[116]

A Queenly Cold Warrior

Diana, in contrast, was determined to write like a man. In 1949, after nearly a decade at *The Nation*, she resigned. She wanted to write longer, more critical pieces for journals like *Partisan Review*, which she had never published in. Diana's decision to leave *The Nation* also likely had to do with politics. Throughout her years at the magazine, Diana's "anticommunism was seldom far from the surface of [her] reviews."[117] But *The Nation*'s longtime editor, Freda Kirchwey, was a fellow traveler who called for accommodation with the Soviet Union. *The Nation*'s literary editor, Margaret Marshall, was anti-Stalinist. Kirchwey, "to her credit, believed in free speech. We said whatever we wanted in the back of the book, which contradicted everything she said in the front of the book," Diana later recalled. "It was really two magazines," Diana said. But the result was a "schizophrenic enterprise in the 40s." By the late 1940s that tenuous arrangement could no longer hold. Diana resigned from *The Nation*, ostensibly to pursue longer writing projects, but politics likely had something to do with it as well.[118]

Facing the prospect of freelancing rather than having a regular book review column to write, Diana initially struggled over what topics to write on. Throughout the 1940s, even though "the women's movement had not yet begun, all the publishers who took me to lunch in the hope of signing me up for a book wanted me to write about women," Diana wrote in her memoir.[119] A book on the topic never materialized. But after leaving *The Nation*, Diana put together an outline for a "series of articles on the American Female."[120] But Diana likely concluded that writing about women would not establish her as a serious critic and writer. Her outline languished for much of the decade. When she finally returned to it in the late 1950s, she published those articles in women's magazines and mainstream glossies.

In the early 1950s Diana needed to demonstrate that she could write like a man. So she turned to anti-communism, a subject she was passionate about and one that she knew would establish her as a serious writer. "The anti-communist intelligentsia was not at all monolithic. Opposition to communism, coupled with the will to weaken or defeat Soviet communism, could reflect an infinity of ideas," as one scholar notes.[121] Diana, along with Lionel, occupied the center-right of this spectrum. But Diana was by far the more vocal and forceful of the two in print but also through her involvement in the American Committee for Cultural Freedom (ACCF), an anti-communist group spearheaded by Sidney Hook in the early 1950s. Diana became a "queenly Cold Warrior" among a sea of male anti-Stalinist New York intellectuals.[122]

Like many of the older New York intellectuals, Diana and Lionel briefly flirted with communism. Hook had "converted" them to communism in the summer of 1931 while they were at Yaddo together, the retreat for writers and artists in Saratoga, New York. Hook "did not remain a communist for long: he soon confronted the character of the Soviet regime, its absolutism and injustice and cruelty, and for the rest of his life he was a passionate opponent of communism," Diana wrote in her memoir. "But at Yaddo in the summer of 1931 he was still ignorant of the range of Stalin's power and the means by which it had been arrived at and was maintained." When the Trillings returned to New York, they joined the National Committee for the Defense of Political Prisoners (NCDPP), a communist-front group that Elliot Cohen was also active in after leaving the *Menorah Journal*.[123]

Their involvement with the NCDPP, however, quickly disabused them of any illusions that communists stood for social justice. Of the NCDPP's handling of the Scottsboro case in 1931, which involved five Black teenagers falsely accused of raping two white girls on a freight car in Alabama, "it soon became clear," Diana wrote in her memoir, "that the Communist Party was not concerned with the justness of their cause. It had come into the case for its own political motive." The Party cynically took on the case to amass support from Black Americans.[124]

In such opportunism, American communists "paralleled" the treachery and self-interest of Stalin and the Party based in Moscow, Diana said. Like most of the other New York intellectuals, she and Lionel became avidly anti-Stalinist. There was not one moment that marked their break from the Party. But by the Moscow show trials and purges of 1936–37, they were done. "Lionel's and my intimacy with the radical movement of the early thirties would have a deep and lasting effect on our thinking about politics and society and on the kind of work we did for the rest of our lives," Diana wrote in her memoir. "It made anti-Communists of us."[125]

The New York intellectuals contributed much to America's anti-communist liberalism of the postwar years. They championed a liberalism severed of any illusions toward the Soviet Union and communism. It was a "mature" liberalism that disavowed its naive dalliances with the Popular Front of the 1930s.[126]

Calls for "maturity" were ubiquitous in postwar America. "'Maturity' was promoted as the hallmark of the well-adjusted male and men were urged to fulfill their responsibilities as breadwinners and fathers," writes historian K. A. Cuordileone.[127] The nuclear family, with its stay-at-home mother and breadwinning father, secluded in affluent suburbs and raising their children in houses stocked with the latest consumer goods, was upheld in these years—in mass culture and by politicians, including Vice President Richard Nixon—as a bulwark against communism.[128] Anti-Stalinist liberals called for a mature liberalism bereft of any connections to the radical idealism of the Popular Front. Arthur Schlesinger Jr.'s classic 1949 book, *The Vital Center*, was perhaps the most famous example. "In this remarkable cold war composition," writes Cuordileone, "the 'vital center' emerges in the text not just as the locus of a tough-minded liberalism whose leaders bring a 'new virility into public life,' but also as the home of a secure and restored American masculinity."[129]

Lionel Trilling in many ways set the tone for that liberalism in his influential 1949 compendium of essays, *The Liberal Imagination*. "Often associated with the 1950s, the decade in which *The Liberal Imagination* had its deepest influence," writes Kimmage, "if *The Liberal Imagination* was of a decade, it was of the 1940s, recording the arc of Trilling's early anti-communism."[130] The essays in the book were written between 1946 and 1948. Lionel had never been a Trotskyist. In this way his political "maturity" came earlier than many other New York intellectuals. In *The Liberal Imagination* he called for a "mature" liberalism bereft of childish illusions that socialists—or any political movement—could remake the world, by revolution or politics.[131] "Maturity" was a theme that greatly influenced anti-communist writings in the postwar years, particularly criticisms of the Soviet Union, the People's Republic of China, and those in the West who sympathized with those regimes.

Lionel focused more on literature than politics, however. He disparaged social realism and the fetishization of Stalinism in the arts and literature during the Popular Front. His "literary criticism was pivotal to the anti-Stalinism of *Partisan Review*," writes Kimmage. But his cultural and literary bent also made him seem less political, less confrontational than the more aggressive and polemical Cold War liberalism of the other New York intellectuals.[132] He was seemingly more restrained.

Diana was the opposite of restrained. According to Jason Epstein, she once stood behind her husband's chair at a dinner party and told the other intellectuals in attendance, "None of you men are HARD enough for me!"[133] Whether Epstein's recollections are reliable is debatable. But Epstein undoubtedly spoke to Diana's reputation. "She had a passion for polemic against all possible dupes of the Soviet Union that in the McCarthy era and the heyday of the American Committee for Cultural

Freedom was to make her the scourge of all mistaken ill-thinking 'anti-anti-communists,'" Alfred Kazin recalled.[134] Epstein's remark highlighted the subtext of a woman accusing men of not being virile or "hard" enough. It was through an aggressive anti-communism that Diana came to embody secular Jewish masculinity.

Diana's first long, original essay for *Partisan Review* dealt with Alger Hiss. William Phillips had approached Diana about writing on the Hiss case for the magazine shortly after she left *The Nation*. She "was flattered but badly frightened." [135] She had never written for *Partisan Review*. Over her "own protest of inadequacy," she recalled, Phillips convinced her to take the subject on.[136]

Diana wrote as the Hiss case unfolded. Hiss had been charged with perjury after denying charges of espionage before HUAC in August 1948. He could not be charged with treason because of the statute of limitations. His first trial ended in a hung jury in 1949, but in a second trial he was found guilty of two counts of perjury in January 1950. Diana's piece appeared a few months later, as Republicans seized on Hiss's conviction to portray Democrats as "soft" on communism and as Joseph McCarthy, a junior senator from Wisconsin, rose to prominence by capitalizing on the issue.

Diana's article was part of a larger effort by anti-communist liberals to defend and redefine liberalism as masculine. Like many other Cold War liberals, Diana depicted Hiss as impotent. Hiss was the "prototype" of the New Deal liberal, she argued: "well-educated, eager, sensitive, charming." Like so many men of that generation, he was idealistic. But idealism could be emasculating. "In our own century, the source of all idealism," Diana argued, "has been socialism," and especially in the era of the Popular Front, "idealism" had led to cooperation with communists. Given the "ideological atmosphere of the time," Hiss did not have to perform "much intellectual acrobatics" to become an "undercover Communist." His "practical idealism" allowed him to believe that he "could both think like a Communist and act like a good servant of American Liberalism."[137]

Like several other New York intellectuals, Diana argued that liberals had a responsibility to disavow Hiss and other unrepentant left-wingers. To do so was to show political maturity. But many refused to do so. Unrepentant liberals criticized anti-communist liberals like Diana for turning into "strange bed-fellows" of right-wing reactionaries like Senator McCarthy. This was a "distasteful" union, Diana argued, but difficult to avoid.[138] "Hiss' defenders warned us that his conviction would be a signal for a grand-scale hunt for Communists in government, and one in which innocent liberals would be tarred with the Communist brush. The way McCarthy conducts himself confirms this fear," Diana wrote. But the fear was predicated on the "belief that Hiss was himself an innocent liberal." For those who believed "Hiss was guilty, you must still continue to fear that innocent liberals will be smeared by McCarthy," Diana argued. "But you must also acknowledge the awkward fact that had it not been for the Un-American Activities Committee Hiss's guilt might never have been uncovered. And you reserve the possibility that a McCarthy, too, may turn up someone who is as guilty as Hiss. What you lament is the tragic confusion in liberal government which leaves the investigation of such crucial matters to the enemies of liberalism, like McCarthy."[139]

A year later, Diana followed with another essay in *Partisan Review*. Titled "A Communist and His Ideals," Diana had first delivered it as a speech at a symposium sponsored by the American Committee for Cultural Freedom (ACCF) in May 1951. Idealism in and of itself was not bad, Diana argued. "By idealism we mean the dedication to goals beyond self-interest."[140] The trouble was that communists manipulated the idealism of "unthinking" people on the left. Idealists were foremost concerned with "virtue." But virtue without intelligence was reckless and emasculating. "Living for virtue and without pride, the idealist is forced always to keep his eyes elsewhere than on himself. Himself is, by assumption, a weak and faulty vessel, and he can find good only where he is not—in the country which is not his country, in the class which is not his class, in the races and religions which are not his race and religion, in the occupations which are not his occupations, in the advantages which are not his advantage, even (sometimes) in which the sex is not his sex." The idealist, she continued, finds sustenance in "the principle of self-deprecation."[141] This was a "psychology of subservience; we become servants. And where there are servants, there are masters. This is the path by which an ideal politics, a politics of supposed freedom, becomes a real politics of repression. It is the path by which Communism has become a totalitarianism as bad as fascism," she warned.[142]

Anti-communism preoccupied Diana for much of the 1950s. Though she created an outline for a series of articles about the American female after leaving *The Nation*, it was not until 1958 that Diana published articles on that subject. Diana had drawn from that outline in a review of Margaret Mead's 1949 book, *Male and Female*. It was her first byline in *Partisan Review*. Her longer original essay on Hiss (not a book review) appeared a month later. Diana chose not to write about women's issues, even when reviewing the work of one of the most discussed feminists of the period: Simone de Beauvoir. In 1953 Diana wrote about Beauvoir, the French existentialist, for the journal the *Twentieth Century*. She did not, however, discuss *The Second Sex*, Beauvoir's landmark study of women, published in French in 1949 and translated to English in 1953, which became a groundbreaking work of feminist theory. Rather, Diana wrote about Beauvoir's recently published journal, *America Day by Day*, which chronicled the writer's four-month visit to the United States in 1947.

Diana took aim at the book's "hostility to America," its "inaccuracies and distortions," which she attributed to Beauvoir's preconceived views, informed by her politics. "Her journal is a faithful testimony of what she saw because she saw only what she wished to see," Diana wrote. Beauvoir's views were "nourished by a political doctrine . . . Communism." She was an unrepentant fellow traveling liberal, Diana argued.[143] "We look for a name by which to call this blindness: sometimes we call it Stalinoidism; sometimes we call it Stalin-liberalism," Diana wrote. "But none of these labels is precise as applied to the phenomenon that shows itself so variously, and anyway, what to call it is less important than how to combat it." Diana continued:

> Why, we ask ourselves, should people who think of themselves as liberals prefer to throw their weight on the side of an established tyranny, rather than on the side of an established democracy, however faulty? Why, despite the inescapable fact of Soviet totalitarianism, do people who think of themselves as nothing if not fact-facers persist in the illusion that Communists are more their allies than are anti-Communists? Why, and particularly in the learned professions throughout the democratic world, is it so steadily part of conscience and enlightenment to see an absolute evil in America's every lapse from democratic perfection, while glossing over the absolute evil which is the Soviet Union? Why do supposed liberals cling to the notion that to attack a Communist is somehow to attack their own better selves?[144]

Diana headily devoted herself to these questions in the 1950s. Not just in her writings but also through her involvement with the American Committee for Cultural Freedom.

The ACCF and Women

Founded in late 1950, the ACCF was the American affiliate of the Congress for Culture Freedom (CCF), established six months earlier in Berlin in the summer of 1950. Both groups sought to galvanize anti-communist intellectuals in opposition to Stalinism and in defense of cultural freedom.

Diana eagerly joined the ACCF soon after it formed. "It was the group she had been waiting for," according to her biographer. She felt it was "where she belonged."[145]

The ACCF was organized by Sidney Hook, who served as the group's executive chairman from its founding through 1955. According to Hook, at its height in 1952–53, "the membership list of the ACCF consisted of several hundred of the most distinguished men and women in the cultural life of the nation."[146] Sol Stein, the ACCF's executive director between 1953 and 1956, later recalled that, "there was no question as to the cultural stature of an organization that included Arthur Schlesinger Jr., Lionel Trilling, Reinhold Niebuhr, J. Robert Oppenheimer, A. Philip Randolph, David Riesman, Upton Sinclair, John Steinbeck, James Johnson Sweeney, Bruno Walter, Robert Penn Warren, Thornton Wilder, James T. Farrell, Robert Motherwell, W. H. Auden, Richard Rovere, Norman Thomas, Dwight Macdonald, Peter Viereck, Saul Bellow, Norman Cousins, John Dos Passos, Arthur Koestler, James Baldwin, and George Balanchine, among many others elected by their peers from the political spectrum except for die-hard extremists at either end."[147]

But contrary to Hook's proclamation that the group included "several hundred of the most distinguished men and women," most of its members were men.[148] Out of the hundreds of intellectuals listed as members in the group between 1952 and 1955 barely a dozen were women.[149] Only three women ever served on the group's board or as officers: the novelist Grace Zaring Stone, Pearl Kluger, and Diana. Stone served as the group's first treasurer executive secretary. But she rarely attended meetings and by 1953 seems to have dropped out of the group. Pearl Kluger had a more enduring presence. She served as the group's executive secretary. Her job related to the group's finances, however, and she was minimally involved in its intellectual activities.

Diana was really the ACCF's only active woman member. Not only did she serve on the group's executive board for multiple years but following the noisy resignation of James Farrell as chairman of the executive board in the fall of 1956 (Farrell succeeded Hook), Diana was elected as chairman.[150] While Lionel had lent his name to the ACCF when the group was "in formation" in the last months of 1950 and joined the group once formed in 1951, he was much less involved in its activities.[151] "He was not one to join a movement, not even one of his own making," writes Kimmage.[152] Diana was far more active.

Founded in the same year that Senator Joseph McCarthy rose to prominence, the ACCF continuously struggled over the issue of McCarthyism.

In its first meeting the group acknowledged "the danger of certain men and groups who represent themselves as militant opponents of Communism, but who make use of devices or strategies which have considerable affinity with totalitarianism, and which are wholly inappropriate to democracy."[153] But how to treat McCarthy was a subject of constant consternation. Daniel Bell later recalled that there was "a small group" who "wanted a specific attack on McCarthy." But "the majority view," which prevailed, "was that one should denounce violations of cultural freedom in general (see resolutions passed) and name McCarthy only where specific instances were warranted."[154]

Diana leaned toward a "harder" anti-communism but was more measured than others in the group. In late 1952 she criticized those members who maintained that "their fight against the anti-anti-Communist position" was not an endorsement of McCarthyism, a position she found "specious." Such "anti-anti-McCarthyites" were mistaken not to confront the excesses of McCarthy. "Why don't you come out against McCarthyism as I have," she told Arnold Beichman, one of the group's "hard" anti-communists, "indicating your agreement with him that Communists are an evil, even the chief evil, but asserting your disagreement with his methods and motives."[155]

Yet after McCarthy was censured in the fall of 1954 and as domestic anti-communist furor began to wane, Diana remained steadfast in her commitment to a "hard" anti-communism. In her 1993 memoir she wrote that McCarthy's "procedures and those of the House Un-American Committee were a serious threat to freedom and an offense against the democratic process. But they were not a witch hunt, as they are so often said to have been. Witches do not exist. Communists and Communist fellow travelers did exist, the latter in abundance."[156] It was a point she had made forty years earlier in her review of *America Day by Day*. Beauvoir "is a victim of the prime liberal fallacy of our time," Diana wrote. "Mme. de Beauvoir sees no resemblance at all between Communism and Fascism. In her opinion, Communists are, in fact, not only no threat, they are not *real*; they exist only in the reactionary imagination; they are the witches of the witch hunt."[157]

By the time Diana was named chairman of the Executive Committee of the ACCF, the group was on the verge of collapse. In January 1957 it suspended its activities.[158] Between 1954 and 1957, many ACCF members resigned from the organization. There were some conservative right-wing anti-communists in the group who felt the ACCF had lost its will to combat domestic communism, while others felt that communism was no longer a threat in the United States. Diana was never a part of that group. On the contrary, she continued to insist on the dangers of communism through the early 1960s.

The ACCF resurfaced in 1959 to take over the publication of *Partisan Review* for tax-exempt purposes.[159] That led to Diana's acrimonious resignation. Diana had initially "strongly favored the proposal that the committee take over the publication of *PR* and without editorial interference of any kind," as she later told Phillips. She "foresaw possible difficulties" with the connection, but at the time they struck her as "minor . . . compared with the importance of keeping *PR* in existence as an independent journal."[160] By 1960, however, Diana felt *Partisan Review* was no longer sufficiently anti-communist. Its "cultural-political attitudes" had shifted away from her own and for these reasons she felt she could no longer serve on the board of the ACCF.[161] "There was something thoroughly unsound about my being in a position in which I appeared to be sponsoring a point of view which I deeply disapproved," she later told *PR* editor William Phillips.[162] Rather than demand the magazine find a new sponsor, she resigned.

Diana had clashed with *Partisan Review*'s editors over politics in preceding years. After she published an article critical of the Beats in the magazine in 1958, she observed a "notable breach" between her and the magazine. It "became unmistakable to me that my contributions to *Partisan Review* were no longer welcome."[163] The magazine was leaning leftward while Diana remained firmly in the liberal anti-communist camp. At the ACCF board meeting in December 1960, William Phillips acknowledged that "there had been a lot of trouble and criticism over her article on the 'beats' in *PR*." But he denied that she was barred from the magazine. The differences between the editors and her were "literary, not political or cultural." Phillips argued that the article was poorly written and executed.[164] Diana disagreed. "William says the difference is literary," she wrote in yet another statement about her resignation, read to the board on January 10, 1961. "I say the difference is cultural-political."[165]

Diana's resignation catalyzed a broader discussion among the ACCF's Executive Board about the group's sponsorship of the magazine. "There was too much secrecy" when it came to the relationship between the ACCF and *Partisan Review*, Arnold Beichman stated at a December 19, 1960, board meeting. "Such a relationship could only lead to increasing dissatisfaction." But many board members were angry at Diana in ways that are difficult to explain. "It is justifiable criticism of Mrs. Trilling that she wanted to raise these issues," Hook exclaimed, but he accused her of raising "these issues without taking responsibility for raising them." Other board members agreed, and they voted to reject her resignation. They feared her resignation would sully the reputations of both the ACCF and *Partisan Review*.[166]

Diana wrote several long letters and statements in response to the board's position. "The fact that my move has brought to the surface doubts and questions about the tendencies of *PR* in the last year or two which might otherwise have remained unvoiced," she wrote in a second resignation letter, "does not imply, and should not imply, that it is my personal situation with *PR* which creates these doubts and questions."[167] Diana reiterated that she did not take issue with the ACCF's sponsorship of the magazine, but instead was uncomfortable with *Partisan Review*'s shift to the left. The magazine's "response to communism," she explained, had "considerably altered from what it was a few years ago. A magazine which once viewed the struggle between Western democracy and Soviet Communism as an inevitable and unending cold war until one side or the other had a decisive victory no longer believes in cold war."[168] She disapproved of *PR*'s embrace of the "zeitgeist" of the early 1960s. *Partisan Review* was swinging left, like *Commentary* under Podhoretz's new editorship. "The line that developed at *Commentary* is typical," she complained to Arthur Schlesinger Jr.[169] Looking back on the controversy years later, Diana explained that "toward the end of the 50s," as the New Left emerged, there "was a new kind of activity for which one had to have a new political vocabulary and certainly a new cultural vocabulary, and the old terms of reference," by which she meant anti-communism, "weren't quite the same."[170]

Many prominent male intellectuals had resigned from the ACCF between 1954 and 1960. They elicited responses ranging from frustration to a silent shrug; Diana's resignation was met with unanimous and vitriolic condemnation, however. The members of the board were insulted that she questioned the anti-communist stance of *Partisan Review*, but also the ACCF's commitment to anti-communism. According to the board's minutes, Sidney Hook said that "Mrs. Trilling is conceited about many things," and he could understand why *PR* didn't want to publish her. "Her letter was like somebody throwing a stone and saying he didn't mean to break a window." Diana later recalled that Hook told her that her "whole project of a quiet resignation from the board was indicative of my lack of political sense—if I disagreed with the magazine policy as I (and now he) did, then I should make a big open fight and destroy the magazine," she wrote in a 1980 letter to William Phillips.[171] At the ACCF board meeting, Bertram Wolfe "called for the rejection of Mrs. Trilling's resignation." He declared, "She ought to be asked to come to a future meeting and explain her position like a man."[172]

Diana was the only woman on the ACCF board. It is hard not to see some sexism in the vitriol directed at her. William Phillips characterized Diana as "crazy" after her resignation. In a 1969 letter in which she recalled the whole affair, Diana wrote that "you [Phillips] reported to me that when you went to England a short time later you were asked about the situation and your reply to these inquires was that Trilling was crazy but you loved her anyway."[173] Phillips managed to remain friends with Diana over the years—unlike Hook, whom Diana rarely spoke to. Williams later apologized. "On the crazy bit, I did not realize you were upset by this," he wrote, "and I must now somewhat belatedly apologize." Phillips hedged a bit, however. "I thought you knew I used the term loosely, extravagantly, as a metaphor for inconsistencies, self-indulgence or temperament, the way I do about so many of my friends."[174]

Years later, Diana still felt slighted. The "gossip routes in the literary community" were filled with the news that "Diana Trilling had taken to destroy *Partisan Review*," she recalled in a 1979 interview.[175] A decade earlier she had told Phillips that the descriptor "crazy" was unwarranted. "You called me crazy rather than call me wicked." Though she made no mention of sex, she did observe that "objectively, the whole damn thing turned out to be a mess. But the worst of which I can accuse myself in the situation was stupidity, a lack of recognition of the kind of people I was dealing with on the Board."[176] The kind of people she was dealing with were combative, aggressive male intellectuals.

———

In the early 1950s Diana established herself as a New York intellectual through her aggressive anti-communism. Anti-communism, as the next chapter will show, was also how the New York intellectuals proved their American and masculine credentials in the early years of the Cold War.

Diana's "hard" anti-communism showed she could write like a man. Like other women in the group, however, she was derided as a result. But even more so. Diana seemed especially pugnacious in part because she was married to Lionel, who outwardly embodied a more tamed and genteel masculinity that some New York intellectuals admired, and others scorned. Diana, meanwhile, was deemed "difficult" and "crazy." Her frustration, combined with her growing resentment at being treated as secondary to her husband, would eventually lead her into sympathy with second-wave feminism, a subject taken up in chapter 5.

CHAPTER THREE

Jewish Cold Warriors and "Mature" Masculinity

IN 1952, OVER the course of three issues, *Partisan Review* ran a symposium called, "Our Country and Our Culture." Its editors explained the theme and cultural watershed they wished to underline: "American intellectuals now regard America and its institutions in a new way." They "feel closer to their country and its culture." In the postwar era intellectuals regarded America "not merely [as] a capitalist myth but a reality which must be defended against Russian totalitarianism." Their new political accommodation also involved embracing mainstream culture and relinquishing once deeply held convictions that intellectuals were, by definition, disaffected outsiders. "For better or worse," the editors wrote, "most writers no longer accept alienation as the artist's faith in America; on the contrary, they want very much to be a part of American life."[1] This marked a sharp shift away from the radical politics of the 1930s, when intellectuals harshly critiqued American society and its consumer capitalist ethos.

Partisan Review then asked the contributors to assess the attitudes of intellectuals toward America, its institutions, and its culture. More than half of the nearly two dozen intellectuals who participated in the symposium were Jewish.[2] All were men. Leslie Fiedler's opening statement summed up the majority of responses. "The end of the American artist's pilgrimage to Europe is the discovery of America. That this discovery is unintended hardly matters; ever since Columbus it has been traditional to discover America by mistake."[3]

Many contributors argued that the postwar embrace of America by intellectuals represented a journey from boyhood rebellion to adulthood. "Writers and artists must achieve enough maturity to recognize the profound difference between creative dissidence and mere negative self-alienation," Newton Arvin wrote. "The negative relation" of intellectuals to society was "simply sterile, even psychopathic, and ought to give way, as it has done here, in the last decade, to the positive relation. Anything else suggests too strongly the continuance into adult life of the negative Oedipal relations of adolescence."[4]

Immaturity and maturity were common themes in mid-century American discourse. Coming at the high tide of mid-twentieth-century revisionist Freudianism or neo-Freudianism, "maturity" was integral to the postwar zeitgeist in its fever to restore the nuclear family and "traditional" gender roles.[5] "Maturity itself required the predictable, sober ingredients of wisdom, responsibility, empathy, (mature) heterosexuality, and 'a sense of function,'" writer Barbara Ehrenreich has observed, "or, as a sociologist would have put it, acceptance of adult sex roles."[6] For intellectuals, maturity meant more. "The critical attitude of American intellectuals toward American culture," pervasive in the early decades of the twentieth century, Reinhold Niebuhr argued in the *PR* symposium, "was rooted in adolescent embarrassment."[7] Intellectuals had to abandon the radicalism of their youth, Niebuhr and others in the symposium implied. For Jewish intellectuals, the stakes were even higher. In brandishing their anti-communist credentials, they would show that Jews were both loyal insiders and properly manly in Cold War America.

As many scholars have pointed out, the New York intellectuals played a crucial role in defining Cold War liberalism as a "mature" ideology bereft of any illusions when it came to the Soviet Union. "No one seemed better equipped to undertake this mission," historian Richard Pells writes, "than the intellectual who had been exposed to the disease of Communism in the 1930s and was now immune to further infection."[8] As anti-Stalinists who opposed the Popular Front, they were "premature anticommunists," Nathan Glazer recalled, who "suffered from no allusions" when it came to the Soviet Union.[9]

Their deep knowledge of Marxism and their visceral experience with "the God that failed" made them especially effective critics of communism. "I cannot understand why American intellectuals should be apologetic about the fact that they are limited in their effective historical choice between endorsing a system of total terror and *critically* supporting our own imperfect democratic culture with all its promises and dangers," Sidney Hook wrote in his contribution to *PR*'s symposium. Democracy and prosperity were proof of America's superiority over Russia, and intellectuals who remained tied to socialism were "incapable of learning from experience." They were immature. The stubborn ones took comfort "in the belief that their sincerity atones for their stupidity," Hook continued. "The task of the intellectual is still to lead an intellectual life, to criticize what needs to be criticized in America, without forgetting for a moment the total threat which Communism poses to the life of the free mind."[10] For the New York intellectuals, reared in an ideology of secular Jewish masculinity, not just immaturity but also "stupidity" implied weakness and an inadequate masculinity.

There were a few dissenters. Philip Rahv complained that the sycophantic tone among intellectuals was more a result of prosperity than maturity. He derisively termed this development the *"embourgeoisement* of the American intelligentsia." Rahv argued that a new "group of parvenu conservatives" had emerged, who "having but lately discovered the pleasures of conformity, are now aggressively bent on combating all dissent from the bourgeois outlook and devaluating the critical traditions of modern thought."[11] Norman Mailer complained that, "Everywhere the American writer is being damned to become healthy, to grow up, to accept the American reality, to integrate himself, to eschew disease, to re-value institutions. Is there nothing to remind us that the writer does not need [to] be integrated into his society, and often works best in opposition to it?"[12] Irving Howe found "much of the *PR* statement . . . unacceptable."[13] Howe, Mailer, and Rahv believed intellectuals needed to remain independent outsiders and espoused a different vision of Jewish masculinity in postwar America.

Two visions of masculinity collided in this debate. On the one side was maturity, which meant, among other things, embracing a virile anticommunism and assimilating to mid-century American norms of masculinity. On the other side was an outsider's faith and a deeply held conviction that an intellectual needed to be a critic. That alienated status undergirded the New York intellectuals' ideology of secular Jewish masculinity in the 1930s. "A war was being fought in American culture between two styles of asserting one's seriousness as an intellectual: the old style of 'alienation,' represented by the ideal of Revolution and an apartment in Greenwich Village on the one hand," Norman Podhoretz—too young to have been asked to participate in the *Partisan Review* symposium—reflected five years later in 1957, "and, on the other, the new style of 'maturity.'" The New York intellectuals, with some exceptions, veered toward the new maturity.[14]

This maturity reached its apogee at *Commentary*, a journal founded in November 1945 by the American Jewish Committee (AJC). Its inaugural editor, Elliot E. Cohen, first helped mold the New York intellectuals' ideology of secular Jewish masculinity as managing editor of the *Menorah*

Journal from 1924 to 1931. At *Commentary*, Cohen worked to make a virile and "hard" anti-communism central to the magazine and the meaning
of postwar American Jewish masculinity. *Partisan Review* contributed to
this project, too. Yet "the main difference between *Partisan Review* and
Commentary," Cohen once quipped, "is that we admit to being a Jewish
magazine and they don't."[15]

Commentary

Commentary grew out of an initiative at the end of World War II to widen
the appeal of the AJC's prior journal, the *Contemporary Jewish Record*.
The AJC was the oldest of the big three Jewish defense organizations
in the United States, which also included the Anti-Defamation League
(ADL), founded in 1913, and the American Jewish Congress (AJCongress),
founded in 1918. Established in 1906, the AJC drew its membership from
so-called "uptown" Jews from German-speaking lands who had assimilated after coming to the United States in the middle of the nineteenth
century, as opposed to the much larger wave of Eastern and Central
European, or "downtown," Jews who came in the 1880s–1910s.[16] The
AJC functioned "as its name declared, as a committee," historian Hasia
Diner notes, made of members with "prestige, status, and connections."
This elitism shaped policy. The AJC was more reserved in its approach
to combating anti-Semitism, generally relying on a strategy of working
quietly behind the scenes, lobbying government officials, and forming alli-
ances with non-Jewish organizations to shape public opinion.[17] The *Record*, however, marked a departure from this strategy. With anti-Semitism
raging on both sides of the Atlantic, the AJC founded the bimonthly in
1938 to chronicle the plight of world Jewry. The *Record* functioned like
"an archive, devoted to information, research, and documentation of Jewish life and Jewish affairs throughout the world," writes historian Nathan
Abrams. But it struggled to attract a broader readership.[18]

In 1943 the AJC hired a new editor, Adolph S. Oko, a trained librarian
who was also for many years an associate editor at the *Menorah Journal*.
Oko worked to make the *Record* "less-Jewish oriented, and less of a record of events, more a vital and thought-provoking periodical." He even
recruited Philip Rahv, one of the founding editors of *Partisan Review*, to
help make it a more intellectual journal. Rahv edited five issues between
1943 and 1944.[19] He also helped organize "Under Forty: A Symposium
on American Literature and the Younger Generation of American Jews,"
which brought in contributors like Saul Bellow, Delmore Schwartz, Isaac

Rosenfeld, David Bazelon, Nathan Glazer, Clement Greenberg, Hannah Arendt, and Lionel Trilling—all of whom later wrote for *Commentary*.[20]

When Oko died suddenly of a stroke in 1944, the AJC sought to accelerate the trends he had started at the journal. The AJC wanted its magazine to reach a wider audience. Moreover, the AJC felt a pressing need to remedy the shocks of World War II and to counter anti-Semitic stereotypes of Jews as weak and timid. "If the Jew refuses to accept himself with dignity and awareness of his achievements and religio-cultural contributions to the main stream of Western civilization," John Slawson, the AJC's executive vice president explained, "it is difficult to ask others to do so for him." As the war came to an end, the AJC wanted its magazine to cultivate an invigorating self-confidence in Jews while also solidifying American Jewry's "full adjustment as American citizens."[21]

The AJC was unsure the *Contemporary Jewish Record* could achieve those goals. So, it created a subcommittee to discuss its future after Oko's death. The AJC tapped Cohen to serve on it. "It was quite clear" from the beginning that "Elliot himself had a blazing desire to run a magazine, and his own intensity communicated itself to everyone else in the committee," Daniel Bell, then a junior editor at the *New Leader*, who also served on the committee, later recalled.[22] The AJC ultimately appointed Cohen editor of a new magazine and gave him free rein to run it. Anti-communism was the only prerequisite. But the AJC knew that "Cohen inhaled Communism and exhaled anti-Communism," as *PR* editor William Phillips later put it.[23]

In the 1930s Cohen had traveled the well-trod path from communist to anti-Stalinist radicalism among many secular Jewish intellectuals. After leaving the *Menorah Journal* in 1931, he took a job with the National Committee for the Defense of Political Prisoners (NCDPP), a subsidiary of the Communist Party's International Labor Defense (ILD), founded that year to mobilize artists, intellectuals, and writers on behalf of political and racial persecutions. Cohen rose through the ILD's ranks to become its executive secretary, but he never joined the Communist Party. Like Lionel and Diana Trilling and many of the burgeoning New York intellectuals, he was a fellow traveler until the Moscow show trials, when out of revulsion with Stalinism, he resigned from the NCDPP.[24]

Cohen tried to eke out a living as a freelance writer. But he suffered from debilitating writer's block, as well as chronic depression (which would ultimately lead to suicide in 1959).[25] He was better at molding other people's prose than writing. After the birth of his son in 1934 he needed a steady income. So he took a job as the director of public information at the Federation of Jewish Philanthropies (FJP). Cohen excelled at his work but hardly found it fulfilling. "Cohen was an intellectual," writes Abrams, "he loved books, and he had a talent for editing and nurturing young writers. These skills lay dormant for a decade." But the FJP connection brought him to the attention of the AJC, which ultimately appointed him editor of its new magazine.[26]

Like he had at the *Menorah Journal*, Cohen attracted an outstanding group of writers and editors to *Commentary*. Many were young and just starting their careers. Cohen hired Nathan Glazer, a recent graduate of CCNY (1944), who was working as a researcher at the AJC, as an editorial assistant. He also hired Clement Greenberg as managing editor. An art critic soon to be renowned for championing abstract expressionism, Greenberg was in fact a holdover from the *Record*. Other new staff included Robert Warshow, a twenty-eight-year-old son of Russian immigrants and graduate of the University of Michigan (1938), who served as code breaker in the US Army Signal Corps during World War II. Warshow came to Cohen's attention writing for the *New Leader*, a socialist and anti-communist magazine edited by Sol Levitas. Irving Kristol joined the editorial staff in 1947, hired on the recommendation of Glazer, a friend from CCNY, and his brother-in-law Milton Himmelfarb, another researcher at the AJC. By the early 1950s Glazer, Greenberg, Warshow, and Kristol were all listed as associate editors.[27]

According to Daniel Bell, "Elliot had a rather clear purpose in mind" when he became editor of *Commentary*. "He wanted to take a generation of young Jewish intellectuals who had been foundering about in radicalism, and finding little meaning any more in radicalism, and give them not just a forum to discuss their ideas and travails, but more positively, to give them an appreciation of the virtues of America, and the possibility of being a Jewish intellectual or more broadly an intellectual in the United States without being alienated from the country. He did not deny the critical roles of the intellectual, but he insisted that one could be a critic of one's country without being an enemy of its promise."

Much as he had done at the *Menorah Journal*, Cohen fostered a masculine camaraderie at *Commentary*. "Elliot wanted a magazine not for its readers, but for its writers. He wanted to build a community," Bell recalled, "and for a while he did. It broke up, for a variety of complex reasons; in some measure the 'sons,' as all prodigals do, ultimately have to go their own way."[28] Other writers made the analogy of father and sons. After Glazer left *Commentary* in the mid-1950s, he recalled that "it was as if [Cohen] were a father losing his son. I should have been more aware of how much we meant to him, but like so many sons, I was not."[29]

There were women at the magazine but in supporting roles.[30] Evelyn Shefner, a writer from Chicago, was initially hired as an editorial assistant alongside Glazer but stayed at the job for only a few issues.[31] Two other women, Hanna F. Desser and Anne Magnes, worked as junior editors in 1946. But by 1947 they had been replaced by Warshow and Kristol.[32] Midge Decter started her career as a secretary to Robert Warshow and later Cohen, but in 1955 she left to work at the magazine *Midstream*. Sherry Abel joined the staff in 1950 as an editorial assistant. She was married to Lionel Abel, a *Partisan Review* contributor. Francis Green was the longest-serving woman at the magazine under Cohen. She was its business manager from 1945 until her retirement in 1963.[33]

The name *Commentary* pointed toward this male orientation. "Commentary" was a reference to the Jewish Talmud, the oral commentary, or rabbinic discussions, of the Torah. Traditionally halakhic law barred women from studying both.[34] "Our ancient scribes and sages, as we know, only wrote commentaries on the revelation which was the Law," Cohen wrote in the magazine's first issue. "But we know that these ever-changing interpretations of the past by the men of wisdom and men of insight of each generation, became for that generation more than merely commentaries. It became the truth that men lived by. Truth, as someone has said, is an ever changing, ever flowing, ever-renewing stream. . . ." Like the Talmud, *Commentary* would be a place for contestation, argumentation, and debate—masculine traits in Jewish tradition. "*Commentary*, as its name implies, aims to be many-sided," Cohen added. "We will present significant discussion by many minds on the basic issues of our times." Cacophony and dispute would animate its pages. The editors would function like "well-diggers," Cohen wrote. "We roll up our sleeves and in the sweat of our brows we dig." Under Cohen's leadership *Commentary* promoted a cerebral Jewish masculinity but also an image of brawn.[35]

The name *Commentary* also signaled a new vision: no more radical naysaying from the sidelines, but a constructive *comment* on American life and politics. The title "symbolized the accommodation that had been reached with America," according to historian Nathan Abrams.[36] It signaled maturity. Cohen envisioned *Commentary* as a place where formerly radical Jews could come to terms with their identity as intellectuals and Americans. In stark contrast to postwar intellectuals in Europe, *Commentary* eschewed the alienation that had been such a popular theme among Jewish intellectuals in the 1930s. Jewish insecurity was "imagined," one *Commentary* writer noted in 1948. "The fact is that, in spite of their uneasiness, American Jews are American in the full and best sense of the word."[37]

An Act of Affirmation

Cohen spoke of "our" country at the end of the war as the saving force and hope for the future: "Our country has demonstrated a giant's strength, in production, in cooperation, in planning, in courage" during the war, he wrote in *Commentary*'s first issue, published three months after V-J Day. The prefix, "our," marked a sea change in the views of radical Jewish intellectuals. *Partisan Review*'s "Our Country and Our Culture" symposium made this point seven years later, in 1953. Cohen did it in November 1945. He envisioned *Commentary* as a symbol of Jews' survival and as an affirmation of their place in the United States.

Cohen was unflinching when it came to the near decimation of European Jewry.[38] "As Jews, we live with this fact: 4,750,000 to 6,000,000 Jews of Europe have been murdered. Not killed in battle, not massacred in hot blood, but slaughtered like cattle, subjected to every physical indignity—*processed*," Cohen wrote in his inaugural editorial. Jews were not killed on the battlefield heroically defending themselves. Rather, Jews had been slain, "processed" in concentration camps. And they could not rely on others for help. "There was a strange passivity the world over in the face of this colossal latter-day massacre of innocents," Cohen wrote.[39]

Cohen's observations echoed those made by Zionists who called for the establishment of a Jewish state and the cultivation of new "muscular" Jews who could protect their own. "Cohen sought nothing less than to produce a new American Jew arising out of a new American Jewish culture," writes Nathan Abrams. "In many ways, Cohen's project mirrored that of the first Israeli Prime Minister, David Ben-Gurion, who was seeking to breed a 'new man' in Israel." [40] *Commentary* was initially cold toward Zionism, reflecting the AJC's long-standing antagonism since it raised the specter of dual loyalty and implied that America was not a home for Jews.[41] But there was a sense at *Commentary* that not only did the Jewish people need to be reaffirmed but so too did Jewish masculinity.

Cohen cast *Commentary* as a symbol that Jewish masculinity had endured and that it would thrive in the United States. "It is an act of faith of a kind of which we seem peculiarly capable, we who, after all these centuries, remain, in spite of all temptation, the people of the Book," Cohen wrote. "We believe in the Word. We believe in study—as a guide to life, for the wisdom it brings to the counsels of men, and for its own sake. We have faith in the intellect, in the visions of visionary men, in the still, small voices of poets, and thinkers, and sages." A robust Jewish culture in America was essential after the Holocaust. American Jewry, Cohen argued, had a special responsibility to revive Jewish life. "With Europe devastated, there falls upon us here in the United States a far greater share of responsibility for carrying forward, in a creative way, our common Jewish cultural and spiritual heritage." To this end, *Commentary* was "an act of faith in our possibilities in America."[42]

At the same time, Cohen also sought to show that Jews were as manly as any other group in the United States. It was a project he had begun at the *Menorah Journal*. Back then Cohen "filled his columns with instances of Jewish physical triumphs in track and field, football, wrestling and boxing."[43] But that mission took on added urgency in the postwar years. At *Commentary* he created a section, "From the American Scene," which he described in 1953 as "nearest of all to the heart of the magazine's purpose." Made up of "informal [character] sketches" and "written by Jews about Jews," some of the essays harkened back to Jewish immigrant life "under the caftan in the ghetto." Others focused on the suburbs and new locales in which Jews settled in the postwar years, including in the South and West. While women writers too contributed to this section, essays often highlighted modes of masculinity, featuring stories about Jewish servicemen, street corner bravado, and the "Lost Young Intellectual," the title of a young Irving Howe's first article in the magazine.[44] Taken together they showed how "Jews, that most desperate of people," Cohen wrote, could "look at their lives [in America] with a new ease—an ease that comes from the realization that here they, like a hundred other kinds of people, are at home."[45] The essays in "From the American Scene" showed that "Jews are like everybody else—only more so."[46] According to sociologist David Riesman, "From the American Scene" revealed "the enormously different ways there are of being at the same time both Jewish and American."[47]

In 1947 Cohen gave a series of talks to local Jewish communities and college audiences, culminating with a keynote address to the Assembly of the National Council of Jewish Federations and Welfare Funds about fostering a strong Jewish culture. Cohen published the talk under the title, "Jewish Culture in America: Some Speculations by an Editor," in the May 1947 issue of *Commentary*. Cohen argued that culture strengthened a community. "To a human being, culture is not a luxury. It is a necessity— indeed the deepest necessity. It is not the marmalade added to the bread and butter of daily life. It is, rather, those components of our daily life that provide its hidden and essential vitamins. Lacking these vitamins," Cohen continued, "our community suffers from all kinds of spiritual diet-deficiency diseases. We become irritable and confused. Our movements become disoriented and uncoordinated. We fall prey to delusions and hysterias; we suffer from community battle fatigue." Without a strong culture, American Jews would be weak and enervated. This was not an option in the wake of the destruction of European Jewry.

Cohen called for an American Jewish culture that was equally Jewish and American, that was not apologetic, or defensive. "The choice that lies before us is not whether we will have a Jewish culture or not in America—we have one today," Cohen explained. "The question is whether we shall have a first-rate culture or a tenth-rate one. The question is whether we shall have a Jewish culture conceived and nurtured in imitativeness, apologetics, nationalist separatism, and mediocrity, or whether we shall have a culture that we respect and that enhances our self-respect."[48] To have a first-rate culture, Jewish leaders needed to embrace intellectuals.

For Cohen, intellectuals were key to a virile masculinity. Cohen had been making this argument since the 1920s. In "The Intellectuals and the Jewish Community: The Hope for Our Heritage," published in *Commentary* in 1949, he provided a postscript to his 1925 *Menorah Journal* manifesto, "The Age of Brass." As he had two decades earlier, Cohen made the case that intellectuals were indispensable to strengthening the Jewish community. "For obviously, if we are interested in the Jewish heritage in America," Cohen wrote, "that future depends primarily on [young intellectuals], and only secondarily on us. No bees, no honey."[49]

Twenty-five years earlier Cohen had derided Jewish communal leaders, including organizations like the AJC, for their pandering to gentiles and ultimate emasculation of American Jewry. Cohen had argued that there was an unbridgeable chasm between intellectuals and Jewish leaders. Twenty-five years later he called on the two groups to work together. As editor of a magazine sponsored by the AJC, Cohen now belonged to the very establishment that he had previously criticized. But his calls for a rapprochement were not just personal. Intellectuals and Jewish leaders shared a host of pertinent concerns, most notably totalitarianism. Cohen, therefore, called for "the marriage of true minds, that match between Jewish institutional life and the Jewish intellectual." Using a Yiddish word for matchmaker, Cohen explained that "so many self-appointed shadchans," like himself, "are anxiously seeking to bring it about."[50]

Such a union was possible because intellectuals had matured. They were no longer blinded by radicalism. Their choice of intellectual craft reflected their newly found "maturity." "In contrast to his prototype of the 20's, he is not likely to be a novelist, short-story writer, or, least of all, dramatist," Cohen wrote. "His turn of mind seems to be reflective and analytical, and, as you would expect, his talents are directed toward philosophy, psychology, literary criticism, the social sciences, and religion." Maturity was also evident when it came to his Jewish identity. "There is no longer the emotion and the struggle over the problem over Jewish identification which gave so much of the color and drive to the Jewish intellectuals' mentality of the 20s," Cohen argued. "'Jewishness' is accepted." Part of the reason why intellectuals embraced their Jewishness was that totalitarianism made evasion no longer an option. "One is a Jew because, after Hitler and the six million exterminated, how can one repudiate the bond?"[51]

But Cohen argued that the Jewish community needed to act differently from the way it had in the 1920s. The community needed to welcome its intellectuals, even when they dissented from the community's norms and traditions. Overcautiousness or defensiveness would lead to "self-imposed censorship on honest recording of Jewish experience and decent self-criticism, lest the *goyim* hear and 'use it against us.'" Such attitudes would lead once again to Jewish emasculation. Cohen warned that, "much of the mediocrity, vulgarity, and low standards that intellectuals complain of within the official Jewish culture represent the corruption of Jewish values via the imitation and wholesale adoption of the values of mass communication, advertising, and propaganda." With their own critics and philosophers to guide them, "we may well see the intellectual-religious tradition flower in ways that will stand in comparison with Spain, Germany, Eastern Europe, and elsewhere." That would happen even in America, and even in the twentieth century—despite "the frightful casualties Jews have suffered in recent years in scholarship, learning, art, and, in particular, in irreplaceable creative personalities."[52]

Intellectuals were particularly important in the postwar era because of their keen insights into the most pressing issue of the time, totalitarianism. "Call it trauma or insight," Cohen wrote, "the core of the intellectual's concern seems to be the facts neither of depression nor war but his fright at something else—the menace of totalitarianism." This was especially true for Jewish intellectuals. "It is his special experience as a Jew, in which the concentration camp is the culmination and the symbol," Cohen wrote, "that he continues to find himself in a kind of strategic center of this whole question."[53]

Cohen's call for conciliation reached fruition through *Commentary*. Within a few years it became a leading intellectual journal, respected both within and outside the Jewish community. Of its success, the AJC noted in an internal 1950 memo, that within "four short years *Commentary* had achieved a paid circulation of 20,000." It had surpassed the 7,000-person circulation of the respected liberal Catholic weekly, *Commonweal*.

Commentary's circulation numbers were more akin to *Foreign Affairs* (19,000 subscribers) and *The Nation*, which had 30,000 subscribers but was established nearly a century earlier in 1865. Much more "important" than numbers, the AJC noted, was "the quality of the readership." The magazine had "a larger percentage of business, professional, civic and intellectual leaders than any other magazine in the country," a readership survey completed by an outside firm had found. "According to this survey every copy of *Commentary* is read by four people, making the actual readership of the magazine 80,000." Mainstream publications, like *Time* and *Life*, picked up articles in *Commentary*, and it was "quoted more often in magazines and newspapers than any other general magazine, to say nothing of a Jewish organ of opinion." Its articles were assigned in college classrooms and circulated in the highest echelons of the US government. The State Department "reprinted, translated, or broadcast through its Voice of America in Europe and Asia the high total of twenty articles," the AJC reported, "which, we are told, is the highest number of articles from any magazine."[54]

Its success had much to do with the magazine's alignment with the zeitgeist and in shaping a "hard" liberal anti-communism. In a 1952 report for the American Committee for Cultural Freedom (ACCF), Cohen bragged of *Commentary*: "The recognizedly [*sic*] top spokesman among magazines in the English-speaking world on behalf of democratic ideals and against totalitarianism, left and right, happens also to be the world's leading Jewish magazine, sponsored, moreover, by a Jewish organization."[55]

Under Cohen, anti-communism was a major prerogative of the magazine. Cohen was "one of the most obsessive of the anti-Communists," according to *Partisan Review* editor William Phillips. "It is hard to determine the connection between politics and psychology, but it did seem that Cohen's neuroses were channeled into this extreme and sometimes perverse politics." Central to Cohen's psyche was proving the anti-communist and manly credentials of American Jewry. "No one seemed to be anti-Communist enough for him, and he was forever fulminating against the fuzzy-minded liberals and radicals," as Phillips later recalled.[56]

Anti-communism

Commentary emerged in lockstep with the Cold War. As Cohen sought to use the magazine to project a vision of Jewish masculinity, anti-communism became a central element. In his inaugural editorial in November 1945, Cohen warned that "the *ignis fatuus* that lured the German people to their doom" was not vanquished. The challenge in the postwar era would be "to resist it; to learn how to stamp it out; to re-affirm and restore the sense of the sanctity of the human person and the rights of man."[57] Though he did not explicitly name the Soviet Union, Cohen drew a direct line between Nazism and communism as forms of totalitarianism from that first issue.[58]

Within two years of the magazine's founding, the United States and Soviet Union were engaged in a global conflict for political and ideological supremacy. In 1947 President Truman made containment of communism the guiding force of American foreign policy. After the horrors of World War II, liberals had concluded that democracy needed to be protected against totalitarian threats, which in the postwar years shifted from Nazism to communism. This necessitated both a strong military and the constant projection of strength. Defense spending would also deliver social benefits, fueling economic growth and the expansion of the middle class—further tools in the fight against the Soviet Union and the spread of communism. Finally, fighting communism necessitated embracing civil rights at home. As Secretary of State Dean Acheson argued in 1947, "discrimination against minority groups in this country has an adverse effect upon our relations with other countries."[59]

A second red scare swept the nation as Republicans and Democrats wrangled over who was "harder" on communism. The Republican-controlled House Un-American Activities Committee (HUAC) held widely publicized hearings on alleged domestic communist subversion. HUAC first formed in 1938 to investigate alleged communist influence in New Deal agencies and within the labor movement. During the war it investigated Nazis and was known as the Dies Committee, for its chairman between 1938 and 1944, Congressman Martin Dies Jr. of Texas. In 1946 HUAC became a permanent House committee but did not gain much traction until the start of the Cold War. In 1947 it achieved widespread influence when it held hearings on supposed communist subversion in Hollywood.[60] Then in 1948 HUAC turned its attention to alleged communist subversion in the State Department.

This second red scare intersected with postwar anxieties about gender and sexuality. Concerns about a softened male self were widespread as politicians, writers, and social commentators worried that emasculated men were unable to meet the challenges of the atomic age. They fretted over the effects of suburban conformity and corporate jobs on traditional American notions of manly individualism. A perceived rise in juvenile delinquency and homosexuality was blamed on overbearing mothers and independent women influenced by prewar feminism and the expanding economic opportunities created by the war. Homosexuals, real and imagined, were deemed "security threats," fired from government jobs in a Lavender Scare that was part and parcel of the second red scare. Politicians on both sides of the aisle "conflated fears of domestic political subversion and foreign aggression with anxieties about the maintenance of a domestic and sexual order." Republicans were especially aggressive.[61]

In 1948 HUAC subpoenaed Alger Hiss to testify in front of the committee after Whittaker Chambers accused him of spying and passing secrets to the Soviets in the 1930s. A former State Department official in the Roosevelt administration, Hiss could not be tried for espionage because of the statute of limitations. But he was found guilty of perjury in January 1950. The Hiss case, along with several other sensational spy trials in the late 1940s and early 1950s, gave ammunition to Republican charges that communist subversives had infiltrated the federal government under the Democratic Party.[62]

Republicans seized on the Hiss case to discredit Democrats as "soft" on communism. They portrayed Hiss as an effete "cookie-pushing" Ivy League internationalist intellectual type and tarred the entire liberal foreign policy establishment with the specter of communist subversion and homosexual "perversion." They insinuated that an alleged effeminacy among eastern establishment elites made liberals susceptible to Russian spies who could seduce them and threaten to expose their "perversion" to their employers and families. In anti-communist rhetoric "hard" signified toughness and resolve as well as heterosexual virility. "Softness" denoted the opposite: timidity, weakness, and effeminacy. Republicans implied that being "soft" on communism was also analogous to the appeasement of Hitler. Ruthless imperialist dictators like Hitler and Stalin could not be reasoned with. All they understood was force, and force was something only virile men could credibly deliver.[63]

Liberals responded to charges of being "soft" by brandishing their own anti-communist credentials. Less than two weeks after announcing the policy of containment in March 1947, Truman established a loyalty-security program for government employees, authorizing the attorney general to formulate a list of organizations deemed subversive. Democrats and liberal groups like Americans for Democratic Action (ADA), founded in 1947, worked in these years to sever liberalism from the Popular Front and thus the Democratic Party's connection to communism.[64]

In the presidential election of 1948, a pivotal year, the Democratic Party split into three factions. Harry Truman, the former vice president, ran for the first time after becoming president in 1945 following the death of Franklin D. Roosevelt. Henry Wallace challenged Truman under the Progressive Party ticket. Wallace, FDR's former vice president, called for conciliation between the two superpowers in what he described as a "common man" approach to world affairs. Finally, the staunch segregationist Strom Thurmond ran as a "Dixiecrat" in protest against the Democratic Party's embrace of a civil rights plank. With the Democratic Party split three ways, nearly every pollster predicted that Republican Thomas Dewey would handily win the election. In one of the biggest upsets in US presidential politics, Truman eked out a victory, cementing the ascendancy of a Cold War liberalism over the Popular Front "common man" liberalism that Wallace personified.[65]

The 1948 election was a rejection of the "common man," Cohen argued in one of a handful of articles he wrote as editor of *Commentary*. He described the idea of the "'common man' . . . as the fine demagogic flower of totalitarian politics, both on the Right and the Left." The notion of a "common man" presumed that people did not think for themselves, which Cohen saw as emasculating. "The 'common man' approach," he wrote, "looks upon the vast majority as the *masses*, the untutored many, an undifferentiated glob of nameless, mindless, and will-less beings—a lot of guys named Joe." But ultimately, Americans rejected this approach in 1948. "As against all this, Americans voted that they were men—not 'common men'—and they intended to govern themselves accordingly," Cohen wrote.[66]

But Cohen warned that the Democratic Party needed to embrace antiStalinism unequivocally or would surely lose future elections, to say nothing of the Cold War. "No more crucial problem faces the American people today than to learn just what is 'Left' and what is 'Right'; that is, what policies will enhance freedom and which will lead to the totalitarian path. The Stalinists have capitalized most heavily on the current confusion."[67] Stalinists had done that, in effect, by emasculating all the individuals they could treat as a *mass*. Wallace and other Stalinist dupes in the West were helping legitimate that view of human nature. Liberals needed to wise up, and fast. "American liberalism has been reluctant to leave the garden of its illusion," Leslie Fiedler warned in *Commentary* a few years later, "but it can dally no longer: the age of innocence is dead."[68]

Cold warriors like Cohen and Fiedler were intent on repudiating Wallace's and Hiss's brand of liberalism, with its connections to the Popular Front in the 1930s, and replacing it with a tougher, more pragmatic, and virile liberalism. Arthur Schlesinger Jr.'s bestseller of 1949, *The Vital Center*, provided one of the clearest and most explicit articulations of the new tough Cold War liberalism. Schlesinger characterized Wallace and his supporters as weak-minded "doughfaces."[69] He "heaped scorn on progressive 'wailers' whose femininity had sullied the manly reform tradition that Franklin Roosevelt and the New Dealers had inherited from Theodore Roosevelt." *The Vital Center*, argues historian K. A. Cuordileone, "placed a ban on 'soft' utopian thinking, reinvented the liberal's relationship to power, and in the name of liberalism seized the masculine high ground for a tradition too long associated with bleeding hearts, effete intellectuals, and striped-pants diplomats."[70]

Schlesinger was not Jewish. But in the postwar years he traveled in New York intellectual circles.[71] The son of the esteemed Harvard historian Arthur Schlesinger Sr., he had a different upbringing from the New York intellectuals. Schlesinger Jr. attended the elite Phillips Exeter Academy and graduated from Harvard at age sixteen in 1938. Schlesinger never embraced radicalism. He was drawn to New Deal liberalism in his youth. During World War II, he served as an intelligence officer in the Office of War Information (OWI) and the Office of Strategic Services (OSS).[72] Primed by his patrician schooling and his service in the OWI and OSS, Schlesinger was a product of what one historian describes as an "imperial masculinity" that shaped a generation of Cold War foreign policy makers. It was a patrician masculinity with roots in the late nineteenth century that valued martial virtues, athleticism, and heroism, especially on the battlefield. He became acquainted with the New York intellectuals, in part, through his affiliation with the American Committee for Cultural Freedom (ACCF), founded in late 1950 as the US offshoot of the Congress for Cultural Freedom (CCF). Schlesinger served as an important link between the New York intellectuals and the patrician foreign policy establishment. Both groups remade liberalism into a fighting Cold War ideology—masculine, tough, and intellectually combative.

It was these two groups, however—patrician eastern elites and Jews—whom right-wing conservatives homed in on for being most prone to communism. Senator Joseph McCarthy rose to prominence in February 1950 by attacking the liberal foreign policy establishment. He and other right-wing conservatives blamed Secretary of State Dean Acheson (who had defended Hiss) and the "dilettante diplomats" who worked at the State Department for a series of Cold War foreign policy "blunders," most recently the "fall" of China in 1949. In their view, these men had rendered America "impotent." They were effeminate, weak, and pampered—too sissified to effectively counter communist aggression.[73]

Right-wing discourses, meanwhile, had long tied Jews to effeminacy and subversion. Stereotypes of Jewish men as unmanly abounded in these years, as they had for decades in anti-Semitic discourse. There was the "shlemiel: the pale, bespectacled, diminutive vessel of Jewish anxieties," as one historian describes it, as well as the nebbish "sissy" intellectual type who now blended with the effeminate dandy and the communist dupe of the 1950s.[74] These stereotypes, combined with the fact that Jews had long been attracted to radicalism and leftist political causes, posed an acute political problem in the Cold War era. In the late nineteenth and early twentieth centuries Jewish immigrants had joined the labor movement in large numbers, and many in the immigrant generation were socialists or leftists of one sort or the other. At least since the second wave of immigration began in the 1880s, American anti-Semites tended to see recent Jewish immigrants behind all revolutionary socialist and anarchist action.[75]

Although Jews had cemented their allegiance to the New Deal and Democratic Party in the 1930s, the stereotype of the Jew as radical persisted. "As political liberals, Jews articulated positions that many Americans considered suspect," writes historian Hasia Diner. "Jews had been over-represented among the supporters of left-wing causes in the United States throughout the twentieth century. Jews had played an inordinately large role in organizations and endeavors that to many Americans deviated from basic American values. Many Jews in America and elsewhere had, in fact, supported socialists and communist organizations."[76] Only a small minority of American Jews ever joined the Communist Party. But they made up a disproportionate number of Communist Party members, so they were especially visible.

Even when second-generation Jews moved to the suburbs and exchanged urban radicalism for middle-class values and consensus liberalism, the stereotype of the radical Jew endured.[77] Matters were not helped by the fact that in 1947 HUAC turned its attention to Hollywood, an industry founded by immigrant Jews. Six of the so-called Hollywood ten— those who refused to answer HUAC's questions after invoking their First Amendment rights, an argument the Supreme Court ultimately rejected, were held in contempt of Congress and sentenced to prison time—were Jews.[78] Then in the summer of 1950, Julius and Ethel Rosenberg were arrested for sharing secrets about the atomic bomb with the Soviets.

Leslie Fiedler referenced the connection between patricians, Jews, and communists in the American psyche in a 1951 article in *Commentary*. Writing a year and a half after Hiss had been convicted of perjury and a few months after the trial and sentencing of Julius and Ethel Rosenberg to death, he observed how initially Hiss, with his "boyish charm," was "just the type" who could "slip past the ordinary Congressmen, to whom Red really means loud-mouth or foreigner or Jew."[79]

What Hiss and the Rosenbergs had in common, Fiedler argued, was their immaturity and inability to take responsibility for their actions. "The qualifying act of moral adulthood is precisely this admission for the past and its consequences, however undesired or unforeseen," Fiedler wrote. Hiss had refused to take that step into moral adulthood. Then there were "the fantastic affirmations of innocence by Julius and Ethel Rosenberg." Both were gutless. "In the past," Fiedler continued, "such political idealists welcomed their trials as forums, opportunities to declare to the world the high principles behind their actions, the loyalty to the march of history and the eventful triumph of socialism that had brought them to the bar. They might have been, in some eyes at least, spectacular martyrs; they chose to behave instead, before the eyes of all, like blustering petty thieves."[80] More than thieves, they were cowards.

For the New York intellectuals, dissociating Jews from communism involved proving the masculinity of American Jews. Looking back on the appeal of Joseph McCarthy in 1955, a year after his colleagues censured him in the US Senate, David Riesman and Nathan Glazer marveled how the senator had combined "the image of the homosexual with the image of the intellectual," which resulted in the "State Department cooky-pusher Harvard-trained sissy" becoming "the focus of social hatred," while "the Jew becomes merely one variant of the intellectual sissy—actually less important than the Eastern-educated snob!"[81] While Jews might not have been the only "sissies" in the American imagination in the early 1950s, Glazer and Riesman understood how fearful and anxious American Jews were in the early years of the Cold War.

Anti-communism and Jewish Masculinity

Cohen once quipped that "*Commentary* had been created by the American Jewish Committee to prove to the world that there were anti-Communist Jewish intellectuals."[82] Indeed, abolishing any connections between Jews and communism in the minds of Americans was an equally important and overlapping project at *Commentary*. In 1948 Cohen wrote an internal report for the AJC, "The Problem of Disassociating Jews and Communism in the Public Mind." He asked the AJC "to organize a direct campaign, using whatever media and channels available, designed to counteract the association of Jews and Communism frequently found in the public mind."[83] Cohen saw *Commentary* as central to that initiative. According to Norman Podhoretz, who succeeded Cohen as editor in 1960, "The increasingly hard-line articles that he regularly published on Communism and the Soviet Union, while reflecting his own extreme anti-Stalinism, were also part of a secret program to demonstrate that not all Jews were Communists—even though, as all the world knew but as *Commentary* would have folded before admitting, Jews were disproportionately represented in the American Communist Party."[84]

The situation for American Jewry was especially perilous after the arrest of Julius and Ethel Rosenberg on suspicion of espionage in the summer of 1950. Found guilty in March 1951 for passing secret information about the atomic bomb to the Russians, the couple was executed by electric chair on July 19, 1953. Though Julius's guilt was established years later, following the release of declassified US and Russian documents after the collapse of the Soviet Union in 1991, Ethel's death sentence remains controversial. In any event, evidence of the Rosenbergs' crimes was kept from the public at the time. Many leftists and American Jews believed they were innocent, and that anti-Semitism undergirded the case.[85]

The Rosenberg case terrified and divided the American Jewish community. It was "a definitional ceremony," according to historian Deborah Dash Moore, "in which opposing versions of American Jewish identity competed for ascendancy." On one side was a left-wing labor radical tradition "informed by Jewish and universal values." On the other side was Cold War liberalism and an assimilated middle-class Jewish community. Nearly everyone involved in the case was Jewish, from the defendants to the attorneys on both sides, and even the judge. As Moore argues, it was a Jewish drama that played out in front of a gentile jury and public. The Rosenberg's "death represented a symbolic atonement demanded to signify the loyalty of American Jews to the United States and its ideals," writes Moore.[86]

In the spring of 1953 Roy Cohn, an assistant US attorney in Manhattan and a prosecutor in the Rosenberg espionage trial (and also Jewish), received a letter from a concerned citizen asking why so many communists were Jewish. He forwarded it to the AJC. While this sender had "always prided [herself] on lack of prejudice against minorities," she felt she "would be blind if [she] did not take note that the pro-Red or Red witnesses before Senate hearing[s] were at least 75% Jewish" and that most of the people convicted of subversion were Jews.[87] The AJC responded that an individual's political orientation was not informed by race or religion and that "adherence to the Communist Party or its tenets is purely a personal, individual matter." The Communist Party, the AJC wrote, "tried very hard to make it appear that Communists are Jews and vice-versa in order to shield themselves behind spurious charges that the attack on Communism is anti-Semitic."[88]

But public statements notwithstanding, the AJC was deeply concerned by the public perception that Jews remained more tied to communist organizations than other groups. "Judging from names connected with the American Labor Party and the organizations dominated by Communists," worried one AJC official, "it would appear that the proportion of Jews who are active in Communist and fellow-traveler circles is probably even greater than it was. Their numbers have not increased—but because the members of other groups have fled the party in droves, Jews are more conspicuous."[89]

In the midst of the Rosenberg case, as the couple appealed its conviction, the AJC created a committee to deal exclusively with domestic communism. It named Solomon Andhil Fineberg, a trained rabbi and the AJC's national community relations director since 1939, as its head.[90] Elliot Cohen was also tapped to serve on that committee.[91] At its first meeting in March 1952, Fineberg announced that the AJC was putting everything on hold to deal with "an emergency situation created by the vigorous efforts Communists are making to interpret the decision in the Rosenberg case as anti-Semitic."[92] Cohen argued that the AJC should "avoid the civil liberties issues" and focus on fighting communist propaganda, "exposing the new world-wide anti-Semitic campaign emanating from the Kremlin and increasingly obvious satellite countries." The stakes could not be higher. The Soviets were waging a battle for hearts and minds by portraying themselves as arbiters of peace and civil liberties while depicting the United States as a nation that treated its minorities as second-class citizens. "Today we have a historic opportunity to give testimony as Jews that this is but another totalitarian big lie," Cohen wrote.[93] It was critical to dissociate the Rosenbergs from communist propaganda that linked the case to anti-Semitism.

Cohn made sure *Commentary* was at the forefront of that mission. When the Committee to Secure Justice in the Rosenberg Case, a group of left-wing supporters of the couple, argued that anti-Semitism was the basis of the government's case, the magazine went on the attack. It was a claim "with breath-taking mendacity and impudence," Lucy Dawidowicz wrote in *Commentary*. The campaign wanted to "persuade the world that the American government is in the hands of an anti-Semitic conspiracy which is inexorably working up to the extermination of American Jewry." It insinuated that the conviction of the Rosenbergs was "a 1952 version of the [Nazi's] Reichstag fire, prelude to an American version of Auschwitz." Compared to the New York intellectuals who leaped into the controversy after her, Dawidowicz's assessment was relatively mild.[94]

Six months before the Rosenbergs were scheduled to die in the electric chair, the case became not just a political but an intellectual controversy, involving the publishing world and the politics of literary criticism. The Rosenbergs were allowed to exchange letters throughout the two years they were under custody before their execution. In January 1953, *The Death House Letters of Ethel and Julius Rosenberg* appeared in print. The New York intellectuals found the publication both laughable and terrifying. The "Jero Publishing Company" claimed the letters would "establish the Rosenbergs as popular heroes whose letters would be recognized as 'world classics of democratic eloquence and inspiration.'" To the New York intellectuals, it was a ludicrous assertion. These letters, published by a fake publishing house, were an all too transparent propaganda ploy.[95]

After the execution of the couple in the summer of 1953, Leslie Fiedler and Robert Warshow published essays excoriating the couple and the *Death House Letters*. Fiedler's appeared in October 1953 in the inaugural issue of *Encounter*, a London-based journal founded by the Congress for Cultural Freedom (CCF) and edited by Irving Kristol, who left his position as an editor at *Commentary* and as the American Committee for Cultural Freedom's (ACCF) first executive director to take the job.[96] Robert Warshow's followed a month later in the November 1953 issue of *Commentary*. Both men derided the Rosenberg letters for their communist duplicity. Both men denied that the couple's conviction had anything to do with anti-Semitism or Jewishness, and both depicted Julius as emasculated.

Fiedler and Warshow both argued that the couple referred to their Judaism throughout their letters only because it served their cause. "There were no limits to the absurd masquerades," Fiedler wrote. "Julius [was] draped after his death, not with a red flag, but with the ritual prayer shawl." Rosenberg, the communist, had arranged for psalms to be sung at his funeral and for "a rabbi to intone unbelieved-in prayers at the grave." To Warshow, "the continual display of Judaism and Jewishness" in the Rosenberg letters was entirely contrived. "Since the propaganda built up around the case emphasized the fact that the Rosenbergs were Jewish," he sniped, "they simply adopted the role that was demanded of them."[97]

Out of the hundreds of *Death House* letters, Fiedler and Warshow both homed in on a letter Julius wrote to Ethel on July 4, 1951, in which the condemned man celebrated "this holiday for freedom." Julius told his wife he had clipped a copy of the Declaration of Independence, where he read about "free speech, freedom of the press and of religion." Rosenberg was playing the innocent child who believed in the promise of the American Revolution. Perhaps at the behest of party representatives, he tugged on readers' heart strings. These were the rights "our country's patriots" died for, Rosenberg said, and they "can't be taken from the people even by Congress or the courts." But Rosenberg had the wrong document. "Does it matter that the Declaration of Independence says nothing about free speech, freedom of the press, or freedom of religion," Warshow wrote in relishing disdain.[98] Fiedler similarly decried how Julius "had stuck up in his cell a copy of the Declaration of Independence clipped out of the *New York Times*." He referred to the document "as if in passing so that all the world will know he is really a misunderstood patriot." But Julius was at best a "poseur and a hypocrite," Fiedler argued. More accurately, he embodied "something much more devious."[99]

The Rosenberg letters were evidence of the couple's inability to think for themselves. "One is forced to wonder whether the literal truth had not in some way ceased to exist for these people," Warshow wrote.[100] "The Rosenbergs thought and felt whatever their political commitment required them to think and feel," he wrote. "They were able to commit their kind of treason because they were incapable of telling treason from devotion, deceit from honesty," Fiedler wrote. "These two people moved always like puppets from above."[101]

But especially in the case of Julius, Warshow and Fiedler highlighted his most conspicuous shortcoming aside from being a communist—his simple-mindedness. As part of a cohort that viewed intellectuality as masculine, Warshow and Fielder were effectively saying that cooperation with communists did not just make you a traitor, it exposed you as a "sissy." They implied that Julius Rosenberg did not have the mental strength to see Russian spies as the liars and swindlers they were. Julius, in short, wasn't much of a man.

Ethel was also inane, though seemingly the more steely of the two.[102] She was "hopelessly the victim not only of her politics but of the painfully pretentious style" that was the "literary equivalent," of communist politics, Fiedler wrote. Her bland prose was perhaps to be expected of a middlebrow woman, but the trouble was that her strength only made her husband's weakness stand out more. "Julius manages from time to time to seem more sincere and touching," than his wife, Fiedler added. "One is moved by this feeling for his wife, which is more than love—an almost frantic dependence and adulation."[103]

The New York intellectuals felt they understood Julius Rosenberg more than most. Julius attended CCNY in the 1930s. "It is now about seventeen years since the Communists told the truth about themselves," Warshow wrote. "The 'popular front' was inaugurated during Julius Rosenberg's student days at City College," a period between 1935 and 1939 when communists would recruit, support, and try to take advantage of just about anybody—not just Communist Party members. Communists at CCNY might be shrewd but they were not smart. Julius certainly was not an incisive thinker or a forceful debater. "At the risk of being accused of smugness," Kristol wrote years later, only Julius Rosenberg from Alcove No. 2 "made a name for himself."[104] Rosenberg's treason was not based on principle. It was based on his susceptibility to the forceful ideas of others, his slavishness.

In February 1950, Senator Joseph McCarthy made a speech at the Republican Women's Club in Wheeling, West Virginia, where he claimed to have the names of some two hundred known communists in the State Department. It was a claim of breathtaking mendacity. When he submitted his speech to the *Congressional Record* eleven days later, it included fifty-seven names. Those names were likely based on a State Department internal report from 1946 and 1947 and were nothing new. McCarthy, however, continued to inflate the number in public speech and made wild charges with no evidence. Coming at the heels of the Soviets acquiring the atom bomb and what Republicans described as the "fall" of China, McCarthy capitalized on and exploited American fears of communism at home and abroad. For four years he skillfully manipulated the media with his outrageous, unproven accusations. "The blatant disregard for the accuracy of his charges," writes historian Ellen Schrecker, "distinguished him from other politicians," who came to fear and loathe him. But Republicans initially found him useful. "His extravagant charges amplified their own allegations that the Truman administration had lost China" and that Democrats were "soft" on communism.[105]

The New York intellectuals criticized McCarthy. Irving Kristol called him a "vulgar demagogue," for example. But within the pages of *Commentary*, they downplayed the threats McCarthyism posed to civil liberties. Kristol also wrote that, "there is one thing that the American people know about Senator McCarthy: he, like them, is unequivocally anti-Communist. About the spokesman for American liberalism, they feel they know no such thing. And with some justification."[106] In 1952 Cohen wrote that the senator from Wisconsin "remains in the popular mind an unreliable, second-string blowhard; his only support as a great national figure is from the fascinated fears of the intelligentsia."[107] In 1953 Nathan Glazer suggested that, "all that Senator McCarthy can do on his own authority that someone equally unpleasant and not a Senator can't, is to haul people down to Washington for a grilling by his committee. It is a shame and an outrage that Senator McCarthy should remain in the Senate," Glazer continued, "yet I cannot see that it is an imminent danger to personal liberty in the United States."[108] Cohen did publish some opposing views in

Commentary.[109] But by and large they took the position that McCarthy was preferable to being "soft" on communism.

Following the Senate censuring of McCarthy in the summer of 1954, after he accused the army of harboring communists, several New York intellectuals began to reflect on how anti-communism had evolved in the previous years. "In these strange times," Daniel Bell wrote in the introduction to his edited volume, *The Radical Right*, first published in 1955, "new polar terms have been introduced into political discourse, but surely none as strange as the division into 'hard' and 'soft.'" Bell noted how "presumably one is 'soft' if one insists that the danger from domestic Communists is small" while "the 'hard' anti-Communists insist that no distinction can be made between international and domestic Communism." To Bell's exasperation, figures like Reinhold Niebuhr and Arthur Schlesinger Jr., unimpeachable anti-communists behind the formation of Americans for Democratic Action (ADA) and "early intellectual antagonists of the Communist, before McCarthy ever spoke up on the subject, have been denounced as 'soft.'"[110] Bell knew the terms of the debate had been perverted.

In another essay that appeared in *The Radical Right*, originally published in *Partisan Review*, Nathan Glazer and David Riesman argued that McCarthy's appeal centered on his masculinity. They described a "discontented class" of white Americans who saw in McCarthy someone who was virile and tough. Especially when compared to liberals who came from "the older educated classes of the East, with their culture and refinement, with 'softness' and other amenities he does not yet feel able to afford." These effete Ivy educated eastern establishment liberals had appeased Stalin at Yalta and let China "fall" to communism in 1949. To this "discontented class," liberals were at best "do-gooders and bleeding hearts—the grown-up version of that unendurable taunt of being a 'sissy,'" Glazer and Riesman wrote. At worst, they were guilty of treason. McCarthy appealed to the discontented class precisely because his "methods" were so "obviously not sissified."[111]

The American Committee for Cultural Freedom (ACCF)

The same year that McCarthy came to prominence, many New York intellectuals became active in the American Committee for Cultural Freedom (ACCF). Founded in December 1950 as the American affiliate of the Congress for Cultural Freedom (CCF), the ACCF was the brainchild of Sidney Hook. But Elliot Cohen played an important behind-the-scenes role.

At the outset, any discussion of the CCF and ACCF should begin by acknowledging what everybody learned about in 1967. That year, *Ramparts*, a magazine closely associated with the New Left, and the *New York Times*, simultaneously published exposés that revealed the CIA covertly funded the CCF and its affiliate groups and magazines in various countries. The history of the CCF and ACCF has been recounted by numerous scholars. So too has the heavy involvement of the New York intellectuals in its activities. Scholars have debated at length whether they were "witting" or "unwitting" recipients of CIA funding and whether CIA funding affected the group's intellectual activities.[112] "Whatever it was that the New York intellectuals in the ACCF knew or did not know about the CIA's hand in their affairs," historian Hugh Wilford has argued, "it did not prevent them from treating the organization as if it were a genuine, privately run committee, indeed, as if it were their own."[113]

In June 1950 Cohen traveled to Germany as part of the American delegation to the first Congress for Cultural Freedom. The CCF was organized to galvanize intellectuals around the world "to take up the totalitarian challenge posed by the Soviet Union." The American delegation, led by Hook, included some twenty intellectuals. They included the writer James T. Farrell; historian Arthur Schlesinger Jr.; Sol Levitas, editor of the anticommunist journal *The New Leader*; the Russian émigré composer Nicolas Nabokov; playwright Tennessee Williams; George Schuyler, editor of the influential African American weekly, the *Pittsburgh Courier*, and later to emerge as perhaps the nation's most prominent Black conservative; and the Black activist and journalist Max Yergan, among others.[114] With Hook and Cohen, they joined "118 distinguished writers, artists, philosophers, and scientists from 21 countries," according to a CCF brochure, who "met together at the thin edge of the divided world" between June 26 and 30, 1950, and "pledged themselves to defend the freedom most gravely menaced in our century: freedom of critical and creative thought."[115]

Cohen gave a speech on that trip at a meeting "held under the joint auspices of the newly formed Gesellschaft für Christlich-Jüdische Zusammenarbeit and the Congress for Cultural Freedom."[116] *Commentary* printed Cohen's speech in its September 1950 issue. It provided a prefatory note: "Introduced as the 'first American Jew to speak in Berlin since the war on the relations of Germans and Jews,' Elliot E. Cohen delivered this address to a German audience of almost a thousand in the Rathaus Schoeneberg, the city hall of West Berlin." Cohen addressed German-Jewish relations, which he described as "a chasm as wide as an ocean—and over the abyss no sign of a bridge." He did not shrink from mentioning the atrocities committed by

Germany under Nazi rule. "Germany still lies behind a smoke curtain—the smoke that still seems to hang over the concentration camps," he said. But Cohen emphasized two major points: Jewish resilience and strength, and the need to reconcile strained relations. Cohen echoed the points he made in the first issue of *Commentary*—that Jews were not emasculated victims. "Surely it would be understandable if from so colossal and uncanny a victimization a group would emerge traumatic, hysterical, almost unhinged of reason," he said. "But with some pride I note this has not happened." Jews had survived and "intend to survive as a distinctive group in the West, and they will survive."

Cohen turned to the role of Germany in the postwar order. Relations between Germany and world Jewry could not "be bridged by a few kind words and pious resolutions, or even by certain necessary financial or diplomatic arrangements," he said. German-Jewish relations were not just "another problem to be reported on and memorandized about and filed away with other postwar problems in a portfolio (lettered, I suppose, EJ: Extermination Jews)." But Germany, he knew, needed to be integrated into the anti-communist West. He might have reflected that the Nazis had been soundly defeated, their industrial base wiped out, and their economy crippled. He might have reflected that the Nazis had won barely over a third of the German electorate's support in the last free election, and that the non-Nazi majority had surely learned the lesson that a totalitarian insurgency cannot be tolerated or appeased—just as Germany's neighbors to the east *and* west had learned, and paid a similar price for learning it, alas, too late. So, despite enormous challenges and the justified misgivings of Jews, Cohen called for reconciliation. Germany, he argued, could find redemption by being on the right side this time in the fight against totalitarianism during the Cold War.[117]

When Cohen returned home, he helped found the ACCF as another venue to press for and expand a "hard" anti-communism along the lines already appearing in *Commentary*. The ACCF's first official meeting took place six months after the CCF meeting at New York University's Faculty Club on December 14, 1950. Some two dozen intellectuals attended, including James Burnham, William Barrett, Arnold Beichman, Elliot Cohen, James T. Farrell, Clement Greenberg, Sydney Hook, Arthur Koestler, Sol (S. M.) Levitas, Nicolas Nabokov, William Phillips, Philip Rahv, Richard H. Rovere, George Schuyler, Norman Thomas, Bertram D. Wolfe, and Max Yergan. The organization would grow to several hundred members by 1953.[118] Membership, however, did not mean active engagement. One became a member through nomination by other members in the group. Once voted in, membership did not require any tangible commitment. For many anti-communist intellectuals, the ACCF was a prominent group doing important work to which they were happy to add their name, but which required little of them.[119] Diana Trilling later commented of joining the ACCF that, "all decent people in the community felt it was the proper thing" to do.[120]

The ACCF had its roots in earlier attempts by Sidney Hook to organize anti-Stalinist intellectuals. One of the oldest and most fiery of the New York intellectuals, Hook was known as a "brilliant, pugnacious [and] a fearsome polemicist; poet Delmore Schwartz nicknamed him 'Sydney Chop' for his impeccable performances of logical argumentation."[121] Born in 1902 to Eastern European Jewish immigrants, Hook grew up in Bushwick, Brooklyn. He attended CCNY and studied under Morris Cohen, graduating in 1923. He earned a PhD in philosophy in 1927 from Columbia, training with the pragmatist philosopher John Dewey, and thereafter secured a job at NYU's philosophy department, where he spent most of his career.

Hook was the leading American Marxist theoretician of his generation. In the early 1930s he was a fellow traveler but turned against communism in the wake of the Moscow show trials. Thereafter he organized a number of precursors to what became the ACCF. In 1937 he put together a committee, chaired by John Dewey, to investigate Stalin's charges that Leon Trotsky, then exiled in Mexico, was guilty of an anti-Soviet conspiracy. The Dewey Commission, as it became known, cleared Trotsky of all charges. But when many leftists rejected the group's findings, Hook organized the Committee for Cultural Freedom in 1939 to counter the influence of the Popular Front among intellectuals and cultural figures.[122]

Ten years later Hook galvanized anti-communist intellectuals to protest so-called world peace conferences sponsored by the Soviet Union. The first of these conferences took place in Poland in November 1948. Two more followed soon, in Paris and Stockholm.[123] But the one that galvanized Hook to counterorganize was the so-called Cultural and Scientific Conference for World Peace held in March 1949 at the Waldorf-Astoria Hotel in midtown Manhattan.[124] Some of the Waldorf Conference's well-known sponsors included Leonard Bernstein, Marlon Brando, Charlie Chaplin, Aaron Copland, W. E. B. Du Bois, Dashiell Hammett, Lillian Hellman, and Langston Hughes, among other luminaries.[125] The sheer star power troubled the anti-Stalinist New York intellectuals. So, when Hook learned of the Communist Party's plan for the Waldorf Conference, he contacted many anti-Stalinist intellectuals and artists, hoping to make a public show of their opposition to Stalin and the Communist Party's attempt to monopolize and control leftist dissent. With the many who responded, Hook formed an ad hoc group called Americans for Intellectual Freedom (AIF), which picketed the hotel.[126] AIF would eventually morph into the ACCF.

The New York intellectuals became the ACCF's most committed and active members. Many served on its Executive Committee. Hook was "designated president or chairman of the organization" and served as a liaison between the ACCF and the CCF.[127] Irving Kristol was hired as the ACCF's first executive director, a position he held from 1951 to 1953, when he departed for London to edit the new CCF magazine there, *Encounter*. Other New York intellectuals who served on the Executive Committee included Elliot Cohen, Daniel Bell, William Phillips, and Diana Trilling. These "core" members of the board were "relatively consistent," Phillips later wrote.[128]

Out of hundreds of intellectuals listed as members, barely a dozen were women.[129] Only a few women served as board members or officers. Diana Trilling was the group's most active woman member, as chapter 2 chronicled. The novelist Grace Zaring Stone, part of the American delegation that traveled to Berlin for the CCF in the summer of 1950, served as the group's first secretary treasurer but rarely attended meetings.[130] Pearl Kluger had a more enduring presence. She served as the group's executive secretary. She was an ex-Trotskyite who had helped run the Dewey Commission in defense of Leon Trotsky in 1939. According to one scholar, Hook trusted her enough to make her "witting" about the ACCF's funding sources. Kluger handled the group's financing, transferring money from the CCF and the various front groups the CIA set up to support anti-communist publications and organizations, such as the Fairfield Foundation.[131] "Thanks to the enterprise and political intelligence of Pearl Kluger, the organization operated on a very modest budget," Hook later wrote in his memoir—adding "supplemented by the voluntary services of the spouses of active members."[132]

But wives were scarce, certainly at Executive Board meetings. In January 1954, Executive Committee members' wives were allowed to attend "by invitation." But Elliot Cohen "wanted his objection recorded to the discussion at meetings attended by wives of Committee members." Daniel Bell replied that, "the meeting was purely for discussion and that no decision would be made." There were men at the meeting also listed in the minutes as there "by invitation." But no objection was made on that count.[133] The ACCF was dominated by men.

There was also a Jewish dimension to the group.[134] Hook likened the ACCF to a Jewish defense organization. "The policy of the ACCF," Hook told legal scholar Milton Konvitz, "is to act openly but on some occasions, it has to act discreetly—like the Anti-Defamation League. We do not dispute the right of Communist front groups to hold meetings, etc., but we believe it in the public interest [that] deception should be exposed."[135] In 1952 Cohen reported to the AJC that, "almost every important Jewish writer, scientist, scholar, university figure, or intellectual is not merely non-Communist, but openly anti-Communist—one needs only examine the lists of the executive committee and the membership of the American Committee for Cultural Freedom, the U.S Government-approved pro-democratic and anti-Communist organization in the professional and intellectual fields: they are full of Jewish names."[136] The ACCF, like *Commentary*, functioned as a masculine Jewish space.

Cohen also played an important behind the scenes role linking the ACCF to *Commentary* and the AJC. In 1952, the AJC and ACCF discussed jointly organizing an event at Carnegie Hall to denounce Soviet anti-Semitism in the wake of the Rudolf Slánský show trials that targeted Czechoslovakian Jewish communist leaders. The proposed conference would bring together "various religious denominations and civil liberties groups" to "protest against racism, genocide, religious persecution, and the denial of liberties behind the Iron Curtain."[137] Cohen was the main conduit between the two groups. The AJC ultimately reneged because it worried about publicly appearing too entwined with the ACCF. It asked the ACCF to remove its name as a sponsor but remain involved in the planning. The ACCF declined, not wanting to "continue as an anonymous behind the scenes agency."[138] Ultimately, plans for the conference were scrapped. But Cohen continued to provide a link between the established Jewish community and the ACCF.

Between 1951 and 1955 the ACCF planned conferences and talks and released statements on important issues pertaining to anti-communism and intellectual freedom. "Its well-publicized statements," the Democratic Socialist Michael Harrington observed in a 1955 article critical of the group in the magazine *Dissent*, "are often taken as the quasi-official opinion of intellectual liberalism."[139] The ACCF, however, was always "more interested in sustaining and promoting anti-Communism than in polishing and protecting an ideal of open intellectual analysis," as historian Neil Jumonville observed.[140] And by the middle of the 1950s the group was increasingly divided over whether domestic communism continued to pose a threat and over the tactics of Senator McCarthy.

By 1955 the group faced a slew of resignations from intellectuals on both the right and left of the anti-communist political spectrum. Conservatives George Schuyler, James Burnham, and Max Yergan resigned in 1954 because they felt the organization was too critical of McCarthy. In his resignation letter, Burnham told the Executive Committee "that over the past year and a half the Committee has developed into a narrow and partisan clique."[141] Schuyler echoed Burnham's "clique" comments in his own resignation letter, complaining that "the ACCF has remained a small in-grown group of some three hundred self-styled intellectuals largely concentrated on the Eastern seaboard and influenced chiefly by the ideas and prejudices predominating in that area."[142] While they did not say so explicitly, Yergan and Burnham likely had Jewishness in mind.

On the other end of the political spectrum, by 1954 Cold War liberal stalwarts like Arthur Schlesinger Jr. clashed with the leadership of the ACCF over their "hard" anti-communism. Schlesinger took issue with the ACCF distribution of a *Commentary* article, "How Insure [*sic*] Security in the Government Service: Past Failures and Present Remedies," calling it "tendentious," "nonsense," and a "preposterous defense" of Congressman Martin Dies, founder of the House Un-American Activities Committee (HUAC), and "its equally preposterous apologia for the Eisenhower security program."[143] Schlesinger argued that the ACCF had played an important role in exposing domestic communism when it first formed, but by 1955 he felt that time had "largely passed." "The ACCF in recent months," he wrote in a letter to the ACCF executive board, "has somehow lost track of its original objectives," which were to "strengthen the social and political conditions of cultural creativity and free intellectual inquiry."[144] By the mid-1950s there was not "any serious resurgence of pro-Communism" in the United States, Schlesinger said, so the ACCF needed to shift its priorities.[145]

Schlesinger was not alone in resigning from the ACCF because of its hard anti-communism. Others took issue with how it excluded opposing points of view and blinded the organization to other important issues that had to do with cultural freedom. David Riesman, for example, resigned from the ACCF because the "expenditure of Committee energies . . . appeared disproportionate." Furthermore, he wrote that "quite apart from the substantive issues, the meetings have a polemical, even fanatical quality, which seems to render systematic procedure impossible and which cannot be justified by the importance of the issues involved." Elsewhere, Riesman wrote that ACCF meetings were full of "malice." "I have never been to an academic meeting as disagreeable as the A.C.C.F. meetings appear to be from the minutes and my own limited experience."[146] Another ACCF member, referring to the issue of communists in schools, wrote in his resignation letter that, "the committee looks from one point of view which may not be entirely in accord with the balance of judgment we are seeking to establish."[147] In 1957, the ACCF suspended its operations.

———

Notably, New York intellectuals on the left of the anti-communist spectrum never joined the ACCF. Irving Howe and Alfred Kazin were never nominated. Others refused to join. Meyer Schapiro, the Columbia University art historian, turned down his invitation to the ACCF because in his view it was not "a 'Committee for Cultural Freedom' but an organization for fighting the world Communist movement."[148] So did the art critic Harold Rosenberg.[149] Jason Epstein, meanwhile, later claimed he never joined the group. After attacking the ACCF in the *New York Review of Books* in 1967 following CIA funding revelations, Irving Kristol and Diana Trilling were incensed because Epstein had been "unanimously elected" as a member in 1954 after Nathan Glazer nominated him.[150] "What you say about my unanimous election is news to me," he told them. "I may have been elected to the Politburo. But I didn't belong to that either."[151]

Irving Howe ultimately founded the magazine *Dissent* in 1954 to counter what he saw as the excessive conformity of the group and its abdication of the intellectual vocation by celebrating rather than criticizing society. They "were a tiny minority within the intellectual world," Howe later recalled. "We fought hard for our opinion that, while Stalinism was the major danger internationally, in domestic life it was necessary to focus energies against McCarthyism."[152] Their disagreement over the ACCF had to do with politics—the appropriate response to the threat of communism and McCarthyism but also the proper role of intellectuals. *Dissent* stood against the "flabbiness of spirit which characterized a good many American intellectuals during the McCarthy period, particularly those who were associated with the ill-named Committee for Cultural Freedom and who dominated the editorial staffs of *Commentary* and *The New Leader*," Howe explained in 1960.[153] The proper role of the intellectual was also a debate about how to be Jewish and masculine in America after World War II, and is the subject of the next chapter.

CHAPTER FOUR

World of Our Fathers, World of Our Sons

IRVING HOWE AND JEWISH MASCULINITY ON THE LEFT

Whatever distinction can be assigned to the New York intellectuals during the 30's lies mainly in their persistence as a small minority, in their readiness to defend unpopular positions against apologists for the Moscow trials and the vigilantism of Popular Front culture. . . . Their best hours were spent on the margin, in opposition.[1]

—IRVING HOWE

SO WROTE IRVING HOWE in a 1968 chronicle of the group he designated the New York intellectuals. For Howe, the 1930s was the decade when the New York intellectuals responded to the Great Depression by embracing radicalism and criticizing the status quo. Congregating as Trotskyists in Alcove One of the City College cafeteria, they opposed Stalinism and thus dissented from the Popular Front that the Communist Party initiated in 1935, which united many American leftists and liberals in the fight against fascism.[2] Those were the years when the New York intellectuals began, sometimes consciously, to embrace their ideology of secular Jewish masculinity.

Howe recalled that although he abandoned the Trotskyism of his youth, he remained a leftist. More importantly, he remained a critic. To have an intellectual vocation—to offer honest and critical assessments of the society in which one lived—meant, according to Howe, detachment from centers of power and maintaining an outsider perspective. Howe complained that in the postwar years, however, many intellectuals had abdicated their role as critics to become defenders of Cold War America. "In the 40's and 50's," he said, "most of the New York intellectuals would abandon the effort to find a renewed basis for socialist politics—to their serious discredit. . . . Some would vulgarize anti-Stalinism into a politics barely distinguishable from reaction."[3]

Irving Kristol took Howe to task for "an unexamined premise." Howe took it for granted, Kristol complained, that an intellectual was almost by definition "politically radical, a man of the Left." That premise led Howe to see Kristol and others as "deviants or dropouts (or cop-outs)," and to see their post–World War II change of political views as "a form of apostasy." Kristol insisted that "there was nothing mysterious or sinister" about his own "political transition." Maturity had simply led him past radicalism. "I resigned from the Left a long time ago—and Mr. Howe has been expelling me ever since," Kristol quipped. "It's a sterile exercise, and I wish—more for his own sake than mine—that he would cease."[4]

Howe stood firm, however. "Many of the intellectuals who then dropped—dropped, rather than turned away from—their socialist convictions, were scurrying along as part of 'the herd of independent minds.'"[5] Intellectuals, he said, "are not supposed to run in packs."[6]

By 1968, Howe and Kristol, one-time friends at City College, were politically at odds. In 1954 Howe founded *Dissent* magazine to promote democratic socialism and, as the first issue declared, "to dissent from the bleak atmosphere of conformism that pervades the political and intellectual life of the United States; to dissent from the support of the *status quo* now so noticeable on the part of many former radicals and socialists."[7] Kristol, in contrast, became an editor at *Commentary* and then *Encounter*. In 1965 he founded *The Public Interest*, a magazine that along with *Commentary*, edited by Norman Podhoretz, led a small but vocal minority of New York intellectuals into the Republican Party.

Both Howe and the *Dissent* group, and Kristol, Podhoretz, and emerging neocons, were critical of the New Left and the most radical manifestations of the social movements of the 1960s. Podhoretz and Kristol would both become key architects of neoconservatism and stewards of the Reagan revolution. Though no longer an orthodox Marxist, Howe remained a man of the left. The differences between the two groups centered not only on politics but on the meaning of Jewish masculinity.

In 1968 Howe also began work on what became *World of Our Fathers*, his magisterial and beautifully written account of immigrant Jewish life in New York, published eight years later in 1976. The book was, to Howe's utter surprise, a bestseller. One of the first books to explore the history of the Eastern European Jewish migration to the United States, it appeared at a moment when many ethnic and racial groups were celebrating their pasts. Alex Haley's *Roots: The Saga of an American Family*, was also published that year and adapted into a hugely popular television series in 1977, helping to account for *World of Our Fathers*' success.[8] Although his book was ostensibly about the immigrant Jewish past, Howe undoubtedly had the present in mind as he wrote it. He was thinking about Jewish sons and the turmoil of the 1960s. *World of Our Fathers*, as historian Gerald Sorin has observed, "celebrated secular Jewishness and its manifestation in a Jewish socialism which held to values [Howe believed were] sadly missing in the 'socialism' of the New Left of the late sixties."[9]

World of Our Fathers venerated a Jewish masculinity that embodied intellectuality and combative debate, which Howe ruefully felt the New Left lacked. Howe focused not on rabbis and religion, as critics have noted, but on intellectuals, workers, and leftist movements. Though he wrote some about Jewish women—especially Jewish mothers and the role Jewish women played in the labor movement—overall he focused on male intellectual activity.[10] The book was an ode to a secular Jewish masculinity that Howe felt was disappearing by the 1970s, both among his contemporaries and younger leftists—a masculinity that was combative, intellectual, argumentative, critical, and firmly on the outside.

From the Bronx to the Sect

Irving Howe was born Irving Horenstein on June 11, 1920, in the Bronx, the only child of David Horenstein and Nettie Goldman, immigrants from Moldova, which was then part of the Pale of Settlement in western Russia. His parents came to the United States in 1912 as teenagers, probably on the same boat, but did not meet until a few years later. Their marriage lasted more than thirty years, until Howe's mother died in 1946.[11] The family lived in the Bronx, in "a self-contained little world" of Yiddish-speaking neighborhoods. They initially lived in the West Bronx, where Howe's father owned a couple of grocery stores. But when the Depression hit, they went bankrupt. The Horentsteins were forced to move to the East Bronx to take up a residence with extended family. "The move from the prosperous West Bronx to the East Bronx came to no more than a few miles, but socially the distance was vast," Howe wrote in his memoir. "We were dropping from the lower middle class to the proletarian—the most painful of all social descents."[12]

The family's descent into poverty profoundly shaped Howe's worldview. "To be poor is something that happens to you; to experience poverty is to gain an idea of what is happening," Howe explained in his memoir, *A Margin of Hope*. Both his parents found work in the garment industry, "my mother an operator, my father a presser." They struggled to put food on the table. They were *"folksmassen*—ordinary people, you know—with a little bit of religion and a little bit of leftist feeling, but hardly political at all." That changed when the International Ladies Garment Workers Union (ILGWU) organized a massive strike in 1933. His parents unflinchingly supported the strike. As Howe explained, "for a Jew to scab was as unthinkable as to become a Christian convert." The ILGWU secured his parents higher pay and better working conditions, which amounted to some semblance of economic security and dignity for the family. The experience shaped Howe's commitment to the labor movement. "One reason that I've always been strongly attached to unions is that they made an enormous difference in my own life."[13]

Books also shaped Howe's political consciousness. "The sense of my own deprivation grew keen after I learned about the troubles of people I did not know," he later wrote. "And this was typical of many other boys and girls in my generation, in whom family trouble and intellectual stirring joined to create a political consciousness." Books also provided a respite from the working-class toughness of the East Bronx. "In the West Bronx I was gregarious, on the street, carefree, a baseball player," Howe recalled, but in the East Bronx he rarely ventured outside because he feared the various street gangs, the "'toughies' on the street."[14]

In his teenage years, Howe forged an alternative kind of masculine camaraderie, not through street gangs or sports but through politics. He first became active in the Young People's Socialist League (YPSL) while at the famed all-male DeWitt Clinton High School, which after 1929 was in the Bronx.[15] He was part of a "little clique of twelve or fifteen kids" who spent their after-school time at street-corner meetings. These meetings were "a remarkable institution that formed part of Jewish life," Howe later recalled. Novice orators competed for attention with seasoned ones, preaching to gathered crowds or debating issues with one another. Howe described the street-corner meeting as "a training school where young speakers could learn to talk quickly and to cope with skilled hecklers." At this stage he was a "cocky Jewish boy, a talkative little *pisher*." But he cultivated his polemical skills, cutting communists and the occasional "right-winger" down to size.[16]

Howe attributed his interest in books, politics, and debating to Jewish tradition. "Some heritage of Jewish sensibility or incipient trace of intellectuality" led him to find "a home of sorts" in the YPSL. Jewish-ness centered for Howe not on religion but a secular Yiddishkeit culture and radical politics. Even the rules of polemical combat among leftists came out of Jewish tradition.[17] There was an "unwritten understand-ing" in the neighborhood. "No violence," Howe recalled. "That was very Jewish."

> I remember that one of our girls had her glasses broken jostling with a Communist lady, a Jewish woman. The girl burst out crying: her mother would give her hell and where would she get the money to have those glasses fixed? The Communist lady who had been denouncing her in the most vitriolic terms suddenly became a Jewish mother who forgot that she was facing an adversary. She offered to pay for the new glasses.[18]

Though women were active in the Left, the radical sects of the 1930s functioned as masculine spaces. "On nights after branch meetings, we often relapsed into a kind of male bonding," Howe wrote years later, in the shadow of second-wave feminism. There were certainly "bright and strong girls in the movement," but men did not take them seriously. Some were mere "vanguard groupies," but even the most intellectual ones were treated with "subtle and not-so subtle sexual condescension." Women in the movement of the 1930s were confined to menial tasks, Howe observed, like giving out leaflets and typing stencils, and they "didn't yet have the feminist vocabulary or sense of solidarity that might get them through rough times." Moreover, as socialists they were "determined to behave as if our proclaimed belief in sexual equality had been realized, while in fact of course it was not."[19]

In 1936 Howe entered City College. Two years later he joined the Socialist Workers Party (SWP), founded in January 1938 by followers of Leon Trotsky who were expelled from the Socialist Party. "The Trotsky-ists were not very different politically from socialists on the left," writes Sorin, "but according to Irving Howe, they brought with them 'an aura of certainty' about why the Russian Revolution had succeeded initially, why it had been betrayed, and how it might yet reoccur."[20] Howe became the "theoretician" of the Trotskyist contingent at CCNY. "A real Commissar," according to Daniel Bell. Other CCNY Trotskyists included Philip Sel-znick, Seymour Martin Lipset, and Irving Kristol, whom Howe recruited. He later described that recruitment as "a big mistake." Kristol "wasn't, let's say, good material."[21]

Howe graduated from City College in the spring of 1940 into a world mired in depression and war. Sitting next to Irving Kristol and Earl Raab at graduation, the three young men, dressed in their black gowns and graduation caps, could not help but "burst out laughing" when the commencement speaker alluded to the "careers lying ahead of you." In 1940 Howe also began his journey from sectarian radicalism to democratic socialism. He followed Max Shachtman out of the SWP that year into a tiny left-wing group called the Workers Party. Shachtman formed the Workers Party to protest "the more orthodox Trotskyists, who continued to see the Soviet Union, even under Stalin, as a socialist entity."[22] In 1949 the SWP became the Independent Socialist League (ISL). Howe remained connected to the group until 1952, when he finally broke from the sectarian Old Left. Thereafter, he referred to himself as simply a democratic socialist.[23]

Between 1940 and 1952 Howe also began to figure out what he was going to do with his life. He aspired to be a political organizer and writer but feared the combination was unlikely, since "Marxists had always regarded intellectuals as 'unstable'—desirable allies, but inclined to vanities of independence."[24] There were also few jobs to be had in 1940. The Depression lingered, and the United States had not yet entered the war. The summer after he graduated, Howe worked a number of short-term jobs, including one at a pinball-machine factory on Long Island. He was fired within weeks, however, for trying to organize a union.

In late 1940 he began writing for *Labor Action*, a four-page weekly published by the Workers Party.[25] In 1941 the paper named him managing editor. He was twenty-one.[26] He wrote nearly half the articles in each issue, using various pen names. It was "the best training of my life," he later explained, "and one of the happiest periods, too."[27]

As editor of *Labor Action* Howe opposed America's entry into the war. That was the Trotskyist position: fascism was the last stage of capitalism. It did not matter "whether the bourgeois democracies or fascism" triumphed in the war, as Sorin explains. In the end, "capitalism will be the winner and the working-classes the losers." Looking back on his editorship at *Labor Action* and the many articles he wrote, Howe was embarrassed by how "cocksure" he was. He also later tried to hedge on his opposition to America's entry into the war, claiming that he had moved toward "a position of implicit 'critical support of the war'" by 1941. Sorin, in his biography of Howe, maintains that Howe "overstated his case." Howe did serve in the army after the United States entered the conflict in December 1941, unlike many radicals and many New York intellectuals, who never served.[28]

World War II and the New York Intellectuals

World War II was a watershed for American Jews. Throughout the 1920s and '30s, American Jews were a racial and religious minority, "outsiders" in many ways, to American society. World War II ushered in a new era of acceptance. Scientific racism and anti-Semitism were discredited during the war, setting the stage for American Jews to prosper in the postwar era. A tri-faith America became a common self-description during World War II, and seemingly axiomatic in the wake of Will Herberg's bestseller, *Protestant, Catholic, Jew* (1955). Catholicism and Judaism joined Protestantism in a new "Judeo-Christian tradition."[29] Finally, Jews became "white," and, like many white ethnics, they moved out of working-class immigrant neighborhoods into middle-class suburbs.[30] In the process most abandoned the radicalism of the immigrant generation and embraced consensus Cold War liberalism.[31]

Significantly, and especially in retrospect, the war also fundamentally transformed perceptions of Jewish masculinity. Military service has long been tied to the cultivation of masculine traits like strength, athleticism, bravery, and heroism—the traits that anti-Semites most pointedly denied to Jewish men. By serving in the military during World War II, Jewish GIs challenged long-held anti-Semitic stereotypes that depicted Jewish men as feeble, weak, and effeminate. Jewish GIs proved to non-Jews, and to themselves, that Jews were "fighters." "The skills they acquired in the army and navy, how to handle weapons and defend themselves" became, argues historian Deborah Dash Moore, "part of their understanding of manhood, an understanding that would accompany them back to civilian life."[32]

That was true of huge numbers of Jewish Americans—more than half a million American Jews, men and women, served in the US military during World War II. This number constituted more than 11 percent of the American Jewish population. "Jewish men made 8 percent of those in uniform, about twice their proportion to the population as a whole." Moreover, 50 percent of American Jewish men between the ages of eighteen and forty-four served in the military during World War II.[33] After the war, Jewish veterans took advantage of the Service Men's Readjustment Act (1944), also known as the GI Bill, just as quotas limiting the number of Jews at universities crumbled. The ramifications for Jewish male presence in sports, entertainment, business, and the professions of law and medicine, were huge. Most significant for our story here, however, is that most *intellectual* Jewish men who attained cultural prominence in the 1950s and '60s missed the straightforward and seemingly irrefutable masculinization—and Americanization—of combat.

Most New York intellectuals either did not serve or, if they did, did not see combat during World War II. There were exceptions. Irving Kristol was an infantryman in the 12th Armored Division, which took heavy losses invading Germany and helped to liberate Dachau, and Leslie Fiedler volunteered for the navy, serving as a cryptologist and Japanese language interpreter in Iwo Jima, Okinawa, and China.[34] But for most, the war did little to redefine their understanding of masculinity.

Rather, the war made their development of a cerebral and exaggeratedly verbal masculinity all the more urgent and even poignant. Alfred Kazin, for example, sought to enlist. He wanted to serve as a lecturer, what he called "soldier-brain instructors" in a 1942 journal entry. Kazin felt his brain would serve him better than muscle in the military. In a painful twist, the military classified him as 4-F, unfit for military service, because of an undescended testicle. Kazin underwent a series of operations in September 1943 to fix the problem. According to biographer Richard Cook, the operations were "successful—removing a longstanding source of anxiety and embarrassment."[35]

Howe spent the war in Alaska. Drafted in June 1942, he attended basic training at Camp Upton on Long Island that summer and then was sent to Fort Richardson in Alaska. "Army ways are mysterious and opaque," he later reflected. "Why it sent me to places where there was no active fighting I would never discover." Rather than fighting, Howe spent the war reading. "In nearly two years in Alaska I must have read a solid 150 books." Howe compared those years to "graduate school."[36] Similarly, Clement Greenberg spent the war stationed in Oklahoma, where he too read voraciously and even had time to publish reviews. Nathan Glazer graduated from CCNY in 1944. He got an exemption from military service for health reasons and went to work for the *Contemporary Jewish Record*, a journal sponsored by the American Jewish Committee, relaunched as *Commentary* in 1945. Robert Warshow served as a code breaker in Washington DC in the US Army Signal Corps. And so on.[37]

Some of these budding intellectuals went to great lengths to avoid military service. Daniel Bell spent more than a year and a half fighting his 1-A (acceptance for military service) classification. He was working as managing editor for the *New Leader* when drafted in December 1942. Its editor, Sol Levitas, wrote numerous letters seeking a permanent draft deferral for Bell. Levitas told the draft board that Bell was essential to running the magazine, which he argued contributed to the war effort by covering fascism. "The paper will be in jeopardy if Mr. Bell is drafted, and I believe that in the interests of national defense it is of vital importance

FIGURE 7. Irving Howe stationed in Alaska during World War II.
Courtesy of Nina Howe.

that Mr. Bell be kept in his present position," Levitas wrote.[38] When that
line of argument failed, Levitas submitted medical documentation that
Bell suffered "from acute anxiety neurosis," "migraine and conversion hys-
teria," and poor eyesight.[39] The army ultimately granted Bell a permanent
deferral.[40]

Even Norman Mailer, who would go on to publish one of the great
American war novels, *The Naked and the Dead*, in 1948, did not see
combat. He had enlisted in the army hoping to find inspiration for his
writing. But when offered the opportunity to serve on the front lines he

declined. In a letter to his wife, he explained "that he chose office work because he thought to himself, 'You ass, you're playing around with your life.'" That Mailer and others did not see the front lines made them no different from many enlisted soldiers, who worked as "clerks, dentists, base cooks, logistic officers, and members of support staff, and so on." But given the strong association between combat and masculinity, it is noteworthy.[41]

It was with a pen rather than a rifle that many of these intellectuals contributed to the war effort. Bell reported on the war for the *New Leader*. He later felt somewhat ashamed that he evaded service, partly because it was a masculine rite but also because of the fate of European Jewry.[42] Kazin's attempt to enlist was stymied, but he reported on the army's effort to educate soldiers for *Fortune* magazine in 1943. In 1944 the Rockefeller Foundation sent him to London "to observe and report on the education of soldiers and war workers in England" and also to "give talks and lead discussions on America and American literature for the Office of War information." It was the closest he got to the war.[43]

Howe, for his part, counted himself "lucky" to find himself posted "in Alaska, away from the killing, safe and sluggish, almost indifferent to ego, sex, or thought of the future." Revealingly, it was in Alaska that he decided to be an intellectual rather than "a socialist tribune or leader." At Fort Richardson he began "the habit of mumbling to oneself that is the occupational disease of intellectuals. Here I came to see a little of what I really was, rather than what I had tried to will myself into becoming. Words held me; so did ideas."[44]

The Academy

When the war ended Howe returned home to begin a career as a freelance writer. "Like many returned soldiers—it seems almost a moral obligation—I join the '52–20 club'" (a year's unemployment insurance at twenty dollars a week).[45] Part of the GI Bill, this unemployment money allowed him to resume working at *Labor Action* for no pay and support his writing for other small and obscure publications that paid very little. In 1946, when his GI benefits ran out, Dwight Macdonald hired him as an editorial assistant at *politics*, the independent radical magazine Macdonald founded in 1944 after becoming disillusioned with *Partisan Review*. The pay was poor—only fifteen dollars a week—but it was good experience, and good mentorship under Macdonald.[46]

In its brief life from 1944 to 1949, *politics* had a great impact on Howe. When Howe began thinking seriously about launching his own magazine

a decade later, *politics* served as an example.[47] In the late 1940s the magazine served as "a kind of halfway house for independent leftists who were
bored with sectarian Marxism but thoroughly opposed to postwar conservatism."[48] Howe was undergoing his own political transformation. "As to
your question about my politics, I haven't considered myself a Trotskyist in
any strict sense of the word for some time now," he wrote to Macdonald in
the summer of 1948. "I've been undergoing a rather painful soul-searching
and will probably be able to arrive at a terminus soon."[49] Howe did not
officially break from Trotskyism until 1952 when he resigned from the
Independent Socialist League and the editorial board of *Labor Action*. But
working at *politics* put him well on his way toward democratic socialism.

In 1947 Howe moved to New Jersey with his new wife Thalia Phillies,
who had secured a well-paid teaching position at a private day school in
Princeton after graduating with a doctorate in Classics from Columbia. It
was in fact Howe's second marriage.[50] He had married a fellow Trotskyist in
1941, "a marriage of convenience," recalled Howe's former student, professor of literature Judith Walzer. Though whose convenience was unclear.
They separated after a year and divorced in 1946. Howe's marriage to
Phillies lasted until 1960. They had two children: a daughter born in 1951
and a son in 1953.[51] When they moved to Princeton, Phillies's salary was
significantly higher than Howe's at *politics*. Howe sought out better paying work. He, like so many men in the 1950s, faced societal pressures to
provide a "family wage."[52]

In 1948 he accepted a position as a book reviewer at *Time*, Henry
Luce's "middlebrow" newsweekly, which Howe detested but which paid
extremely well. Up to that point Howe had only worked for left-wing
organizations and obscure independent publications. He rationalized taking the job at *Time* because it freed up time to advance his writing career
in the highbrow journals, such as *Partisan Review*, that he aspired to publish in. Macdonald himself had worked at *Time* back in the 1930s, and
at Henry Luce's more business-focused *Fortune*. Macdonald might have
told Howe that working for a major weekly that vast numbers of ordinary
people actually read was excellent training. It was a "good job in most
ways," Howe told a friend. It brought in "a good income and takes less
than half a week. I don't like the work and don't like the association; yet
it's been immensely convenient, allowing me to get all my work done."[53]
Howe later put it this way: "By working on the time provided by *Time*, I
managed to break loose from its grip—indeed, from all it symbolized."[54] It
symbolized, of course, acceptance of the capitalist consumer society that
America was becoming with too little critical self-consciousness, too little

cultural and literary refinement, and virtually no inclination to question American power.

The *Time* salary also relieved Howe of relying on Phillies as breadwinner. As he told a friend when he accepted the job, he felt it "more wretched to be supported by a wife."[55] Although it was common for the New York intellectuals to depend on their "working wives" in the 1930s and 1940s, as Daniel Bell later recalled, "so they could be supported while they wrote their esoteric essays," by the postwar years they were not immune to societal expectations that men be breadwinners.[56] Indeed, Howe was not the only New York intellectual to take a well-paid job in the postwar years. Many worked for what they disparaged as "slick" magazines. Bell, for example, was the labor editor at *Fortune* from 1948 to 1958. In 1959 Bell joined the sociology faculty at Columbia University, indicating the future trajectory of many once independent intellectuals. "Why did I give up a career in journalism for academia?" Bell famously quipped: "Three reasons: June, July and August."[57]

Many New York intellectuals joined the academy in these years when it was still relatively common for universities to hire people who did not have a PhD. With anti-Semitism discredited and the expansion of higher education catalyzed by the GI Bill and the new subsidies of the Cold War, opportunities arose in universities that just fifteen years earlier had discriminated against Jews, including traditionally genteel fields like English.[58] In 1953 Howe was offered a position at Brandeis, a school founded in 1948 in part because Jews and other minorities still faced discrimination in higher education.[59] Howe worried that dependence on the comforts of university life might corrupt him and that his new employer's public relations strategies might impinge on what he could say in the classroom and in print. What would happen to the intellectual's hard-won independence after becoming a mere employee of a large bourgeois institution like a university?

When Max Lerner, a well-known journalist who had taken a position at Brandeis, approached Howe in late 1952 about teaching at the university, Howe hesitated. He contacted an old friend, Lewis Coser, who had just joined the Brandeis faculty as its first sociologist.[60] Howe had met Coser a decade earlier when both were members of Shachtman's Workers Party. Coser was an émigré who escaped Germany in 1939. He ended up writing a weekly column in *Labor Action* when Howe was editor, despite not being proficient in English. Howe needed whatever contributors he could get. Coser "didn't, of course, get a penny for his contributions," Howe later recalled, and the two men "didn't become friends." But after the war both wrote for Macdonald's *politics*. Both were also in the process of moving away from sectarian socialism. When *politics* folded in 1949, Coser went on to pursue a PhD in sociology at Columbia University. The decision "roused in me suspicions of 'bourgeoisification,'" Howe recalled. But he had the good sense not to say anything to Coser as the two went their separate ways—Coser into academia and Howe into journalism.[61] When the two reunited on Coser's turf at Brandeis, they became good friends and lifelong colleagues. They founded *Dissent* together in 1954.

Before accepting the position at Brandeis, Howe exchanged a series of letters with Coser. He asked whether Brandeis was even a "serious school." Its reputation in Princeton was "a rural New School." Howe also worried about the school's Jewishness. "Is there a lot of Jewish politicking?" he asked Coser. Howe said he did not want to be seen "as a 'young Jewish intellectual'" but simply a "literary man" more broadly. Howe also asked about rank and pay.[62] He conceded he was no "celebrity," but he felt "a good deal more than a beginner." He had written three books and was "in the process of doing 3 more."[63] Given those accomplishments and "given the other individuals hired at the assistant professor rank," Howe felt he "deserved . . . at least an associate professorship."[64]

More significantly, Howe wanted to know whether being a full-time professor might be too time-consuming. He worried about keeping up with the work he truly cared about, writing.[65] "Would it be possible to continue writing once I got there? How many hours a week does one teach?" he asked Coser. "Is there are a lot of extra-teaching duty, such as student-coddling, committees, etc. etc.?"[66]

Howe also worried about his political independence. The invitation to teach at Brandeis came at the height of McCarthyism.[67] "The one thing that worries me about teaching is the question of academic freedom," Howe confided to Coser. "I anticipate a terribly reactionary period, with a full-scale attack on teachers—and the teachers will run like mice! Will Brandeis back me up in case of attack?" Howe reminded Coser that "I've never been a CP member or sympathizer" and "I've always been violently anti-Stalinist . . . But the McCarthy's don't care for political distinctions."[68] Some of the Trotskyist organizations he had been affiliated with were on the attorney general's list of subversive organizations.[69] "Right now they're on ex-cpers, which is OK," he told Coser in another letter. "But their capacity for making distinctions, or their desire, is very limited. Would it matter to them that someone like myself has always been anti-Stalinist? The question is: what would the likely reaction of the Brandeis people be to any trouble?"[70] Would Abram Sachar, the university's president, come to his defense if the House Un-American Activities Committee (HUAC) targeted him? Coser could offer no solid assurances. Howe later recalled that Coser told him, "If there were minor harassments, Sachar would stand firm; but if there was a direct major assault by McCarthy, well . . ." all bets were off.[71]

The final question was Phillies's career. She had a well-paying job in Princeton. Moreover, she was "really the scholar in the family," with "a PhD in classical archaeology . . . able to teach Latin, Greek, archeology, and art." Though Lerner had told Howe he would find "something part-time for her at Brandeis," Howe asked Coser if he could "patch together two-part time deals," by reaching out to nearby colleges like Wellesley.[72] Coser's wife, Rose, was also a sociologist, who taught at Wellesley and Northeastern.[73] Ultimately, Howe and Phillies moved to Waltham in 1953. Howe began teaching at Brandeis in the fall while Phillies left her well-paying full-time job for a part-time position at Brandeis that Howe called a "raw deal. Twelve hours and low pay. They take advantage of [the] fact she's my wife."[74]

Howe, however, had to reconcile the new reality of his academic institutionalization with his deeply held belief that intellectuals needed to remain detached from institutions in order to maintain their independence, whether those institutions be government bodies, established media outlets, or universities. Though Howe had been thinking about starting a magazine since 1949, when *politics* folded, it is significant that the birth of *Dissent* coincided with Howe's entry into academia. Postwar circumstances might have transformed how intellectuals made a living, but Howe still felt they needed to maintain a critical and combative stance.

Defining the Intellectual in Postwar America

Between 1946 and 1954 Howe struggled to define the intellectual vocation within new postwar circumstances. He explored these tensions in various essays, most famously "This Age of Conformity," which appeared in *Partisan Review* in 1954, just weeks before Howe launched *Dissent*. Howe republished "This Age of Conformity" numerous times over the years. Less well-known is an essay he published eight years earlier, his first long piece in *Commentary*, titled "The Lost Young Intellectual." Howe never republished it in any of the numerous edited volumes he put out over the years. In 1946 he was a neophyte, an unknown—and perhaps he viewed the piece as amateur. But for this reason, "The Lost Young Intellectual" is in some ways more revealing than "This Age of Conformity."[75]

FIGURE 8. Irving Howe teaching at Brandeis in the 1950s. Courtesy of the
Robert D. Farber University Archives & Special Collections Department,
Brandeis University.

In 1946 Howe was twenty-six years old, just out of the army, and trying
to launch his writing career. He published his first book review in *Commentary* that year, a rite of passage for any aspiring young intellectual in
this milieu.[76] *Commentary* paid "fairly well," Howe told Dwight Macdonald. "But I need more outlets—how nepotism rules in the literary world."[77]
The following year he would publish his first piece in *Partisan Review*.[78]

"The Lost Young Intellectual" was clearly semi-autobiographical even
though Howe and the editors at *Commentary* tried to suggest otherwise.
"Irving Howe is a young writer, active in radical politics," the article's accompanying biography stated. "During the war, he served in the army in Alaska.
Any implied resemblance between him and the young intellectuals described
in this article, is, we are assured, quite unwarranted." But anyone who read
the piece could glean it was based on Howe's own experiences. Howe even

switched into first person and included anecdotes from his childhood. But he tried to present it as a broader analysis of "a new social type": the American-born Jewish intellectual, who Howe argued was "a marginal man, twice alienated." He was estranged from both his Jewish immigrant roots and from American society, in part because he did not conform to either Jewish or American expectations of masculinity. *"It is difficult to be a Jew and just as difficult not to be one* [italics in original]," Howe wrote. "He is caught in the tension resulting from conflicts between his society and his tradition, his status and his desires: he suffers as a man, intellectual, and Jew."[79]

The essay was very much a rumination on the meaning of American Jewish masculinity in the postwar era. Howe wrote about generational conflict between sons and their immigrant parents, a theme he would return to thirty years later in *World of Our Fathers.* Jewish immigrant fathers lived vicariously through their Americanized sons, in part because American society had emasculated them. "The father desires in his son the fulfillment of his own undeveloped frustrated ambitions," Howe wrote. Jewish fathers did not want their sons to toil in factories, unable to make enough money to provide for their families, but rather to attain an education. Learnedness was a traditional attribute of Ashkenazi Jewish culture. "The father . . . still feels himself part of a people whose tradition is that of learning (after all, isn't Einstein a Jew?)," wrote Howe, and thus "has an exaggerated reverence for things intellectual; he will literally work himself to death so that his son can go to college." Immigrant fathers viewed education as a path toward economic independence and upward mobility in the United States. They had become "wedded to professional success," Howe complained, something "he learned in America. Learning is an end in itself—provided it is not an end in itself, provided it helps his son become a teacher or doctor."[80]

The lost young intellectual son was scornful of professional success. Jewish sons aspired to a cerebral masculinity untethered to commercial and professional success. The son not only "reject[ed] religious values in general, as many modern intellectuals do," Howe wrote, but also "rebelled against the standards of bourgeois capitalist society."[81] The leftist son had forged his own vision of a secular Jewish masculinity rooted in the intellectual vocation but freed from the capitalist ethos of breadwinning.

Jewish mothers played a significant role in Howe's analysis of Jewish masculinity. They contributed to the emasculation of both father and son. "In most Jewish immigrant families, the father occupies an anomalous position," Howe wrote in 1946. "His education is incomplete." Its incompleteness was a form of castration, severing the father from traditional constructions of Ashkenazi Jewish masculinity. At the same time, Jewish wives dominated the households in immigrant families. The father "is not really the power in the family," observed Howe, because "the mother is often much more 'practical' and 'decisive.'" Mothers were the ones who thwarted their sons' efforts to embody American norms of boyhood. Jewish mothers coddled their sons, stymieing their ability to grow into American men. Citing psychoanalyst Helene Deutsch, Howe wrote that "from infancy on, the child is spoiled by his mother; she keeps him in the feminine pattern as long as possible, delaying the cutting of his baby curls, and later trying to prevent him from entering street relationships by tying him to her apron strings; she inhibits his normal urges towards athletic activity by her fears that he will be hurt, infecting him with the same fears."[82]

How was the lost young intellectual to develop into manhood under such circumstances? Howe didn't have a clear answer. "Some would suggest Zionism; still others a return to traditional Judaism," Howe wrote. But Howe remained "sceptical" [sic] that those avenues would appeal to "intellectualized sons," like himself, who felt like "the 'outsider,' the outcast." "Possibly he can find some alleviation in individual psychotherapy," he mused. Ultimately, the lost young Jewish intellectual would need to develop his own place in American society, including his own vision of masculinity, with the hopes that he would eventually find "integration, security, and acceptance."[83] For Howe that journey ultimately led to *Dissent*. But not before some more soul searching about the meaning of the intellectual vocation and masculinity in postwar America.

In 1952 Howe was one of only three contributors who opposed the underlying assumptions of *Partisan Review*'s famed symposium, "Our Country and Our Culture" (discussed in chapter 3). That symposium posited that intellectuals were no longer alienated from American society, and that this was a good thing. It cast American capitalism as a positive force, which had brought prosperity in the postwar years. Most contributors to the symposium also implied that intellectuals should no longer criticize American democracy. After all, America had defeated Nazism and now stood as the only bulwark against Soviet totalitarianism. Howe took issue with these assumptions. In his contribution to the *PR* symposium, he argued that intellectuals should not support America uncritically. It didn't matter that the United States was less oppressive than the Soviet Union. Capitalism was still an unjust system. In Howe's view, the intellectual vocation required a critical stance. That intellectuals "no longer behave like exiles" was "good" in Howe's view, but that they ceased being "rebels" was "a pity."[84]

Howe took the occasion here to define, for the first time, the intellectual: he "should be an independent man thinking and behaving in terms of his personal integrity, a man who remains free from the dictates of all state power, a critic of cant and convention whom the philistines will not cease to find 'destructive.'"[85] Note that Howe interchanged intellectual with man and that an intellectual's virtues were ones that he associated with masculinity: independence, autonomy, integrity, and rebelliousness.

Howe expanded on these positions two years later in the lengthy polemic titled "This Age of Conformity." It appeared in *Partisan Review* in its January–February 1954 issue but signaled his impending departure from that magazine. On the brink of founding *Dissent*, Howe was laying down the raison d'être for the new magazine. The essay "aroused a quantity of anger, hostility, and irritation," Howe later recalled, "understandably so: it was a scatter-shot polemic, meant to strike a variety of targets."[86]

In "This Age of Conformity" Howe blasted his peers for uncritically embracing affluence, capitalism, and Cold War liberalism. He lamented that intellectuals were no longer part of bohemia but "now sink into suburbs, country homes, and college towns." Howe himself had just moved to a college town and begun teaching at Brandeis. He acknowledged as much. "The pressures of conformism are at work upon all of us, to say nothing of the need to earn one's bread." But Howe nonetheless warned of the "slow attrition which destroys one's ability to stand firm and alone: the temptations of an improved standard of living combined with guilt over the historical tragedy that made possible our prosperity." For Howe, "what was most alarming is that the whole idea of the intellectual vocation—the idea of a life dedicated to values that cannot possibly be realized by a commercial society—has gradually lost its allure."[87]

Howe's concern fit into a broader "crisis of masculinity" that various commentators warned about in these years.[88] But Howe's critique focused particularly on intellectuals and was rooted firmly in a distinctly Jewish construction of masculinity. Intellectuals, Howe warned, were losing their manly edge. "Thirty years ago," he wrote, "'Intellect' was self-confident, aggressive, secure in its beliefs, or, if you wish, delusions." In the postwar years, however, "the ideology of American capitalism" had transformed intellectuals into sycophantic promoters of the American zeitgeist. Intellectuals were no longer "self-confident" and "aggressive" but "conformist" and "timid." They embraced and indeed helped give rise to a "moderate" liberalism that was a "liberalism . . . without confidence or security." According to Howe, "to call oneself a liberal one really doesn't have to believe in anything."[89]

Howe did not refer to Jewish identity in this article. But his main targets were the mostly Jewish New York intellectuals writing for *Commentary* and the *New Leader*, some of whom he mentioned by name. He took Irving Kristol, Sidney Hook, and Nathan Glazer to task for their "hard" anti-communism, arguing it teetered dangerously close to support of McCarthyism. "Marx-baiting, that least risky of occupations, has become a favorite sport in the academic journals; *a whining genteel chauvinism is widespread among intellectuals* [emphasis added]; and the bemoaning of their own fears and timidities a constant theme among professors." Howe's phrase "whining genteel chauvinism" suggested that conformist cold warriors were sissies. If the new Jewish masculinity was to be combative and fierce, genteel chauvinism was decorous and deferential, prim and ultimately weak.[90]

Dissent

"When intellectuals can do nothing else," Howe famously declared in an essay marking the twenty-fifth anniversary of *Dissent*, "they start a magazine." The sentence that followed, though less quoted, is also instructive: "But starting a magazine is also doing something: at the very least it is thinking in common." In the 1950s thinking in common included rethinking democratic socialism. Within the magazine "the idea of socialism was itself to be treated as problematic rather than a fixed piety," Howe wrote.[91] But thinking in common also meant embodying an intellectual masculinity. To a degree this was circumstantial. Most of the founders of the magazine were men. They would work out a local masculinity as any military unit or sports team would. But for Howe, the masculinity—like everything he developed— was thoughtful, an act of conscious opposition to the trends of the outside world. At *Dissent*, Howe strove to develop a way of being intellectual that was combative, polemical, and critical in an era when he believed most intellectuals had made peace with American society and capitalism.

The idea for the magazine that became *Dissent* tangibly took root in 1952. That fall Howe resigned from the Independent Socialist League and terminated his association with *Labor Action*, ending his affiliation with Trotskyism. "*Labor Action* speaks in tones that are strident, dogmatic, and often lifeless," Howe wrote in his resignation letter. "It reflects the desperate intransigeance [*sic*] of its contributors rather than any effort to think about the present world in terms that have some relation to people outside the sect."[92] Stanley Plastrik and Emanuel Geltman, old friends from the Shachtmanite group, also "decided to quit. We had enough of the claustrophobic, depressing existence of a socialist clique," Howe later explained. "But we could not resign ourselves to a complete withdrawal from leftist politics, and so, like others before and after us, we decided to start a magazine." They, along with Lewis Coser, also politically "adrift" in the early 1950s, became the core editors at *Dissent*.[93]

The group began to send out letters to other leftists they thought might feel similarly alienated from politics in the age of McCarthy. "A few weeks ago, Irving Howe and I were talking about the unhappy situation of the few remaining left-wing (i.e., Socialist, anti-Stalinist) intellectuals in this country," Coser wrote in one letter. They wanted to bridge the "isolation and loneliness" many radicals felt in the early 1950s by exploring "the possibilities of some joint intellectual effort, preferably in the form of a serious magazine." Such a magazine would be "polemical; mainly political though concerned also with broad cultural matters; open and eager for discussion of socialist problems; in a word something like the early version of *Politics* before Macdonald discovered the root is man," meaning Macdonald's turn toward pacifism.[94]

They were convinced an audience for such a magazine existed, not only among their contemporaries but also among a younger generation of leftists. "There seem to be enough semi-demi-radicals among the younger people who look for a way out," they noted in their letter.[95] This last point was crucial. They envisioned the magazine as a training ground for a new generation of leftists in radical politics and the art of intellectual combat.[96] As Howe wrote to sociologist C. Wright Mills in an attempt to enlist his support: "the value of the magazine would be to allow younger, less known people to write from a critical, radical slant things which no one else will take. And to serve as a center, a rallying ground for intellectual socialist opinion."[97] By the spring of 1953 they had put together "a mailing list of 1000 names," many of them "young people without political experience," interested in the magazine. This enthusiasm among a younger generation was an exciting contrast to the "apathy" characterized by the response of "many ex-radicals" their age.[98]

To enlist support for the magazine and begin raising funds, Howe and Coser organized a two-day conference in New York in December 1952.[99] "We invited about fifty people, ranging from those with a little money to potential writers," Coser later recalled. "To our great surprise they almost all came, and there was a good deal of enthusiasm."[100] The meeting resulted in the formation of the Committee for an Independent Magazine, chaired by the art critic Meyer Schapiro. According to a fundraising letter, "some 25 socialists" attended the meeting, "almost all of them not

affiliated to any political group and most of them intellectuals by trade."
They held various political positions but were "bound together by common values and ideas; that we all believed in the need for critical, radical
thought; that we all rejected the notion that socialism has become passe
[sic]; that we had no faith in the basic recuperative powers that liberals ascribe to capitalist society; that we believed Stalinism could best be
defeated by means of a political offensive on the left, which would undercut its hold on millions of workers in Europe and discontented nationals
in Asia. Everyone present," Schapiro continued, "felt that civil liberties in
America were in danger; that the bleak rituals of conformism had never
before been so prevalent; that the liberals and ex-radicals who had constituted themselves as a cheering squad for the status quo did little good for
the liberties we all want to defend and extend."[101]

While a full list of attendees at the conference is unknown, undoubtedly most were men.[102] *Dissent*'s inaugural editorial board was also made
up of all men: Howe, Coser, Travis Clement, Emanuel Geltman, Stanley
Plastrik, Harold Rosenberg, and Meyer Schapiro. Contributing editors
included Erich Fromm, Sidney Lens, Frank Marquart, A. J. Muste, and
George Woodcock.[103] Howe often referred to the group that formed *Dissent* as a "fraternal society."[104] In an essay marking the fifth anniversary of
the magazine, for example, he wrote that "for these men to learn to work
together took time, effort and the growth of an attitude of tolerance and
fraternity, such as has not always been present among American radicals
in the past."[105]

Dissent did not consciously exclude women. In an early letter explaining the need for "a new radical magazine," its future editors noted that
"those of us having contact with a new generation now growing up in the
schools and colleges of this country have often felt that these young men
and women are desperately eager to find, somehow, somewhere an organ
which would formulate their vague fears and criticisms, their anxieties
about tomorrow and their rejection of today."[106] When Howe taught at
Brandeis he treated male and female students in an "egalitarian" manner, but he understood "intellect and brains" generally as masculine,
Judith Walzer recalled. But Howe was also fairly conventional when it
came to gender roles, "meaning women take certain roles, take care of
certain things, and men take care of other things, and certainly [in his
view] intellect and running a magazine and all that is male by nature."
At *Dissent* parties at Brandeis in the 1950s, Howe encouraged male students to contribute to the magazine but did not do the same for female
students, despite treating them equally in the classroom. This, of course,

made Howe no different from most male editors in the decades before second-wave feminism.[107]

Dissent, like other New York intellectual journals, functioned as masculine space. But whereas *Commentary* staked out a "hard" anti-communism in these years, which helped masculinize Jewish intellectuals by associating them with the "right" side in the Cold War, Howe and the *Dissent* crew staked their futures on an intellectual masculinity that was critical as well as combative. It was critical of American institutions, mass culture, unfettered capitalism and consumer society. It objected to the stifling of civil liberties and "of intellectuals accommodating themselves to the status quo."[108]

Dissent *and Women*

Women were present at *Dissent* from the beginning. But they were rarely publicly acknowledged. Both Simone Plastrik and Rose Laub Coser (wives of Stanley Plastrik and Lewis Coser) were "larger than life" at the magazine. Yet they were almost never recognized as such.[109] No woman served on the editorial board of *Dissent* until 1972, when sociologist and labor activist Patricia Cayo Sexton joined it. Her husband, Brendan Sexton, an education director at the United Auto Workers, also joined that year. In 1974 Rose Coser and Deborah Meier, a public education activist, became the second and third women named to the board. Rose Coser had published her first article in the magazine in 1959. Patricia Cayo Sexton had first written for the magazine in 1971, Meier in 1968.[110]

Dissent, unsurprisingly, did not have many women writers. In the fall of 1956 Helen Mears, a Japan specialist, became the first woman to write for the magazine. In 1959, *Dissent* published articles by Hannah Arendt and by the French socialist Suzanne Labin. Along with Rose Coser, that was it for articles by women in *Dissent* in the 1950s.[111] Importantly, the dearth of women writers at *Dissent* made it no different from other intellectual magazines. "They were as male dominated as *Dissent* or worse," writer Joanne Barkan, who joined *Dissent*'s editorial board in the 1980s, points out.[112]

Notably, Arendt was the only well-known woman among the New York intellectuals to appear in the magazine in its first years of publication. Her article, a controversial analysis of the liberal strategy of school desegregation, occasioned by the crisis in Little Rock, Arkansas, in the fall of 1957, garnered widespread attention. It was supposed to appear in *Commentary*, but the magazine shied away from its provocative analysis of a delicate subject. Many at *Dissent* shrank away from its challenge, too. But after a protracted dispute among the editors, *Dissent* printed it.[113] Mary McCarthy, Diana Trilling, and Elizabeth Hardwick never wrote for the magazine. These were "very distinguished, large figures," Howe's friend, political theorist, Michael Walzer noted, "women who were not part of *Dissent* at all."[114]

The spring 1966 issue saw the first women listed on *Dissent's* masthead: Edith Tarcov, identified as an editorial assistant. Yet in reality Tarcov "did everything" at the magazine, Judith Walzer recalls, and "Irving was enormously dependent on her." In 1968 she was promoted to managing editor, a position she held until she retired in 1985. Though many people "thought of her as an impossible nudnik," Judith Walzer recalled, "she was a genius" who kept the magazine "going."[115] Tarcov was "an editor of the old school: tireless, exacting, and passionately devoted to clarity," according to writer Brian Morton, who joined *Dissent* in the 1980s. "Like most dedicated people, she could sometimes be difficult. But if she demanded a lot of the people she worked with, she demanded much more of herself. She worked like a demon, for little pay, [and] little reward of any kind."[116]

Howe and the other male coeditors were also not paid in the first decades of the magazine's existence. "No editor ever received a penny in more than the twenty-seven years of publication," Howe proudly stated of the magazine's early history. "We refrained from such bourgeois indulgences as having an office: all editorial and business matters were handled on desks at home."[117] Editorial meetings took place in editors' living rooms while manuscripts circulated by mail. "Irving would put the title on a long sheet of yellow paper, and it went around to everyone on the Board," recalled Michael Walzer. "You'd read the article; you would write your comments and send it on to the next. It was all U.S. mail, and then Irving would get the sheet with all the comments," and make the final decisions.[118] "The whole thing was run like a mom-and-pop grocery store," Michael Walzer said.[119] Yet like many mom-and-pop shops, men were the public faces while women's labor remained largely hidden.

The closest thing the magazine had to an office was the Plastriks' apartment. Stanley Plastrik served as the magazine's general business manager. But in reality, so did his wife, Simone. "The *Dissent* office" in the early years "was her apartment," notes Michael Walzer. She was "very involved" in running the magazine and was "an important behind-the-scenes figure in the magazine's early history."[120] Yet her name never appeared on the masthead. Nor did Howe mention Simone in essays about the magazine's early history.[121] Howe described Stanley in one such essay as "an extremely able man" who managed the magazine's financial affairs and "rejected Keynesian economics not so much on principle as out of an understanding that we couldn't bear the anxiety of owing money. How curious that the old-fashioned virtue of austerity so dear to conservative hearts should have found one of its few homes in our little socialist enterprise!"[122] Although he said nothing publicly about Simone, he was aware that she played a crucial role getting *Dissent* out. "The Plastriks are indispensable to running the magazine," he wrote Coser in the summer of 1961. "They do perform a most efficient, if in some ways limited, job."[123] In an "informal Bulletin of Information" sent to *Dissent* supporters in February 1962, Howe noted that "too much of the work continues to be done by too few people, esp. in New York, where the administrative burden falls on the Plastrik family."[124]

Howe was equally silent publicly about Rose Laub Coser's large role at the magazine. Unlike Simone, however, Rose's name did eventually make it to *Dissent*'s masthead—in 1974, twenty years after the founding of the magazine. A brilliant sociologist trained at Columbia University (PhD, 1957), Rose taught part-time at Wellesley and Northeastern, all the while "carrying forward important work in medical sociology, social psychiatry, and the role of theory at Harvard Medical School." While Howe and Coser were at Brandeis, she "progressed from instructor to assistant professor at Wellesley College between 1951 and 1959 and then went on to the Department of Psychiatry at Harvard University where she became a research associate."[125]

It was Rose who introduced her husband and Howe to Joseph Buttinger, an Austrian socialist émigré married to Muriel Gardiner, a wealthy American heiress with "strong socialist convictions." Buttinger and Gardiner financed the launch of the magazine with "a check for $1000—pretty big money for Christmas 1953," as Howe recalled.[126] After the editors raised another thousand dollars, they had enough money to fund four issues of *Dissent*. "Whether it would make it to Volume II remained an open question."[127] But Rose Coser played more than a networking role. She and Lewis Coser collaborated on their research and shaped each other's work, sometimes writing jointly. "They formed an extraordinary intellectual and intimate partnership manifest in their collective work," *Dissent* contributor Cynthia Fuchs Epstein recalled, and that collaboration extended to the magazine.[128]

Why did it take twenty years for Rose Coser to appear on the editorial board? By the early 1970s she probably just "put her foot down," Judith Walzer suggests.[129] Rose Coser was always "an extremely assertive person, and a staunch feminist."[130] Second-wave feminism probably influenced her. Prior to the late 1960s "her calls to arms were not so much from the soapbox but from written works," according to Fuchs Epstein. In the 1970s Rose Coser became "involved in a women's group, a women's faculty group" at the State University of New York Stony Brook, where she and her husband accepted full professorships in 1969. "She instituted a class-action suit at Stony Brook on behalf of women faculty and staff and engaged in a sit-in at a male-only bar at the hotel hosting the 1972 American Sociological Meeting."[131] By 1974 she was perhaps unwilling to have her labor at *Dissent* remain invisible.

Not until the 1980s was there a concerted effort to recruit women as writers and members of the editorial board. In 1985 when Joanne Barkan joined the board, "everyone was keen on bringing in more women. At every meeting I attended for the next two decades, one or two members called for getting more women writers into the magazine and more women onto the board. Irving often responded, 'Give me names.'" He wanted good writers. "Women or men? It didn't matter." Yet when Barkan once suggested to the editorial board that the magazine strive to have 30 percent of articles in each issue written by women, she was met with "silence." Affirmative action was not something the editors contemplated, in part because it "would require a radical shift of focus and resources."[132]

Dissent *and Feminism*

Second-wave feminism had transformed *Dissent*. But that transformation took time.[133] Women's equality "is one of the oldest doctrines of social democracy," notes Michael Walzer. "August Bebel, the German Social Democrat, said something about the crucial test of a socialist is his position on the emancipation of women, and we all believed that. Everybody believed that, and it may not have manifested itself, but that was our official political position" at *Dissent*. Judith Walzer responded, "I think that makes very clear the space between official position and life habits."[134] Howe admitted as much by the early 1980s. "I had to notice within myself habits of condescension that women had no doubt noticed long before but were only now combative enough to criticize," he wrote in *A Margin of Hope*. "When this happened to me, I didn't like it. I wasn't prepared to admit that in my pure heart—socialist heart of hearts!—there could be so much as a grain of sexual bias. But of course there was."[135]

Howe initially derided much of second-wave feminism. But by the early 1980s "while not an activist for feminism, nor an aggressive recruiter of women writers for *Dissent*," as historian Gerald Sorin observes, "Howe was from the sidelines giving 'two cheers' for women's liberation."[136] Those cheers reflected a significant evolution. In 1970 he fiercely attacked the women's movement. While he supported "most of the immediate objectives of the feminist movement," including equal pay for equal work and legalized abortion, he had "reservations about the ideologues of 'radical feminism,' the extremist wing that was then especially articulate and influential."[137]

Howe did not express his views in the pages of *Dissent* but published a notoriously scathing critique of Kate Millett's *Sexual Politics* (1970) in *Harper's Magazine* in December of that year. Howe's denunciation of Millett was typically "Irving style over the top," in that "it went for the jugular," Judith Walzer recalled.[138] The episode reveals as much about the cultural force of feminism in the late 1960s and 1970s as it does about Howe's own agon with masculinity.

Howe highlighted Millett's limited frame of reference: her middle-class white bias (a criticism that white and Black feminists also made of the women's movement more broadly). Displaying his Marxists roots, Howe derisively labeled Millett "an old-fashioned bourgeois feminist." Millett universalized women's experiences throughout time and place, Howe complained, ignoring differences among women based on race, religion, and especially class. "Has the fact of being female been more important in the social history of most women than whether they were rich or poor, black or white, Christian or Jewish?" Howe incredulously asked. He viewed class oppression as most germane. "Women have been exploited throughout history," he wrote, "but most of the time in ways quite similar to those in which men have been, and more often than not, as members of oppressed or disadvantaged classes rather than as women alone."[139]

Most derisively Howe called Millett a "female impersonator." Because she seemed to question whether there really was such a thing as a biological category of sex, Millett revealed a "rather comic ignorance of essential experiences of her sex, such as the impulse toward the having of children," Howe argued. He seemed to say she was not really a woman, and certainly could not speak for women.

Paradoxically, however, Howe also argued that Millett's femaleness prevented her from seriously engaging with rigorous social theory. He dismissed her use of terms like "chattel" (to describe women's position in modern society) and "sexual object" as "phrases of a little girl who knows nothing about life." Howe put that last sentence at the end of a paragraph in which he lauded the women he knew for being "at one and the same time intellectuals or professionals," "mothers," and "attractive wives (and why not? Since so many succeed)." Howe equated femininity with domesticity, motherhood, and attractiveness. Intellectual work was manly.[140] The women in his professional life wrote like men but otherwise behaved like women. Millett, on the other hand, was neither a real woman because she rejected motherhood and heterosexual marriage, nor an intellectual, because she didn't write like a man.[141] Howe erased Millett's "authority," as one scholar astutely observes, "paradoxically through a construction of Millett as both woman and not."[142] Of *Sexual Politics*, Howe concluded: "In short, we have here an intellectual goulash that could be taken seriously only in a moment when serious standards have collapsed."[143]

The same month that *Harper's* published Howe's review of Millett, *Dissent* ran a sympathetic assessment of women's liberation by Alice Rossi, a feminist sociologist and one of the founders of the National Organization for Women (NOW). Rossi may have been recruited to write for *Dissent* by Rose Coser. In 1969 Rose Coser republished Rossi's influential 1963 paper, "Equality between the Sexes: An Immodest Proposal," in a volume she edited, *Life Cycle and Achievement in America*. Rossi first wrote for *Dissent* in its July–August 1969 issue on the topic of abortion. Then in the November–December 1970 issue, she published "Women—Terms of Liberation." Whereas Howe dismissed Millett's analysis of Freud as "vulgar" and "simplistic," writing that "she simply will not read with care," Rossi wrote that "a number of radical-feminist analyses begin with a good critique of Freudian fallacies concerning female sexuality." Rossi's article was sympathetic and nuanced, even as she contrasted the focus of younger radicals on sexuality with the emphasis on legal discrimination by groups like NOW. "Liberation group discussions" of sexuality, she wrote, "can be enormously helpful for the psychological release of the submerged sexual selves of many women."[144]

Was there discord at the *Dissent* offices over women's liberation? Michael Walzer remembered that a number of editors at *Dissent* thought Howe's review of Millett was "over the top."[145] The editors might have thought Millett's book deserved some criticism—*Dissent* published a negative review of *Sexual Politics* a year later by Sonya Rudikoff—but many felt that Howe's attack was excessive.[146]

Howe's review of Millett's book got a lot of attention. *Time* magazine published a review that echoed Howe's, and even quoted Howe's description of *Sexual Politics* "as a 'farrago of blunders, distortions, vulgarities, and plain nonsense,' and its author is guilty of 'historical reductionism,' 'crude simplification,' 'middleclass parochialism,' 'sexual monism,'

'methodological sloppiness,' 'arrogant ultimatism [*sic*],' and 'comic ignorance.'" That was a significant reassessment on *Time*'s part. Five months
earlier, the magazine had featured Millett on its cover with generally
positive coverage of the women's liberation movement.[147] In this "second
look," however, *Time* quoted Howe's description of Millett as a "female
impersonator," suggesting that he had "sensed a sexual ambiguity" before
she came out as bisexual.[148]

Time mentioned other critics of *Sexual Politics*, notably Midge Decter, an editor at *Harper's*, who had solicited Howe's review. Decter had
just written her own anti-feminist polemic (the first of many) in *Commentary*.[149] Decter was part of a rightward shift underway among a minority of
New York intellectuals, soon to be called neoconservatism. Howe would go
on to denounce the rightward shift of his colleagues at *Commentary* and
vigorously opposed neoconservatism. But in 1970 he fired a major salvo
against radical feminism under Decter's editorship. In the late 1960s and
early 1970s his negative views of other currents in the radicalism of the
1960s at times overlapped with those of his rightward-shifting colleagues.

By the middle of the 1970s, however, Howe was rethinking his assessment of feminism. He republished "The Middle-Class Mind of Kate Millett" only once, in a 1973 anthology titled *The Critical Point: On Literature
and Culture*. Revealingly, Howe omitted the offending lines in which he
called Millett a "female impersonator" and a "little girl who knows nothing
about life." In 1979 he included Rossi's essay, "Equality between the Sexes,"
in an edited volume celebrating the first twenty-five years of *Dissent*.[150]
By the time he published *A Margin of Hope* in 1982, he could admit his
blindness when it came to the women's movement. "Once polemic was
exhausted, the fact remained that feminists spoke for genuine grievances,"
he conceded. "What finally mattered was the strength and genuineness of
the feelings women were displaying—a crucial testimony."[151]

Fathers and Sons: The New Left

One of the reasons why Howe was initially so antagonistic to women's
liberation was because he associated it with the New Left. "Ms. Millett is a
writer entirely of our moment, a figment of the *Zeitgeist*," Howe wrote in
his review of *Sexual Politics*. She is "careless" in her scholarship, "exhibit-
ing a talent for the delivery of gross simplicities in tones of leaden complexity," and "has a mind of great energy but small regard for nuance." For
these reasons, "she is the ideal highbrow popularizer for the politics and
culture of the New Left."[152] Kate Millett did not write like a man, but in

Howe's view, neither did most male New Leftists. Howe, and many other New York intellectuals, believed that New Leftists, their leaders and theoreticians included, tended to lack intellectual sophistication. Specifically, most of them failed to engage robustly in an exchange of ideas. They relied too often on style rather than substance. They were immature, that is they had not won their intellectual spurs through long, hard preparation, and the rigors of verbal combat. They were, to Howe's generation, crude adolescent boys.

Masculinity was at stake in Howe's conflict with the New Left—a masculinity that had much to do with Jewishness. Like the New York intellectuals, the New Left was disproportionately Jewish. "Is it even necessary to point out that close to a majority of the participants at Port Huron [where the founding manifesto of SDS, the Students for a Democratic Society was written in 1962] were secular Jews?" writes historian Michael Kazin, and that "Jews continued to be prominent in the white New Left out of all proportion of their numbers in the American population."[153] Kazin's assessment is both historical and biographical. In the late 1960s he was a leader of Harvard's SDS chapter. He is also the son of Alfred Kazin. Paul Buhle, another noted historian and former SDS activist, has similarly observed that "from its inception in 1960, SDS was Jewish by a proportion so considerable that early SDSers usually shied away from exploring its significance, at least in public."[154]

Like the New York intellectuals, the New Left was also male dominated. "SDS was an organization with a lot of very strong male egos," SDS leader Tom Hayden acknowledged. Indeed, women's liberation emerged in part as a critique of the male chauvinism and sexism within the New Left. "A critical subtext of the revolt of young male students," according to historian Sara Evans, was that they contested the "masculinity of their father's generation." Young male leftists spurned such markers of American manhood as "militarism, financial success, the tradeoff of sexuality for the responsibilities of marriage and family."[155] Evans's observation can be extended to the New York intellectuals and their ideology of secular Jewish masculinity.

New Leftists rejected their elders' habit of debating but never acting. As Hayden later recalled of meeting Howe and the *Dissent* crowd for the first time: "I was not raised in, thankfully, a household of people yelling at each other about the correct line, so I couldn't comprehend the decibel levels that these people would reach," a reference not only to the sectarian battles of the Old Left but also to a Jewish masculine style of disputation.[156] In the eyes of New Leftists, these middle-aged *alte kakers* were passive armchair intellectuals. They endlessly argued, put pen to paper, but never took to the streets to protest—not in the 1960s and not in the 1930s when they were young radical anti-Stalinists who spurned the Popular Front.[157] New Leftists, meanwhile, did not care much for anti-communism, nor were they initially interested in the intricacies of Marxism. They considered themselves incisve thinkers and wrote a great deal, too, contrary to what Howe and other Old Leftists thought.[158] But masculinity and meaningful political engagement for them also meant taking to the streets in protest. It meant putting their bodies on the line, something they felt the New York intellectuals never did.

Both groups were cognizant of each other's Jewishness. Todd Gitlin, an SDS leader turned academic, described the New York intellectuals as "seasoned scrappers, trained in the Talmudic disputation characteristic of Trotskyism." Employing a Yiddish word that combines annoyance and amusement, he noted that "they had little patience for us, young and inexperienced *pishers*."[159] Gitlin's references linked these intellectuals to a traditional construction of Jewish masculinity, that of the learned Talmudic scholar. He was not alone. In 1966 Jack Newfield, a young journalist who reported on the New Left for the *Village Voice*, made a similar observation. These were "Talmudic intellectuals trained in the *Partisan Review* Stalinist guerilla rumbles of the 1930s."[160]

The New York intellectuals were equally aware of the Jewishness of many New Leftists. In a 1969 volume on student radicalism, edited by Irving Kristol and Daniel Bell, Seymour Martin Lipset wrote that "the student left in the United States is disproportionately Jewish." Lewis Feuer, a sociologist who circled the New York intellectual milieu, devoted portions of his 1969 book, *The Conflict of Generations: The Character and Significance of Student Movements*, to the Jewishness of SDS leaders. Norman Podhoretz, writing in 1970, observed that despite the "decidedly Protestant flavor" of some SDS leaders, Jews were the "most visible" in the movement.[161]

Howe, for his part, did not mention Jewishness when he wrote about the New Left. But he often told a story about being taunted by "a gang of New Left kids" while teaching for a year at Stanford in 1969. As he walked across campus "this very bright boy named Cohen, who was the leader of this gang," verbally accosted Howe. Howe had grown accustomed to ignoring the taunts of this group, but that afternoon he turned to Cohen and yelled: "When you grow up . . . you are going to turn out to be a dentist!" Both men understood it as "the most dreadful of insult[s]." There was of course the bourgeois connotation. But it was also emasculating. Although the stereotype of Jewish mothers had them bragging about their sons becoming doctors or lawyers, Jewish leftists—old and new—equated

FIGURE 9. Irving Howe at Stanford, likely in 1969.
Photo credit: Jose Mercado / Stanford News Service.

masculinity with brains, not professional success and wealth.[162] Of his encounter with Cohen, Howe ruefully concluded: "It was very hard because it was like seeing your own children going off the deep end."[163]

When the New Left emerged in the early 1960s, Howe and the editors at *Dissent* were initially optimistic. After all, they had founded *Dissent* six years earlier in part to train a new generation of leftists. The editors might have only been in their thirties and forties—still "young and buoyant," according to Howe, and looking "forward to polemical battle against our rightward-moving friends, especially those who had been less than lion-hearted in standing up to McCarthyism."[164] But they were already looking for "successors."[165] Thus when civil rights activists broke through "the psychic smog of the Cold War," catalyzing a political awakening among young white college students in the process, the editors at *Dissent* were excited and "very hopeful."[166]

Dissent covered the New Left intently. It devoted its spring 1960 issue entirely to "The Young." Michael Walzer provided the magazine with a first-person account of the Southern student-led sit-in movement.[167] Walzer had graduated from Brandeis in 1956. In 1959 he joined *Dissent*'s editorial board as its youngest member. He was a good ten to fifteen years younger than the other editors. Then enrolled in a doctoral program in government at Harvard, he became the magazine's point man on the New Left.[168]

The New Left brought new readers to the magazine and revitalized the left in the United States. In the spring of 1962, *Dissent* held a symposium on "The Young Radicals." Beginning that year subscriptions rose precipitously. In 1962 the magazine had 2,500 subscribers. It was not much, Howe conceded, but it was the "most successful year" since the founding of the magazine in 1954.[169] Over the course of the decade the numbers continued to rise. By 1966 the magazine was able to change from a quarterly to a bimonthly publication.[170]

Yet from the beginning, anti-communism divided these two generations of leftists. For the *Dissent* group, anti-communism was essential to any leftist politics. When they announced the formation of the magazine in 1954, the editors specified that it would "be open to a wide arc of opinion, excluding only Stalinists and totalitarian fellow-travellers on the one hand, and those former radicals who have signed their peace with society as it is, on the other."[171] Six years later their position had not changed.

As early as 1961, Howe and Coser were pressing the New Left on its anti-communist commitments. In the fall 1961 issue of *Dissent*, they observed that these young activists had "no particular attachment to Russia or Communism" and rightfully questioned Cold War orthodoxy. But they were dismayed that they were "not very interested in distinguishing between kinds of anti-Communism, whether on the right or left." Howe and Coser, moreover, warned that the New Left risked repeating the mistake of "Popular Frontism of two decades ago" if it ignored the issue.[172]

Howe and Coser titled their article "New Styles in Fellow-Travelling," an extended version of which became the epilogue of a revised 1962 edition of their book, *The American Communist Party: A Critical History*, originally published in 1957. Fellow traveling was a reference to leftist support of the Communist Party in the 1930s and the failure of many Old Leftists to distinguish between Marxism and Stalinism. Just as Old Leftists ignored the murderous authoritarianism of Stalin, Howe and Coser warned that young leftists were romanticizing authoritarian Marxist revolutionaries like Patrice Lumumba of Congo and Fidel Castro of Cuba. Castro in particular appealed to young radicals because he "dared tweak Uncle Sam's nose, fought heroically, spoke rhetorically and dressed spectacularly."[173] Howe and Coser suggested that due to outward appearances these revolutionaries seemed heroic to younger radicals, and manly. But their appeal was all a performative masculinity. Moreover, their hip style obscured their authoritarianism and Leninism (and Soviet backing).[174]

Foreshadowing what would become the major critique of the New Left by the *Dissent* crowd, Howe and Coser argued that New Leftists focused on "style" at the expense of intellectual sophistication. When they "turn to politics," Howe and Coser argued, "they have little concern for clear or precise thought. What attracts them is the surface vitality, the appearance of freshness, the gesture of drama. They care more for style than conviction, and incline more to outbursts than sustained work."[175] For a group that understood intellectuality and thought as central to masculinity, this was an argument that had much to do with gender. The New York intellectuals' ideology of secular Jewish masculinity was cerebral and involved meticulously debating ideas. For New Leftists, however, masculinity also meant something different. It meant acting and protesting.

These tensions between the *Dissent* group and the New Left exploded at a 1962 meeting between the magazine's editors and leaders of SDS. SDS had just issued its Port Huron Statement, and the editors at *Dissent* organized the meeting with the hopes that it might lead to the "joining of two generations of the Left." Gitlin later described the scene as: "five SDS leaders met with five *Dissent* editors in a mansion right off Central Park," probably the home of Joseph Buttinger.[176] Gitlin, Hayden, Paul Potter, and Paul Booth represented SDS. "They came with a sense of reverence, and antagonism, combined," Gitlin later recalled. "These were the fathers we were meeting, and at the same time they were the proprietors of the left such as it was."[177] Howe, Buttinger, Plastrik, and Geltman were probably the editors who represented *Dissent*. Walzer did not attend. But he quickly heard about the meeting. "It became a thing. Everybody heard about it."[178]

Anti-communism divided these two generations of radicals, but so did competing constructions of masculinity. The *Dissent*ers maintained that anti-communism was essential to the success of any democratic leftist movement.[179] Yet as they pressed the SDSers on their views of the Soviet Union, China, and Cuba, the younger radicals balked. In forming SDS, they wanted to transcend the sectarian battles of the Old Left and the stale and debilitating anti-communism of the postwar era. Moreover, what mattered to them was action—protesting racism and inequality—not debating anti-communism. "It was very puzzling," Hayden later recalled: "If you said, 'I think students should have the right to vote, I think students should be able to write opinion pieces in the Ann Arbor paper without them being censored, I think black citizens should be able to vote, I think we should desegregate the South,' if somebody then said 'but how anti-Communist are you?' it would just seem that they were on another planet."

The SDSers had taken part in sit-ins in the South, risked their lives protesting racial injustice. What had these middle-aged intellectuals ever done besides bellow? "They reminded you, in a sick way, of your father," stated Hayden. "This was paternalism beyond Abraham—paternalism to an extreme that I've never heard of. People pointing at you and lecturing to you. They didn't appear to be doing anything. And we were going to jail. So at least we knew we were on the right track."[180]

Thus, two different visions of masculinity collided that day— rebellious sons versus cerebral Jewish fathers. For the *Dissent*ers, arguing and debating embodied masculinity and hashing out political differences was a form of masculine camaraderie. When Howe was at CCNY in the 1930s, "he'd been accustomed to paying his friends the compliment of a rigorous political bashing if they strayed, however briefly, from the correct line to which he adhered," notes historian Maurice Isserman.[181] New Leftists didn't see it that way. They felt admonished and infantilized. Howe later conceded as much. "We tended to seem to them people who knew everything or thought they knew everything. We had become a little fixed in our views, a little rigid in our postures," Howe said. "We were impatient; we scolded."[182] But after the meeting Howe told his friend and fellow Democratic Socialist Michael Harrington that "political positions need to be argued." Yet "these fellows," meaning the New Leftists, "haven't much dialectical capacity. They don't even believe in the need for arguing."[183]

In 1965 Howe published a full-blown critique of the New Left, "New Styles in Leftism." The article first appeared in *Dissent* and thereafter in various edited volumes. For readers in the know, the title played on Howe and Coser's 1961 essay, "New Styles in Fellow-Travelling." Howe now expanded on the concerns that he and Coser had raised in 1961. But at forty pages, it was a much longer polemic—a diatribe against the New Left. Howe no longer cast his concerns as a warning of what could happen, but rather as a description of reality. New Leftists were "ideologues and desperadoes," he argued, some of whom verged on authoritarianism. He cast theirs as a politics of "impotence . . . because movements that are powerful, groups that are self-confident, do not opt out of society: they live and work within society in order to transform it." In Howe's view, New Leftists were nothing more than immature adolescent "desperadoes." He and his fellow editors had offered to give them the training and leadership to become men of intellectual substance, but they shrank away from the challenge. Their show of rebellion curdled, for Howe, into an escape from politics—from engagement with ideas and with reality—altogether.[184]

Howe identified a number of troubling "characteristic attitudes among the 'new leftists.'" Their disdain of liberalism and their refusal to learn about the past, including the mistakes of the Old Left when it came to Stalinism. Howe admonished the New Left's "vicarious indulgence in violence, often merely theoretic and thereby all the more irresponsible." Once again, he took them to task for idealizing "third world" revolutionaries who embodied a dangerous and superficially virile masculinity. Their "heroes" on the international front were "figures like Lumumba, Nasser, Sukarno, Babu and above all Castro," while at home they looked up to civil rights militants who advocated violence, including Robert Williams and especially Malcolm X, who "neither led nor won nor taught."[185] Theirs was a masculine politics of style and outward appearances but not substance. New Leftists had made "style the very substance of [their] revolt."[186]

Howe wrote that New Leftists "displayed a tendency to regard the political—and perhaps all of—life as a Hemingwayesque contest in courage and rectitude." By that he meant that outward appearances of virility mattered more than stepping up like a man to deliver intellectual substance. "People are constantly being tested for endurance, bravery, resistance to temptation," Howe complained, "and if found inadequate, are denounced for having 'copped out.' Personal endurance thus becomes the substance of, and perhaps even a replacement for, political ideas."[187]

New Leftists took offense to the essay. Marshall Berman described it as an "extravagant acting out" against a younger generation that would not follow Howe's lead. According to Berman it was Howe who "was a man obsessed with style" and "only people with THE RIGHT STYLE were allowed to play." The right style was the masculine debating style of the New York intellectuals.[188]

In 1966 Howe reprinted the essay in his volume *Steady Work* and acknowledged that his tone angered many readers. But he found that criticism "irrelevant":

> For what is the use in telling people who feel strongly about an intellectual matter that they should keep their voices low and sweet? In the political tradition from which I derive, it has been common to write with polemical sharpness—hopefully an impersonal sharpness—and then to expect one's opponents to reply in kind. You argue, you let some heat come through, and you don't pretend that gentility is the ultimate virtue.[189]

This was a Jewish masculine style of arguing. Morris Dickstein, one of the youngest and arguably last of the New York intellectuals, who like Michael Walzer was closer in age to New Leftists than others in the group, described Howe's essay as "an inventory of bullet points, each of them like a jab to the ribs or an uppercut to the jaw."[190] The boxing metaphor was evocative of the New York intellectuals' ideology of secular Jewish masculinity.

Ultimately, Howe and *Dissent*'s concerns about the New Left proved prophetic. By the late 1960s, SDS had descended into violent sectarianism. The Vietnam War, racial unrest, the election of Richard Nixon in 1968, all tore the movement apart. By 1970 Howe was denouncing the New Left's "quasi-Leninist fascination with violence." Groups like the Weathermen, meanwhile, stood for a "mixture of violent adventurism, staged desperation, and even hooliganism." Howe conceded most New Leftists were not Weathermen. But "the cult of violence, the celebration of bombs," and "the adulation of charismatic authoritarian leaders" could all "be found in most New Left tendencies."[191]

The New Left, Howe argued, embodied a stylized and performative masculine politics run amok. Taking over university buildings, irrational hostility toward liberalism, and "carrying guns" had "nothing to do with the socialist, or radical tradition," Howe wrote in 1970. Rather, that was all "a strange mixture of Guevarist fantasia, residual Stalinism, anarchist braggadocio, and homemade tough-guy methods."[192] While Howe and the *Dissent* group sympathized with many New Leftist reactions to the outrages of the late 1960s, they felt that protest had to be accompanied by reasonable thought and analysis, which they felt the New Left lacked. "We too thought it callous to prolong the [Vietnam] war. We too wanted to demonstrate against it," Howe wrote in his memoir. "But we took the trouble to read the materials issued by the organizers of the antiwar demonstrations, and what we saw dismayed us."[193] The New Left's shallow intellectual engagement was infuriating. These were traits that Howe and the *Dissent* group first warned of in 1961. That they came true was dispiriting.

The self-destruction of the New Left dashed the *Dissent*ers' hopes for the resurgence of a leftist politics in the United States. "There are signs today of a massive withdrawal from political involvement, a spreading mood of cynicism about the possibilities of political success," Michael Walzer ruefully wrote in *Dissent* in the spring of 1972. "It is clear that any sort of sustained leftist activity is going to be extremely difficult. *In the New Left fall/We suffered all.*"[194]

Howe touched on Jewish masculinity in the encounter with the New Left in his 1984 memoir, *A Margin of Hope*. Was his, and the *Dissent*ers', reaction to the New Left perhaps a "case of unrequited love?" Howe asked. "Hadn't middle-aged Socialists like you set for yourselves the role of mentor to the young, and weren't you now reeling from blows of rejection?" He conceded that there was some truth in that notion. He also admitted that he "overreacted" to the New Left, "becoming at times harsh and strident." Howe was argumentative because he took the New Left seriously and wanted them to succeed where the Old Left had failed. He also embodied secular Jewish masculinity, something that he obliquely acknowledged in his memoir and is worth quoting at length:

> Friends began to hint in the kindliest way that I was becoming a little punch-drunk. I found myself wondering why Michael Harrington, who expressed criticisms of the New Left close to mine, was not regarded as so dastardly an opponent. The generous-hearted Harrington was a Christian of sorts, while I was a polemicist in the old style. So, in a conversation painful to both of us, Michael Walzer gently told me. Couldn't I make my criticisms more temperate? Someone should, I could not.
>
> The truth is that the "kids," as the phrase goes, "got to me." I might score in polemic, but they scored in life.[195]

For Howe, there was a real sense of kinship with the New Left, which made the situation between the two groups all the more tragic. Howe admitted in his memoir that the New Left's attacks on older liberals and radicals like himself felt personal. "They wanted to deny our past, annul our history, wipe out our integrity." When New Leftists painted "the slogan 'Up against the wall, motherfuckers!' on campus buildings," they not only had police and the political establishment in mind but "parents of the New Deal generation who had raised them." It felt like a schism between fathers and sons, a theme that animated *World of Our Fathers*.[196]

Howe and the *Dissent* group remained on the left and deeply tied to democratic socialism and an ideology of secular Jewish masculinity, even as they failed, at least initially, to join two generations of the Left. In the 1980s these fathers and sons would reconcile to counter the intellectuals at *Commentary*, who forged neoconservatism and in the process embraced a gendered politics centered on conservative family values and hawkish foreign policy (the subjects of chapter 6 and 7).

CHAPTER FIVE

"Lady" Critics

WOMEN NEW YORK INTELLECTUALS
AND FEMINISM

*Although it will indeed be a significant day for women when they are
appointed to full professorships at our leading universities on the same
basis as men, that is, on the basis of their merit, it will be an even better
day when, in their own living rooms, they are naturally paid the same
heed, given the same credence, as men can now count on for their opinions
and speculations.*[1]

—DIANA TRILLING

IRVING HOWE WAS not the only New York intellectual irritated by Kate
Millett's 1970 book, *Sexual Politics*. Shortly after Howe published his
scathing review of Millett in *Harper's Magazine*, Midge Decter talked to
Nachem Malech "Norman" Mailer about "women's lib." He said, "I ought
to write about it." "God, you certainly ought to," she responded.[2] Millett
had described Mailer as a misogynist and "a prisoner of the virility cult"
in her book.[3] Decter had solicited and published Howe's review in *Harper's*, where she had worked as an editor since 1968. But she knew that a
response from Mailer would generate even more publicity.

Mailer's article, "The Prisoner of Sex," appeared in the March 1971
issue. It soon became "the biggest-selling issue in *Harper's* history."[4] Decter resigned from the magazine a few weeks later, however, as did other
senior staffers in response to the departure of Willie Morris, the magazine's young brash editor. Morris said he was forced out because Mailer's
article "deeply disturbed the magazine's owners."[5]

Decter went on to become one of the most formidable critics of the women's liberation movement and a leading neoconservative ideologue (the subject of the next chapter). But she was not the only woman New York intellectual to criticize feminism. *All* of them did, even if most did not become neoconservatives as Decter and her husband, Norman Podhoretz, notoriously, did.

The New York intellectuals viewed male-female distinctions as fundamentally and inescapably biological, not social constructions as feminists argued. Diana Trilling once observed of her "equal love of cooking and writing: 'The cook is the feminine side and the critic, the masculine, and I don't know which one to turn to.'"[6] Like the men in the group, the women New York intellectuals also took it as axiomatic that the intellectual vocation was masculine. This was a view shaped by Jewish tradition and undergirded by Freudianism. The New York intellectuals embraced Freud in the late 1930s and 1940s as they abandoned Marxism. While Freudianism was a disparate and evolving set of theories, Freudian categories generally prescribed men as "active" and women as "passive." Intellectual work was active. The women New York intellectuals transcended these prescriptions by performing secular Jewish masculinity in the public sphere.

All the women in the group were known for being acerbic, combative, and sharp. That made them little different from the men. But because they were women they were often maligned as cold, difficult, heartless, and yes, bitchy.[7] "It is difficult to find . . . a similar roster of male writers and intellectuals who lived through and beyond their characterization as unfeeling," literary scholar Deborah Nelson observes. Aggression and pugnacity were desirable in the New York intellectuals' culture of secular Jewish masculinity. But for the women in their ranks, those qualities could be cast as a form of "castrating bitchiness."[8]

Second-wave feminists called attention to these paradoxes. More than any of the radical social movements of the 1960s, they fundamentally challenged the New York intellectuals' ideology of secular Jewish masculinity. Tough and brilliant as they were, the women New York intellectuals encountered what feminists called sexism. But they remained, at best, indifferent to feminism; most were critical of the movement.

Only Diana Trilling emerged as an exception. While she too criticized women's liberation, she did not shun the label *feminist*. "Throughout my adult life I have thought of myself as a feminist, alert to discriminations against my sex," Trilling said in a 1974 speech she titled "Feminism and Women's Liberation: Continuity or Conflict?" While feminism and women's liberation were often "used interchangeably," Trilling said, they were "not identical." Feminism had long been concerned with the "overt," she argued, which meant the political and economic equality of women. Women's liberation, by contrast, focused on the personal, what Trilling described as "the implicit." Trilling identified with an "older feminist tradition."[9] In 1981 she told a reporter she "once considered herself 'the last living feminist,'" referring to this "overt" definition.[10] Trilling later described herself as a "family feminist," by which she meant "a woman who believed that women in concert with men and their families will transform modern life." According to Diana Trilling's biographer Natalie Robins, Trilling "became a pioneering feminist, although she was rarely acknowledged as such."[11]

Few of Trilling's contemporaries remember her as any sort of feminist, however. "Diana Trilling," the novelist Ann Birstein recalled, "never openly exhibited any feminist impulses."[12] In a review of Robins's biography, writer Vivian Gornick retorted that Trilling's concept of "family feminism" "was a dubious definition of modern feminism, to say the least, and one that in reality ate away at whatever genuine self-regard she might otherwise have attained." As a feminist who had been active in women's liberation, Gornick was unconvinced. "One might have thought that a devotion to analytic insight would produce some understanding of, if not sympathy with, those liberationist movements of the 1970s—especially the women's movement," Gornick wrote of Trilling. "But such was not the case. Like her illustrious husband, Diana was a self-styled 19th-century liberal and saw the movement only as disruptive."[13]

Trilling never liked the radical style of women's liberation. But over the course of the 1970s, feminists convinced her that sex roles—the term then used for what we now refer to as gender—were not biologically rooted but largely social constructions, thus diminishing her faith in Freud. "For many years my own view of the relation between the sexes was substantially shaped by Freud's perception of the differing biological natures of the sexes and the consequent differences in their psychological lives and social roles," Trilling explained in 1970.[14] Though many feminists found Freud useful in fleshing out the intellectual implications of feminism—the intellectual history of feminism would not be complete without the Freudian feminism of Juliet Mitchell, Dorothy Dinnerstein, and Nancy Chodorow, and neither would the intellectual history of Freudianism—women's liberation convinced Trilling that Freud had been wrong on some subjects.[15] In doing so, these younger feminists ultimately convinced Diana that one did not need to write like a man.

Town Hall:
The New York Intellectuals v. Women's Liberation

A few weeks after the publication of "The Prisoner of Sex" in March 1971, Diana Trilling and Norman Mailer found themselves on stage with feminists at Town Hall on West Forty-Third Street in New York City. Mailer had been tapped by Shirley Broughton, the director of the Theater of Ideas, to "moderate" "A Dialogue on Women's Liberation." Founded in 1961, the Theater of Ideas was a consortium of some "one hundred heterogeneous intellectuals—writers, artists, [and] scholars" who gathered periodically to discuss "the arts, culture, and politics." Many New York intellectuals participated in its programming; Elizabeth Hardwick and Robert Silvers, cofounders of the *New York Review of Books*, sat on its board of directors.[16] The intrigue at *Harper's* only fueled the hype for the whole affair. Three feminists—Jackie Ceballos, president of the New York chapter of the National Organization for Women (NOW); Jill Johnston, a radical lesbian and the *Village Voice* dance critic; and Germaine Greer, an Australian author of the recent bestseller, *The Female Eunuch* (1970), agreed to participate. Trilling rounded out the panel.

Most Theater of Ideas events were by invitation only. "A Dialogue on Women's Liberation," however, was a fundraiser, so tickets were sold to the general public. They were expensive: twenty-five dollars for floor seats and ten dollars for the balcony. But all 1,500 tickets sold out quickly. "I don't know how many seats there are in Town Hall," Diana later told Mailer biographer Peter Manso. "But all week people had been calling me to ask if I could get them in. God what an evening."[17] As NOW's Ceballos said that night: "It looks like Shirley Broughton's Theater of Ideas had the best idea of the year. It's too bad that we didn't think of it so we could have made some money for women's liberation too."[18]

Recruiting feminists for the event had not been easy. Many refused to share a stage with Mailer. Millett turned down several requests from Broughton. She had no interest in debating the premise of women's rights, let alone with Mailer. The whole event struck her as "sensationalism, making a kind of pugilism out of the whole issue of feminism."[19] Ti-Grace Atkinson, Gloria Steinem, and Robin Morgan also declined invitations. Martha Shelley of the Radicalesbians and Gay Liberation Front, and *Village Voice* contributor Ellen Willis, one of the founders of the women's liberation group Redstockings, dropped out at the last minute.[20]

Greer agreed to take part despite the misgivings of American feminists. Several prominent feminists had asked her to "boycott the whole shindig."

They said, she recalled, "But why . . . should we give an account of ourselves to Norman Mailer? Why should he run the show, he adjudicate?"[21] For Greer, however, the spectacle of Mailer refereeing a debate on feminism was an event she could hardly resist. She relished public clashes and could also bend this one to her own purposes, which were never narrowly ideological. She arrived at Town Hall "dressed for the party in a long slinky black gown with a dead fox slung over one shoulder," as one journalist quipped.[22] Trilling later described it as "a floozy kind of fox fur that trailed over her shoulder to the floor. It was mangy. I expected moths to fly out of it."[23] Greer claimed that "the humorless New York press" had assumed her outfit was expensive. In reality, her "fox fur" "cost a pound" and was worn "for fun and satire."[24] There was no shortage of fun or satire that night. It was the "most lurid" and "extraordinary of evenings," Trilling later recalled, "the last gasp of the sixties really."[25]

"A Dialogue on Women's Liberation" combined the feel of a 1960s New York "happening" with that of a Hollywood premiere. Mailer had arranged for the entire evening to be filmed by documentarian Donn Pennebaker. He didn't bother, though, to tell any of his co-panelists in advance. "Everywhere, all around—tape recorders, movie cameras, flashbulbs, press pencils scribble," one reporter wrote of the scene.[26] Pennebaker's film, *Town Bloody Hall*, was not released until 1979. But Mailer had signed a book contract for a longer version of his article. Little, Brown and Company released *The Prisoner of Sex* a month later.[27] "The Mailer–Women's liberation title fight," Greer later quipped, "was being set up for maximum exploitation."[28]

One journalist characterized the evening as a "commedia dell' arte," complete with eccentric cast and attention-grabbing histrionics. Mailer cast himself as the lead, as the "punk, genius, proctologist, Brooklynite, multiple divorcee, dressed in a nice-looking business suit."[29] Greer disagreed, characterizing Mailer instead as the "carnival barker who had drawn in a crowd of diamond-studded radical chic New Yorkers."[30]

The audience was part of the show. "The hecklers—oh the hecklers! They were the best," one reporter noted.[31] The many literary "celebrities" in attendance included Susan Sontag, Jules Feiffer, Jack Newfield, Stephen Spender, Elizabeth Hardwick, Betty Friedan, Robert Brustein, Philip Roth, Richard Gilman, Norman Podhoretz, Midge Decter, Anatole Broyard, and John Hollander, among others.[32] "America's intelligentsia," another reporter wrote, had gathered "for a festival as gorgeous as any glamour industries."[33] Town Hall was filled with an "elite of a thousand intellectual battles," according to another.[34]

Mailer began the debate with the story of his own article and how *Harper's* fired Morris over it. "The Prisoner of Sex" had tried "to pull the tail feathers of women's lib," he said, since women's liberation was "the most important single intellectual event of the last few years." Mailer was met with loud laughs from the audience—either because they didn't agree with his assessment of women's liberation as an intellectual force or because they thought Mailer was being disingenuous.[35]

Either way, secular Jewish masculinity collided that evening with a younger generation of feminists who challenged the basic axiom of New York intellectual life: that the intellectual vocation was by definition masculine. Greer began her remarks by stating: "I do not represent any organization in this country, and I daresay the most powerful representation I can make is of myself as a writer for better or worse. I'm also a feminist," she continued, "and for me the significance of this moment is that I am having to confront one of the most powerful figures in my own imagination . . . that being, I think, most privileged in male elitist society, namely, the masculine artist."[36] Later that night, during a raucous question-and-answer session, the novelist Cynthia Ozick chided Mailer as an especially conspicuous example of literary masculinity. Referring to his 1959 collection of essays, *Advertisements of Myself,* she asked Mailer: "you said, quote, 'a good novelist can do without everything but the remnant of his balls.' For years and years, I've been wondering, Mr. Mailer, when you dip your balls in ink, what color is it?"[37]

It was not the first time that night that Mailer's genitalia came up. "The whole question of how much liberty men and women can find with each other, and how much sharing of those dishes that they can do, goes into the center of everything," Mailer said at the start of the question-and-answer session. Women's liberation, he argued, would come at the expense of masculinity. Changes in women's roles would only encroach on men and chip away at masculinity, he implied. Mailer thus implored the audience to take the discussion seriously. But Mailer was as interested in stoking the entertainment value of the evening. He added: "I'm perfectly willing, if you wish me to act the clown, I will take out my modest Jewish dick and put it on the table. You can all spit at it and laugh at it, and then I'll walk away and you'll find it was just a dildo I left there. I hadn't shown the real one," he continued. "But if we're going to have a decent discussion, we all got here tonight at great, various efforts to ourselves, let's have it at the highest level we can."[38]

The Jewish phallus was an apt metaphor for the evening. Gender and Jewishness joined at the hip at that evening's Town Hall. Three of the five panelists were Jews: Mailer, Trilling, and Greer. Greer later revealed that Mailer told her backstage that evening that she was better looking than the author photo for *The Female Eunuch*, which in his view "looked like any other uppity Jewish girl." When they met, he seemed "relieved to see that I was a shiksa (except that was wrong too—I am like God in his last despairing suspicion, half Jewish)."[39] The audience, meanwhile, was made up of a cross section of feminists and New York literary people, two groups with disproportionate numbers of Jews.[40] Jewish women were so visible in second-wave feminism that historian David Hollinger has wondered, "In what sense is Women's Liberation, as it was called at the time, a Jewish story?"[41] At Town Hall, Jewish women dominated the question-and-answer session. Sontag, Ozick, Betty Friedan, Lucy Komisar, and Ruth Mandel all spoke. Mailer called Friedan a "lady," eliciting boos from the audience. At one point he was exasperated: "You know I'm not going to sit here and listen to harridans harangue me." Mailer might as well have said Jewish mothers.[42] The writer Ann Birstein, married then to Alfred Kazin, wrote to Greer later that month, "I hope you didn't feel you were drowning in chicken soup," referencing the undercurrent of Jewishness that night.[43] She later described Mailer at Town Hall as "a Jewish mama's boy, who longed to be taken for a tough Irishman."[44]

It was not the only time that evening that Mailer referred to a woman writer as a "lady," either. One of the most memorable moments came after Jill Johnston gave her prepared remarks, which the *New York Times* described as "a free verse, free association, pun-infested, Bible-belting cry for the rites of lesbians."[45] After she finished two women jumped on stage and embraced Johnston. The three fell to the floor entwined in an apparent ad hoc make-out session. If they meant to shock, it didn't work. "It was a miscalculation to have thought that a Lesbian exhibition could break up a meeting like ours—in New York City, 1971," Trilling later recalled.[46] Mailer responded by yelling: "Come on, Jill, be a lady." The audience had not paid "25 bucks to see 3 dirty overalls on the floor when you can see lots of cock and cunt for $4 just down the street."[47] While Mailer's profanity barely registered, his use of "lady" reverberated.

After Johnston and her friends left the stage, Mailer introduced the final speaker of the night as: "the lady of much soul and much establishment who has been one of our leading, if not our leading, literary lady critic for many, many, many years, Miss Diana Trilling." Trilling took little notice of Mailer's introduction. The two were friends. Trilling did later say she felt a "lack of respect" from Mailer. He was too consumed with the spectacle of the evening and with Greer, who Trilling learned was passing notes under the table with Mailer while she gave her formal remarks, fueling rumors that the two would sleep together.[48] Sexual innuendo defined the evening. "Anything that went on between Greer and Norman had an enormous subtext," Jules Feiffer later recalled. Trilling later said she felt like "the token straight, the sacrificial lamb of the evening."[49]

After Trilling sat down the stage was opened to questions and comments from the audience. Susan Sontag asked Mailer about calling Trilling a "lady" critic. Sontag wondered why it was necessary. "If I were Diana, I wouldn't like to be introduced that way. And I would like to know how Diana feels about it. I don't like being called a lady writer . . . It seems like gallantry to you, but it doesn't . . . it doesn't feel right to us. It's a little better being called a woman writer," Sontag mused, but that too was problematic. "If you were introducing James Baldwin, you wouldn't say foremost Negro writer. And we certainly wouldn't say a man writer." Sontag then turned to Trilling for her response. "I recognize the point you're making very well," Trilling told her. "But sometimes I think it's a bit like saying lady runner or lady high jumper, something of that kind . . . and so I permit it on that basis."[50]

Diana's comparison of herself to a "lady" runner or high jumper is revealing. She understood writing and criticism as masculine—akin to athletics, where one flexed one's cerebral muscles and where, like in sports, men were the norm, women the exception. In that respect, she was like other New York intellectuals. Trilling acquiesced to the prefix "lady," however, because she felt, in the context of the evening, it denoted that she was unique in the field as a woman critic. When Hardwick pressed Trilling on the same issue later that evening, she responded, "I'm not quite sure that I find the word lady as offensive as so many people here do. It doesn't hit me viscerally."[51] Trilling wasn't bothered by the term lady; at least not that night in the spring of 1971 at Town Hall.

That these questions came from two other women New York intellectuals is also interesting. Both Hardwick and Sontag implied that if a woman was a good writer, she should be known as a writer—with no "woman" or "lady" prefix. Neither positioned herself as a feminist, however. Both women accepted the masculinist terms of literary excellence articulated by the New York intellectuals. A good writer wrote like a man. Their views were typical of the women in their milieu.

Hardwick, Sontag, Trilling, as well as Mary McCarthy and Hannah Arendt, were at best ambivalent toward feminism. Perhaps because their generation fell between first-wave feminism (1848–1920) and second-wave feminism (often dated to 1963, the year Betty Friedan published

The Feminine Mystique), and because they had become successful writers, they felt "gender had been no impediment in their own careers." They concluded they "didn't *need* 'liberation,'" as one chronicler of this group argues.[52] Friedan said as much about McCarthy in the 1980s. "The first-wave of feminism stopped not long after the winning of the vote in 1920 and the second wave began in the sixties. Mary McCarthy was in the generation in between."[53]

But there was more to it. Part of that generational experience for Trilling, Hardwick, McCarthy, and Arendt, as well as Decter, Gertrude Himmelfarb, and even the younger Sontag, was the thrill of public success as women in the world of secular Jewish masculinity. A successful "writer," in their experience, was a writer who wrote about serious topics with masculine drive and ruthlessness, and one who could bear rough treatment from critics and rivals. They earned their fame by meeting the highest possible standards. Any hint of a double standard was shameful to the writer and a disservice to the craft. In their view, feminists did not meet this standard. They were, essentially, mere "lady" writers who wrote like women.

———

Jewish tradition had long classified intellectual activity as the domain of men. So did Freud, the Jewish doctor from Vienna who reprogrammed the West's high culture on a new foundation: the discovery that sexual experience and sexual fantasy informed human personality. Freud had a disruptive "ism" named after him, as liberating for its partisans and as offensive and dangerous to its opponents as those of Darwin and Marx, the other two distinguishing intellectual turns of "modernist" culture in the West.[54] Freud's theories of sexuality and human development, radical as they were, did not initially disrupt the traditional view that women were passive and men active. "The Freudian tale of femininity centered on penis envy," as historian Jane Gerhard writes. "Since women had no penis, no organ for their aggressive pleasure-seeking libido," healthy sexuality for women meant transferring their leading genital zone from their "castrated" clitoris to their passive vagina. Freud's followers applied these ideas about human sexuality and development to the public sphere as well. Freudianism, as it developed in the twentieth century, posited that healthy heterosexual development for women meant accepting their natural passivity.[55]

The New York intellectuals were some of Freud's "chief advocates" at mid-century.[56] When *Partisan Review* was reborn in 1937 as the flagship of American anti-Stalinism, its editors and contributors "were all more or less saturated with psychoanalytic jargon," William Barrett, a junior editor at the magazine, later recalled. Freud had replaced Marx as a lens for understanding the world. Freud also validated their ideology of secular Jewish masculinity: that intellectual activity reflected a healthy "active" and masculine self-mastery and achievement in world affairs.[57]

Lionel Trilling was perhaps the most fervent Freudian in the group.[58] His 1940 essay "Freud and Literature" celebrated an "Apollonian Freud" as "the guardian of civilization" who "worked to bring the irrational under control," historian Dorothy Ross writes. This was in contrast to the "Dionysian" Freud of sexual liberation, who had captured the American imagination in the early twentieth century. "Trilling's Freud also legitimated a new political voice. In 1940 this was the anti-Stalinist voice of American left liberals disabused of their utopian hopes and anxious to reform America's simplistic optimism."[59] The New York intellectuals, informed as well by the social scientists of the Frankfurt school who immigrated to New York in the 1930s, incorporated Freud into their analysis of the Cold War, mass society, and the dangers of totalitarianism at home and abroad.[60]

Like her husband Lionel, Diana Trilling was steeped in psychoanalysis. "Diana was a very aggressive believer in Freudianism" and "a fanatical believer in psychoanalysis," according to Sidney Hook. Hook once recalled that when he criticized Freud in front of Trilling, she responded: "Well, I don't see why you're a critic of psychoanalysis since it gives such an obvious explanation to your career and behavior." When Hook asked her what she meant, Trilling quipped, "Well, you're very aggressive, you're very analytical, and you're very argumentative, so it's obvious this is compensatory." Hook then asked, "'What is it compensatory for?' 'A small penis,' she said!"[61] In her own memoir, Trilling also wrote about discussing Freud with Hook. Intellectuals tended "to voice their opinion of analysis in the language of religion: one 'believed' or did not 'believe' in it," Trilling explained. "I recall once questioning Sidney Hook on his opinion of Freud in such language: Did he or did he not believe in psychoanalysis? He hedged and I laughingly cut in: 'Of course you believe in it, Sidney. But only for women, not for men.'"[62]

The recollections of Hook and Trilling point to a gendered dichotomy among the New York intellectuals when it came to Freud. The men applied Freud to political issues but were reticent to openly embrace psychoanalysis. Women like Diana were more forthright about undergoing analysis and applied Freudianism to understanding everyday life. It irked Diana that many male New York intellectuals were reluctant to admit they underwent psychoanalysis. "Yet the fact is within the New York literary-intellectual community of the time it seemed to be the men rather than the women who first sought analytic help," Diana wrote in her memoir. "Many of them were exempt from military service because their analysts attested to their emotional instability." Lionel was equally guarded. Though he underwent therapy for most of his adult life, he "regarded his own recourse to analysis," according to Diana, "as a sign of weakness." For these reasons his outward "approach to analysis was intellectual and even literary rather than clinical." For Lionel, Freud "was a giant figure in intellectual history, the author of an original and powerful set of ideas," Diana said. That "was the opposite of my own approach to psychoanalysis."[63]

Whereas Lionel applied Freudian categories to literature and politics, Diana applied them to understanding relations between men and women. "Freud's use of the words, 'passivity' and 'activity'—female passivity, male activity," might have been "misogynistic," Diana argued as late as 1970, but it was rooted in "an irrefutable fact in nature."[64] This Freudian lens would inform her views of feminism and sex roles, which she began writing on in the 1950s.

"Female-ism" v. Feminism

In 1949 Diana Trilling resigned from *The Nation*, where she had had a book review column for nearly a decade. She left *The Nation* because she wanted to write longer articles.[65] She wanted to publish in venues like *Partisan Review*, the litmus test for New York intellectuals, and to be seen as more than just a book reviewer.

Trilling published her first two articles in *Partisan Review* in 1950, when she was forty-five years old. Two years earlier in 1948, she had given birth to her only child. She thus embarked on motherhood and career right as American society was directing young women to devote themselves entirely to marriage and motherhood. Trilling was not young. But she was a mother. And this emphasis on old-fashioned nineteenth-century Victorian femininity irritated her.

Shortly after leaving *The Nation* in 1949, Diana put together an outline for "a series of articles on the American female." Diana wanted to write about America's "woman problem," which she described as "a conflict between feminism and female-ism."[66] "Female-ism" was the term Diana used to describe the effort to put women "back" home after the emergency of World War II drew them into the industrial workforce in unprecedented numbers. Hollywood, Madison Avenue, and the State Department—with sweeping amnesia about how industrialization in the nineteenth century brought women into the workforce in droves, a trend that continued unabated into the twentieth century—launched a new cult of domesticity in the 1950s. This was the powerful set of cultural values and ideals that Betty Friedan termed the "feminine mystique" a decade later in her best-selling book. This "feminine mystique" defined women solely as wives and mothers and directed them to find self-fulfillment and happiness through their husbands and children in homes laden with consumer goods in the postwar suburbs.[67]

A decade before Friedan published *The Feminine Mystique* in 1963, Trilling noted that women's roles had changed in the postwar years. There had been a "shift in consciousness" from "the 19th century American ideal of the wife as helpmeet," she wrote in her outline, to "our present-day ideal of the wife as validation of her husband's right to succeed." Trilling lamented how in postwar American society "only in the home is woman validated as a woman." She noted that a woman was treated not as an individual but as a "social instrument" defined only "in terms of function" as a wife and mother. Modern marriage had become "a kind of mental hospital," she argued, in which a "successful marriage" was "measured in terms of the wife's ability to supply whatever emotional support her husband may require, or whatever emotional strengths he might lack, at the same time that she maintains the socially-required image of her emotional dependence."[68]

Like Friedan did ten years later, Trilling targeted the mass media. She noted "the various myths of American womanhood created by advertising, merchandising, and the popular arts." They were behind many of "the hypocrisies and self-deceptions prevalent in our sexual culture" when it came to women's roles. Trilling was particularly perturbed by how advertisers sold a specific vision of women's roles in the 1950s: that as solely of wives and mothers. She planned to write about what she described as the "tyranny of advertising in creating the American female's image of herself." Trilling asked in her outline: "Does the American woman achieve fulfillment as a woman by her efforts of conformity to the advertising image?" The answer: "Obviously not."[69]

Trilling, however, appears to have concluded that if she wanted to be taken seriously as a writer and critic she should not write much on women. In 1949, William Shawn, editor at the *New Yorker*, rejected a lengthy piece she wrote about baby nurses, modeled on her own experiences after giving birth to her son Jim in 1948. Shawn "suggested she try a magazine where 'the feelings and the very personal treatment would more acceptable.'

But Diana didn't try other places (she knew Shawn meant she should try a woman's magazine, which just didn't interest her at the time)," writes her biographer Natalie Robins.[70] Her first contribution to *Partisan Review* in 1950 was a review of Margaret Mead's *Male and Female* (discussed below). But her other pieces for the magazine dealt with more "serious" topics like liberal anti-communism. Her first long piece for *Partisan Review* was on the Alger Hiss case (she deemed him guilty), affirming her credentials as a "hard" anti-communist and establishing her as a formidable polemicist.

"Although I liked to boast that wherever I wrote, my work was the same, I think I was deceiving myself," she later reflected about the difference between *Partisan Review* and women's magazines. "Where one cannot assume that one is writing for people with the same education as oneself and the same intellectual concerns, one is bound to limit one's range of reference and to relax the tensions in one's prose." In the early 1950s Trilling focused on establishing herself as a serious writer among the New York intellectuals.[71]

It was not until the late 1950s that Trilling published articles about women, drawn from her outline conceived years earlier. These pieces all appeared in women's or popular magazines. In 1958 Trilling submitted an article, "Women and Their Minds," to *Charm*, a magazine that billed itself as "the Magazine for Women Who Work." In March 1959, *Look* magazine featured Trilling's, "The Case for the American Woman," as its cover story. In June 1960 *Mademoiselle* published Trilling's "Female-ism: New and Insidious."[72]

These articles published between 1958 and 1960 anticipated many of the arguments Betty Friedan made a few years later in *The Feminine Mystique*. Trilling argued that women needed to be able to pursue careers and use their minds. She lamented that "motherhood" had become "a profession" after World War II. Like Friedan, she attacked the idea that educated women would abandon their roles as wives and mothers if they pursued careers. "There is small danger that women will cease to be wives and mothers," Diana wrote. "There is imminent danger—the signs are all about us—that the women of America will sacrifice their gifts of mind on the altar of spurious notions of femininity, and that one of the rationalizations they will offer for this sacrifice is the duty of good citizenship, the duty, as they see it, to meet the spoken and unspoken demands of their society at whatever cost in personal ambition, personal preference or endowment."[73] Trilling defended feminism for bringing educational opportunity and legal equality to women. Feminism had "taught women to think of themselves as full-fledged members of the community instead of second-class citizens, and it offered them the chance to use their extra-domestic abilities if they wanted to," she wrote in her piece for *Charm*.[74]

Building on her anti-communism, Diana connected her arguments about women to the Cold War. In an era when the United States was fighting for ideological and technological superiority with the Soviet Union, she warned that sidelining women was both dangerous and ill-considered. "We are in a situation of national crisis, in which we need all the brains we can muster," Trilling wrote. "Yet we throw away the at least potential contribution of half of our population, the female half, by conspiring in a culture in which women are made to feel less womanly if they employ their full intellectual powers." Directing women to devote themselves entirely to domesticity was dubious for other reasons. "All of our current propaganda to the contrary notwithstanding, we have little proof that either husbands or children are better off because of the kind of attention our new female-ism focuses on them."[75]

Like so many social critics in the 1950s, Trilling believed that the United States was facing a crisis in masculinity.[76] "All around us today we see a male sex which, if not yet defeated in its ability to control our human destiny, is certainly frightened by the gigantic tasks it faces," Trilling wrote in her cover story for *Look*. She argued that this emasculation had little to do with women. Rather, it was a reaction to larger economic and technological changes in the twentieth century. American men could no longer assert a rugged individualism and independence as they once had. They felt enervated, weak, and "powerless," because "individual man" had become "mass man—a smaller and smaller cog in an always vaster machine, denied the kind of test and confirmation of his masculinity which enabled his grandfather to take the competence of *his* women all in his manly stride."[77]

Yet women were blamed for all the problems men faced, Trilling lamented. "For some years now, the American woman has been under persistent attack as the cause of the major ills of modern American life," Trilling wrote in the first paragraph of her *Look* article. "She is blamed for the marked decline in masculine self-esteem and for the nervous tension that seems to characterize both men and women. The instability of the modern home, the rise in juvenile delinquency and male homosexuality, even the alarming increase in heart disease among American men—all of these are blamed on the American woman's distortion of her traditional female role."[78]

Trilling did not presume to offer a cure for the crisis, which may simply be another way of saying she refused to substitute any oversimplification for the emerging scapegoat of Hollywood and the mainstream magazines of Madison Avenue: feminism. On that point, she was clear. Feminism was not to blame. "The fact is, of course, that long before feminism was anything but a gleam in the eyes of a few social visionaries, there had been planted the seeds of self-doubt which now bear fruit in the extreme conflicts and frustrations we blame on female emancipation," she wrote in *Look*.[79] Women, more generally, were not to blame. "At the heart of this new domestic emphasis," Trilling ruefully observed in *Mademoiselle*, "is the belief that one important reason why the American man is not swinging his full weight on behalf of his country is that his authority is being undermined by women."[80]

Trilling thus situated the nation's female-ism within this postwar crisis of masculinity. She called on society "to stop thinking of women as a force to be deployed merely for male ego-building." The American man would find relief from all his difficulties only if "he pulled himself up by his own emotional bootstraps and refused to be passive before history."[81] American men needed to find a way to reassert a healthy and robust masculinity on their own and stop blaming women for their failings. The health of American society depended on it. "No matter how strong our belief in sexual equality," Trilling wrote in *Look*, "we all of us operate on the premise that men are the more important sex, whose condition determines the fate of society. While we grant that women exert a variety of subsidiary influences in the world, we have only to consult the record of Western civilization to see that it is men who steer the course. The way women behave or are treated in a society may be a sound index to its health. But social survival depends neither on the virtue nor the achievements of women. It depends upon the force and vision of men."[82]

In this way, Trilling turned assumptions about masculine malaise on their heads in these articles. But without challenging the idea that biological sex difference had serious cultural and social consequences. If women seemed more aggressive and assertive, she argued, it was their reluctant response to the enervation of modern American men. Manly weakness had caused the defeminization of women, not vice versa: "No woman— no reasonably normal woman—wants to assert superiority over men, let alone dominate them," Trilling wrote in her cover story for *Look*. "On the contrary, women want to be cherished and protected by men and dependent on men's superior strength. It is by this that they are made to feel most feminine." Trilling continued:

> But modern man seems incapable of the traditional assertions of masculinity. He cannot give a woman the emotional support she desires because he has come to believe that it is he who needs supporting, from

a woman. Instead of exercising the authority, which was once thought to define a mature man, he tries to impose himself by demands for deference and attention which are essentially childish. He often retreats into passivity, forcing women into attitudes alien to their sexual disposition—and then he resents them for being more active and positive than he.

"In short," Trilling concluded, "if the modern woman is defeminized, she believes she has the right to say that it is not of her own free choice. It is because she has inevitably responded to the demasculinization of the modern man."[83]

In this way Trilling differed from Friedan. In 1959–60 she believed sex roles had a biological basis, whereas Friedan would argue they were largely social constructions. Their contrary views reflected in part their different interpretations of Freudianism. Friedan dismissed "the sexual solipsism of Sigmund Freud," arguing that the Austrian psychoanalyst—and especially his mid-century Neo-Freudian followers—were central to propagating "the feminine mystique." As Friedan wrote, "much of what Freud believed to be biological, instinctual, and changeless has been shown by modern research to be a result of specific cultural causes."[84] Trilling, in contrast, believed that passive femininity and active masculinity were biological facts that Freudianism only further proved.

But Trilling and Friedan stood on common ground in that they both targeted anthropologist Margaret Mead with their ire. Their critiques, however, came from opposing arguments about the implications of biological sex differences. In the 1930s, Mead had pioneered the theory that sex roles were socially constructed, freeing sex roles from a Freudian paradigm. Yet in her 1949 book, *Male and Female*, Mead seemed to backtrack by arguing that women's maternal capabilities should be more valued. As historian Mari Jo Buhle notes, Mead gave biology greater power in the later book and "even went so far as to refer to maternity as woman's 'biological role.'"[85]

Friedan was disappointed with Mead's reversal. She devoted an entire chapter to Mead in *The Feminine Mystique*. Friedan argued that *Male and Female* undercut all of Mead's previous work, which had done so much to advance women's equality. Because Mead was so well-known and respected, the publication of *Male and Female* became a "cornerstone of the feminine mystique." Friedan argued that "what the feminine mystique took from Margret Mead was not her vision of woman's great untested human potential, but this glorification of the female sexual function."[86]

Trilling had criticized Mead, too. In her 1950 review of *Male and Female*, published in *Partisan Review*, she wrote that although Mead tried to build on her earlier theories that sex roles were a product of culture, she was now falling back into biological determinism. Mead rejected Freud's theory of penis envy, Trilling argued, but embraced womb envy, a theory advocated by neo-Freudian psychoanalyst Karen Horney. "Refusing the Freudian castration theory, which of course is of major importance in the whole Freudian system," Trilling wrote, "Dr. Mead elaborates the quite opposite idea of a pervasive masculine sense of inadequacy engendered by the male's incapacity to actually bear children." In this way Mead simplistically reversed "the concept of female organic inferiority" that underlay Freudian thought. Yet ultimately Trilling argued that Mead fell back on Freudian definitions of masculinity and femininity as biologically rooted.[87]

Trilling, in contrast to Friedan, thought Mead was insufficiently Freudian. "Although Dr. Mead gives evidence of extensive grounding in Freudian theory and procedure, she has a fashionable aptitude for using, bending, or discarding Freudian principles at will." Trilling pointed out that Mead had embraced Freudianism when she defended her own "femininity" in a "long and unhappy" forty-seven-page introduction, which amounted to "a woman's apology for being in the field where, by for reason of her sex, she fears she ought not be." Mead's introduction assured her readers "that despite her 'masculine' activity, the author has the delicate feelings appropriate to femaleness." Trilling concluded that, "the shuttle Dr. Mead runs between being a popularizer and being a professional is also the shuttle every sensitive professional woman in our culture runs between the need to protect and the wish to transcend her femininity."[88] But ultimately femininity could not be easily transcended because it was rooted in biology.

Trilling argued that the goal of feminism in the early twentieth century was never to dismantle women's biological and innate femininity. "Never, except perhaps at some pathological extreme," she wrote in "Women and Their Minds," did feminism "propose that men and women were socially and psychologically the same and interchangeable. Properly understood, [feminism] never tried to coerce women into an equality with men which would be tantamount to sexual identity." Feminism always respected "this natural distinction between the sexes" and a tradition of "great womanliness" in the United States. "It was the purpose of feminism to increase the range of female competence and give women a more secure legal and economic base from which to develop their large capacities—but without sacrifice of their distinctly female emotions and preoccupations."[89]

Trilling's articles in *Charm, Look,* and *Mademoiselle* make clear she identified with feminism years before Friedan published *The Feminine Mystique* in 1963. She shared many views in common with Friedan, but not when it came to Freud. Trilling did not write about Friedan, or *The Feminine Mystique*, and she was critical of second-wave feminism, like the other women New York intellectuals. But her writings on women and feminism in the late 1950s and early 1960s made her different from McCarthy, Hardwick, and Arendt. So too did the fact that she wrote for women's magazines, which were seen as venues for "lady" writers. Trilling later said that she suspected she was *Partisan Review*'s "first contributor who had also appeared in *Glamour*."[90]

"Lady" Writers

For most women New York intellectuals nothing was more insulting than being described as a "lady" writer. Ted Solotaroff, who worked as an assistant editor at *Commentary* in the early 1960s, characterized "lady" writers as those whose "daydreams . . . are quite rightly consigned to the *Ladies' Home Journal*."[91]

In 1963 Norman Mailer and Norman Podhoretz did just that to Mary McCarthy. Both called her best-selling book, *The Group*, "a trivial lady's novel." McCarthy's story centered on eight brilliant and charismatic women who graduated from Vassar College in 1933. *The Group* followed these women through the outbreak of World War II as they tried to make their way in a world shaped by rapid changes in industry, medicine, social organization, and mass communications. "No male consciousness is present in the book," McCarthy explained in a 1959 application for a Guggenheim fellowship to complete the book (which she won).[92] Written entirely from the perspective of women, the book provided intimate details of the inner workings of women's lives. McCarthy confronted questions having to do with sex, motherhood, politics, and ambition. But it was precisely that attention to detail and to women's intimate lives that shocked audiences and irked the New York intellectuals.

McCarthy had first conceived of what became *The Group* in 1951–52. But she long struggled to complete the manuscript. In 1954 she sold one chapter to *Partisan Review*, which published it under the title "Dottie Makes an Honest Woman of Herself." That story centered on a young unmarried woman getting fitted for "a pessary."[93] It created a sensation. "There *was* nothing new about getting a diaphragm in 1954; Margaret Sanger had been dispensing them in her clinics since the 1930s," writes one scholar. "What *was* new was reading about it in fiction."[94] For young unmarried women in the 1950s getting a diaphragm was also more difficult than it had been twenty years earlier, when the story took place. They clamored for information about this form of birth control. McCarthy provided it.

The story "also created a strong desire to see what befell Dottie's seven classmates."[95] In 1963, as McCarthy neared completion of the book, the *New Yorker* serialized what became two chapters. Published in June 1963, "Polly Andrews, Class of 33," whetted the appetite of readers.[96]

When McCarthy's book was finally published in late August 1963, it was an instant bestseller. By early October it had risen to number one on the *New York Times* best-seller list, with 95,000 copies in print. Published right as a new feminist movement was getting off the ground and the sexual revolution heated up, it sold more than 300,000 copies in its first two years. Early reviews were mixed, but many critics praised it for its great literary artistry as well as McCarthy's unflinchingly honest and sometimes graphic details of women's lives. The *New York Times Book Review* featured it on its front cover a few days before its publication date. "In her persistently reasonable, acutely amused way, Miss McCarthy knows everything about these girls," the reviewer stated. She had made the subjects "all too human." Another *New York Times* reviewer called it a "multipaneled story with an eye for style." It was "startling" in the best sense of the word. "Miss McCarthy has once more achieved the continuing aim of her dazzling literary career."[97]

But the New York intellectuals savaged McCarthy's novel. Podhoretz lumped the author in with "the whole tribe of contemporary lady novelists." By that he meant she was "an intellectual on the surface, a furniture-describer at heart." He reduced *The Group* to a "trivial lady's novel that bears scarcely a trace of the wit, the sharpness and the vivacity which glowed so often in her earlier work."[98] Mailer quoted Podhoretz in his own review for the *New York Review of Books*, describing Podhoretz as "a villainous, impressive, and magnetically disdainful prosecutor." But Mailer went a step further, writing that McCarthy "failed and even failed miserably to do more than write the best novel the editors of the women's magazines ever conceived in *their* secret ambitions." Mailer charged that McCarthy's reputation as a writer had long been overstated. She never had the wherewithal to "get tough enough to go with the boys," he wrote. Mailer mocked McCarthy, long feared for her acerbic prose and sharp wit, for having "been a very bad girl these years, mean and silly, postured and over-petted, petty in the extreme." Perhaps McCarthy would one day write a great novel, Mailer quipped. But only if "the Saints will preserve our Mary-Joan and bless her with a book which can comprehend a man."[99]

No doubt McCarthy's commercial success rankled her male rivals, as when Tess Slesinger achieved similar mainstream success thirty years earlier with *The Unpossessed* (1935). Mailer, who valued the novel as an artistic form above all else, had not written his own novel since *The Naked and the Dead* (1948). *The Group* spent two years on the best-seller list and was a finalist for the National Book Award.[100] Hannah Arendt made the obvious point in a letter to McCarthy, "That the 'boys' have tried to turn against you seems to me only natural and I think it has more to do with 'the Group' being a best-seller than with any political matters."[101] Arendt, for her part, praised the book. "I like the Group very very much," she wrote McCarthy in the early fall of 1963. "I don't need to repeat what anybody who knows anything says—," Arendt continued, "that it is beautifully written (the inner balance of the sentences is extraordinary) and often hilariously funny."[102]

But not all the women New York intellectuals appreciated McCarthy's achievement. Hardwick, one of the founders and an advisory editor at the *New York Review of Books*, played a part in the book's hostile reception at that magazine. "I am afraid Elisabeth [*sic*] had the brilliant idea" to choose Mailer to review the book, Arendt told McCarthy. "I asked her, and she said 'yes'—so no doubt. But she probably would not have done it if there had not been fertile ground for precisely this kind of stab-in-the-back."[103] McCarthy had angered Mailer a year earlier at the Edinburgh Festival's International Writer's Conference when she refused a paid invitation by the BBC to debate him on television. Hardwick was aware of the animosity between the two writers.[104]

Three weeks earlier the *New York Review of Books* had also published a scathing parody of *The Group* it titled "The Gang."[105] In three short paragraphs the author, Xavier Prynne, mocked a scene in *The Group* where one of the characters loses her virginity. Prynne turned out to be a pen name for Hardwick. The parody and "terribly hostile" reviews upset McCarthy. "I confess I'm depressed by what seems to me the treachery of the *New York Book Review* [*sic*] people," McCarthy wrote to Arendt. "I find it strange that people who are supposed to be my friends should solicit a review from an announced enemy but even stranger that they should have kept pestering me to write for them while hiding from me the fact that the Mailer review was coming. As for the parody, they have never mentioned it to this day, perhaps hoping that I would not notice it," McCarthy continued. "I can't put myself in the place of Elizbeth Hardwick or even Bob Silvers," referring to the magazine's editor and advisory editor.[106]

McCarthy did not initially know who wrote that parody. But gossip moved quickly among New York intellectual circles and she soon found out. What made it worse was that Hardwick was a longtime friend, who had faintly praised the book in an earlier letter. In August 1963 Hardwick told McCarthy she had "wangled a copy from Harcourt" before its official release. She described *The Group* as "very full, very rich." Hardwick's main critique was that she was disappointed none of the characters seemed based on McCarthy. "The only thing I miss in it is YOU," she wrote. Hardwick also mentioned that "there are technical aspects that perplex me a little." But she was vague about those. She concluded: "What I want to say is Congratulations. I'm so happy to have this wonderful book finished and so happy you will make money on it as we all knew you would! Your long, brilliant career had to bear money fruit as well as all the real fruit."[107] The "real" fruit presumably meaning respect as a serious writer while "money fruit" was commercial success. But as Ann Birstein later quipped, "best-selling (equals frivolous) female novelist."[108]

After McCarthy learned Hardwick was behind the Xavier Prynne parody, Hardwick apologized. "I am very sorry about the parody," Hardwick wrote to McCarthy in late November 1963. "It was meant as simply a little trick, nothing more. I did Not mean to hurt you and I hope you will forgive it." Hardwick told McCarthy she hoped the parody would not have long-term ramifications on their friendship.[109] The two friends eventually reconciled.

But reception of *The Group* showed the limits of female solidarity within the circles of the New York intellectuals. Only Arendt defended McCarthy. Earlier that year Arendt had published her own controversial book, *Eichmann in Jerusalem* (1963), which first appeared as a series of articles in the *New Yorker* in 1962 (discussed in greater detail in chapter 7). McCarthy described the negative reviews of *Eichmann* among the New York intellectuals as "assuming the proportions of a pogrom."[110] She promised to "write something to the boys for publication," which she did for *Partisan Review*.[111] Arendt, meanwhile, told McCarthy, "Your ears must be burning too, because of the many discussions about your book."[112] McCarthy and Arendt bonded over the intensely hostile reaction both their books generated. Their bond was unique among the women New York intellectuals.

Sisterhood?

Betty Friedan published *The Feminine Mystique* in 1963, the same year McCarthy and Arendt had published their books. The New York intellectuals ignored Friedan's book, even as it climbed best-seller lists and sparked a movement. They might have talked about it at cocktail parties—Friedan sometimes ran in the same literary social circles—but "the talk was not deemed spirited or important enough to merit any notice in print."[113] *Partisan Review* did not publish a review of the book, nor did *Commentary* or *Dissent*. Diana Trilling never wrote about it. Nor did any other women New York intellectuals.

Few of them could relate to the concept of sisterhood, which animated the early years of women's liberation.[114] "What is this nonsense about sisterhood," Trilling quipped in an interview late in her life, referring to the slogan that many feminists applied to social bonds between women. "There's much more brotherhood than there is sisterhood," certainly among the men and women in her circle, she observed.[115] She never felt connected to the other women New York intellectuals, especially those of her generation: McCarthy, Hardwick, and Arendt. Those three were the "*PR* girls" of the 1940s. They prided themselves on having made it in this boys' club—sometimes referring to the men in the group as the "*PR* boys and their thugs." They were friends. But that friendship did not stop Hardwick from mocking *The Group*. While Trilling was part of this first generation, for years many of the "*PR* girls and boys" dismissed her as a mere wife. Diana had married Lionel Trilling in 1929, years before McCarthy, Hardwick, and Arendt joined their ranks in the late 1930s and early 1940s.

Diana Trilling and Mary McCarthy first met around 1937 at a Trotsky-ite meeting, when McCarthy was dating *Partisan Review* editor Philip Rahv. McCarthy had been writing reviews for *The Nation* and *New Republic*, and Trilling "very much envied Mary as a writer. There was a shine on everything she wrote, and whatever she wrote was always a statement of her sense of her own power," Trilling wrote in her memoir.[116] According to *Partisan Review* junior editor William Barrett, after McCarthy published *The Oasis* in 1949, a satirical novel that caricatured the *Partisan Review* circle, Trilling called McCarthy "a thug." "Neither she nor her husband, Lionel Trilling, had been lampooned in McCarthy's story," Barrett wrote in his memoir *The Truants*, "but Mrs. Trilling felt it necessary to deliver her disinterested moral judgement."[117] Trilling wrote to McCarthy after Barrett published his memoir denying she ever said such a thing. "Did I write that?" Trilling dismissively asked. "I have no recollection of having said it and I doubt that I said it." She challenged Barrett to produce any evidence. "More than thirty years passed since then," Trilling continued. "I knew Barrett as I knew you, through being at the same PR parties. I was never in his house. I don't think he was ever in mine," she retorted.[118] But Trilling was not a fan of McCarthy. She described McCarthy as a "starry-eyed opportunist" in an interview late in her life.[119]

When McCarthy first laid eyes on Trilling at that Trotskyist meeting in the 1930s, she noticed her "dark eyes and flaring nostrils," which McCarthy apparently meant as a compliment. "She looked like Katharine Cornell," the striking stage actress. "Among Stalinist males . . . the Trotskyists were believed to have a monopoly on 'all the beautiful girls,'" McCarthy wrote, in which she included Trilling.[120] McCarthy saw Trilling as a possible rival. At least when it came to looks. But she never took her seriously as a writer.

The two women never got along. They fought publicly over anti-communism and Vietnam, for example, in the pages of the *New York Review of Books* in 1968. The magazine had sent McCarthy to Vietnam in the winter of 1967 to write about the conflict. Her articles, collected in her 1967 book, *Vietnam*, became touchstones for Americans who became disillusioned with the ineptitude, recklessness, and naivete of liberal foreign policy in Vietnam and elsewhere during the Cold War.[121] Alluding to "that old, vexed question of the responsibility of intellectuals," Trilling chided McCarthy for "limiting the political role of the intellectual wholly to that of dissent." Trilling opposed US intervention in Vietnam and conceded that "America was and is careless of certain deeply important consequences of going to Vietnam." The point to her was, however, that that did not justify "being similarly careless of the consequences of our getting out."[122]

McCarthy thought Trilling's anti-communism was rigid and unreasonable. "What Mrs. Trilling wants is a prize-winning recipe for stopping the war and for stopping Communism at the same time," which in McCarthy's view was impossible. "The power of intellectuals, sadly limited, is to persuade, not to provide against contingencies. They are not God, though Mrs. Trilling seems to feel they have somehow replaced Him in taking on responsibility for every human event." In McCarthy's view, Trilling was accusing her of having "forgotten the old lessons" of Stalinism and of having "gone soft." McCarthy replied that she would rather be "soft" on communism than be found on the "letterhead . . . of the American Committee for Cultural Freedom, which in its days of glory, as Mrs. Trilling will recall . . . was actually divided within its ranks on the question of whether Senator Joseph McCarthy was a friend or enemy of domestic liberty."[123]

In a letter to Arendt, McCarthy complained of Trilling: "that woman is such a fool; if she didn't occupy her absurd place in the New York establishment, they would have thrown her letter in the wastebasket."[124] McCarthy dismissed Trilling again as merely Lionel's wife. Ten years later, McCarthy described Trilling in an interview as "a kind of Mrs. Grundy," referring to a Victorian English character who was morally self-righteous and prudish.[125]

Trilling did not like Arendt, either. While McCarthy could at times be "rude, it was not with the purposeful rudeness of her good friend Hannah Arendt," she wrote in her memoir. "Year after year Hannah made believe that I did not exist even when we were a few feet apart, staring into each other's face."[126] She suspected an ulterior motive. "Hannah Arendt never said hello to me in her life. She probably wanted to go to bed with Lionel," she told an interviewer late in her life.[127] Trilling "lived in perpetual fear that he might get involved with someone else," Sidney Hook later said. "And, I think, she kept him on a pretty tight leash. Not obviously, but wherever he went, she went."[128] So much of this was petty gossip. But clearly, friendships among women were not easy to maintain. They were often pitted against each other, which impacted their views of feminism.

The Other Women

Other wives of New York intellectuals disliked Arendt, too. Alfred Kazin's wife, Ann Birstein, felt shunned by Arendt, who seemed only interested in friendships with men. She made the wives of those men feel invisible. At an American Academy of Arts and Sciences ceremony, for example, at which Arendt received a prize, she greeted Kazin and Birstein, who attended the ceremony because Kazin had previously been a recipient. Arendt "began to drag Alfred down the aisle to sit with her," leaving Birstein to sit alone. Birstein made her way to their seats in the balcony, "until I asked myself what I was doing up there, relegated to a place where even the women in my father's synagogue were no longer required to sit." Birstein's father had been an Orthodox rabbi, "the beloved spiritual leader of the Actor's Temple off Times Square."[129] Birstein left in the middle of that ceremony and took the subway home. Birstein was also not partial to Trilling, whom she described as one of the "West Side intellectuals" and "always absurdly self-important."[130]

Two types of women emerge clearly from these clashes: those who got credit for being intellectuals and those who did not. Those who did not included wives who did not write for a living. But more revealing was the number of women who were writers or scholars who never ranked among the "New York intellectuals." This category includes Ruth Slotkin Gay, married to Nathan Glazer from 1942 to 1958; Lionel Abel's first wife, Sherry Abel, who worked as an editor at *Commentary*; Irving Howe's second wife, Thalia Phillies, a classicist who published widely in scholarly journals; and his third wife, Arien Mack, a professor of psychology at the New School and editor of its quarterly, *Social Research*, beginning in

1966.[131] Phillies and Mack were academics who did not write for or edit the group's magazines. But Sherry Abel was a longtime editor at *Commentary*, and Ruth Gay contributed reviews and stories to *Commentary*'s "From the American Scene" section when she was known as Ruth Glazer and married to Nathan Glazer. In 1959 Ruth married the historian Peter Gay and never stopped writing.[132]

Birstein, the novelist and essayist who was married to Alfred Kazin for nearly thirty years, and Kazin's younger sister, Pearl Kazin Bell, who married Daniel Bell in 1960, are particularly instructive contrasts. In her 2003 memoir, *What I Saw at the Fair*, Birstein chronicled her difficult marriage to Kazin. "He was handsome and brilliant. An extraordinary writer. He had justified my existence."[133] She also said Kazin was verbally and physically abusive. Birstein wrote about how she was never viewed as "an intellectual, only an unknown fiction writer" among the "Jewish West Side intellectuals." Although many men in the group viewed writing a novel as the most manly of activities—Lionel Trilling and Norman Mailer, for example—Birstein maintained that "even well-established novelists were given short shrift in these circles." Birstein felt the group prized the writing of criticism over fiction. Criticism, she implied, was considered masculine. "Criticism was where it was at. Criticism about criticism."[134]

Birstein ultimately was drawn to the women's movement in the 1970s. She first befriended women in the movement after participating in a PBS program on "Women Writers," which included feminists like Germaine Greer, Adrienne Rich, Rosalyn Drexler, and Susan Brownmiller. "By the end of the program this group of us," Birstein recalled, were all "united in exhilaration and heady sense of freedom." They went out for drinks afterward, "talking in a bar until we closed the place." Thereafter, Birstein began going to "Women's Rights marches" and attending consciousness-raising sessions. "Listening to other women's stories, so like my own, though still nobody mentioned *physical* abuse, I finally understood I wasn't crazy after all, that maybe I had never been crazy." She learned that other female writers "swept [their] accomplishments under the rug." Through feminism, she also ultimately found the courage to divorce Kazin.[135]

Pearl Bell, in contrast, was more ambivalent toward feminism. In a December 1970 review of major feminist books for the *New Leader*, where she had a book review column, Bell described Kate Millett's *Sexual Politics*, which began as a PhD dissertation in English at Columbia, as having "quickly shed its plain academic wrapper and became a Holy Book." Bell found Millett's analysis underwhelming. *Sexual Politics* was a book that began with a "portentous intellectual pronouncement" about the

FIGURE 10. Daniel and Pearl Bell, holding their son David, 1961.
Courtesy of David A. Bell.

all-pervasiveness of patriarchy and sexual domination across time and space, she wrote. "The brilliant unpersuasiveness of her arguments" was matched by her "style (much of the time relentlessly pounding invective, irritating prolix, and repetitious)." Millett's book, Bell wrote, had "replaced such earlier bibles of feminism as Mrs. Friedan's *The Feminine Mystique* (1963)." Bell did not admire Friedan, either. She described her as "that tireless ideological yenta" who "talked a batch of middle-class militants into demanding equal rights for women NOW (National Organization of [*sic*] Women)." By using the phrase "yenta," Bell alluded to the Jewishness of feminist circles. "After Millett" came "the deluge," Bell wrote in her sweeping review of feminist literature. "Shulamith Firestone's *The Dialectic of Sex*, Eva Figes' *Patriarchal Attitudes*, Robin Morgan's *Sisterhood Is Powerful*, and so on." Morgan's book was a popular anthology of writings that many feminists considered to be foundations of the movement. Bell dismissed it as "vitriolic dogmatism."[136]

But Bell, who long stood in the shadow of the men in her life (her older brother, Alfred Kazin, and her husband, Daniel Bell), understood why the women's movement had emerged. "Amid the rhetorical excess and the thunder of resentful obscenity heard so loudly from the fulminating Miss Morgan," Bell conceded in her review, "one can easily lose sight of some basic truths: that women have, indeed, been discriminated against, their talents wasted or misused by many institutions and many men for a very long time, and that an end to this inequality is still not in sight." Bell likely had her own situation in mind when she wrote that, "women have been unpaid or underpaid, overworked or unthanked, and the ordinary boring dailiness of domestic and professional life would be much more bearable if the traditionally defined roles of men and women were less tamely and uncritically accepted by people of both sexes." But like many New York intellectuals, she took issue with the movement's radicalism, its stridency and militancy. "To call for a total metamorphosis of personality and society, in a barbaric howling for blood, is a form of melodramatic self-indulgence. To insist on the impossible is to seriously and willfully diminish all prospects of effecting realistic change."[137]

———

Aside from Trilling, the women New York intellectuals entirely dismissed feminism. In 1963, before *The Group* appeared in print, McCarthy told an interviewer for *Vogue* magazine that, "I really don't have much [of a] suffragette side." She was interested in "ideas" and their intersection with politics, but she had no interest in the budding "sex war," as the interviewer described the political climate. "I think of myself as a person, not as a woman; belonging, you know, to the world, not to a lot of other women," McCarthy said. She had no interest in movements—certainly not feminist movements. "I can't stand people who hold themselves together, in pressure groups and interest groups, and are motivated usually by envy of other people. I can't stand feminine envy—envy of men," a descriptor of feminism she would hold throughout her life. "I am for equality, but, at the same time, with the idea of equality envy inevitably quickens and can become absolutely ferocious," she warned.[138]

In the 1980s McCarthy would describe feminism as nothing more than "self-pity, shrillness, and greed."[139] In 1985 she told a San Francisco audience that she was "incapable of true sympathy" for a movement undergirded by "envy and self-pity." "I wouldn't be a man for anything in the world. I do not envy them, including the responsibilities that they have, including the clothes that they wear."[140] McCarthy had traditional sex roles in mind. She felt it proper that men were breadwinners and she embraced feminine standards of beauty.

Hardwick too shunned feminism. "I don't like aggressiveness and I detest anger, a quality some feminists and many psychiatrists think one should cultivate in order to express the self," she told an interviewer in 1979.[141] When another interviewer pointed out that Hardwick was an aggressive writer, Hardwick conceded that "writing is what I do, it's the center of who I am." But she separated her writing from her femininity. "Men writers write, that's all they do. It's the source of their income, it's how they support a family. But there's also a feeling that men have that they must go to the studio every morning and come home every night *because* they are men. Somehow men have to make it clear, even to them-selves, that they can say 'I am a writer.'" For these reasons Hardwick also said, "I think men are more ambitious, don't you? Perhaps I shouldn't say that."[142]

Men were more ambitious in Hardwick's view because they were more "vigorous." Hardwick made that argument twenty-five years earlier in a 1955 review of Simone de Beauvoir's *The Second Sex* (1949), which had recently been translated into English. "Are women 'the equal of men'?" Hardwick asked rhetorically, before dismissing that as "an embarrassing subject." Beauvoir had famously argued that "one is not born but rather becomes a woman." Hardwick elaborated, paraphrasing Beauvoir's point as follows: "what we call the feminine character is an illusion and so is feminine 'psychology,' both in its loose meaning and in the psychoanalytical view." Hardwick disagreed. Sex roles to her were a biological fact, not a social construction. "Women are certainly physically inferior to men, and if this were not the case the whole history of the world would be different," Hardwick wrote. "No comradely socialist legislation on women's behalf could accomplish a millionth of what a bit more muscle tissue, gratu-itously offered by nature, might do for this second being."[143]

For these reasons Hardwick was also unconvinced that female writ-ers suffered because of their "situation." Beauvoir erred in thinking that society or men "trapped" women, she wrote. Hardwick could not see women's literary ambitions the way Beauvoir did—as somehow "'natu-ral' and inevitable." Hardwick took it to be self-evident that women were less ambitious than men. They lacked experience in comparison to men, in part, because "a woman's physical inferiority is a limiting reality every moment of her life." Ultimately, women could not write as well as men because they lacked "*vigor.*" Vigor was masculine. "Who can but help feel that *some* of [Henry] James's vigor is sturdily rooted in his masculine flesh and that this repeatedly successful creativity is less likely with the 'weaker sex,'" Hardwick wrote. "It is not suggested that muscles write books, but there is a certain sense in which talent and experience being equal, they may be considered a bit of an advantage." Women could be marvelous writers, Hardwick argued. But they had to have vigor, which was a quality by nature in short supply among women. "Of course the *best* literature by women is superior to *most* of the work done by men," Hardwick wrote. But "it is only the whimsical, cantankerous, the eccentric critic, or those who refuse the occasion for such distinctions, who would say that any literary work by a woman, marvelous as these may be, is on a level with the very greatest accomplishments of men."[144]

Twenty years later Hardwick's views had not changed. She retreated from some of her criticism of *The Second Sex*, telling an interviewer in 1979 that "it's a wonderful, remarkable book. Nothing that has come since on the matter of women stands [in] comparison to it." Hardwick was aware that women's lives had changed dramatically since the 1950s. But she wasn't convinced that the changes were positive. Women could now "sleep in the streets if you like," just like men, "and go to Arabia in your jeans and knapsack." Yet women were "still weaker than men in muscular force." No amount of change could alter that biological fact.[145]

Nor was it certain that women could afford not to rely on men to be breadwinners. Hardwick was relieved that she did not have to be "self-supporting" when she was married to the poet Robert Lowell from 1949 to 1972. Her writing never paid the bills. Nor was she prolific. She only divorced Lowell after his habit of cheating became untenable: he impregnated another woman. She taught writing at Barnard College from 1965 to 1985 to help make ends meet.

Arendt, meanwhile, did not think feminism rose to the level of serious intellectual inquiry. She once told a student wearing a women's liberation pin, in her thick German accent, "this is not *serious*."[146] She too understood masculinity and femininity to be biological categories and writing to be masculine. "I have always thought that there are certain occupations that are improper for women, that do not become them, if I may put it that way," she told an interviewer in 1964. "It just doesn't look good when a woman gives orders. She should try not to get into such a situation if she wants to remain feminine." When it came to her own femininity, Arendt was unconcerned. "I myself have lived in accordance with this more or less unconsciously—or let us rather say, more or less consciously. The problem itself played no role for me personally. To put it very simply, I have always done what I like to do."[147] Arendt implied that she transcended these categories, and she wrote like a man.

Even Susan Sontag, the youngest member of the group, was largely uninterested in feminism. She joined the ranks of the New York intellectuals in the early 1960s after divorcing Philip Rieff, a sociology professor she met while studying at the University of Chicago. They married in 1950 when she was seventeen and divorced eight years later. Sontag then made her way to New York, where she began publishing theater reviews in *Partisan Review*. Her first long essay in the magazine, "Notes on Camp," appeared in its fall 1964 issue. It established Sontag as a new force among the New York intellectuals. She was barely thirty.[148]

Sontag was much more of a political activist than her senior colleagues at *Partisan Review* in the mid-1960s. Her ties to the Old Left, from which the New York intellectuals emerged, remained strong, even as she embraced the New Left, from which women's liberation emerged. She showed little of her elders' reservations about the younger generation's political initiatives. But Sontag abided by the rules of the New York intellectuals. According to biographers Carl Rollyson and Lisa Paddock, she "played a male game." She too shunned feminism. Her one essay on the subject was "The Third World of Women," published in *Partisan Review* in 1973.[149] While it indicated tacit support for feminism, overall, the movement was a subject that did not particularly interest her. But it was also an issue "she could not ignore," write Rollyson and Paddock.[150] "The Third World of Women" was thus an anomaly in Sontag's writings—not the beginning of a sustained engagement with feminism. "Determined not to be held back by a description that she found limiting," writes biographer Benjamin Moser, Sontag wrote little else on feminism. "In her aspiration to universality, her example was Hannah Arendt, who would make her contribution to the cause of women by achieving equality—and, indeed, superiority—by talent alone."[151] Sontag, like Arendt, would write like a man—indeed, better than a man.

A "Shove" Toward Women's Liberation

Diana Trilling alone moved away from the ambivalence toward feminism that characterized her fellow women writers. In many ways she seemed as ambivalent as they. "What women's liberation actually turned out to be," she told a reporter in 1981, "is a kind of open season on gunning for men."[152] But while critical of women's liberation, younger feminists managed to convince Trilling that sex roles were social constructions and that women did not need to write like men.

Trilling did not write much about women or feminism in the 1960s. Her most well-known publication in that decade was a stinging critique of the student uprising at Columbia University in 1968, which appeared in *Commentary* under the editorship of Norman Podhoretz.[153] In late April that year, students occupied five campus buildings. They were protesting what they viewed as Columbia's racist policies toward the surrounding Harlem community and the university's complicity in the Vietnam War through a military research consortium called the Institute for Defense Analysis (IDA). After six days, a faculty committee that included Lionel Trilling and Daniel Bell failed to broker a resolution between the protesters and the administration. On administration orders, the police forcibly removed students from the buildings. Police injured nearly 148 and arrested 720.[154]

For many spectators across the country, the protests at Columbia personified the nihilism and destructiveness of New Left protesters in the late 1960s. For the New York intellectuals, Columbia hit close to home. Diana and Lionel had lived in Morningside Heights for more than three decades. Lionel was one of Columbia's most renowned faculty members. Columbia was their backyard. By the 1960s Lionel was far from the only New York intellectual in academia. Many were college professors. Recalling their own educations as liberating and enriching opportunities, which so many of their Jewish ancestors had been denied in Eastern Europe, they watched with sadness, dismay, and anger as similarly violent protests erupted at other campuses: Berkeley, Harvard, Cornell, and others. While most of the New York intellectuals had come to oppose US intervention in the Vietnam War in the late 1960s, they were defensive and protective of institutions they felt were most worth preserving—chief among them the university. Why, they wondered, did students attack the institution that nurtured their freedom of expression and was largely responsible for their critical understanding of history and power?

Although a minority of New York intellectuals shifted politically rightward in response to what they viewed as the callow militancy of many antiwar protesters and Black Power activists, some, like Dwight Macdonald and Robert Lowell, sympathized with student protestors.[155] The vast majority, however, neither supported the student protesters nor became neoconservatives. Lionel and Diana Trilling were at the center of that broader camp. Though Podhoretz and others tried to claim Lionel as a harbinger of the neoconservative movement, Diana always claimed that Lionel would never have supported neoconservatism had he lived into the 1980s. Yet in the 1960s and early 1970s, what separated the neocons from the New York intellectuals who remained liberal was not always clear.

Diana Trilling viewed women's liberation in the late 1960s warily. She saw it as an extension of the excessive radicalism of the New Left. Women's liberation, after all, called for revolution and the overthrow of established norms and institutions. In the spring of 1971, when invited to participate in the Town Hall forum, she was spending nine weeks in Cambridge, Massachusetts, living in the dorms at Radcliffe with Lionel, interviewing current students and doing research in the Radcliffe archives. "I was concerned to trace, through the evolution of one educational institution, a distinguished college for women, something of the general course of the American female fate," she later wrote. To make it to Town Hall, she took a train from Boston to New York. Her conversations with students at Radcliffe and Harvard undoubtedly framed her thinking that night.[156]

At Town Hall, Diana argued that the women's movement, like other visible offshoots of the New Left, had descended into an "authoritarianism . . . advanced in purpose and efficiency." Diana directed most of her remarks that night to radical feminist critiques of sex and heterosexual intimacy. "Among those efforts of the women's liberationists which I find most impoverishing, most absolutist, are the doctrines now being promulgated on the female orgasm," she exclaimed. "Surely it is remarkable that the same people who properly criticize our society for its harsh and unimaginative treatment of homosexuals have no hesitation in dictating to women—and it is dictation, make no mistake about that," she said, "where they are to find their single path to sexual enjoyment. I'm talking, of course, about the campaign now being mounted to persuade women that there is no such thing as a vaginal orgasm, and therefore they might as well dispense with men."[157]

Three years later, in a 1974 speech titled, "Women's Liberation: Continuity or Conflict," she put it this way: "women's liberation, like gay liberation, is really a new sexual consciousness. Its logic cannot but lead us to the overthrow of the established organization of the way we live together in society." Its "revolutionary culture," she complained, "encourages in us ill-will [and] in hatred of men." Trilling identified herself as part of an "older feminist tradition." Women like her "felt impelled to back away from the women's liberation movement: we are not political revolutionaries. And no more are we revolutionaries in personal life—we are, dare I say the word, reformers; or even worse, liberals."[158]

Trilling indicated, however, that her view on women's liberation had evolved between 1970 and 1974. She harkened back to the events at Columbia to make her point that while she did not condone violent and destructive outbursts of radicalism, the substance undergirding women's liberation in fact had more depth. "The distinguished critic, Dwight Macdonald, gave his support to the university uprisings" in 1968, she noted, because "he said they 'shoved' the society and that our society needed shoving. I opposed this position at the time and I still do," Trilling explained. She still had little patience for overindulged college kids. But by 1974 Trilling "gave approval to the 'shove' of society by . . . women's liberation."[159]

"Women's liberation exhilarated me," Trilling told an interviewer in 1977, because it went beyond traditional feminist goals of equal pay for equal work. The movement "delve[d] into something deeper," she explained, including examining "the real miseries and sense of inferiority that women suffer in these subtle ways in which they're downgraded." Yet Trilling abhorred what she felt "very quickly turned into a kind of field day of hatred" of men. She also did not like the style and tactics of women's liberation. Yet at the same time she had been convinced by their arguments, particularly that sex roles were social constructions, not biological facts. Freud—and a generation of social critics before him—had in fact been wrong about that.[160]

This was a significant reassessment on Trilling's part. Just four years earlier, in 1970, she still adhered to biological determinism. In a speech on women's liberation at Radcliffe in 1970 she homed in on Freud. It was "both appropriate and ironic to talk about our present movement for women's rights," Trilling said, "in conjunction with Freud." The irony lay in the fact that Freud "had such an invidious view of the female sex," which he extended to culture. "And no doubt it is an extension of his view of women's basic biological inferiority that Freud makes his forthright statement in *Civilization and Its Discontents* that it is men who are the makers and carriers of culture; he adjures women not to interfere with man's adventures in this sphere." By 1970 her views were no longer as fixed in Freudianism as they had been in 1959, the last time she wrote at length about women and sex roles. Trilling now gave "more weight" than she "once did to the cultural, as opposed to the biological, determination of our sexual attitudes."[161]

Yet Trilling still believed Freud was partly right. His "castration theory" was condescending to women and understandably "irritating, especially when we contemplate some of the activities which men regard as proper life in culture, like inventing the hydrogen bomb or claiming the moon for their own country." But no one had disproven Freud's theory or come up with a better explanation to account for sexual differences. "There is nothing in Freud's formulation of the castration fear that I'd be prepared to fault or which people far more competent than I am, have yet succeeded in refuting," Trilling explained. Neither Karen Horney nor Margaret Mead was ever able to prove womb theory. "This appealing reassignment of biological advantage," Trilling explained, "is supported neither by men's literary metaphors, their dreams, nor their free associations during psychoanalytical theory."[162]

Trilling argued that biology had to have something to do with it. Female passivity and male activity could not merely be cultural constructs because these roles were ubiquitous. They were multicultural: "this distinction between the active and passive sexual roles is an irrefutable fact of nature," she said.[163] "To put the matter at its crudest the male has the biological capacity to rape; the female has not." Women's liberationists too glibly dismissed biological difference. "We may, if we wish, accuse Freud of drawing too many, or mistaken, inferences from this primary biological difference. But to try to ignore the difference, as some women's liberationists do, is to narrow rather than widen the prospects opened up to us in dealing with biology."[164]

At the Town Hall that night in 1971 Trilling upheld Freud and "sexual duality." As she later explained, "my impulse to defend was not in favor that night, the idea that there were two sexes." Trilling was critical of America's "sexual culture." She opposed what feminists described as sexism, and Mailer's defense of America's sexist culture in "The Prisoner of Sex." But at that Town Hall, she proclaimed that she "would gladly take even Mailer's poeticized biology"—his views that men and women had distinct roles because of their sexual organs—"in preference to the no biology at all of my spirited sisters." Women's liberationists, she argued, "seek a culture which will invalidate the biological differences between the sexes." Yet Freud—and mountains of anthropological evidence and biology itself—could not be so easily dismissed. "I defer to none in my high regard for Freud," Trilling declared.[165]

But by 1974, however, she no longer believed that Freud was right about much of anything. "I yield to biology only the significant differing roles of the sexes in reproduction; everything else I give to culture." While she did "not deny physiology" and "happily acknowledg[ed] the existence of two sexes," she now believed that women's liberationists had been right that sex roles—what we now call gender roles—were "a social construct, and an unhappy one." She did not like the style of women's liberation—its glibness, its hostility toward the male sex, and its dismissal of a vaginal (heterosexual) orgasm. But she no longer could argue that the movement was flat-out wrong. This was "a contradiction and a dilemma" for someone like her. "The contradiction is between the distaste one might feel for the

personal and social style of women's liberation, also for its political implications, and the recognition of its usefulness. The dilemma is a personal
one: how [to] choose between two destructive attitudes in culture, that of
the old sexual authority . . . and that of the new?"[166]

———◆———

When Mailer introduced Trilling as a "lady" critic at Town Hall in 1971 she
did not take offense. Looking back on the evening six years later, Trilling
conceded that her response had been "careless." She had been too preoccupied with criticizing women's liberation to consider Susan Sontag's point.
"At a meeting in which all sexual differences were being wiped out . . . I
felt the need to separate my position from the other women panelists and
their audience and, at any cost, to put myself on the side of sexual duality,"
Trilling explained. She continued:

> It was only when the dust of the evening had settled and I was no lon-
> ger moved to counter the extremity of opinion and behavior which had
> characterized the discussion that I let myself see that the question was
> of course not an expression of concern about the genteel connotations
> of the word "lady"; it had seriously to do with professional condescen-
> sion to women. It was addressed to the pejorativeness in the mechani-
> cal sexual differentiation Mailer had indulged in, and its point was not
> negligible: to be a lady writer, a women writer, a female writer is not the
> same as being a writer. It is a professional value judgment; implicitly, a
> *de*value judgement. . . . No man is a man writer, he is *a* writer.[167]

Writing was masculine. Sontag had pointed that conventional assumption out, and it was a view that the New York intellectuals, female as
well as male, had long defended. Some women's liberationists (and, as
that distinction faded, many other kinds of feminists) challenged such
dichotomies, rejecting the notion that women need to perform like men
to be taken seriously. Who was an intellectual? On what terms? At whose
expense? Liberationists asked those questions.

Like nearly all the New York intellectuals, Trilling was steeped in
Freudianism. According to the entire Jewish tradition that rumbled
behind the Jewish Doctor Freud was an ancient habit and internalized
command: writing and intellectual activity were masculine. Women in
the group performed a secular Jewish masculinity in the public sphere.
But in their private lives they largely adhered to Victorian definitions of
femininity. Freudianism would undergird Midge Decter's fierce critique

of women's liberation, the subject of the next chapter. Freud led Decter to family values and the New Right. But Diana Trilling had embraced a deeper Freud—one might say a more Talmudic Freud, a more psychoanalytic Freud who proceeded through dialogue and interaction. Freudians might see that supple and resilient Freud as a more experimentally scientific Freud. Some sort of living Freud led Trilling to relinquish Freudianism by 1975. Women's liberationists had convinced her that sex roles were cultural, not biological. They convinced her that one did not need to write like a man.

In 1975 Lionel died of pancreatic cancer. Diana was aware that his death had something to do with her writing. Between 1949, when she left *The Nation*, until his death, she "wrote for a wide variety of periodicals and large-circulation magazines, as well as serious literary journals." "But I never wrote a book of my own," she reflected in an unpublished 1996 essay. While she had thought at length about why that might be the case, she did not have an easy answer. "It is exceedingly difficult for me to explain the limitations I put on myself as a professional writer; it involves untangling a variety of influences, those of my family culture, those of the general culture of my young womanhood, [and] the particular conditions of my marriage."[168]

In 1981 Diana published her first original book: *Mrs. Harris: The Death of the Scarsdale Diet Doctor*. She had published only anthologies of previous articles: the *Claremont Essays* (1964), while Lionel was still alive, and *We Must March My Darlings* (1977), shortly after he died. *Mrs. Harris* was not a highbrow essay but in the vein of "the new journalism." It followed the sensational murder trial of Jean Harris, a headmistress of an exclusive girls' school in Scarsdale, New York, for the murder of her lover, Dr. Herman Tarnower. It was a finalist for the Pulitzer Prize in general nonfiction and garnered mainstream attention. Then in 1993 she published her memoir of their marriage, *The Beginning of the Journey*. No longer in Lionel's shadow and with the insights of women's liberation, she was freed to write any way she wanted—like a woman or a man.

CHAPTER SIX

Midge Decter

THE "FIRST LADY OF NEOCONSERVATISM"

IN DECEMBER 1970 Midge Decter met Gloria Steinem in a packed ball-room in Union Square to debate the women's movement. Decter was an executive editor at *Harper's Magazine* while Steinem, a writer and jour-nalist, was quickly becoming the most well-known face of women's libera-tion. They were brought together to tackle the question, "What Do Women Want?" The ensuing debate "was a lively 2 1/2 hours with frequent hoots, heckles, and cheers from the 300 people—one third of them men—who paid $2 a head to hear the discussion," the *New York Times* reported. Its coverage focused mostly on Decter. The reporter described her "big gold earrings swinging over her bright orange dress" as she railed against the women's movement. Decter told the crowd that evening that women already had equal rights, so feminists did not have any legitimate grievances. They "used the women's liberation movement to 'escape from responsibility.'" "The feminist's problem," Decter said, "is her refusal to grow up."[1]

While the *Times* dwelled on Decter's appearance, Decter herself found Steinem's ensemble to be the more eye-catching. Thirty years later, she vividly remembered what Steinem wore. Her outfit was "unforgettable, for she turned up in a crotch-high skirt and knee-high suede boots." Her clothes, in Decter's view, discredited her position from the start. "Look-ing at that skirt [I] had to control my impulse to giggle: how to issue men a stern warning to back off while affording them a juicy glimpse of thigh. Where I grew up, we used to call that 'teasing.'" [2] Steinem's outfit encapsulated Decter's distaste not only for the women's movement but also the sexual revolution and the loosening of cultural mores in the 1960s. It spoke to her support for what conservatives soon called "family values."

Two months before the debate with Steinem, Decter had published "The Liberated Woman," a scathing critique of women's liberation in *Commentary*, a magazine edited by her husband, Norman Podhoretz.[3] Podhoretz was then emerging as a key architect of neoconservatism. That word, originally pejorative, was first coined by Michael Harrington to describe formerly liberal intellectuals who became conservatives in the early 1970s.[4] According to the standard neoconservative narrative, reified in Podhoretz's memoir, *Breaking Ranks* (1979), and adopted by many scholars since then, these intellectuals shifted rightward in the late 1960s in response to New Left militancy, especially the violence associated with the antiwar and Black Power movements.[5] Many were disillusioned by the expansion of President Lyndon B. Johnson's Great Society and other reform programs, which they argued were expensive and only exacerbated lawlessness and crime. By 1972 they felt the Democratic Party catered too much to New Left radicalism in its "New Politics" platform, with policies like affirmative action and the nomination of antiwar candidate George McGovern for president that year.[6] Some of these incipient neoconservatives voted for Republican Richard Nixon in the 1972 election. Though most backed Democrat Jimmy Carter four years later, by 1980 the neocons were stalwarts of the Reagan revolution.

Decter was integral to the making of neoconservatism but is rarely mentioned in either scholarly or journalistic accounts of its history. Podhoretz and other brash male intellectuals, including Irving Kristol, the so-called godfather of neoconservatism, upstage her in the literature. When mentioned at all, Decter is usually cited as executive director of the Committee for the Free World, an anti-communist organization she founded in 1981. Her abundant writings on women, feminism, and sexuality, however, have gone largely unexamined.[7] That is in part because scholars of neoconservatism have tended to lump the women's movement into a broader analysis of neoconservative derision of the New Left, focusing more on these intellectuals' responses to Black militancy, the antiwar movement, and campus radicalism, than feminism. While women's liberation was part of the "movement of movements" that constituted the New Left, second-wave feminism was also its own phenomenon.[8] Similarly, while Decter's critiques of feminism shared much in common with broader neoconservative critiques of the New Left, her analysis of gender was distinctive, and singularly important.[9]

Like Diana Trilling, Decter began writing about women and sex roles, what we now refer to as gender, in the late 1950s—*before* Betty Friedan published *The Feminine Mystique* in 1963, widely considered to have started second-wave feminism, and which critics charged was an assault on the traditional nuclear family. Decter defended "traditional" gender roles and heterosexuality long before her husband turned against 1960s radicalism and transformed *Commentary* into a mouthpiece for neoconservatism. Her writings challenge a central tenet of the neoconservative narrative: that the conservatism of these intellectuals was provoked only by the excesses of late sixties radicalism. Decter's writings point to an earlier and more complex trajectory for neoconservatism, one in which gender anxieties were as important to its development as was disdain of sixties radicalism.

———◆———

When Decter published "The Liberated Woman" in *Commentary* in October 1970, the article elicited a slew of angry letters from many feminists. Decter's "liberated woman" amounted to a "biased and prissy caricature," wrote Sue Wimmershoff-Caplan, chairman of the Equal Opportunity Commission. Her conclusions, moreover, "[flew] in the face of continued discrimination against women in all areas of public life, in training for the professions, and in all levels of employment." Ann J. Lane, a pioneering feminist historian, wrote a letter to *Commentary* complaining that Decter's "preaching gets us to a kind of inapplicable Puritan admonition to work hard, shape up, and stop whining. Her supercilious comment that both men and women have choices," she continued, "is reminiscent of Anatole France's observation that it is forbidden equally to the rich and to the poor to sleep under the bridges across the Seine." Vivian Gornick, a *Village Voice* writer and feminist, lambasted Decter "for sounding like a Jewish mother, arms folded across fat breasts, mouth compressed into fat face, saying: 'After everything I've done for you, this is what I get back!'" Gornick's comparison of Decter to an overbearing and shrill "Jewish mother" points to how Jewishness underlay the confrontation between the New York intellectuals and some feminists. Gornick was not alone. "Miss Decter's vindictive attitude toward her passive girl protagonist," wrote feminist scholar Madelyn Gutwirth, "reveals the bias of one who has internalized that [Jewish] prayer in which God is daily thanked for His goodness in not having created man a woman."[10]

Decter was unfazed by her critics. "Tut Tut Miss Gornick," Decter responded in *Commentary*'s letter section, "she who screams of 'painfully threatened reaction' ought to bethink herself about the use of such imagery as that of Jewish mothers with fat breasts and fat faces in the place of argument." Feminists like Gornick, Decter implied, were incapable of marshalling intellectually sophisticated arguments—their views and theories were frivolous and short on substance. To another critic, Decter wrote: "I plead guilty to thinking it right and proper that a woman should do domestic chores. Somebody has to make the bed—just as somebody has to do all the other joyless tasks in this world. Why is there so much fuss, so much insistence on the problem of 'roles,' over perfectly simple and practical reciprocal services men and women do for one another?"[11]

Decter, in many ways, reflected the views of most New York intellectuals. This was a group that understood male-female distinctions as deeply and inescapably biological, not social constructions, as younger feminists argued. They also viewed intellectual work as masculine. Their views were shaped partly by Jewish tradition, which long classified study and scholarship as the domain of men. But it was also informed by Freud. Before feminist Freudians emphasized and developed Freud's insights (and those of contemporary anthropologists) that masculinity and femininity were taught to children, and thus precarious cultural constructions, American Freudians tended to see Freud as supporting the idea that social distinctions between masculinity and femininity were fixed with the anatomical distinctions between male and female. Freud's own works sometimes echoed these long-standing traditional views.[12]

Freudianism was an evolving and contested set of theories. Revisionist Freudians at mid-century deviated from the radical implications of Freud's theories. By the 1940s many stressed that heterosexuality, adaptation, and control of libidinal impulses within marriage were central to the well-adjusted person. Decter (like many anti-feminist men) drew from this peculiar brand of mid-century revisionist Freudianism and its advocacy of "maturity" through heterosexuality and marriage.[13] That reading of Freud would ultimately lead Decter to the "family values" of the Republican Party by the 1980s. Whereas most women New York intellectuals dismissed feminism with a shrug, Decter went on a crusade against it. And that crusade fundamentally shaped her political trajectory.[14]

In the early 1970s Decter was arguably the most formidable anti-feminist in the country. Her first book, *The Liberated Woman and Other Americans* (1971), was an anthology of her essays from the late 1950s through 1970, most of which focused on the topics of women and sex roles. A year later, Decter published a book-length attack on the women's movement, *The New Chastity and Other Arguments against Women's Liberation* (1972). Three years later she published *Liberal Parents, Radical Children* (1975), a broader critique of the New Left that devoted a chapter to women's liberation and the sexual revolution.[15]

In 1972 the New York chapter of the National Organization for Women (NOW) "awarded" her book, *The New Chastity*, "Horrible Mention" in its "Keep Her in Her Place" competition. The national office of NOW extended Decter an "Aunt Tom" award. That year Decter told an interviewer she was "'happy' to be identified as Public Enemy No. 1 of women's liberation." A year later, in 1973, she boasted that she was "the figure at the center of resistance to the movement."[16]

Decter, however, is not remembered as the leading anti-feminist of her generation. That designation ostensibly goes to Phyllis Schlafly, the "first lady of conservatism," as the *New York Times* described her in a 2016 obituary.[17] A longtime conservative activist, Schlafly first gained national attention in 1964 when she wrote *A Choice Not an Echo*, endorsing Barry Goldwater's presidential campaign. But it was not until late 1972 that Schlafly turned her attention to feminism, when she founded STOP ERA, an acronym for Stop Taking Our Privileges, to halt the passage of the Equal Rights Amendment (ERA). "Her involvement in the ERA came about accidentally," writes historian Donald Critchlow, after she was asked to participate in a local debate on the subject. Schlafly initially knew little about it. But thereafter she used the ERA to galvanize conservative grassroots women, turning this "single-issue movement," historian Marjorie Spruill argues, "into a more enduring, profoundly anti-feminist, and—in [Schlafly's] words—'Pro-Family' movement."[18]

Decter did not initially think highly of Schlafly. In a 1979 *Washington Post* interview, Decter retorted: "just because 'Bella Abzug doesn't represent men,' doesn't mean that Phyllis Schlafly does either. They deserve each other."[19]

Decter's dismissal of Schlafly is curious because the two women espoused similar views. Both fiercely defended traditional gender roles, even as both led very public professional careers: Decter as a writer and editor, Schlafly as a lawyer and political organizer. Both lauded the family wage system, with breadwinning men providing for dependent women and children. Both maintained that American women in the middle of the twentieth century were incredibly privileged to not have to work for wages. Both exalted domesticity as a sign of postwar affluence and strength, and both viewed the nuclear family as the bedrock of a healthy society. Both criticized the sexual revolution and the loosening of cultural mores in the 1960s. Finally, both women warned that, along with feminism, the gay rights movement irrevocably harmed American norms of masculinity.[20]

Why, then, did Decter dislike Schlafly? Decter later claimed not to recall that interview. She said she might have made those remarks because she was not "a movement person." Schlafly, therefore, "seemed very distant" and "culturally from somewhere else." But in the 1980s Decter felt compelled to issue Schlafly a public apology for "not paying sufficient attention" to her. "I was now publicly wishing to say that I owed her something, that the country owed her something."[21]

For reasons Decter herself highlights, she does not fit easily into the historiography of conservative women. That scholarship has emphasized the grassroots mobilization of ordinary white Christian women and the networks they built from their living rooms and kitchen tables in suburban communities across the country, particularly in the Sunbelt. Propelled to political activism by their Christian faith—Schlafly was Catholic while other conservative women were part of the newly politicized groups of Evangelicals, Fundamentalists, and Mormons—these white suburban women first organized politically in the 1950s around fears of communist infiltration of their communities, especially in public schools. They also castigated permissive parenting, which they felt exacerbated the problem of juvenile delinquency. But they did not initially cast their ire on feminism. Rather, they focused on what they saw as an expanding secular state displacing the Christian values that they believed undergirded the nation. Thus, they inveighed against the 1962 Supreme Court decision in *Engel v. Vitale*, which rendered school prayer unconstitutional. In 1964, they mobilized behind Barry Goldwater's presidential campaign, playing a critical role in his successful bid to become the Republican nominee. It was not until late 1972 that they turned their attention to feminism, with the anti-ERA campaign.[22]

Decter was not a Christian housewife. She was a New York intellectual and a Jewish writer who lived most of her adult life in Manhattan. Her politics thus developed within an entirely different set of parameters. Rather than canvassing PTA meetings in the suburbs, Decter wrote for highbrow magazines like *Harper's* and *Commentary*.

Decter contributed to two histories tied to the rise of conservatism in the late twentieth century: she and Podhoretz were among the initial wave of "neoconservatives," and she was an advocate of "family values," a socially conservative agenda linked to the rise of the New Right.[23] Significantly, though, Decter's political metamorphosis predated the standard timelines of both these strands of conservatism by at least a decade. She did not so much react to the radicalism of the late 1960s as balked at it from the beginning. She was also a champion of "family values" before the term even existed.

The Gay Divorcee

Decter was born Midge Rosenthal in St. Paul, Minnesota, in 1927 to middle-class Jewish parents. Her mother nicknamed her the Yiddish word for "mouth" because she talked a lot, "an expression half of pride, talking being a true mark of achievement in Jewish children and half of disapproval, because I didn't seem to 'know my place.'" The youngest of three girls, Decter was "a kind of honorary son" to her parents, which meant that "more was expected of me and at the same time I was given a longer leash." After spending one year at the University of Minnesota she dropped out and moved to New York City to pursue Hebrew studies at the Jewish Theological Seminary (JTS). She quit after a year because she "hated going to school" and she needed a job to help support her husband, Moshe Decter, a veteran completing his education on the GI Bill, whom she married in 1948.[24] Her first job in 1950 was as a secretary to Robert Warshow, the managing editor of *Commentary*. After getting pregnant in 1951, she quit working. Like many young couples in the 1950s, the Decters moved to the suburbs.[25]

Yet Decter's first marriage was short-lived. Decter gave birth to a second daughter in 1952 but divorced in 1954. She writes very little about her divorce in her memoir, not even mentioning her first husband by name. She simply notes that the divorce "saved my life." In 1962 Decter broached the subject in a thinly veiled essay titled "The Gay Divorcee," which scrutinized the definition of modern marriage as an institution centered on love, sexual fulfillment, and high hopes. Decter adhered to an older view of marriage. She argued that the institution worked best when understood as a "sensible economic and physical arrangement." Writing of the "gay divorcee," her hypothetical heroine, who, like Decter, would remarry, she ended with advice: "One can only hope that her new pretensions—to the marriage of limited expectations—will serve her better than the old ones."[26]

Following her divorce, Decter returned to Manhattan to work again at *Commentary*, this time as a secretary to the magazine's editor in chief, Elliot Cohen. There she was reintroduced to Norman Podhoretz, whom she had first met when they were both students at JTS. Podhoretz had taken classes at JTS while studying at Columbia University, from which he graduated in 1950. Over the next few years, he pursued graduate work in England and completed a stint in the army. They stayed in touch while he was abroad. When Podhoretz returned to the States, he worked as junior editor at *Commentary*. After a short courtship, they got engaged. They married in October 1956.[27]

Planning the wedding "was the worst of all nightmares," Decter reported to her friend, the writer Bernard Malamud. Podhoretz and Decter considered eloping but concluded they needed "some ceremony" because of Decter's children from her previous marriage. Podhoretz's family also did not initially support the union. While divorces were "perfectly commonplace" in literary circles, Podhoretz's immigrant parents viewed their son's decision to marry a divorcee as a "scandal, disgrace, misery, etc." His parents ultimately relented, but not before the wedding "had to be planned and replanned a dozen times," as Decter explained to Malamud. "First covering for kashrut [Jewish dietary laws] of an aging grandfather, then disregarding it as he refused to come, then regarding it again because he was coming, first inviting half the world, then the whole world, then no-one." The whole experience left Decter feeling rather ashamed: "shame that my years and few gray hairs couldn't protect me from all that folly, no more than if I had been a virgin, a fitting match for my young virginal bridegroom."[28] While Decter later said she felt little opprobrium for being a divorcee in literary circles, she herself would come to defend traditional views of marriage.[29]

After their nuptials Podhoretz and Decter settled into an apartment on the Upper West Side, "just half a block from the Hudson River." She was relieved to be living in Manhattan. They were "very happy," Decter told Malamud, but also "very broke."[30] In 1958 Decter gave birth to another daughter, followed by a son in 1961.

During her first marriage, Decter had yearned to return to the city when affordable housing became available. She did not like living in the suburbs. But she did not view her suburban sojourn with disdain. She was troubled, she later said, by the denunciations of the suburbs made by social critics in the late 1950s and early '60s. They marked "the beginning of a more general assault on the way ordinary Americans had come to live in the postwar world."[31]

Decter was particularly appalled by the image of the suburbs "made famous, one might even say indelible" by Betty Friedan in *The Feminine Mystique* (1963) "as a society in which women were systematically excluded from the interesting and important lives being led by their husbands, who all unfeelingly hopped aboard a magic train and headed for the Emerald City."[32] Friedan's thesis, in Decter's view, was "intellectually and stylistically very crude" and "unbelievably insulting to ordinary

housewives." While Decter herself "may have not wished to settle permanently in some fresh built community of nice homes far from the center
of town," Decter claimed that the vast majority of postwar Americans
did. As she told an interviewer in 1973: "My original point was that the
movement was putting women down. The young housewife with three
little kids is not doing something inferior to her husband; she's doing
something different. It was her own choice and her own doing—and
what's wrong with that?"[33]

Decter, Friedan, and Freud

The New York intellectuals did not initially take Betty Friedan seriously
as a writer. They never bothered to review *The Feminine Mystique* in any
of their journals. But their circles overlapped with Friedan's. In the introduction to his biography of Friedan, historian Daniel Horowitz writes of
having dinner with her in the 1990s at the Woodrow Wilson International
Center for Scholars at the Smithsonian Institution in Washington, DC,
where Friedan was then serving as a scholar in residence. "After dinner—
the people from the next table—Gertrude Himmelfarb, Irving Kristol,
Seymour Martin Lipset, and Sydnee Lipset—came over and engaged
Friedan . . . in cordial chat." These veteran neocons were by the 1990s well
integrated into conservative think tanks and government circles.[34] "That
moment," Horowitz wrote, "impressed upon me the importance of thinking of Friedan not only in the context of American feminism; I also became
interested in comparing her writings with those of neo-conservative New
York intellectuals to examine how postwar writers grappled with moral
and political issues." Horowitz did not follow this point through in his
excellent biography of Friedan. But it was an apt connection.[35]

More than any other New York intellectual, Decter and Friedan shared
much in common. Both women were raised in middle-class Jewish families in the Midwest. Born in 1921 in Peoria, Illinois, Friedan was six years
older than Decter. She too went east for college, graduating from Smith
College in 1942. Both women began their careers working at magazines in
New York City. Both stopped working after marrying and having children
(Friedan was fired from her job after the birth of her second child). Both
moved to the suburbs at the height of the postwar baby boom. Both women
disliked living in the suburbs. Both women also divorced.[36]

But they held starkly different views of feminism. Decter's and
Friedan's contrasting views of women's roles in society and their place in
the labor market reflected, in part, their different views of Freud. Friedan

would condemn Freudianism, especially its mid-century revisionist mode, for promoting the idea that women belonged at home solely as wives and mothers. Decter, in contrast, embraced mid-century revisionist Freudianism and its calls for "maturity" through heterosexuality and marriage, which ultimately undergirded her conservative politics.[37]

In the early decades of the twentieth century, Freud's ideas aimed to free women and men from the guilt and anxiety that resulted from sexual repression. Initially, they attracted the attention of only a handful of medical doctors, bohemian artists, and intellectuals.[38] Freud himself had also written little about women as a group, though he had written a great deal about the individual female patients he treated.

It was left to his followers, particularly two influential female analysts, Helene Deutsch and Karen Horney, who beginning in the 1920s "reworked Freud's theory of femininity to emphasize the biological basis of women's heterosexual identity."[39] Horney argued that women's heterosexuality was achieved not through fear of castration but vaginal sensations that women had from infancy. Like Freud, she rejected the clitoris as an important site of women's sexuality. But Horney provided a radical reinterpretation of Freud's theories of female sexuality by granting women bodily autonomy. In addition to discarding Freud's theory of "penis envy," she replaced it with "womb envy." Horney argued that men suffered from a "femininity complex" since they could not birth children and projected their inadequacy onto women. Thus, social factors, more than innate biological difference, accounted for female neuroses. Horney would go on to influence feminists in the 1970s.[40]

Deutsch's work, however, was initially more influential. Deutsch too focused on the vagina as the site of healthy female sexuality. But unlike Horney, she did not entirely discard Freud's theory of penis envy. She theorized that girls suffered from a sense "organlessness" after they experienced the "genital trauma" of discovering "their clitoris was an 'inadequate outlet' for [women's] 'active-aggressive instincts.'" Like other psychoanalysts before her, Deutsch suggested that women who did not accept their innate and natural passivity suffered from a "masculinity complex." In the 1940s she fused her theories of women's sexual development with the turn to ego psychology in American psychoanalysis. Ego psychologists focused on the role of mothers as primary caregivers in the development of their children. They "attributed to mothers an inordinate psychic power," blaming overbearing mothers for emasculating their sons and causing juvenile delinquency and, especially, homosexuality. In her 1944 book *The Psychology of Women*, Deutsch argued that only when women accepted their "natural femininity" would they repress any masculine tendencies and devote themselves healthily to the role of wife and mother.[41]

This more conservative version of Freudianism trickled into the broader culture. It underpinned the golden age of psychoanalysis in the United States in the two decades following World War II. Philip Wylie, in his 1942 best-selling book, *Generation of Vipers*, coined the pseudo-Freudian term "momism" to describe overbearing mothers and wives who emasculated their sons and husbands. "It was only a matter of degree that separated Wylie," historian Mari Jo Buhle argues, "from the more restrained psychoanalysts who provided the theoretical fortification for his main argument." Benjamin Spock's 1946 child-rearing bible, *The Common Sense Book of Baby and Child Care*, instructed women to devote all their energy to raising young children, bringing revisionist Freudianism to the masses. Two years after the end of World War II and in the midst of a sweeping effort to send women out of the workforce and back home, journalist Ferdinand Lundberg and psychoanalyst Marynia F. Farnham published *The Lost Sex* (1947), a bestseller that argued that higher education and careers "masculinized" women to the detriment of children, husbands, and society at large.[42]

Friedan targeted all these writers in *The Feminine Mystique*. Her 1963 book began as a series of articles meant to disprove Lundberg and Farnham's thesis. To gather evidence, Friedan had sent a survey to her classmates from Smith. Their responses led her to write *The Feminine Mystique*. Friedan devoted an entire chapter to "the sexual solipsism of Sigmund Freud," writing that "much of what Freud believed to be biological, instinctual, and changeless has been shown by modern research to be a result of specific cultural causes." She took particular aim at his mid-century revisionist followers. Of Deutsch, Friedan wrote that "this brilliant feminine follower of Freud states categorically that women who by 1944 in America had achieved eminence by activity in their own various fields had done so at the expense of their feminine fulfillment." Friedan lamented how passages from *The Lost Sex* had been "paraphrased ad nauseum in the magazines and marriage courses, until most of its statements became part of the conventional truth of our time." These writers were central to propagating the feminine mystique. "Freud's popularizers embedded his core of unrecognized prejudice against women ever deeper in pseudo-scientific cement," Friedan wrote.[43]

Decter, in contrast, did not challenge revisionist Freudianism. Rather, she used it to buttress her arguments about women and sex roles. When Decter said feminists were women who refused to grow up, she was repeating conventional Freudian wisdom about "maturity" in the postwar years.[44] While Friedan chastised these theories for bolstering the feminine mystique, Decter would lean on them to discredit the women's movement.

Crucially, Decter developed her views years before Friedan published *The Feminine Mystique*. In a 1959 article sparked by an advice manual, *American Marriage* by Ruth Shonle Cavan, Decter lamented that such a book was necessary since it indicated that "elementary biological functions and social institutions so universal as to be almost a condition of nature must now become objects of full consciousness." She complained that marriage, once "an institution founded on solid rock which creates a rational economic organization for the family" and an "institution whose function is to thrust [a man] into adulthood and responsibility," had evolved into something focused more on "relationships" and "we-feelings." Marriage was an economic and psychological necessity, Decter argued, ensuring healthy masculinity by turning men into providers for dependent women and children.[45]

Modern marriage was an unfortunate feminization of traditional marriage, Decter argued. This new marriage had "been set up to disadvantage" man, she wrote, and "his natural talents." Under this new arrangement, a man's "virtues as a lover will be found in his ability to submit to female terms and desires; and those as a father will be measured by his capacity for participating in his wife's pregnancy, delivery, and physical care of the children." For Decter, the concept of companionate marriage, which emerged in the 1920s in response to Freud's acknowledgment of female sexuality, women's growing independence, and civic equality following the passage of women's suffrage, had gone too far. This more modern definition was emasculating and led to a higher rate of divorce, "or at least to a restlessness and discontent staggering in their dimensions."[46]

Echoing revisionist Freudians, as well as moralists of nearly all backgrounds, Decter argued that female sexuality had to be contained within heterosexual marriage and within clearly defined sex roles. Marriage was psychologically essential to women because it guaranteed maturity by turning them into wives and mothers. In a 1964 essay titled "Secrets," published as the sexual revolution heated up, Decter warned that for women "premarital sexual activity" had "not at all been liberating." Whereas women used to worry about not getting married before they were considered old maids, they now contended with more ominous threats like male desertion, unwanted pregnancy, and abortion. As a result, Decter warned that women's response was increasingly to opt out of heterosexuality altogether.[47]

Decter broached the topic of lesbianism several years before it came to animate discussions within women's liberation. Decter argued that lesbianism was "one of the responses to the modern difficulties of womanhood" and "a growingly popular form of female chastity." Lesbians were not "sexual deviants," she wrote in 1964, but women who refused to grow up. Their rejection of heterosexual marriage indicated that they were "merely retreating to a point of girlishness from which grown-up life in the world cannot really make its full and painful demands on them." These were arguments rooted in Freudianism, and Decter would repeat them verbatim in her critiques of the women's movement a decade later.[48]

Women and Work

Between 1951, when Decter gave birth to her first child, and the mid-1960s, when her youngest (born in 1961) reached grade school, Decter worked intermittently. While married to her first husband, Moshe Decter, she was a stay-at-home mother in suburban New York, working only twice during those years in part-time jobs for short periods. "Both times it had been a matter of needing some extra money while my then husband had been between jobs." During the two years between her marriages, she worked full time when she "needed a job simply to live on."[49]

After marrying Podhoretz in 1956, she quit her job at *Commentary* to take a position at the magazine *Midstream* because the pay was better and both Decter and Podhoretz wanted to avoid an office romance. But after the birth of their first child in 1958 (Decter's third), she quit working altogether because the cost of hiring a nanny combined with her commute amounted to nearly as much as her salary. "The discovery that my job was costing us money, then, came as something of a welcome relief. I could just stay at home and hang out with the children and at the same time even feel that I was adding to the family coffers," she wrote in her memoir.[50]

Decter did not appear to question why her wages were low, nor was she troubled by the postwar family wage system and its ideology of a male breadwinner. While she knew that many women worked out of necessity, she felt that her "story of working and not working" was not "different in any significant respect from the stories that could be told by countless numbers of working mothers today." In her view, the challenges women faced in the workforce were not systemic. "The true Woman Problem," she wrote in her memoir, was "not the oppression of women, to say the least a laughable proposition in the United States, nor the glass ceiling . . . but rather a seemingly never-to-be mediated internal clash of ambitions: the ambition to make oneself a noticeable place in the world and the ambition to be a good mother."[51]

Decter also diverged from Betty Friedan (and other feminists) when it came to the issue of sex discrimination. Friedan founded the National Organization for Women (NOW) in 1966 to fight for women's equality under the law and ensure the enforcement of Title VII of the 1964 Civil Rights Act, which barred discrimination in employment based on race, religion, national origin, and sex.[52] While Friedan served as the group's first president, Decter had dismissed the issue of sex discrimination in a 1961 essay.

In "Women at Work" (1961), Decter examined popular fears about the increasing number of women working since World War II, a number that the United States Department of Labor predicted would only keep growing. Decter commented on the same fears that Friedan analyzed in *The Feminine Mystique* two years later, but with drastically different conclusions. While Friedan condemned such fears as part of the "feminine mystique," Decter downplayed the idea that most women even wanted to work outside the home. "Such figures, stated flatly," she wrote, "tend to conjure up an image as misleading as it is frightening to the popular imagination of men and women coming to be less and less differentiated, elbowing one another for room in some kind of sexual and occupational jungle."[53]

According to Decter, a woman's relationship to "salaried employment" differed from a man's. "As a general rule," she argued, women "do not define themselves by what they do, or try to be as successful as possible." Rather, they worked briefly during certain stages in their lives because most desired to be married, keep house, and raise children full-time. "In the very teeth of their emancipation and hard-won freedom," Decter concluded, "girls go on dreaming of being married and loved and happy, in fact, more than girls have ever done before."[54]

Decter's article appeared the same year that President John F. Kennedy assembled a Presidential Commission on the Status of Women to study how "prejudices and outmoded customs act as barriers to the full realization of women's rights." Kennedy hoped the committee, the first of its kind to study the status of women, would appease women voters and make good on the Democratic Party's promise in its 1960 platform to provide equal job opportunities and equal pay for women. Yet when the committee issued its report in 1963, it reflected societal assumptions about women's primary roles as wives, mothers, and homemakers, even as it made recommendations to address workplace discrimination.[55]

Decter's analysis shared these biases, minus the committee's liberal prescriptions. While she acknowledged that there was "a good deal of prejudice against women in the men's world," she also argued that most employers had "sound reasons" to not hire women. They justly hesitated "to invest the time, and the money, required for training women to assume responsibilities which they will chuck for marriage, or to have a baby, or to answer the urgency of some other family need." Decter did not see this as a form of sex discrimination but as a reflection of women's natural life cycles, and as a feminine advantage. "If women suffer the disadvantages of being deprived of opportunities to hold the best jobs in the highest echelons," Decter wrote, it was because of "this irrevocable privilege: they always have a place of retreat when failure threatens—this is not what they really are, what they really do."[56]

In her 1971 debate with Steinem, Decter had declared that "there is no sex discrimination in the field of writing." There is only "*quality* discrimination in the field of writing." Sex discrimination, she continued, "no longer exists in law schools and medical schools, either." Decter was greeted with "howls of derisive laughter" along with the shout, 'Where have you been?'"[57]

Decter was a New York intellectual, and by 1971 she was an executive editor at *Harper's*. She was a gifted writer and editor. But like other conservative women, including Schlafly, whose husband's "legal practice allowed his wife the financial freedom to pursue her political work," Decter did not have to work for wages when her children were young.[58] She also had social connections, something she rarely acknowledged but which made navigating her career and motherhood less difficult. In the late 1950s and early 1960s, Decter wrote occasional reviews, mostly for *Commentary*, where her husband became head editor in 1960. In 1961 Podhoretz hired Decter as an "acting managing editor," a job that likely allowed for flexible hours. Thereafter she worked as an editor at the Hudson Institute (1965–66) and at CBS Legacy Books from 1966 to 1968, likely part-time.[59] Revealingly, Decter argued in her 1972 book, *The New Chastity*, that one of the benefits of marriage for a woman was that her husband "automatically confers upon her membership in his social class or—what may be more precisely to the point—his social milieu."[60]

Decter at Willie Morris's Harper's

Decter entered the workforce full time in 1968 when her youngest son had reached grade school. This time her position was not as a secretary but as an editor at *Harper's*, under its newly minted head editor, Willie Morris. In his memoir, Morris described Decter as "one of the accomplished women of the city." She was "the mother of four children and had long become established in the city as a reputable book and magazine editor with broad and serviceable contacts in the Jewish intellectual community, the city and nation."[61]

Decter got the job through Podhoretz. In 1963 he befriended Morris, a white Southern Protestant who arrived in New York that year to work at *Harper's*. Within four years he had "risen like a multistage rocket from his hometown of Yazoo, Mississippi, without missing a beat and became at thirty-two the youngest editor in *Harper's* history," Podhoretz recalled.[62] Just three years earlier in 1960, Podhoretz had been named the head editor of *Commentary* when he was just shy of thirty years old.

Morris had settled into an apartment on the Upper West Side upon arriving in Manhattan, which was where many New York intellectuals lived by the 1960s. On those "Upper West Side benches," he later recalled, he imbued the "spirit of Yiddish [that] pervaded the city, these park benches, the delis, the most serious salons of the intelligentsia, *Commentary*, *Partisan Review*, *Dissent*, where I often found myself the solitary goy, or one of two if one counted Dwight Macdonald. The Anglo-Saxon *émigré* could not wholly survive without a little touch of Yiddish." He would look to bring that spirit to *Harper's*. Podhoretz helped him. The two men became fast friends. Podhoretz "was indeed for a while my best friend, very much a part of the magazine scene and my own life," Morris wrote.[63]

Despite their disparate upbringings, Morris and Podhoretz shared much in common. Both men were young, gregarious, and ambitious— eager to make some noise for their respective magazines. They would meet often after work at Le Moal, a joint not far from *Commentary's* offices on East Fifty-Sixth Street and Third Avenue, which "Murray Kempton called 'the *Commentary* commissar,'" to gossip, talk shop, and drink. "The Pod," as Morris called him, "was irreverent, amusing, bawdy, and courageous." "There is an adage that Jews cannot drink: Pod was the proof of that lie," he wrote. "Of course almost everyone, including me in those days, drank too much," Podhoretz recalled. "For literary people it went with the territory. A writer was expected to drink and suspected if he didn't; and far from being frowned upon, drinking heavily was admired as a sign of manliness, and of that refusal of respectability that seemed necessary to creative work."[64]

Podhoretz shared his knowledge of the New York publishing scene with Morris. "Pod edified me about the jostling intellectual life of the town, the rivalries and grudges, the jeopardies of driven ambition," Morris wrote. When Morris was promoted to head editor at *Harper's* in late 1967, it was

Podhoretz who suggested he hire Decter. "'You'd be a fool not to hire her,' Podhoretz confided to me in those days of our friendship. 'She's a better editor than I am.'"[65]

Upon taking over the magazine, one of Morris's first acts was to hire Decter. He looked to her, along with Robert Kotlowitz, a former editor at *Show Magazine*, whom he hired as managing editor, to help him transform *Harper's* from an outmoded and stale periodical into a leading magazine that published the nation's most well-known and celebrated writers. "Bob Kotlowitz, Midge Decter, and I worked hard—I have an honest recollection of our sitting down at some point and making a master roster of whom we really wanted—to make this list of good writers and artists grow: courting agents, cornering writers, martini lunches, letters, phone calls," Morris wrote. Many had never written for the magazine. New York intellectuals like Irving Howe, Alfred Kazin, Elizabeth Hardwick, and Philip Roth started to appear in its pages. It was Decter's connections that lured those writers to *Harper's*.[66]

One of Decter's biggest coups for *Harper's* was editing Norman Mailer's 1968 essay, "The Steps of the Pentagon," which became part of his book, *The Armies of the Night* (1968). Mailer had attended the MOBE (National Mobilization Committee to End the War in Vietnam) March on the Pentagon in October 1967, where he deliberately got arrested. When Morris heard that Mailer planned to write about the experience, he was determined to get the piece for *Harper's*. He turned to Decter, a longtime friend of Mailer's, to get the deal done. Together they pitched a plan to Mailer's agent to publish the piece first as an article in *Harper's* and then deliver the manuscript to a book publisher a month later.

As Mailer worked on the article, Morris and Decter flew to his house in Cape Cod to edit as he wrote. "I would read fifteen or twenty pages, then give them to Midge Decter in another room," Morris recalled. "Midge, who was a resilient editor in every facet of the trade, had no difficulty with the handwriting. She was erasing many of his interpolations and reprinting them legibly so that certain pages would not need to be retyped. From time to time she and Mailer would sit down and do minimal editing, then he would retire upstairs again to finish."[67] The article, both knew, was "clearly something extraordinary. It was 'an event,' [Decter] later said. 'An event, an editor's dream come true.'"[68] It appeared in the March 1968 issue of *Harper's* and "was the longest magazine article ever published (John Hersey's 'Hiroshima' in the *New Yorker* having previously had that distinction)."[69] *Armies of the Night* went on to win a Pulitzer Prize and the National Book Award.[70]

Three years later, *Harper's* published Mailer's polemic against women's liberation, "The Prisoner of Sex" (1971).[71] Again, Morris and Decter flew to Cape Cod and Decter edited the piece as Mailer wrote. It was the last piece she edited for *Harper's* and the last issue Morris oversaw. He was forced out by the magazine's publisher as the issue hit the stands. Decter and the other senior editors resigned in protest.[72]

While at *Harper's* Decter also wrote for the magazine. "Her *Harper's* pieces would be significantly rooted in the Sixties and addressed to many of its excesses and severities," Morris later wrote. "Although herself a left-of-center intellectual," she assailed intellectual supporters of the New Left "for contemporary fashion-mongering and self-destructive postures."[73] Her views of sex roles however were never particularly left-of-center. Nor did they change all that much over the course of the 1960s.

In the 1970s, when Decter would get invited to speak to young women about careers in publishing, her number one piece of advice was to know how to type. "For all intents and purposes that ended the session," Decter recalled. "They were too outraged to say another word." Decter told them that most women in publishing had started their careers as secretaries. Moreover, that was no different from men starting out "in the publicity office," an entry-level job in which "the pay was not great" but which gave them a foot in the door. Decter believed she had achieved a "much higher level of professional status and pay than [she had in her] first two" secretarial jobs through hard work. But Decter lacked a college degree. In that way her situation was not analogous to young college-educated women, and she viewed such young women, receptive as they were to the women's movement, as entitled and dilatory.[74]

The Liberated Woman

Decter made that view clear in "The Liberated Woman," her first major broadside against the women's movement. Though she was then working at *Harper's*, the article appeared in *Commentary* in October 1970, a few months after Podhoretz had begun attacking the New Left in a monthly column he reinstated in June 1970.[75] The title of her article was sardonic. "The liberated woman," Decter wrote, sought "a freedom demanded by children and enjoyed by no one: the freedom from all difficulty."[76]

The essay provided an unflattering portrait of the type of woman supposedly attracted to the women's movement. It chronicled the life of a fictional protagonist, a woman who is not given a name. She was white, middle class, privileged, and entitled. Raised in a "self-centered world" under "the idea that she must not be made to suffer in any way, physically, emotionally, mentally," her parents and teachers catered to her every whim.[77] When she went to college, she chose an elite women's school "free of everyday male competition." Upon graduating, she moved to New York City to pursue a writing career and landed a "junior position" at a fashion magazine. She did not make enough money, so her parents continued to support her financially. But she found the magazine "just not her kind of place." It was "staffed mainly by women who were or were becoming technical experts in one or another of the phases of fashion-and-food presentation the publication specialized in." She had been naive to think she could begin a serious career as a journalist there, as the magazine "had nothing to teach her." So she quit to become a freelance writer.[78]

As Decter chronicled her protagonist's professional and personal travails, her prose dripped with sarcasm. Decter's character was a freelancer who "inevitably had to sit down all by herself and face her typewriter, the product of this confrontation had to be judged immediately and found adequate or inadequate." But the young woman was incapable of handling criticism or rejection. Like other women of her generation, she professed to want a career but was unwilling to handle the demands involved. Part of the problem was she had been coddled her entire life. Her parents and teachers had catered to her happiness since she was an infant and taught her neither how to work hard nor how to handle failure. "In high school, then college, she had heard nothing but praise for whatever she was able to do. Now she was often criticized: editors rejected her," Decter wrote. So "she began to tell herself that the real difficulty lay in the world's expectations of her." Moreover, she suspected employers did not take her writings seriously because she was a woman.[79]

Decter also wrote about her fictional protagonist's relationships. There were many, since she was freed by the sexual revolution to pursue sex outside the confines of marriage. She struggled to recall which of her male friends "she had once slept with and which merely exchanged deep confidences with." Her most promising relationship should have led to a "fairy tale ending." The young woman finally found herself in "the arms of, if not Prince Charming, then at least the kind of man her great-grandmother might have mistaken for him." But her happily ever after was not to be, because she discovered women's liberation by way of a successful female editor in the publishing industry.[80]

Decter's heroine soon began attending consciousness-raising groups and reading movement literature. There she learned that "like blacks, women were an oppressed class; that more than blacks, they had been oppressed throughout history."[81] Decter's protagonist brought this new-found knowledge home and soon began to quarrel with her boyfriend, a successful newspaper photographer, about mundane issues like who was responsible for household chores to the more serious charge that her boyfriend was not supportive of her career. The two broke up. In their final argument, he told her that "if she were a writer she would simply write, rather than spend half her time telling anyone who would listen about all the things that made writing difficult for her."[82]

Women's liberation was intoxicating, Decter argued, because it told women that they were victims of male supremacy and sex discrimination. In reality, however, women did not suffer from discrimination. They just did not work as hard as men. But that was because they did not have to. Harkening back to her 1961 essay, "Women and Work," Decter argued that not having to work was a privilege young women took for granted. Women could choose not to attend college or have a career "with none of the opprobrium attaching to what for a young man would have constituted the very definition of failure, future as well as present," she wrote.[83]

Women's liberation turned this "female freedom" not to work into a grievance that women were victims of male supremacy. This idea of victimhood was a self-fulfilling prophecy, Decter argued. "Movements like Women's Lib always have some degree of circularity about them. Which is to say, in addition to being expressions of a deep dissatisfaction, they do themselves constitute a culture of dissatisfaction."[84] Far from identifying any real problems, the women's movement actually taught women that they were inferior to men while at the same time excusing female indolence. "It's undergraduate girls in the best Ivy League colleges," Decter explained in a 1973 interview, "who are saying that they have been discriminated against, and it's just a way of saying 'Take it easy on me.'"[85]

Decter's fictional protagonist in "The Liberated Woman" bore some resemblance to Gloria Steinem. In her memoir Decter noted that she met Steinem "in her previous life as a very beautiful, very sexy, friendly and pleasant young journalist around town with a so-so talent and a decent if not distinguished career."[86] Steinem had claimed that when she began her career as a journalist, after graduating from Smith College, she was assigned to cover fashion and beauty rather than serious political stories.

Decter's fictional "liberated woman" also reflected stereotypes about the Jewish American Princess (JAP) that began to circulate in the 1950s and '60s.[87] Decter's liberated woman "changed her style of presenting herself, which is to say her wardrobe, with regular frequency." Her clothes, Decter was sure to note, were always expensive. Like Philip Roth's fictional

Brenda Patimkin in *Goodbye Columbus* (1959), one of the earliest JAPs in literature, Decter's protagonist was sexually precocious, and she eventually "entered into a full-blown affair" with one of her boyfriends. "For this she was equipped by her family doctor with a diaphragm—later she would be given the Pill."[88] Patimkin obtaining a diaphragm is one of the plotlines in *Goodbye, Columbus*, which ultimately leads to the end of her summer romance with Neil Klugman.[89] She leaves her diaphragm at home when she returns to college, only for her disproving mother to find it. Like Brenda Patimkin, Decter's liberated woman was spoiled, materialistic, and coquettish—seemingly liberated by the sexual revolution but also deeply confused and unhappy in her relationships.

"The Liberated Woman" also introduced a method Decter employed throughout the 1970s and early 1980s to discredit feminism, gay rights, and the New Left more broadly. She constructed a composite of young radicals and framed her arguments around these fictional but ostensibly realistic portraits. The technique predictably inflamed her critics. One reader wrote to *Commentary* that Decter "indulged in the sort of instant social research where wit outscores research." Another critic called Decter's approach "fictionalized sociology" or "in other words, fiction. New Journalism at best."[90]

Decter defended her method in her 1975 book, *Liberal Parents, Radical Children*, which was composed entirely of four such extended portraits. While she admitted that her composite characters were "not 'true' stories, in the sense of being about individuals known to me or interviewed by me or whose case studies have been presented to me," she asserted, "they are, as I have said before and as I believe, true stories nonetheless." She used this method to illustrate that radicals were spoiled and expected employers and audiences to give them the attention they craved without doing anything to earn it.[91]

In a 1975 interview with *People* magazine promoting *Liberal Parents, Radical Children*, Decter criticized "a liberal system of upbringing" that she believed fostered a nihilism among young people in the 1960s. "These parents, imbued with the very best of intentions and with the aid of Spock and Freud's followers, believed they had a secret formula for bringing up children who would not be neurotic, aggressive, competitive, sexually inhibited, and who would be full of love." But in the process, "they brought their children up with the idea that any pain or difficulty was a form of outrage that had to be fixed immediately—first by mommy and daddy, and later by society."[92] By the 1970s, conservatives were chastising Spock for "what they considered to be his 'permissive' parenting advice." Ignoring his more conservative message about mothers' roles, they blamed Spock for helping turn young people into radicals, "because parents (mainly mothers) had failed to establish discipline in the home."[93]

Decter, in contrast, criticized Spock for placating feminists. In a 1971 interview, Spock conceded that when he wrote *The Common Sense Book of Baby and Child Care* in 1946 he was "just as prejudiced as the next man." He told the *New York Times Sunday Magazine* he would adopt more gender-neutral pronouns in revised editions of the book, alongside other changes. In "a scathing letter" to the editor, as a *New York Times* reporter later described it, Decter disparaged the demise of Dr. Spock's "once considerable dignity." Years later, however, Decter concluded that Spock had been "given a bum rap" while Freud was "often caricatured and perverted." In her memoir she wrote that "Freud himself had unquestionably had something else in mind than the spectacle of certain [baby boom] child-rearing practices."[94]

Decter anthologized "The Liberated Woman" and her other early essays in her first book *The Liberated Woman and Other Americans* (1971). Decter was "a wife and mother, a writer and editor, a Jew born and bred in the Middle West but now a significant figure in literary New York," one reviewer noted of her book. "She has made it in what was once called a 'man's world' without neglecting the older conventions of womanhood." But as this reviewer astutely observed, "On the evidence of her essays, Midge Decter knew from the start that there was no future in the new hopes and enthusiasms of the sixties."[95]

The New Chastity

By the time Decter published her book-length attack on the women's movement, *The New Chastity and Other Arguments against Women's Liberation*, in 1972, her criticisms of second-wave feminism were well established. While the book reiterated ideas she had long advanced, her methodology was new. Rather than create fictionalized composite characters, as she did in "The Liberated Woman," Decter addressed the major theorists of the women's movement head on. But she generalized, treating the women's movement as "a monolith that doesn't accommodate different points of view," as *Ms.* contributor Barbara Harrison noted in a review of the book. "Anyone who takes the trouble to talk to feminists—as opposed to reading mimeo'd sheets of rhetoric run off in someone's attic," Harrison continued, "knows that we have individual, eccentric points of view, that being human, we differ in opinions like other human beings."[96] In the *New York Times*, Christopher Lehmann-Haupt accused Decter of "lump[ing] together into a single point of view . . . such varied spokeswomen as Simone de Beauvoir, Betty Friedan, Kate Millett, Germaine Greer, Caroline Bird, Shulamith Firestone, Robin Morgan, Gloria Steinem, Juliet Mitchell, and others."[97]

Decter began *The New Chastity* with an extended critique of *The Feminine Mystique*. She called Friedan's book a "critical document" of the movement and one that "was borrowed from so freely (to the point, in some cases, of cannibalization) in the flood of literature" that "poured forth from the Women's Liberationists."[98]

Interestingly, Decter agreed with some aspects of Friedan's argument, even as she sought to discredit the book. She acknowledged that many women found domesticity mind-numbing and that a "daytime career" provided a "welcome means of escaping from the house." But she castigated Friedan for convincing women that careers were a means of self-fulfillment. "Far from making the daily routines of household management less irksome—as Betty Friedan had predicted it would—work outside the home in the society of men was, it seemed, only making them more so. The woman who returned home after working all day in the office found that she merely had a double burden to bear." Feminists sought to restructure the workplace and home to accommodate the changing needs of working women, but Decter chastised the movement for trying to alter sex roles and what she saw as the gender-neutral workplace.[99]

Decter's views were premised on the ideal of a middle-class model of the family. "Married women work because it pleases them. They are free to earn less money if doing so provides them with an opportunity to do something more interesting or satisfying to them. They are free to leave a job whose conditions are not to their liking. They are free, that is, to continue to behave like dependents," Decter wrote. Like some white feminists initially, Decter overlooked women who worked out of necessity. Many postwar American families could not subsist on a single income, particularly families of color.[100] At one point in *The New Chastity* Decter acknowledged her middle-class bias. She wrote that "women's connection with work and the making of money, at least among the middle-class who constitute the movement's basic constituency, is that of volunteers." She believed that most women in the movement were white and middle class, a simplification by 1972. Even if there was some truth to the observation, Decter essentialized sex roles. "A woman wants to be married for the simplest and most self-evident of reasons," Decter wrote. "She requires both in her nature and by virtue of what are her immediate practical needs (if indeed the two can even be separated) the assurance that a single man has undertaken to love, cherish, and support her."[101]

Decter devoted significant space to lesbianism in *The New Chastity*. While she had been writing on this subject since the early 1960s, she could not have predicted that lesbianism would become central to the politics of women's liberation. "Lesbians brought profound insights to the feminist movement," argues historian Nancy MacLean, "because they derived no benefits from the old system of gender hierarchy" and were therefore "in a better position to identify and act on its ugly underpinnings." This focus on sexuality distinguished women's liberation both from first-wave feminism and its precursor in the nonpartisan liberal feminism espoused by Friedan and NOW. "By 1970, radical *lesbian* feminism, a feminism in which women worked principally with and for other women," writes historian Claire Bond Potter, "had become a visible alternative to liberal feminist institutions that hoped to succeed by persuading men that they too would benefit from a societal justice agenda grounded in gender equality." When this shift took place within the women's movement, Decter was ready with critiques informed by years of writing about sexuality and sex roles through a Freudian inflected lens.[102]

In *The New Chastity* Decter repeated the view that lesbians were immature women. Harkening back to her 1964 essay, "Secrets," she wrote that lesbianism "creates lasting forms and significance for the girlish inconsequences of adolescence." She reiterated how lesbianism "represents a demand for the return to female chastity," a phrase she used to title this second book. According to Decter, the increasing visibility of lesbianism was a response to the sexual revolution and its dismantling of norms that had governed relations between men and women. Sex had long provided women with a bargaining chip, forcing men to commit to marriage and to the role of provider. The sexual revolution demolished these old rules. "Women's liberation is indeed nothing less than a demand on the part of those women most completely conditioned by it to repeal the sexual revolution altogether," Decter wrote. "It is a cry for the right of women to step back, retire, from a disagreeable involvement in, and responsibility for, the terms of sexual equality with men."[103]

Decter argued that in its embrace of lesbianism, the entire women's movement revealed itself as anti-men. Lesbianism embodied the "enmity towards men" that was a "basic" and "founding, passion of the movement." Lesbianism in fact provided "a very useful ideological underpinning for dispensing with men," she wrote. While some radical feminists did call for female separatism, Decter disparaged lesbianism vis-à-vis revisionist Freudianism rather than engage with radical feminists' actual arguments. Decter concluded that women's liberation focused on a clitoral rather than

FIGURE 11. Midge Decter and Norman Podhoretz in December 1972.
From the *Times-Picayune*, December 8, 1972, Capital City Press /
Georges Media Group, and Baton Rouge, LA.

vaginal orgasm because it "is a necessary step in renouncing the intervention of men." The clitoral orgasm was a "masturbatory orgasm, produced
by one or another means of external manipulation." Therefore lesbians,
"sexually speaking," had not "submitted to the penis" but "escaped it." "The
fundamental impulse of the movement," Decter argued, was "an impulse
to maidenhood—to that condition in which a woman might pretend to
a false fear or loathing of the penis in order to escape from any responsibility for the pleasure and well-being of the man who possesses it."[104]
Lesbianism was a way for women to remain both chaste and immature.
For Decter, like Helene Deutsch and other revisionist Freudians, sex had
to involve a phallus. In eschewing heterosexual sex, lesbians remained in
perpetual adolescence and rejected their natural femininity.

Decter also briefly addressed male homosexuality in *The New Chastity*
as a means of comparison to lesbians. "Female homosexuals are different
from male homosexuals," Decter wrote, "in that they slip far more easily,

according to convenience, both into and out of homosexual practices." Decter argued that lesbians were childlike and prudish. Male homosexuals, on the other hand, exhibited "a disabling terror and hatred of the cunt." Male homosexuals were especially dangerous because by rejecting women they rejected procreation and life itself: a "woman's physical being most powerfully represents—birth, which is to say morality and death." Decter maintained the main purpose of sexual intercourse was to produce children. Rejecting "the moist conjunction of sperm and ovum and all the attendant unseen paraphernalia and sticky conjoinings [*sic*] necessary for it to happen," Decter wrote, "is the rejection of mortality itself. Each act of love between two men is a denial of sonhood [*sic*], which is also to say, of fatherhood." Decter's conceptions of homosexuality in *The New Chastity* remained firmly rooted in revisionist neo-Freudian theories regarding sex, sex roles, and marriage.[105]

The Boys on the Beach

Eight years later, Decter expanded on the subject of male homosexuality in a notorious 1980 *Commentary* article, "The Boys on the Beach." She examined Fire Island, a gay-friendly beach community off Long Island, where she had long vacationed with her family. As in her analysis of the women's movement, Decter drew on revisionist Freudianism to construct her thesis. She also engaged in gross generalizations, caricatures, and stereotypes of gay men.

Homosexuals, according to Decter, were not real men. That was because "by definition" they were "males undomesticated by women." Real men were only those who accepted the "mature" responsibilities of marriage and fatherhood. Homosexuality "represented a flight from women far more than a wholehearted embrace of men," Decter argued. Homosexuals also impersonated women. They did so through the adoption of female dress and manners in order to "appropriate the advantages of girlishness."[106]

Decter maintained that homosexuals cunningly circumvented the responsibilities of both men and women, all while ruthlessly mocking both sexes. They taunted straight men. "Their smooth and elegant exteriors, unmussed [*sic*] by traffic with the detritus of modern family existence," Decter wrote, "constituted a kind of sniggering to their striving and harried straight brothers. See what you have got yourself into, they seemed to be saying, no wonder you have so much less for yourself—and look it." At the same time, homosexuals tormented women by competing with them and "putting their very existence as women on the line." Thus, they were especially dangerous because they mimicked and derided both sexes. Not only were gay men immature, but they also sought nothing less than to rid society of the "human condition which necessitates a division into two sexes." Without deference to distinct sex roles and their containment within marriage, Decter argued that homosexuals threatened the stability of "the heterosexual world" and the entire social order.[107]

Critics assailed Decter for her coarse views of homosexuality and for perpetuating inaccurate and harmful stereotypes of gay men. Decter said that homosexuals indulged in drugs, alcohol, and compulsive sex. But "so do many heterosexuals," Lewis Coser retorted in *Dissent*. Decter failed to "account for the causes of such pathologies," Coser argued, such as the difficulties homosexuals faced because of police brutality, assault, blackmail, ridicule, disdain, and entrapment. Decter ignored all these causes and "instead of attending to the victimizers who are largely responsible for whatever pathologies may be found among gays, she attacks the victims."[108]

Other commentators identified her outmoded Freudian theories as particularly troublesome. Gore Vidal, writing in *The Nation*, quipped that Decter "knows her Freud, and reality may not intrude." He continued: "Decter accepts without question Freud's line (*Introductory Lectures on Psychoanalysis*) that 'we actually describe a sexual activity as perverse if it has given up the aim of reproduction and pursues the attainment of pleasure as an aim independent of it.'" Vidal also took Decter to task for stereotyping all gay men as effeminate. "Decter should take a stroll down San Francisco's Castro Street, where members of the present generation of fags [*sic*] look like off-duty policemen or construction workers. They have embraced the manly," he wrote. "But Freud has spoken. Fags are fags because they adored their mothers and hated their poor, hard-working daddies. It is amazing the credence still given this unproven, unprovable thesis." Decter's essay, he concluded, was "a vicious attack on homosexuals" and on their politicization of gay rights in the 1970s.[109] He was right. By 1980 Decter was far from alone.

Family Values

By the later 1970s opposition not just to feminism but also to gay rights had moved to the center of a politics of "family values" within the burgeoning New Right. In 1976, Anita Bryant launched a campaign to thwart a gay-rights antidiscrimination measure in Miami-Dade County, Florida. "One of the first evangelical spokespeople to make homosexuality into a national political concern," writes historian Emily Suzanne Johnson, "Bryant's early campaigns helped situate this issue at the very core of the 'family values' politics that would come to define the New Christian Right." In earlier years, few Christian conservatives spoke out against gays and lesbians. "Evangelicals' relative quiescence" on the subject, writes historian Seth Dowland, "depended on the vast majority remaining in the closet, concealed from public view."[110]

That began to change with the Stonewall riots in 1969. When the American Psychiatric Association removed homosexuality from its list of mental illnesses in 1973, conservatives were convinced that gay men preyed on children not only for sex but because they chose a homosexual lifestyle and needed recruits. Their views of gay men were rooted in their interpretation of the Bible. "The creation story of Genesis, in which God created man and woman to live together, served as the template for family life," Dowland explains. "Conservative evangelicals recognized ways that sin wrecked that first family, but they insisted that humans—not God—brought sin into the world. Since they thought of homosexuality as a sin, they insisted God did not create people as gay or lesbians."[111]

By then, conservatives had taken note of Decter's writings. One of the first was Ernest van den Haag, a European refugee who came to the United States during World War II and became a regular contributor to *National Review* beginning in 1956. In 1972 he had praised Decter's analysis of feminism in "The Liberated Woman" as "not only sensible—all of her stuff is—but a virtuoso performance. It is the best I've read on the topic." Van den Haag had studied psychiatry at the Sorbonne and earned a doctorate in economics at NYU. But "the fields of sociology, psychology, and social philosophy interested him more. During the 1950s and 1960s, he was a rara avis in academia: a credentialed social scientist and an unabashed conservative," writes historian George Nash. "Even more improbably, after being psychoanalyzed he became a psychoanalyst himself—a profession he practiced on the side for nearly three decades."[112]

In 1980 Van den Haag again praised Decter. Her article, "The Boys on the Beach," showed that "homosexuality, though not demonstrably a disease, is a developmental defect, minor and well-managed in some cases, crippling in others." Other conservatives found Decter useful on sexuality, too. Sociologist Robert Nisbet wrote that "The Boys on the Beach" revealed how "the self-serving, proselytizing voices of Gay Liberationists ally themselves naturally with the same voices from the radical Women's Liberationism [*sic*]." Both movements' "single objective is the devastation—through contempt, ridicule, and derision—of the family."[113]

Decter had long argued that the two movements were connected and endangered men and American masculinity. In a 1979 *Washington Post* interview, Decter made this connection explicit. She argued that American men had been "robbed of 'manliness'" over the course of the 1970s. She laid the blame for this emasculation mostly at the feet of the women's movement, which had removed "traditional demands such as having to support a family." But homosexuality was equally culpable. "Now everyone chooses his role," she complained. That had resulted "in a generation of men who are neurasthenic, narcissistic, they're running all the time greasing their bodies and doing this that and the other thing to go through the substitute motions of manliness."[114]

In a 1984 *Commentary* essay titled "Liberating Women: Who Benefits?" Decter quipped that the women's movement "unexpectedly brought about the liberation of men" by releasing them from their long-standing responsibilities to women. Men were now free to "withdraw emotionally, physically, and in the end financially," she wrote. "Call a man a pig often enough," she continued, "and he will soon discover there is little advantage in not behaving like one." Decter argued that feminists' attempts to restructure sex roles, marriage, and the family wage system had emasculated men to the detriment of both sexes and of society at large. Men were no longer required to support wives and children, "their own primary 'responsibility' being to themselves." But Decter warned that "in the long run or not so long run, they are beset by the symptoms of a decisive diminution of self-respect." Women too suffered from "male withdrawal." They complained of men who were "wimps and tell stories . . . of sick vanity, of self-preoccupation, of fears and narcissistic anxieties—in other words, of unmanliness." All of this boded ill for American society. It exacerbated the problem of single motherhood, weakened the social order, and rendered America impotent.[115] Decter's analysis of sex and gender touched on most issues that came to define the Republican Party by 1980.

Neoconservatism and Foreign Policy: The Culture of Appeasement

Decter's analysis of gender also filtered into neoconservative foreign policy. Throughout the 1970s, neoconservatives warned that the foreign policy establishment was too influenced by leftist propaganda, which had maligned the use of military force after Vietnam. With the election of Ronald Reagan in 1980 they hoped to reverse this impotency. Neocons opined that the administration should not just restore the policy of containment but roll back and ultimately defeat communism.

Three years before Reagan's election, Norman Podhoretz attacked homosexuals for causing a broader societal impotency in the United States. In an article titled "The Culture of Appeasement," which appeared in *Harper's* in October 1977 (Decter was no longer an editor there), Podhoretz blamed homosexuals for emasculating America on the world stage, something he linked to its post-Vietnam American foreign policy. Podhoretz, as the next chapter shows, had also long been preoccupied with sex and gender. Many of his own writings were fixated on masculinity. But the language he used in the "Culture of Appeasement" was different from any of his past writings. It had clear parallels to Decter's writings. Decter claimed that the two never collaborated nor read each other's work while in progress. "Sometimes we made suggestions but for the most part not," she said.[116] "The Culture of Appeasement," however, reflected Decter's influence.

Podhoretz began "The Culture of Appeasement" with an observation: "successive traumas of Vietnam and Watergate brought Americans a decade of self-doubt, self-criticism, [and] self-loathing." This enervation was particularly evident in the "undifferentiated fear, loathing, and revulsion that the prospect of war now seems to inspire." A "naive pacifism," he continued, had taken hold, which advanced the view that "nothing good was accomplished by American troops and American arms, only evil: only destruction, misery, murder, and guilt." Such "pacificist ideologues," Podhoretz argued, had also "Vietnamized" the past. Popular 1960s novels like *Catch 22* and *Slaughterhouse-Five* convinced many Americans that "not even World War II, the war against Hitler, was worth fighting." Podhoretz then turned his attention to the future. "Have we," he asked, "been plunged by Vietnam into so great a fear of Communism that we can no longer summon the will to resist?" The answer, he feared, was yes. The inability to deter Soviet aggression and the refusal to flex military muscle abroad, what neoconservatives began diagnosing in 1975 as a "failure of nerve," was akin to emasculation.[117]

Podhoretz's article was part of a larger discourse that emerged among conservatives in the late 1970s that sought to discredit a so-called "Vietnam syndrome". "Vietnam conferred a deep wariness," writes historian David Greenberg, "about military intervention" among many Americans, especially those on the left who did not want to see the United States engage in conflicts abroad unless national security was at stake, and national security needed to be more narrowly defined than it had been after World War II. Vietnam also "chastened many Cold Warriors" by demolishing "the domino-theory logic that had transformed the moderate policy of containment into an untenable duty to police the world for Communist influence."[118] Conservatives, however, maintained that the United States lost in Vietnam not because of an overly expansive vision or because of bankrupt or immoral policies but rather because of "a failure of political will." They believed that had the United States applied military force more effectively it could have prevailed in Vietnam. Moreover, they warned that a Vietnam syndrome risked impeding future American military actions abroad and thus would discredit American power and prestige on the world stage. Conservatives of many stripes railed against the Vietnam syndrome but neoconservatives led the charge.[119]

Podhoretz's analysis of the Vietnam syndrome echoed Decter's writings on sex roles, feminism, and sexuality. Podhoretz argued that emasculation underlay the Vietnam syndrome and explicitly blamed homosexuals for sapping American resolve. To make this argument, he compared America in the 1970s to Great Britain after World War I. Although the United States lost Vietnam while Britain was on the winning side of its war, it was an apt comparison, in Podhoretz's view, since "World War I took so great a toll of lives and ideals that for all practical purposes it was experienced by the British as a defeat." This feeling of defeat, Podhoretz argued, provided space for homosexual writers in the 1930s to bemoan English society and incite a general contempt among English youth toward "middle-class or indeed any kind of heterosexual adult life." These attitudes, moreover, directly contributed to Britain's appeasement of Hitler a decade later. "No wonder, then, that so many of those who resented their own country to the point of pledging never to fight for it and even, in a few instances, to the point of joining forces with its enemies, should have been, or should have chosen to become, homosexuals," Podhoretz wrote. He continued:

> For whatever else homosexuality may be or may be caused by, to these young men of the English upper class it represented . . . the refusal of fatherhood and all that fatherhood entailed: responsibility for a family and therefore an inescapable implication in the destiny of society as a whole. And that so many of the privileged young of England "no longer wanted to grow up to become fathers themselves" also meant that they were repudiating their birthright as successors to their own fathers in assuming a direct responsibility for the fate of the country.[120]

Podhoretz then blamed homosexuals for propagating America's pacifist attitude toward war after the defeat in Vietnam. Like Britain during the interwar years, "homosexual apologetics" were ubiquitous in 1970s America, Podhoretz wrote. Gay American writers like Allen Ginsberg, James

Baldwin, and Gore Vidal, he argued, inspired "the same combination of pacifism (with Vietnam standing in for World War I), hostility to one's own country and its putatively dreary middle-class way of life, and derision of the idea that it stands for anything worth defending." The result was an emasculated America unprepared to guard itself against the Soviet Union and Third World insurrections. "A generation raised on pacifism and contempt for the life of its own society," Podhoretz warned, would be unable to mount the necessary defense against communism and any other threats. In "The Culture of Appeasement," Podhoretz reiterated Decter's view that homosexuals rejected the mature responsibilities of fatherhood. But he raised the stakes by blaming homosexuals not only for the emasculation of domestic society but America's position on the world stage.[121]

Decter and the Fusion of Postwar Conservatism

In the early 1980s, Decter too turned her attention to foreign affairs. She founded the Committee for the Free World in 1981. Her goals in that initiative were to "alter the climate of confusion and complacency, apathy and self-denigration, that has done much to weaken Western democracies" and to embolden the United States and NATO to defend "the non-communist world against the rising menace of totalitarianism." She had concluded, as she told scholar John Ehrman in 1991, that "domestic policy was foreign policy, and vice versa."[122]

By 1995 Decter felt the category *neoconservative* was obsolete. "There are no more neoconservatives," she declared, so ingrained were they in the conservative movement.[123] Decter spoke too soon. Since the US invasion of Iraq in 2003, neoconservatism has referred mainly to an aggressive, regime-changing idealism in foreign affairs closely aligned with the administration of George W. Bush.[124] While a militant, "hard" anticommunism was always central to their politics, neoconservatives initially focused more on domestic than foreign affairs. "How the term 'neoconservatism' morphed from a political tendency that dealt almost entirely with domestic social policy to one that deals almost entirely—indeed, entirely—with foreign policy is an interesting question," Nathan Glazer, who had ties to the original architects of neoconservatism, wondered in 2005.[125] Decter's writings provide a crucial link. The gender anxieties she first articulated in articles about feminism filtered into neoconservative discourses on foreign affairs. After Vietnam, neoconservatives lamented a "failure of nerve" in American foreign policy and warned that a resistance to flex military might had rendered America impotent. Podhoretz, the subject of the next chapter, was central to shaping this discourse. But this emasculation had begun at home, and Decter first identified it.

Decter's writings on social issues also played a decisive role in integrating the neocons into the larger conservative movement. So-called paleoconservatives, some reared in the anti-Semitism of the Old Right, were initially wary of this group because they had so recently been Democrats and because so many were Jews, a religious community long associated with liberal and leftist politics in the United States. Decter's long-standing conservative positions on what became "family values" issues helped assuage those concerns.[126]

That Decter arrived at "family values" through Freudianism, not through conservative Christianity, was ultimately helpful to the broader movement. In 1980 the Heritage Foundation named Decter to its board of trustees. According to its president Edwin J. Feulner Jr., Decter exemplified that "common ground" existed within the strands of the movement and that "the old divisions among conservatives" made "no sense."[127] Founded in 1973 as "a nonpartisan public policy research institution dedicated to the principles of free enterprise, limited government, individual liberty and a strong national defense," the Heritage Foundation sought "to be a 'fusionist' think tank," according to historian Jason Stahl, one that could "speak for all the impulses of postwar conservatism at once."[128] Decter embodied this objective.

When Decter first "went to the Heritage Foundation Board meeting and sat down," she later recalled, "there was nothing I heard, or nothing that was discussed, or nothing anybody said, or advocated, or wondered about, that was the least bit alien to me." She had become a fierce defender of "family values," which she said meant "among other things no condoms and no introduction to homosexuality and no teaching about anal sex in the schools."[129]

In 1998 the Heritage Foundation published a collection of essays by what it considered the fifteen most influential conservative thinkers. It included Decter alongside such luminaries as Milton Friedman, Whittaker Chambers, and Ronald Reagan. According to Feulner, Decter had "made at least three major contributions to the development of conservatism in America." First, "an insightful, timely critique of feminism" that extended "beyond a critique of feminism to a defense of the family." Second, she provided "a resolute defense of democracy against tyranny." Finally, Decter had "a keen understanding of those commitments which unite every element of the conservative movement." She was, according to the Heritage Foundation, "the first lady of neoconservatism."[130]

CHAPTER SEVEN

"'Sissy,' the Most Dreaded Epithet of an American Boyhood"

NORMAN PODHORETZ AND JEWISH MASCULINITY ON THE RIGHT

IF ANY NEW YORK INTELLECTUAL could take the concept of writing like a man to its limits, it was Norman Podhoretz, editor of *Commentary* magazine from 1960 to 1995. One of the most pugnacious intellectuals in the group, he helped forge what came to be known as neoconservatism in the early 1970s. Podhoretz famously charted his political conversion from self-identified radical to neoconservative in his 1979 memoir, *Breaking Ranks*. According to his version of events, after he took over as editor of *Commentary* in 1960, he moved the magazine in a leftward direction. Drawn to popular attacks on conformity and anti-communist orthodoxy that sprung up in the late 1950s, he broke free from the "new liberalism— the kind that was at once pro-American and anti-Communist"—of his predecessor generation of New York intellectuals and embraced the emerging New Left. Podhoretz inaugurated his editorship of *Commentary* by serializing the social critic Paul Goodman's trenchant critique of American life in *Growing Up Absurd*, thereby announcing his and the magazine's turn toward the youthful future and his rejection of the stodgy liberal establishment that occupied America from the center.[1]

By the late 1960s, however, Podhoretz's association with radicalism ended. Dismayed by the violent militancy of the New Left and what he viewed as the movement's anti-Americanism, Podhoretz shifted politically

rightward. In *Breaking Ranks*, he concluded that the radicalism of the sixties was an "infection of self-hatred and self-contempt" so perilous that it
jeopardized everything from American foreign policy to traditional gender
roles. He characterized the radicalism of the decade as a "plague." Symptoms first appeared among the "white young," who refused "to assume
responsibility for themselves by taking their place in a world of adults,"
and among Blacks "in the form of a refusal to accept any responsibility
whatsoever for their own condition." By the late 1970s, the plague was
spreading "among the kind of women who do not wish to be women and
among those men who do not wish to be men." These radicals fostered a
culture of "sterility." Here, he distilled his horror over society's embrace
of the New Left and its spawn—feminism and gay rights—all the more
horrifying since he believed he had initially led the embrace. "This identification of sterility with vitality is what links the new narcissism of the Me
Decade to Women's Lib and the gay-rights movement, and it's what links
all of them to the radicalism of the sixties," Podhoretz warned.[2]

Other New York intellectuals shared Podhoretz's disdain of sixties radicalism. But few became Republicans. Diana Trilling was appalled by the
style of younger activists but remained a committed liberal. Irving Howe
and the *Dissent* crew were harshly critical of the New Left but maintained
a steadfast commitment to leftist politics.

In 1965 Irving Kristol and Daniel Bell founded the *Public Interest*, later
also edited by Nathan Glazer, which also became associated with neoconservatism. At the *Public Interest*, they supported the New Deal welfare
state but were critical of some of President Johnson's Great Society programs and other reform efforts. They concluded that such "social engi-
neering" did not always have its desired results of improving opportunities
for work and education but rather tended to encourage rioters and reward
idleness and crime.[3]

Yet few of the New York intellectuals initially associated with this "current of thought" or "mood," as James Q. Wilson later described neoconservatism, remained tied to neoconservatism for the long haul.[4] Daniel
Bell always rejected the neoconservative label. Bell left the *Public Interest*
in 1973 because he took issue with the increasingly conservative politics
of his coeditor, Irving Kristol. In 1972, Kristol voted for Nixon, something
he joked was "the equivalent of a Jew ostentatiously eating pork on Yom
Kippur."[5] Bell maintained that he was "a socialist in economics, a liberal
in politics, and a conservative in culture."[6] Nathan Glazer eventually dis-
tanced himself from the movement, too.[7] Bell once quipped, "When I read
about neoconservatism, I think, 'That isn't neoconservatism; that's just

Irving.'"[8] Kristol famously defined a neoconservative "as a liberal mugged by reality."

Yet Kristol, long known as the "godfather" of neoconservatism, eventually did not fit within the confines of neoconservatism either. While a militant "hard" anti-communism had always been central to the politics of the New York intellectuals, those who shifted rightward initially did so in response to domestic politics—to the violent militancy of New Left radicalism and to what they perceived as the Democratic Party's capitulation to radicalism in the 1970s with policies like affirmative action. But by the early twenty-first century, neoconservatism was almost wholly associated with foreign policy. Neoconservatism now denotes an assertive, critics would say belligerent, approach to foreign policy closely aligned with the Republican administration of George W. Bush and the invasion of Iraq in 2003. Kristol had little to do with foreign policy.[9]

Podhoretz and his wife Midge Decter, the subject of the previous chapter, are the exceptions. The unique durability of their ideological commitment should call our attention to how it developed. Both have spanned the entire trajectory of neoconservatism over the last forty years. Both Podhoretz and Decter were also long preoccupied with gender. Gender, moreover, links the domestic and foreign politics of neoconservatism over the *longue durée*.

Podhoretz's gendered language about "sterility" was not new. It had long been his signature in cultural criticism. Concerns about masculinity—traditionally Jewish and aspirationally all-American—undergirded Podhoretz's interventions in the policy battles and culture wars of the 1970s and 1980s. Those concerns played a central role in the politics of neoconservatism because they were useful to neocons, whether they felt those concerns as deeply as Podhoretz or not. His gender obsessions supply us with a lens to see neoconservatism as Podhoretz was helping to establish it. Far from a late-1960s reaction, his gender fixations were a reservoir that had been filling for years with insights into his own psychic struggle and that of aspiring American men of his generation, Jewish and not.

Podhoretz's concerns about gender also overlapped with Decter's. Decter had been writing about masculinity, sex roles, and sexuality since the mid-1950s. Podhoretz rarely gave his wife credit for her pioneering work in post–World War II sexual conservatism. Rather, he ruminated on his own history of personal affronts and slights upon his masculinity as a boy and young man. But we should never forget that the project was a joint one. Decter, as the last chapter chronicled, was crucial to integrating the neoconservatives into the larger conservative movement.

Scholars have generally been deaf to Podhoretz's gender anxieties, however. Some have warned that "psychological" approaches tend to reduce the political transformation of "lapsed-radicals-turned-neoconservatives" like Podhoretz to head cases "who hate their fathers, and envy the sexual potency of blacks."[10] The point here, however, is to show that for Podhoretz and Decter, gender anxieties played key roles. Thanks in significant part to them, and through their evocative and provocative goading and their guiding talents in the political realignment of the last decades of the Cold War, neoconservative politics tapped into deeper attachments and fears than disdain for the young radicals who dominated the media spotlight of the 1960s.

The only way to avoid exaggeration of the psychological issues—and the equal and opposite error, denial of them—is to examine the language of Podhoretz's preferred writing style closely. And to take it seriously. He used autobiographical forms to explore social issues. After finding his voice, and alighting on a winning formula, in his famous 1963 essay, "My Negro Problem—and Ours," he published three memoirs that hit similarly deep nerves in modern America's collective psyche. In addition to *Breaking Ranks* in 1979, there was *Making It* in 1967 and *Ex-Friends* in 1999. Gender anxieties are evident in nearly all his writings. *Making It* and *Breaking Ranks* unite around Podhoretz's struggle to construct a masculine persona. In the three decades of his prime as a writer, he reflected over his whole past life, which he dared to think typical and hoped would be exemplary. More than any other New York intellectual, Podhoretz wrote explicitly about his experiences as a Jewish man coming of age in mid-century America.

Throughout, he struggled to reconcile the New York intellectuals' ideology of secular Jewish masculinity, which valued combative intellectualism, with more normative American values of toughness, athleticism, and strength. While his struggles on their own do not explain neoconservatism, they do provide insight into Podhoretz's conservative politics and how gender shaped neoconservatism. By 1980, those politics centered on muscular militarism in foreign affairs and family values at home.

From Brooklyn to Manhattan

Podhoretz did not train in the art of intellectual combat at CCNY during the Depression. He was part of the last generation of New York intellectuals who came of age after World War II. Podhoretz attended Columbia University where he studied under Lionel Trilling, who first introduced

him to the New York intellectual "family." Trilling helped arrange Podhoretz's first visit to the offices of *Commentary* in the early 1950s. There he
met Nathan Glazer, Irving Kristol, Clement Greenberg, and Robert Warshow, all associate editors. In *Making It*, Podhoretz connected these men
to a tradition of Jewish Ashkenazi masculinity that had long venerated
Talmudic scholars. These young editors, who surely "numbered" Talmudic scholars "among their forefathers," knew "everything," and "'everything' means *everything*."[11] Podhoretz wanted to join their ranks. He later
recalled thinking they "were exactly the kind of people I was yearning to
be associated with."[12] He thus set out to master their writing style, which
he described as "characteristically hypercritical, learned, allusive"—their
ideology of secular Jewish masculinity. While he "was still a million miles
from the mastery of this art" in the 1950s, he was "practicing it, the first
young man in many years to do so with any authority."[13]

Podhoretz's battle between brains and brawn first took root on the
streets of Brownsville, Brooklyn, where he was born in 1930. Like most
New York intellectuals, Podhoretz was the child of Eastern European
immigrants. His parents came to the United States separately as teenagers
from Galicia, in present-day southeastern Poland and eastern Ukraine.
His father, Julius, was a milkman, an occupation that provided relatively
steady work during the Depression and spared the family the devastating
poverty experienced by many immigrant families. Yet Julius still struggled economically. When trucks replaced horses and wagons, he lost his
job because he did not know how to drive. The "humiliation" lived on in
his son's memory. Podhoretz also felt his father was a "true intellectual."
He read voraciously but lacked an outlet for his intellectual aspirations.
In Podhoretz's view, he was a "defeated man," unable to perform either
American (breadwinner) or Jewish (intellectual) standards of masculinity.
Julius's "influence—dark and underground—," writes Podhoretz's biographer, "is palpable in Norman's fulfillment of the intellectual aspirations he
vaguely harbored."[14]

The Brownsville of Podhoretz's youth was a neighborhood of working-
class Jews, Italians, and African Americans. Masculine competition
among these groups was fierce. In his famous 1963 essay, "My Negro Problem—and Ours," Podhoretz recalled how Black kids in the neighborhood
bullied him because he was a good student. He was smart and obedient,
so they called him a "sissy," "the most dreaded epithet of an American
boyhood." In *Making It*, however, Podhoretz also bragged about gaining
admittance into Brownsville's toughest street gang, the Cherokees. As a
"mediocre athlete and a notoriously good student" it was not easy for "me

to win acceptance from a gang which prided itself mainly on its masculinity and contempt for authority."[15]

Podhoretz saw physical strength as a masculine quality at odds with intellect. He would spend much of his life trying to reconcile these qualities. "What turned you into a writer and not a street fighter," the journalist Al Aronowitz told Podhoretz shortly after the publication of "My Negro Problem—and Ours," was "the fear that left you the loser and victim in the schoolyard." According to Aronowitz, "Every [Black man] who ever beat you up, contributed in some way to whatever success you now have. . . . Somewhere deep inside, you knew you were going to get even for the hurt—not with him, but with the world and it made you work that much harder."[16]

The first few chapters of *Making It* chronicled how Podhoretz got out of Brownsville. "One of the longest journeys in the world is the journey from Brooklyn to Manhattan," Podhoretz wrote in the first line of the first chapter.[17] Podhoretz may have never made it out of Brownsville if not for a teacher who saw his academic potential and made it her mission to turn "a filthy little slum child" into a cultured gentleman capable of getting into an Ivy League university. Though Podhoretz resented this teacher's condescension toward his immigrant roots, he appreciated her efforts.[18] "She was saying that because I was a talented boy, a better class of people stood ready to admit me into their ranks. But only on one condition: I had to signify by my general deportment that I acknowledge them as *superior* to the class of people among whom I happened to have been born. That was the bargain—take it or leave it."[19] In *Making It* Podhoretz cast this choice in terms of class. But it was also about gender. Podhoretz's "brutal bargain" meant he would have to reconcile two different notions of masculinity—Jewish and American.

While Podhoretz was accepted into genteel Harvard, he enrolled at Columbia because it offered a full scholarship with stipend. There he set to work on his masculinity. He imagined that the university, in the Morningside Heights neighborhood of Manhattan, would "make a gentleman out of any young man of 'foreign stock.' . . . In other words, me." Morningside Heights was also the home of the Jewish Theological Seminary (JTS), where Podhoretz simultaneously enrolled to appease his father. But he found the quality of education at JTS lacking. He was put off by "the strident note of apologetics and defensiveness which entered into the least detail of almost every aspect of the Seminary curriculum, the endless pep talks disguised as scholarship, the endless harping on the suffering of the Jews."[20] Here Podhoretz echoed some of the critiques that the *Menorah* writers made of Jewish life in the 1920s and 30s: victimhood and apology emasculated Jews.

Podhoretz was more enamored of the English Department at Columbia, where he studied under Lionel Trilling, F. W. Dupee, and Richard Chase. Those teachers "were our mentors, our models, our gods. In the classroom as on paper."[21] Podhoretz was especially close to Trilling, whom he described as a "foster father."[22] Trilling embodied a less combative masculine persona than most New York intellectuals. The first tenured Jew in the English Department at Columbia, Trilling "lay claim to Anglo-American high culture, even as the son of Jewish immigrants," writes historian Michael Kimmage.[23] While some New York intellectuals resented what they judged as contrived pretensions, others looked up to Trilling as an authentic model of Jewish gentility, Podhoretz included. Yet Podhoretz found it difficult to reconcile his own Jewishness with the gentility his academic advisor seemed so seamlessly to embody. Nor was he sure he wanted to. Columbia sought to turn him into "a gentleman, a man of enlightened and gracious mind!" As he wrote in *Making It*, that "also meant 'Become a facsimile WASP!'"[24]

Podhoretz also struggled socially at Columbia. He aroused "much hostility among certain Columbia types," he wrote in *Making It*. They included "the prep-school boys, those B students" who were jealous of his academic acumen as well as "the homosexuals with their supercilious disdain of my lower-class style of dress and my brash and impudent manner; and the prissily bred middle class Jews who thought me insufferably crude."[25] Though homophobic language was practically universal in the 1960s, it is worth noting Podhoretz's use of it in these early years. He used that language with persistence and relish. By the 1970s, when some liberals were beginning to embrace gay rights, it would flavor Podhoretz's defiantly conservative politics.

After graduating from Columbia, Podhoretz won a two-year fellowship to study at Cambridge University with the famed literary critic F. R. Leavis. Podhoretz hoped to follow in Trilling's footsteps by pursuing a doctorate in English, either at Cambridge or back in the States. But when Leavis asked Podhoretz to contribute to his prestigious literary journal, *Scrutiny*, he began to rethink his career plans. Leavis's invitation to review Trilling's 1949 book, *The Liberal Imagination*, provoked "a crazy succession of reactions," Podhoretz confided in a letter to Trilling: "Excitement, trepidation, but mostly ambition."[26]

After his review appeared in print, Trilling wrote to *Commentary*'s editorial staff to recommend his former student as a contributor. Podhoretz was a "remarkable undergraduate," "a first-class Hebraist (ancient and modern), a good writer, and a brilliant scholar," Trilling stated in a letter to the magazine's editors. "You'll find him [to be] a real intellectual with ambitions."[27] "Lionel Trilling has mentioned your name to us," Irving Kristol, an associate editor at *Commentary*, responded in the winter of 1952, so "naturally, we are more than a little interested."[28]

When Podhoretz returned home from Cambridge to New York in the summer of 1952, he visited the *Commentary* offices. There he met Elliot Cohen for the first time, who gave Podhoretz his first book to review for the magazine. Though Podhoretz returned to England to complete his fellowship, he was increasingly sure he would pursue a career as a literary critic rather than as an academic. "If I have to write literary criticism I want to do the sort of thing you've done," he wrote to Trilling. In a later letter he confided that if "writing is going to be my life. . . . I want to get on with it right away. The only prospect I find attractive for the future is being something instead of preparing to become something."[29]

After he returned home permanently from Cambridge in the summer of 1953, and was ready to begin his writing career, he received a draft summons. Six months later he reported to basic training at Fort Dix, New Jersey. In the intervening six months, Podhoretz wrote as many reviews as he could for *Commentary*.

A particularly scathing review of Saul Bellow's otherwise widely praised novel *The Adventures of Augie March* (1953) caught the attention of Philip Rahv, one of the two "patriarchs" of *Partisan Review*. Rahv invited Podhoretz over to his home for a night of heavy drinking. Among "most of the literary people I knew," Podhoretz later mused, "it was regarded as manly to drink a lot, and one took pride in being able to hold one's liquor."[30] The evening ended with an invitation to write for *PR*, something Podhoretz equated in *Making It* to "a bar mitzvah ceremony." Contributing to *PR* "signified, like that ancient Jewish rite itself, that I had finally come of age."[31] A bar mitzvah is the Jewish ritual that marks when a boy becomes a man at age thirteen after reading from the Torah. Podhoretz viewed publishing in *Commentary* and *PR* in the same way.

Cohen promised Podhoretz a job as an associate editor after he was discharged from the army. He would replace Kristol, who was leaving to edit a new magazine, *Encounter*. At a going-away party before Podhoretz departed for Fort Dix, Cohen gave him a fountain pen. "Now did my cup truly run over. Today, as bar mitzvah boys always say, I was indeed a man."[32] Podhoretz did not just use the bar mitzvah metaphor in retrospect, but as he experienced these events at the time. After Trilling told

Podhoretz he could call him by his first name in a 1955 letter, Podhoretz replied that "I have been calling you Lionel behind your back for years, so I'm glad you made an honest man out of me." The official sanction, however, felt "like a new Bar Mitzvah for me!"[33] Podhoretz felt he had finally entered the covenant of secular Jewish masculinity that bound the New York intellectuals. "To be adopted into the family was a mark of great distinction," he explained in *Making It*. "It meant you were good enough, that you *existed* as a writer and an intellectual." It meant you could write like a man.[34]

But before he could focus fully on his career and further cultivating the New York intellectual's ideology of secular Jewish masculinity, Podhoretz turned his attention to proving his American manhood in the armed services. Unlike most of the other New York intellectuals, Podhoretz claimed he welcomed the opportunity to serve in the military. Most of the others did not serve during World War II and of those who did, few saw combat. The Korean War offered the younger Podhoretz a chance to do what they largely shirked. Podhoretz viewed the army as "a test of masculinity—something like a delayed puberty rite," he wrote in *Making It*. "You weren't a man, in fact, unless you had been in the army."[35]

But when Podhoretz arrived at Fort Dix in the winter of 1954 he was quickly disabused of any romantic notions about military service. He struggled with the lack of freedom, the stifling of individuality, and especially the physical challenges. "I feel pretty miserable," he confided in a letter to Trilling. "I'm a little ashamed of myself for being unhappy."[36] His fellow cadets all seemed tougher and stronger. "They could double-time forever without so much as a pant; they could do a hundred pushups without showing the strain," Podhoretz later wrote in *Making It*, "while I was always an inch away from total collapse." He was embarrassed by his "ineptitude with equipment; as a civilian, I had regarded such ineptitude as charming and perhaps even as a sign of spiritual superiority, but now there was nothing charming in it at all, and if it was a sign of anything, it was a sign of dependency and of my inability to manage the world like a man."[37]

Yet when Podhoretz deployed to Germany, he found his masculinity validated by presiding officers. It was not his physical ability but his intellect that they noticed. "Occasionally, an officer around here discovers that I was a 'professor' and asks me to give a training class to the company, on Communism, on the Meaning of the Cold War, or Our Moral Obligation to Serve," he wrote to Trilling.[38] Podhoretz concluded that intellectuality actually bolstered his manhood in the service. As a kid he "never" was "looked up to as a leader, for being good in school and mediocre at athletics made one's manliness suspect to 'the boys,'" he explained in *Making It*. But in the army "no one seemed to assume that manliness was compromised by education or even cultivation (no doubt my conversational habit of liberally mixing obscenities with big words did something to help this assumption along)."[39] Physical strength was thus not the only mark of manhood. "I've turned out to be a good soldier—I've even been chosen 'soldier of the month,' of our Battalion," Podhoretz told Trilling. "To tell you the truth, I'm prouder of that distinction than of any other."[40]

After two years in the army Podhoretz returned to New York to resume his literary career. Discharged in December 1955, he headed to *Commentary* where he presumed a job as an associate editor awaited him. But *Commentary* was not the same magazine. Most of its younger editors had departed: Kristol had moved to London to edit *Encounter*; Glazer left the magazine for a job as an editor at Anchor Books; and Warshow, whom Podhoretz particularly admired, died tragically of a heart attack in 1955. Most ominously, Cohen was on extended leave as he sought treatment for severe depression. In his place, Clement Greenberg and his younger brother Martin took over editorial responsibilities.[41]

The Greenberg brothers refused to hire Podhoretz as an associate editor but only at the rank of an assistant editor. That made Podhoretz angry. Cohen had promised him a position as an associate editor, which was the rank and title of all the other men on staff. The only other assistant editor was a woman, Sherry Abel. In Podhoretz's view, she had the skills to be an editor but did not want the responsibility. "If she had ever entertained any ambitions for herself in the working world, they had long ago been renounced or perhaps transferred to the men she admired."[42] From Podhoretz's viewpoint women were assistant editors, not men. Demotion made him feel emasculated. He swallowed his pride and took the job, however. He needed the experience and the paycheck.

His tenure at *Commentary* under the Greenberg brothers proved trying. He constantly felt slighted by the Greenbergs, who overruled his editorial work and excluded him from meetings. "I have virtually no autonomy, no authority to move on my own," he complained to a friend in the spring of 1956. Podhoretz felt like "a coward and a fool."[43]

After two years under the Greenbergs, Podhoretz quit. In an interview with the American Jewish Committee (AJC), he accused the brothers of running *Commentary* counter to Cohen's vision, and of secretly plotting a coup. "In thus committing the prime crime of American boyhood, snitching to the authorities, did I feel guilty?" Podhoretz asked in *Making It*.

"A little, but mostly I felt pleased with myself for having acted so selflessly, so nobly. . . . One does not start such a fight without being forced to finish it." Podhoretz cast his actions on a spectrum of masculinity. While being a snitch was the inverse of manly in 1950s America, Podhoretz felt he acted "nobly" and "selflessly" by defending Cohen and the magazine. Moreover, he had recouped his own "power" in the situation and reclaimed the masculine qualities of "sovereignty, autonomy, [and] freedom" when he quit.[44]

The AJC refused to accept Podhoretz's resignation. It launched a six-week investigation that resulted in the firing of Clement Greenberg and the promotion of Podhoretz to associate editor, alongside Martin Greenberg and George Lichtheim. Together, the three would run *Commentary* until Cohen returned.[45]

"Book Reviewing and Everyone I Know"

The situation, however, remained untenable, and Podhoretz quietly quit a few months later. By 1958 he was married with three children. In October 1956, when he was twenty-six years old, Podhoretz had married Midge Decter, a twenty-nine-year-old divorcee with two young daughters. The two first met as students at JTS but reconnected when Decter worked as Cohen's secretary at *Commentary*. They stayed in touch while Podhoretz was abroad and after a short courtship wed. In 1958 Decter gave birth to another daughter followed by a son in 1961.[46]

To support his growing family Podhoretz worked as a freelance reviewer. Book reviews often paid well in the affluent 1950s, especially at larger magazines. Reviews were also a masculine rite of passage for young critics on the make. "If there was a young writer around who wanted to try" to write for these journals, Decter later explained, "the way you broke into this game was doing a book review." They earned "their spurs by writing book reviews."[47]

Book reviews in the "family tradition" had to "relate an aesthetic judgment of the book to some social or cultural or literary issue outside the book itself."[48] The writer used the review not only to expound on the merits and especially deficiencies of a particular book but to show one's mastery of a subject or set of issues. "Everyone I know," Podhoretz wrote in 1963 following the launch of the *New York Review of Books*, a biweekly journal founded by his friend Jason Epstein and dedicated solely to this mode of writing, approached book reviews "quite simply, [as] an occasion to do some writing of their own."[49] In *Making It* Podhoretz likened writing reviews to an athlete exercising his muscles. "I choose the word 'exercise' deliberately, for articulateness on paper is a gift which does not differ greatly in principle from the gift of physical coordination we call athletic skill."[50] For Podhoretz, a strong writer, like "an all-round athlete," had to work his muscles.

In the 1950s, Podhoretz exercised his own muscles by writing reviews of American fiction. He wrote mostly on male novelists, including William Faulkner and F. Scott Fitzgerald. When he turned his attention to Jewish American writers, he was drawn to those who explored masculinity, including Norman Mailer, Saul Bellow, and Philip Roth. Podhoretz's early reviews appeared in *Commentary* and *Partisan Review*. He also published reviews in *Esquire*, the *New Republic*, the *New Yorker*, and *Show*, a high-paying monthly published between 1961 and 1965. Podhoretz was especially proud of simultaneously writing for *Partisan Review* and the *New Yorker*. The former was "the arbiter and embodiment of intellectual sophistication" while the latter was "the arbiter and embodiment of worldly sophistication." His appearance in both magazines proved he could write like a man in the mode of the New York intellectuals and appeal to a more genteel audience.[51]

Immaturity and the Beats

In 1956 Allen Ginsberg sent Podhoretz an advanced copy of *Howl and Other Poems*. Ginsburg and Podhoretz had overlapped at Columbia where both were students of Trilling's. Three years Podhoretz's senior, Ginsberg also published Podhoretz's first piece of writing, a poem, in a college literary journal he edited. Ginsberg cut the poem in half. Ginsberg later suggested that this had enraged Podhoretz so much that Podhoretz could never appreciate the Beats. Podhoretz later denied that, noting that he initially liked "Howl." But between 1957 and 1958 he wrote three reviews of the group, all critical.[52]

In his first review, which appeared in the *New Republic*, Podhoretz characterized "Howl" as "a remarkable poem." But he warned that the Beat writers were driven by an indiscriminate "conviction that any form of rebellion against American culture (which for them includes everything from suburbia and supermarkets to highbrow literary magazines like *Partisan Review*) is admirable, and they seem to regard homosexuality, jazz, dope-addiction, and vagrancy as outstanding examples of such rebellion." Ginsburg was as an exception. His "assault on America," Podhoretz wrote, was "a personal cry that rings true."[53]

In 1957 Podhoretz had been contemplating his own rebellion from middle-class America. In an article for the *New Leader* published that year, he fretted that his generation of writers, men born between 1925 and 1935, had too quickly become "civilized adult[s]: poised, sober, judicious, prudent." Too young to have participated in the radicalism of the 1930s, they came of age instead at the dawn of the Cold War. That conflict demanded "the qualities of *maturity* against the values of youth." Like most middle-class Americans after the Depression, these writers married young, had children, and focused on careers to support their growing families. Society admonished their generation to "stop carping at life like a petulant adolescent . . . and to get down to the business of adult living." Maturity for men in the 1950s meant marriage, family, and providing for a wife and children. Podhoretz initially sympathized with Ginsberg's "howl of protest" because it challenged the exaggerated constraints on 1950s gender roles. But Podhoretz's answer to the confines of maturity was not for his generation to abandon the role of husband, father, and breadwinner. It was to rebel by taking a manly "swim in the Plaza fountain in the middle of the night."[54]

In a December 1958 article for *Esquire*, Podhoretz claimed he favored a loosening of sexual mores. He attacked "the obsolete morality—disguised or not—of the new Victorians" of the Eisenhower era and criticized "the much-publicized religious revival" of the 1950s that had unleashed "the anti-secular forces in our society."[55] In an earlier unpublished draft of this essay Podhoretz elaborated on what he meant: "The idea has been spread around in any number of books and magazines (particularly ladies' magazines) that a man (let alone a woman) who deviates even slightly from the strictest Puritanism is a neurotic and that a wholesome old-fashioned domestic life in the suburbs (complete with a 58 car, presumably) is what Freud meant by psychic health and maturity." He applauded the Beats for drawing attention to the hypocrisy of sexual conservatism in the 1950s. "The conservative drivel that the fears and insecurities of the Cold War period have dredged up" had created space for "the insidious attempt by clerics in psychiatric clothing to make the freer sexual mores of a whole population seem disreputable and unhealthy by calling them 'immaturity.'"[56] In a section that was cut from the final *Esquire* version, Podhoretz explained that one needed only to wave "a copy of the Kinsey Report in the air" to realize that "our middle class has prostrated itself before every cleric in psychiatrist's clothing who uses the word 'maturity' when he really means sex is filthy."[57] Many Americans had sex before marriage and committed adultery. But these transgressions were within the confines of heterosexuality.

Podhoretz, however, opposed the Beats because they advocated an "immature" sexuality that opposed procreation and adult responsibilities.

While he did not explicitly mention homosexuality, he employed revisionist Freudian theories of healthy sexual development when he wrote in *Esquire* that, "The disobedience of a child with a weak father often takes the form of a tantrum, an explosion of undirected, incoherent, inarticulate rage and aggression. This, plus the need to organize the world by setting up authoritative standards in the absence of any provided by adults, is what much juvenile delinquency amounts to. And what juvenile delinquency is to life, the San Francisco writers are to literature."[58]

In *Esquire*, Podhoretz defended normative heterosexual masculinity. A creeping "puritanism" in the 1950s had created a "power vacuum," he warned, for the sexual deviancy of the Beats to flourish. To prevent Beat ideas from influencing young people, Podhoretz implored middle-class America to reject a sexual conservatism that had no basis in reality while affirming mature heterosexuality. "When I say that middle-class culture is flabby and spineless," Podhoretz explained, "I mean that it has grown defensive and timid about its (liberal and 'enlightened') values and has therefore proved unable to assert its authority over the young." The Beats capitalized on the "combination of hypocrisy with a paralysis of parental authority," which "contrived to turn the children loose to make their own rules." (This would again happen in the 1960s.) The Beat generation, Podhoretz argued, amounted to "a conspiracy to overthrow civilization (which is created by men, not boys) and to replace it not with a State of Nature . . . but by the world of the adolescent street gang." Bringing together his fears that the Beats endangered both American and Jewish (intellectual) norms of masculinity, Podhoretz warned: "The San Francisco writers, in their hatred of intelligence, their refusal to respect the requirements of artistic discipline, their contempt for precision and clarity are a perfect reflection of 'the fear of maturity,' the fear of becoming a man."[59]

A few months earlier Podhoretz had addressed the group from the lens of Jewish masculinity. "The Know-Nothing Bohemians," which appeared in the spring 1958 issue of *Partisan Review*, dealt with whether the Beats constituted a real intellectual current.[60] Podhoretz's answer was no. While "the Bohemianism of the 1920's" and "the radicalism of the 1930's was marked by deep intellectual seriousness," Podhoretz wrote, "the Bohemianism of the 1950's is another kettle of fish altogether." The Beats were "hostile to civilization" and expressed only "contempt for coherent, rational discourse which, being a product of the mind, is in their view a form of death." These views of the Beats paralleled the views of other New York intellectuals. For example, while some writers at *Dissent* were sympathetic to the Beats, Ned Polsky argued in 1957 that "the new bohemians' inferiority shows up clearly in its lack of intellectual content."[61] But Podhoretz went further. He heard an "anti-intellectualism" in Beat literature "so bitter that it makes the ordinary American's hatred of eggheads seem positively benign."[62] Podhoretz in turn called into question the intellectual masculinity of the Beats. He argued that the Beats were not only incoherent, but that there was a panicked cry in their collective work to "kill the intellectuals who can talk coherently, kill the people who can sit still for five minutes at a time, kill those incomprehensible characters who are capable of getting seriously involved with a woman, a job, a cause."[63]

Those commitments—woman, job, cause—encompassed the meaning of maturity in Podhoretz's America. Job and cause, perhaps even woman, could serve the artistic and intellectual mission of a changing society. The Beats' live-fast-and-die-young echo of the 1920s was actually stale by contrast. It surrendered to the tyranny of the moment. Their evanescent gestures were, as he said elsewhere, sterile and devoid of maturity. Podhoretz later conceded that his criticism of the Beats was partly personal. By 1958 he was married with three children. "In defending middle-class life against the Beats, I was speaking more personally than politically. In a sense, that is, it was myself and my own experience I was defending rather than my political ideas."[64]

Looking back on these pieces twenty years later, Podhoretz made his views about the Beats more explicit. These writers "feared maturity and the responsibilities it entailed as a limitation of their freedom. In fact, one of the reasons why so many of them were tempted into homosexuality," he added, "was that it allowed them to avoid becoming husbands and especially fathers—it was a way of never growing up, of trying to remain forever young." Though Podhoretz later denied that one could "read a right-wing motivation back into my criticisms of Beat writing," his contempt for that group foreshadowed his views of the counterculture and social movements of the 1960s. They also paralleled Decter's views of sex and gender, topics she started writing on in the late 1950s and early 1960s.[65]

Doings and Undoings

Podhoretz included "The Know-Nothing Bohemians" in his first book, *Doings and Undoings*, published in 1964. An anthology of essays, the book was meant to announce Podhoretz as a formidable voice in American literary life. The full-page author photo on the back cover portrayed Podhoretz as a tough and manly critic. It had Podhoretz looking directly at the camera with a cigarette dangling from his mouth like a literary James Dean.

FIGURE 12. The author photo of Norman Podhoretz in *Doings and Undoings*, a collection of essays and his first book (1964). © Gert Berliner.

Podhoretz included two reviews of women New York intellectuals in *Doings and Undoings*: Mary McCarthy and Hannah Arendt. In 1963 both had published books that garnered significant attention: McCarthy's bestseller, *The Group*, discussed in chapter 5, and Arendt's *Eichmann in Jerusalem: A Report on the Banality of Evil*, which originally appeared as a series of articles in the *New Yorker* in 1962. Podhoretz's review of Arendt was part of a larger controversy, discussed later in this chapter. Of interest here is the way Podhoretz's reviews of McCarthy and Arendt, when juxtaposed, reveal how women in this milieu couldn't win. They were either dismissed as "lady" writers who wrote on superficial topics or accused of trying too hard to be complex, which was how Podhoretz described Arendt.

Like other New York intellectuals, Podhoretz dismissed *The Group* as "a trivial lady writer's novel." The label was meant to sting. He gleefully told Philip Rahv that it was a "very nasty" review.[66] It initially appeared in *Show*, a magazine that paid well but that Podhoretz felt few people read. By including it in *Doings and Undoings*, Podhoretz sought to give it more exposure and make a statement about women writers. "If writers of fiction were forbidden to indulge themselves in elaborate descriptions of dress, furniture, and food—the way freshmen in composition courses use too many adjectives—virtually the whole tribe of contemporary lady novelists would instantly be forced out of business," he wrote in his review of *The Group*.[67]

Podhoretz took a different tack in his review of Arendt's *Eichmann*, published one month earlier in *Commentary*. Arendt held a somewhat distinct place in this group. Her 1951 book, *The Origins of Totalitarianism*, had established her as an unassailable critic of authoritarianism and, among other things, had vindicated the group's long-held anti-Stalinism.[68] Arendt's originality and brilliance, however, did not shield her from the onslaught of criticism that greeted her analysis of Eichmann. According to Podhoretz, Arendt's article was overly analytical and incapable of the potent simplifications that men were in the business of distilling from the disorder of reality. It was "a study in the perversity of brilliance."[69]

By including his reviews of McCarthy and Arendt in *Doings and Undoings*, along with his decision not to engage with any other women writers, Podhoretz conveyed that two of the most renowned women New York intellectuals did not write like men. In the case of McCarthy's fiction, it was superficial, unsophisticated, and shallow. In Arendt's it was the opposite—she spent no time on furniture but was overly academic and fine-grained.

Podhoretz knew some of the essays in *Doings and Undoings* would ruffle feathers, and he fretted over the book's reception. "I am nervous as hell about it," he told a friend. "Not only nervous about it but a little paranoid too: I have a feeling that everyone is lying in wait, eager for the opportunity to get back at me or something."[70] *Newsweek's* review of the book described Podhoretz as "the classic New York Jewish brain-athlete who catches liberal arts scholarships the way the sons of the Pennsylvania coal fields dig out football scholarships."[71] It was undoubtedly the response Podhoretz was looking for. But few other magazines took notice. *Doings and Undoings* made little noise. A more cacophonous reception awaited the publication of *Making It* three years later. The first of Podhoretz's memoirs, it charted how he became editor of *Commentary* and his rise in the New York intellectual "family."

The New Commentary

In 1959 the AJC began looking for a new editor for the magazine after Elliot Cohen lost his battle with depression and ended his life. Podhoretz was not initially high on the list of candidates. The AJC wanted an older, more established figure. Its initial wish list included Daniel Bell, Nathan Glazer, Irving Kristol, Alfred Kazin, Martin Greenberg, George Lichtheim, and Milton Himmelfarb.[72] Most of these men were either not interested in the job or unavailable. Bell "was deeply honored to have even been considered." But he felt Himmelfarb was the best choice. In a letter dated July 1959, Bell wrote that Himmelfarb "has great learning, which he wears lightly; he has a fine mind which is not dogmatic; he has unsurpassed knowledge of the Jewish community, and a deep love of Jewish tradition."[73] The AJC, however, wanted someone who could breathe new life into the magazine and attract a younger readership. Himmelfarb, a longtime AJC researcher, did not fit the bill.

For a while, Leslie Fiedler, an up-and-coming literary critic at Montana State University, was a leading contender.[74] Fiedler's reputation, however, was controversial. "Off the record," David Riesman described Fiedler to the AJC as "a very good example of the man who wants terribly to be fashionable and clever, and who could stand least of all being thought outdated."[75] While the AJC contemplated appointing Fiedler as "visiting editor-in-chief" on a trial basis, it ultimately decided he was too risky to hire.[76] When Fiedler did not get the job, he recommended Podhoretz, whom he viewed as an intellectual "ally." Though Podhoretz's name had previously been mentioned, it was not initially high on the list of possible candidates. Fiedler helped convince the AJC that a youthful vision was what the magazine needed.

Podhoretz told the AJC he would take the magazine in a new direction. He would publish young writers who questioned Cold War orthodoxy and would "make it more general—less parochially Jewish—both in its roster of contributors and in its range of topics."[77] As Podhoretz's name rose to the top of the list of candidates, Bell advised the AJC to split the difference and name Podhoretz and Himmelfarb as joint editors. "Podhoretz would provide the imagination, fire, drive, etc., that would incidentally attract lively contributors," Bell reasoned. "Himmelfarb would provide not only sound scholarship but an element which Podhoretz may lack to some degree, i.e., a continuing deep interest in Jewish communal matters." Ultimately, the AJC offered the position solely to Podhoretz. He was not yet thirty years old.[78]

Podhoretz has long maintained that when he became editor of *Commentary* in 1960, he moved the magazine leftward. He inaugurated his editorship by serializing Paul Goodman's *Growing Up Absurd* and thereafter published other leftist writers like Norman Mailer, William Appleman Williams, Herbert Marcuse, and Norman O. Brown. The inclusion of these writers was proof, Podhoretz wrote in *Breaking Ranks*, that "I was in the final stages of a process that had been carrying me from the liberalism with which I had grown up to the radicalism with which I would be identified for most of the decade ahead": the radicalism of the New Left.[79]

Examination of his work before and after those years is making it increasingly unclear, however, whether Podhoretz ever shared the views of the New Left or even the predecessors they found in Goodman, Marcuse, Brown, and the Beat writers. As a new editor of a major intellectual magazine, he needed to make a strong impression and to distinguish himself from his predecessor. Podhoretz had the "impulse," according to his wife Midge Decter, "to do a little shaking up."[80] He wanted to be at the forefront of cultural trends. In 1960, America was leaning leftward. Diana Trilling sensed as much. She wrote a letter to Podhoretz shortly after he became editor noting his more "modern, flexible" approach to domestic affairs, which she conceded was a "necessary corrective to the sterile anti-Communism of your predecessor generation." But she added, "no doubt the Zeitgeist is with you."[81] Philip Rahv told Ted Solotaroff, an associate editor at *Commentary*, that he believed Podhoretz was "much more a 'political swinger' than he was a radical."[82]

When asked to contribute an introduction for an anthology of New Left writers in the early 1960s, Podhoretz declined. "While I'm on the whole sympathetic to the younger radicals," he wrote in a letter, "I am also highly critical of some of their attitudes and ideas."[83] After *Dissent* magazine published a symposium on the new radicalism in its spring 1962 issue, Podhoretz wrote to one its editors, Lewis Coser, lauding his critical analysis of the subject. "Most of those people are my contemporaries," Podhoretz noted, "but I find myself increasingly out of sympathy with them, and for exactly the reasons you specified in your piece."[84]

Podhoretz also declined to publish essays by Tom Hayden, a founder of Students for a Democratic Society (SDS). In 1961 he rejected Hayden's account of the National Student Association conference at the University of Minnesota.[85] Two years later, he rejected another piece by Hayden. He told Hayden he was "disturbed by the straw-man picture you draw of the liberal. If you want to attack a position effectively," he continued, "surely the thing to do is attack it at its best and not by setting up an unmodulated caricature that makes an easy polemical target." While he told Hayden that "I think the work you are trying to do is important," Podhoretz also declined to publish the *Port Huron Statement*, SDS's formative manifesto.[86] Podhoretz later claimed he felt it was made up of "clichés" and rudimentary regurgitations of critiques made more eloquently by older social critics like David Riesman, C. Wright Mills, and Paul Goodman. In Podhoretz's view, the *Port Huron Statement* was full of "callow and derivative language" and was "stripped of all complexity, qualification, and nuance."[87] His greatest regret in not publishing it was the fame it later acquired as a historical document. But that was long in the future. While Podhoretz published some intellectual gurus of the New Left, he never fully embraced its ideological radicalism.[88]

Significantly, Podhoretz wrote very little during the early 1960s. That makes an assessment of his ideological state of mind difficult. In the early 1960s he was in the midst of an extended writer's block, a "literary impotency."

Podhoretz experienced his inability to write in the early 1960s as emasculating. In *Making It* he compared it to the failure to achieve an erection. For a writer, Podhoretz explained, the act of writing "is not within the power of his will to summon it forth if it refuses to come; nor is he capable of resisting it for long when it starts to demand release." He continued:

> What, according to St. Augustine, the penis is to the body—he said it was the only limb or "member" which defied the control of the will, which, that is, actually had a will of its own, rising and falling of its own accord and not, like the arms or the legs, at the dictates of the "owner's" will—the act of writing is to the mind. In fact, so closely connected in some obscure way are the two phenomena, with the ability to write resembling the experience of sexual potency and the inability to write resembling the experience of sexual impotence, that many men have a strong impulse to masturbate when they are about to start on a piece of writing, as though to persuade themselves that they *are* in control, that they can get it up and make it come.[89]

Podhoretz's "impotency" dissipated when he started to write "monthly reviews for a new not very good magazine called *Show*" in 1962. "They pay a lot and greed seems to have been the effective answer to my writer's block," he told a friend.[90] In *Making It*, Podhoretz explained it this way: "for the first time in my literary career I set out to write not for fame but for money," and in the process "made the wonderful discovery that money could not only buy steak at the Palm but could break through a block as well."[91]

1963

It was not until three years into his editorship of *Commentary* that Podhoretz fully broke through his writer's block. In 1963 he published two significant long pieces: "My Negro Problem—and Ours," followed a couple months later with "Hannah Arendt on Eichmann." The first "wrote itself—over a long weekend at home, in three hot, blissful sessions at the typewriter" in response to James Baldwin's 1963 book, *The Fire Next Time*, which also first appeared in the *New Yorker*.[92] "My Negro Problem—and Ours" was not simply a book review. "The honesty of the essay" made it different from his past writings and established the mode of writing Podhoretz would turn to repeatedly in the future: memoir as a lens to examine social conflicts. As Podhoretz later attested, that essay "was the first piece I had ever written in a voice that belonged entirely to me."[93] Notably, these two articles from 1963 were the only long pieces that Podhoretz wrote between 1960 and 1970, years that he claimed encompassed his radicalism.

Podhoretz long maintained that he commissioned Baldwin to write the essay that became *The Fire Next Time*. He had heard Baldwin speak in the early 1960s on various television and radio programs about the civil rights movement and the growing influence of the Nation of Islam (NOI). After one of these appearances, he approached Baldwin about writing on the topic. Baldwin had written for the "old *Commentary*" under Cohen, and Podhoretz was eager to have him appear in the magazine under his editorship. Podhoretz told Baldwin that he felt "*Commentary* has a real job to do interpreting Negro militancy to the white liberal community."[94] But when Baldwin finished his essay, he sent it to William Shawn at the *New Yorker* for more money. Podhoretz was incensed, angered both by what he saw as a violation of journalistic ethics and by the substance of Baldwin's essay. In an angry confrontation over the essay, he told Baldwin that when he was growing up in Brownsville, it was Blacks who tormented whites. Baldwin listened intently, and then said: "You ought . . . to write it all down."[95]

Podhoretz has repeated this story multiple times over the years. In *Making It*, he described telling Baldwin during their heated meeting that the only reason he got away with selling a commissioned article to another publication was because of liberal guilt toward Blacks. But if Baldwin thought Podhoretz "felt guilty towards him or any other Negro, he was very much mistaken. Neither I nor my ancestors had ever wronged the Negroes; on the contrary, I had grown up in an 'integrated' slum neighborhood where it was the Negroes who persecuted the whites and not the other way round."[96] In *Breaking Ranks* (1979), Podhoretz made a point to mention Baldwin's sexuality, which, while well-known, Podhoretz cast as licentious. "As an open and active homosexual with a taste for the dissolute life," Baldwin should have rejected the NOI, and his seeming endorsement struck Podhoretz as incredible, coming from "so thoroughly integrated a Negro."[97] Finally, in an essay marking the fiftieth anniversary of the article in 2013, Podhoretz described Baldwin's ability to get away with selling a commissioned article to a competing magazine as a violation of journalistic ethics. Moreover, he called it a form of "Crow-Jimism," a term he claimed to borrow from the poet Kenneth Rexroth to describe "the tendency of white liberals to make special allowances for blacks who were guilty of any sort of offense, up to and including violent crimes."[98] Each of these retellings contains an additional dimension of anger and an increasingly right-leaning politics. By the late 1970s, Podhoretz had embraced what the New Right defined as "family values" issues, with opposition to homosexuality and gay rights as a central component.

Podhoretz, however, had actually been thinking about writing on Baldwin for some time. In the summer of 1961, he approached Dan Jacobson, a white South African, about reviewing Baldwin's recent collection of essays, *Nobody Knows My Name*.[99] Jacobson agreed to review the book. But about a month later, Podhoretz asked for a slightly different piece.[100] "I've been thinking about Jimmy Baldwin's book, and it occurred to me that an ordinary review would be less appropriate at this moment (this moment being one of tremendous Negro militancy) than a full-scale article," he wrote. "What I'd really like to see you do is confront Baldwin in his own terms—that is, you might write a personal essay in response to his 'psychic' reading of the race question in America." Podhoretz provided some guiding questions: "How do you, as a Jew and a white South African liberal respond to Baldwin's apocalyptic insistence on the possible consequence of your failure to 'know his name'? Do you really feel the kind of hate and guilt toward him that he ascribes to you? What do you feel towards him? How representative are your feelings?"[101]

Jacobson acquiesced but confided that "the one thing that worries me about the confrontation is that I feel it should be an American who tackles Baldwin, because he writes so much, and quite rightly, as an American."[102] After reading Jacobson's submission Podhoretz agreed. "You're right, of course, in thinking that an American ought more properly to confront Baldwin, but it's almost impossible to think of an American who could. Except, to tell you the truth, for me—and I find it impossible to write anything these days, let alone a difficult article."[103] Podhoretz published Jacobson's review in the December 1961 issue of *Commentary*.[104] But he began mulling his own response to Baldwin in which he would answer the questions he first posed to Jacobson. The response was "My Negro Problem—and Ours."

In that essay Podhoretz set out to convey how he thought white people, and especially Jews who too had experienced discrimination, viewed Black people. He believed his experiences reflected those of other white ethnics who shared city spaces with African Americans. The essay began with a series of encounters Podhoretz had while growing up with Blacks in Brownsville. Once in class, a Black student was unable to answer a teacher's question. "As usual I waved my arm eagerly ('Be a good boy, get good marks, be smart, go to college, become a doctor') and, the right answer bursting from my lips, I was held up lovingly by the teacher as an example to the class." Podhoretz's fate later that afternoon was a baseball bat to the head at the hands of Black bullies. Similar anecdotes peppered the essay, revealing a deep sense of emasculation. His Black peers called him a "sissy," Podhoretz wrote, "the most dreaded epithet of an American boyhood."[105]

Yet to Podhoretz, Blacks were always better off than the white ethnic kids of the neighborhood. Why? Because they were more masculine. They were stronger, tougher, and more athletic. He envied his Black peers because they roamed the streets unrestricted and unbound from family supervision. From Podhoretz's vantage point as a child, they were "free, independent, reckless, brave, masculine, erotic." They were "bad boys," and unlike white hoodlums, "they were *really* bad," explained Podhoretz:

> Bad in a way that beckoned to one, and made one feel inadequate. *We* all went home every day for a lunch of spinach-and-potatoes; *they* roamed around during lunch hour, munching on candy bars. In winter, *we* had to wear itchy woolen hats and mittens and cumbersome galoshes; *they* were bare-headed and loose as they pleased. *We* rarely played hookey, or got into serious trouble in school, for all our street-corner bravado; *they* were defiant, forever staying out (to do what delicious things?), forever making disturbances in class and in the halls, forever being sent to the principal and returning uncowed. But most important of all, they were *tough*; beautifully, enviably tough, not giving a damn for anyone or anything.[106]

Countering Baldwin's description of Black attitudes toward whites, Podhoretz argued that "it was the whites, the Italians and Jews, who feared the Negroes." More importantly, these feelings of emasculation remained in adulthood. "Yet just as in childhood I envied Negroes for what seemed to me their superior masculinity," Podhoretz wrote, "so I envy them today for what seems their superior physical grace and beauty."[107]

At the end of the essay Podhoretz seemed to question the logic of integration as a solution to racism, with some commentators believing he advocated miscegenation.[108] Yet, crucially, Podhoretz maintained that Jews, at least, had a reason to retain a separate identity. "Did the Jews," he asked, "have to survive so that six million innocent people should one day be burned in the ovens of Auschwitz?" Yes, Podhoretz implied, because Jews "were tied to a memory of past glory and a dream of imminent redemption." African Americans, on the other hand, had no such history. He concluded with the following statement: "His past is a stigma, his color is a stigma, his vision of the future is the hope of erasing the stigma by making color irrelevant, by making it disappear as a fact of consciousness."[109] Podhoretz thus placed Blacks on one opposite end of a gendered spectrum that used history to embolden Jewish masculinity. Jews might not be athletic and physically tough like African Americans, but they had a strong intellectual heritage worth preserving, something Black Americans ostensibly lacked.

Podhoretz was not alone in using gender to interpret Black-Jewish relations in the pages of *Commentary* in the 1960s. In 1966 Milton Himmelfarb approached the topic by comparing Jews and Blacks in the United States to Eastern European Jews and muzhiks or peasants in the late nineteenth century. There were "psychosexual reasons" to do so, Himmelfarb argued. Blacks and muzhiks were "emancipated at almost the same time" and perceived within their respective societies "as ignorant, improvident, violent, drunken, incontinent—id figures, embodiments of the untamed instincts." In addition, they were the "other" that Jews interacted with most in society. After drawing this parallel, Himmelfarb surmised that "we may reasonably expect that current Jewish feelings and ways of thinking about Negroes will be affected by older feelings and ways of thinking about muzhiks."[110]

Himmelfarb began his essay with a reference to D. H. Lawrence's 1928 novel, *Lady Chatterley's Lover*, arguing that the peasant gamekeeper lover in Lawrence's novel, with "his animal potency . . . primitiveness and social inferiority," paralleled the Black American male in contemporary America. "In the American imagination, of course, the man-stallion is Negro." Like Podhoretz, Himmelfarb argued that Jews both feared and envied these "others." "The other side of revulsion is attraction, even fascination," Himmelfarb wrote of Jewish perceptions of Muzhiks and by extension African Americans. Jews longed to embody a more virile masculinity. "What all modern Jews in Eastern Europe had in common, transcending any difference of formal ideology," Himmelfarb wrote, "was that they valued action, forcefulness, masculinity, and saw the old Judaism as passive, weak, feminine."[111] The same was true of Jews in contemporary America.

The gendered arguments made by Podhoretz and other *Commentary* writers like Himmelfarb did not go unnoticed by Black writers. In 1967 Ralph Ellison angrily responded that *Commentary* ignored the "fact that we love our Harlems, love to be with other Negroes, marry mostly Negroes, and would consider the loss of such churches as Harlem's Abyssinia a national calamity." Ellison believed Podhoretz, in particular, engaged in a "type of intellectual violence" against the Black community. "It was unfortunate that those young Negroes hadn't considered the possibility that in roughing up a young Brooklyn intellectual to-be," Ellison wrote of Podhoretz, "they were guaranteeing his growing up to balance the score by throwing his typewriter at the whole unsuspecting Negro people."[112] Podhoretz flexed his intellectual rather than physical muscle in response to feeling emasculated by the increasing militancy of the civil rights movement.

Podhoretz concluded "My Negro Problem—and Ours" with a reference to the six million Jews who died in the Holocaust.[113] Three months later, he wrote a scathing review of Arendt's book, *Eichmann in Jerusalem*, which referred to Baldwin in its opening lines. "One of the many ironies surrounding Hannah Arendt's book on the Eichmann trial is that it should have been serialized in the *New Yorker* so short a time after the appearance of James Baldwin's essay on Black Muslims. A Negro on the Negroes, a Jew on the Jews, each telling a tale of the horrors that have been visited upon his people and how these horrors were borne." Both Baldwin and Arendt dealt with evils a minority group faced at the hands of a majority and both used these histories to impart lessons regarding "humankind itself."

The similarities, however, ended there. According to Podhoretz, Baldwin was "eloquent," but his essay lacked intellectual vigor, a critique with gendered connotations for a group that upheld intellectuality as a mark of manhood. Baldwin's was "a black-and-white account" with simplistic categories. "On the one side are powerless victims, on the other the powerful oppressors." Baldwin's was a crude reading of race relations, especially when it came to Jews and Blacks. Arendt, meanwhile, was too theoretical and abstract. "If Baldwin is all eloquence and no cleverness," wrote Podhoretz, "Miss Arendt is all cleverness and no eloquence."[114]

Podhoretz's review was part of a larger uproar over Arendt's coverage of the Adolf Eichmann trial in 1961.[115] Like other New York intellectuals, Podhoretz took issue with both of Arendt's controversial arguments. In response to her claim that Eichmann was not unusually anti-Semitic—the world was full of much more dedicated anti-Semites, who were just not, in practice, as useful to the machinery of the Nazi state as Eichmann was— Podhoretz talked past her by insisting a priori that "no person could have joined the Nazi Party, let alone the S.S., who was not at the very least a *vicious* anti-Semite . . . no banality of man could have done so hugely evil a job so well."[116] He was equally deaf to Arendt's emphasis on how the Nazis used alternately desperate and trapped Jewish leaders against their communities. She spelled out how Nazis manipulated and lied to organizers of the community to make their own jobs easier. They exploited Jewish leaders' efforts to make provisional deals in hopes of buying time. They took advantage of the belief shared by just about everyone, including many Nazis, that many of them could still somehow escape, or at least make themselves unthreatening or even useful enough to be spared. The idea that the Nazis had so much power that trusted Jewish leaders would ever "cooperate" with them was unthinkable. "Why, she is saying that if the Jews had not been Jews, the Nazis would not have been able to kill so many of them—which is a difficult proposition to dispute," Podhoretz exclaimed.[117]

Podhoretz initially worried that his piece did not say anything new. "Lionel Abel's piece on Hannah was very good," Podhoretz confessed in a letter to Philip Rahv, who published Abel's piece in *PR*, "too good, in fact, since he made many of the same points I did."[118] Rahv assured Podhoretz that his article was "quite as good as Abel's, if not better. You hit harder on Hannah's totalitarianism-thesis as well as her mania for profundity at all costs; and your tone is excellent."[119] Many New York intellectuals agreed. "Perhaps the most judicious words in the whole debate were spoken by a writer not afterward to be known for his judiciousness—Norman Podhoretz," Irving Howe later observed.[120]

Podhoretz's focus on Arendt's supposed "profundity" is significant. Even though many of the ideas Arendt presented on the Eichmann trial were drawn from her theories of totalitarianism, which most New York intellectuals had endorsed since she published *The Origins of Totalitarianism* in 1951, Podhoretz charged that she was overly complicated when she applied them to Eichmann. That charge makes particularly strange reading today.

Arendt's writing in her report on the Eichmann trial—perhaps because *New Yorker* editors boiled it down—is actually livelier and more concise than it was in the intricate, and long historical analysis she hammered out in *The Origins of Totalitarianism* back in 1951. But according to Podhoretz, Arendt had taken a simple and unambiguous narrative about evil and "translate[d] this story for the first time into the kind of terms that can appeal to the sophisticated modern sensibility." Thus, "the story as she tells it is complex, unsentimental, riddled with paradox and ambiguity." He continued, "It has all the appearance of 'ruthless honesty,' and all the marks of profundity." But "none of it mattered in the slightest to the final result," Podhoretz wrote. "Murderers with the power to murder descended upon a defenseless people and murdered a large part of it. What else is there to say?" To him, Arendt's analysis was filled with "absurdities" that revealed little except the emasculation of the Jews.[121]

Rarely considered in the same light, "My Negro Problem—and Ours" and Podhoretz's contribution to the denunciation of Arendt's report on the Eichmann trial each articulated uneasiness about Jewish masculinity in a postwar America. Political theorist Jennifer Ring has argued that when Arendt criticized the behavior of Jewish male leaders in Europe, she indirectly drew attention to the inaction of the New York intellectuals during World War II. These intellectuals "felt not only guilty and powerless about their responses to the Holocaust but 'unmanned' by the power of the Nazis and what appeared to be the collusion of the Western world in the face of the slaughter of the European Jews." According to Ring, "it was as though she were exposing the men in all their weakness, a weakness that was experienced by them as impotence, as specifically male sexual powerlessness."[122]

But there was an added gendered dimension to Podhoretz's attack on Arendt. He accused her of engaging in "scholarly pretension" and making her account of the murder of European Jewry overly complex. "Thus, in place of the monstrous Nazi," Podhoretz exclaimed, "she gives us the 'banal' Nazi; in place of the Jew as virtuous martyr, she gives us the Jew as accomplice in evil; and in place of the confrontation between guilt and innocence, she gives us the 'collaboration' of criminal and victim."[123] Arendt's analysis of Eichmann drew on her theories of totalitarianism, which Podhoretz, like many other New York intellectuals, had long endorsed. But at this juncture, he joined them in rejecting Arendt. "Who is Hannah anyway that one should be afraid of her," Rahv insisted to Podhoretz.[124]

Making It—1967

After 1963, Podhoretz did not publish any long essays. He focused on writing what became the first of three memoirs, *Making It*, published in late 1967. Podhoretz wanted the book to make a splash. But early feedback from friends and colleagues did not bode well. While a few praised the manuscript, many took issue with Podhoretz's argument that success, measured in money and fame, was the dirty little secret of American society and intellectual life.

Lionel Trilling advised Podhoretz not to publish *Making It*, telling him "it would take [him] ten years to live it down." Jason Epstein agreed with Trilling. Podhoretz was disappointed by the reaction, partly because he believed his story was their story. *Making It* was "a confessional work" that "deliberately set out to expose an order of feeling in myself, and by implication in others."[125] "While I was writing *Making It*," Podhoretz told Nathan Glazer, "I thought of you as the ideal reader of the book."[126] Podhoretz believed the book revealed his community's psychological and cultural core of secular Jewish masculinity. Yet the community rejected it. The criticism stung. It also struck him as hypocritical. He had been raised "to believe there was something admirable in taking risks," he told an interviewer in 1976. "But the people who raised me, in effect, punished me whenever I did what I was raised to do. I never quite understood why."[127]

Edgar Z. Friedenberg's review in the *NYRB* and Mailer's in *PR* particularly hurt. Podhoretz felt he made Friedenberg an influential voice within the New Left by publishing him in *Commentary* in the early 1960s.[128] That his longtime friend Jason Epstein printed Friedenberg's review in the *NYRB* was another stab in the back. Epstein, however, at least told Podhoretz he did not like the book to his face. "If I were God, I'd drown it in the river," he said.[129] Mailer, on the other hand, said he liked the book when it circulated as a manuscript but then trashed it in print. Mailer twisted the knife by questioning Podhoretz's manhood. Podhoretz's portrait of the group was "so full of sugar," Mailer wrote. Podhoretz indulged in "the one weakness which is fatal to the young novelist: flattery." Mailer implied that Podhoretz was merely performing masculinity, and it showed. Rather than engage in the direct combativeness of the New York intellectuals, Podhoretz played the sycophant. "The kindness palls." It was a mark of "timorousness."[130]

Critics outside "the family" also ridiculed *Making It* and Podhoretz's performance of masculinity. Wilfrid Sheed, in *The Atlantic*, said Podhoretz was "showing off for the grown-ups" and provided an "infantile version of success: comfort, admiration, power for their own sakes, the baby's triumvirate."[131] The *Chicago Tribune*'s review included a cartoon of Podhoretz, cigarette dangling from his mouth, holding his finger up like a gun in front of a silhouette of a cowboy. The headline ran, "Big literary gun aims at self and misses."[132]

As if Mailer's own rejection were not enough, the *Los Angeles Times* rather cruelly emphasized Podhoretz's frank emulation of Mailer. Podhoretz had ended *Making It* with a confession: "For several years I toyed with the idea of doing a book about Mailer that would focus on the problem of success, but in the end I decided that if I ever did work up the nerve to write about this problem, I would have to do it without hiding behind him or anyone else. Writing a book like that would be a very dangerous thing to do but some day, I told myself, I would like to try doing it. I just have."[133] Naturally, the *LA Times* headlined its review, "Hang-Ups of Podhoretz in Aping Mailer," and mocked Podhoretz for imitating the authentically manly writer. Podhoretz was "as trapped in Manhattan as he was in Brooklyn, by a tight little world, in which small men are magnified by proximity to each other."[134]

Scholars have suggested that the negative reviews of *Making It* catalyzed Podhoretz's shift rightward. "The most personal factor driving Podhoretz out of the radical camp came when he published his infamous memoir *Making It* in 1967," writes historian Nathan Abrams. The book was "the pivotal episode in Podhoretz's career," according to essayist Louis Menand. Writer Daniel Oppenheimer has described the book's reception as a "primal trauma" for Podhoretz. Indeed, after the book's negative reception, Podhoretz retreated from social life and drank heavily.[135] He emerged three years later as a staunch critic of the New Left. "When I wrote *Making It* I still considered myself a member, and in some sense a leader, of the radical movement," Podhoretz wrote in *Breaking Ranks*. There he concluded that the negative reactions to *Making It* grew straight out of the influence of 1960s radicalism. *Making It* celebrated "success," but by the end of the decade "this idea that the worship of success lay at the root of a 'sick society' became the central, the organizing theme of the strictly cultural arm of the Movement, variously known as the 'youth culture,' 'the new culture,' and the 'counterculture.'"[136]

In reality, as we have seen, Podhoretz never bought into political radicalism or the various countercultural impulses of the 1950s and 1960s to begin with. Significantly, neither did his wife, Midge Decter, as the previous chapter chronicled. The difference was that there was no longer anything to be gained from promoting the cultural movements that were rising when he took over at *Commentary*. His best hope by the late 1960s was to be on the cutting edge of disillusionment and backlash. He had always been better equipped, by temperament, to cheer on a conservative movement than a rebellious one. In the years that he struggled to discover his own voice, America had sickened of the radical baby boomers. The time had come to bet on the rise and resiliency of the growing middle-class, middle-American, middle-brow reaction against the youth culture—and against the cultural authorities who had, like him, tried to ride the cultural rebellion to commercial success and positions of influence.

He shrewdly decided to make that bet, turning *Commentary* against the youthful impulses he had tried to ally with at the beginning of the 1960s. It was easy because he never bought into those impulses to begin with. But that did not solve his problem of how to become a masculine Jew—a courageous and indomitable authority on the street, with a fighting spirit. Mailer and the others had rejected his masculine pretensions. They had laughed at him, left him feeling exposed. Naturally, he rejected them in turn. Their enemies—the enemies of the counterculture, who wanted to restore order in the streets and teach kids to respect their elders and authority—would welcome him. They would even welcome his claim to have the inside story on radicalism and where its vulnerabilities, dirty secrets, and pressure points were hidden. But he needed a new model of combative masculinity. One quickly came—in a new neighborhood, where the Jews were able to hold their own in street fighting. Where they could swagger credibly, and stare down their challengers.

Israel—1967

Just as *Making It* was about to be savaged by critics, tensions between Israel and its Arab neighbors mounted. On May 14, 1967, a Cairo Radio broadcast declared: "The existence of Israel has continued too long. We welcome the Israeli aggression, we welcome the battle that we have long awaited. The great hour has come. The battle has come in which we shall destroy Israel."[137] As Syria shelled Israel on its northern border, Egypt sent troops to the Sinai Peninsula, then shut the Straits of Tiran and forced United Nations troops out of the region.[138]

By early summer, Jews around the world braced for the Arab armies to push the Jews into the sea. Instead, between June 5 and 10, Israel's army defeated the combined forces of Egypt, Jordan, and Syria in what became known as the Six-Day War. Following Israel's victory, newspapers and magazines across America broadcast images of Israel's military prowess. From mainstream magazines like *Time, Life,* and *Newsweek,* "representations of Israeli Jews as David and their Arab enemies as Goliath," argues historian Deborah Dash Moore, "form a leitmotif in news reporting surrounding the Six-Day War."[139] This celebrated image of muscular militarism was especially marked as the Cold War anti-communist consensus crumbled in the United States. For so many Americans, Jewish and non-Jewish, Israel in 1967 suddenly provided an image of somebody waging war successfully—as Vietnam became an increasingly confusing and unpopular quagmire. As the last of the European empires crumbled, and old imperial powers cut their losses, antiwar sentiment snowballed in the United States. "The fact that Israel was seen as fighting the good fight—and doing it well," historian Melani McAlister argues, "made it an icon of all that the Vietnam War was not for Americans."[140]

In the 1970s Israel became a model for political conservatives, white evangelicals, and some liberal cold warriors of how to wield military power effectively. As they fretted about America's Vietnam syndrome—its growing reluctance to use its military might in the world—they looked to the discipline and training of the Israeli military, and the valor and strategic flair of Israeli generals, as salutary counterexamples. For Podhoretz and others at *Commentary*, Israel also provided a startling new model of Jewish masculinity.

A vision of Jewish military might was new to them, but it had deep roots in Zionism. At the turn of the twentieth century, Zionists like Theodor Herzl and Max Nordau had sought to reconstruct Jewish masculinity, physically, by fighting back against the pogroms and rising anti-Semitism. Herzl and Nordau saw traditional Ashkenazi masculinity, with its emphasis on intellectuality and Talmudic erudition, as powerless in the face of anti-Semitic mobs and propaganda, which fed on the powerful nationalist movements that were transforming Europe. They developed a program for the making of "New Jews," with strong bodies. The New Jews would build the Jews' own strong nationalist state.[141]

After the establishment of Israel in 1948 began to fulfill this program, the state's founding narratives homed in on a masculinity based on youth and strength. The *chalutzim*—pioneers who trekked to Palestine to reestablish Jewish life in the Holy Land—embodied that late nineteenth-century Zionist masculinity. In fact, many of the *chalutzim* were women (including Golda Meir). The socialist-influenced *kibbutzniks* (farmers), who tended the soil and "made the desert bloom," also embodied it, as did the creation of a citizen-army.[142] After the United Nations voted to partition Palestine into separate Jewish and Arab states in the spring of 1948, a massive conscription of able-bodied males expanded the Haganah (the Zionist paramilitary organization formed in the 1920s) from 12,000 to 22,000. The Haganah formed the core of the Israel Defense Forces (IDF) founded that year. Military service became central to citizenship in the new state. The war of independence saw the newly created Israeli forces push back attacks from Egypt, Syria, Iraq, and Jordan, all of whom invaded the new state the day after it was proclaimed and as the British withdrew.[143] "Why," historian Eli Lederhendler has pointed out, "should anyone have been surprised in 1967 to discover that 'Jews are fighters'—as if 1948 had never happened? Yet, this is a point that is made over and over by Jews from various Diaspora communities."[144]

The New York intellectuals took only nominal interest in Zionism prior to 1967. Before the founding of the state in 1948, *Commentary* focused on the "Ihud" vision of Zionism, which supported a binational state.[145] Cohen was not a Zionist, and in the 1950s his views on Israel mirrored the AJC's, the magazine's sponsor. The AJC was "critical of Jewish nationalism and of any political tendency that would cast doubt on the full commitment of American Jews to the United States," Nathan Abrams observes.[146] "*Commentary* has aimed to present a candid, realistic appraisal of Israel and its problems—in its economy, its political, cultural and religious developments, and its relations with the hostile Arab world," according to a 1958 internal AJC report. "Like the AJC it has avoided the polarized positions that characterize some parts of American Jewry. It has maintained a friendly, non-Zionist attitude."[147]

The older New York intellectuals' antagonism toward Zionism was also a remnant of their early Marxism, when they embraced its universalism rather than ethnic and religious nationalism. In the 1930s, as they constructed their ideology of secular Jewish masculinity, most did not look to Zionism.[148] Then in the anti-communist battles of the 1950s, the New York intellectuals were more invested in asserting an American Jewish masculinity devoid of ties to communism. Cohen also sought to document and publicize Jewish athletic achievements and the ability of Jews to labor like all other Americans in order to challenge stereotypes of Jews as weak. He looked to America not Israel for inspiration.[149]

Like Cohen, Podhoretz was initially agnostic about Zionism. He first visited Israel in the early 1950s while on a break from studying at Cambridge. Podhoretz described the Israelis as "gratuitously surly and boorish" and "a very unattractive people," in a 1951 letter to Lionel Trilling. As usual, Podhoretz had a gendered agenda. "Along with other so-called Diaspora habits," the Israelis "rejected courtesy, delicacy, tact, all of which are associated with 2000 years of Jewish servility in their minds." Podhoretz was equally unimpressed with Israeli views of diaspora Jewry. "They suffer under the illusion that Jewish history becomes significant only from the First Zionist Congress onward." Like the older New York intellectuals,

Podhoretz adhered to a Jewish masculinity defined by intellectualism. The Israelis, on the other hand, were "too arrogant and too anxious to become a real honest-to-goodness New York of the East."[150] Podhoretz might have written these words in a bid to impress—Trilling sent Podhoretz's remarks verbatim to Cohen when he recommended him as a contributor to *Commentary*—but they reflected the views of most New York intellectuals in the 1950s.

When Leon Uris popularized the image of the muscular Israeli soldier in his 1958 best-selling novel *Exodus*, *Commentary* dismissed it.[151] The New York intellectuals derided the book and its vision of Jewish manhood, despite the popularity of both and the 1960 film of the same title starring Paul Newman. Uris consciously sought to counter the image of Jews as weak, which he felt dominated the American imagination. He told a journalist in 1958, "We Jews are not what we have been portrayed to be. In truth, we have been fighters."[152] But the New York intellectuals mocked his rendering of Jewish masculinity as middlebrow and inauthentic. Uris presented "a land whose children are blond-haired, blue-eyed descendants of intrepid Biblical heroes; a country, finally, more *Hebrew* than *Jewish*," *Commentary* noted in its 1959 review.[153] Looking back from the perspective of 1967, Robert Alter summarized the views of many New York intellectuals when he wrote that Uris had imagined a "fantasy figure, the Jew as modern buccaneer-adventurer, the pitiless, tough-as-nails Jewish fighter." Uris's Jews were unbelievable because Uris took Jewishness out of the equation. His fictional Jew evoked "the by now familiar paradox, the Jew as *goy*."[154]

The 1967 Six-Day War changed all that. It reconfigured the relationship between American Jews and Israel, propelling Israel from the periphery to the center of American Jewish life. Israel became central to the agendas of nearly all the major Jewish organizations and philanthropic groups and more dominant in the areas of Jewish education and religious services.[155] *Commentary* was in step with that trend. "Following Israel's victory in the war, Podhoretz and many of his fellow editors and contributors were converted to Zionism," notes Nathan Abrams. "From a position of clear non- and even anti-Zionism in the 1940s and 1950s, and coolness and ambivalence in the 1960s, *Commentary* [became] openly 'very supportive' of Israel in the 1970s."[156]

Their newfound interest in Israel—a victorious, muscular, and militarized Israel—transformed their notions of masculinity as well as their position on Zionism. Israel was now triumphant and a success—at a time when America's mainstream culture was questioning its capacity for success, especially in foreign affairs and, more disturbingly, its belief in the moral validity and value of success. This was a painful juxtaposition, just at the moment when Jews had become "insiders" in American life. The New York intellectuals had come from immigrant ghettos and moved to the vanguard of American culture, and at its most dynamic period of development, its postwar boom. Yet the children of America's boom—the New Left—hesitated and soured on American success. This, plus the failure of Vietnam, backed by a once seemingly consensus view of Cold War liberalism, was a striking contrast to events in Israel.

Commentary covered the 1967 War intently. Its August 1967 issue contained several articles on the war, including by Walter Laqueur, Theodore Draper, and the Israeli writer Amos Alon. These articles were more restrained than what would follow in the magazine in proceeding years. They all defended Israel and its security concerns but did not take a hard line on the defeated Arab enemies. They touched on the Palestinian refugee problem and urged a peaceable solution. Such sentiments, one scholar notes, "could still be published in *Commentary* in 1967. The magazine's approach to Israeli affairs would soon flatten to a hardline."[157]

The reasons for this transformation were complex. In part, they reflected the mood of American Jewry broadly. But the *Commentary* crowd was also dismayed when Black Power activists and other New Leftists equated Zionism as a form of colonial imperialism. In August 1967, just as *Commentary*'s first issue on the war came out, antiwar and civil rights activists gathered with left-leaning liberals at Chicago's Palmer House for a meeting of the National Conference of New Politics (NCNP). Organizers of the conference sought to build a broad political coalition among the various groups of the American left that would forge a viable alternative to the Republican and Democratic Parties in the 1968 elections.[158] But discussions of Israel dominated the conference. In a move that shocked and dismayed many Jewish participants, the Black Caucus, led by H. Rap Brown, then the chairman of the Student Nonviolent Coordinating Committee (SNCC), demanded the adoption of a list of resolutions that included a condemnation of the "imperialist Zionist War." Fearful that the New Politics movement would crumble before it ever got off the ground, the NCNP obliged. Outraged that the resolutions passed, many Jews walked out of the conference.[159]

Jews had supported the 1967 War in large numbers. Arthur Hertzberg covered this issue in *Commentary*'s August 1967 issue. Relying on "impressionistic reportage," he noted the unprecedented fundraising effort by the community. He saw a new unanimity of support for Israel among American

Jews. That was in stark contrast to the recent, pre-1967 past, when disagreements over Zionism had divided them. In Hertzberg's view, guilt over American Jewish inaction during the Holocaust undergirded the response of most American Jews to Israel in 1967. He contrasted the behavior of American Jewry in 1967 to the community's "passivity" in the 1930s and '40s, and also to the "passivity" of European Jews regarding Zionist migration to Palestine and subsequent Israeli achievements and development. "'Good' Jews have been largely arguing . . . that this passivity was a distinctly Jewish form of heroism, but it is now apparent that many who have interpreted it in this way never really succeeded in convincing themselves," Hertzberg wrote. "Now, confronted by a threat to Israel's existence, Jews almost universally felt that precisely because of the horrifying prospect that Israel might go down, let it go down fighting."[160] Herztberg, a liberal rabbi who five years later would become the leader of the American Jewish Congress, did not judge this response by American Jews as partisan or politically motivated. But his observations were prescient.

As a writer Podhoretz, fascinatingly, remained silent about Israel in 1967. But Hertzberg's analysis of passivity crept into his thinking on the subject. Over the summer of 1967, he grew increasingly angered by the reaction of New Leftists as well as Jewish intellectuals who criticized Israeli behavior. In late July 1967, right as *Commentary* published its first coverage of the war, David Riesman sent a letter to Podhoretz inquiring whether he would be interested in an article on the American Jewish response to the 1967 Arab Israeli War by Erich Fromm, the respected psychoanalyst and one of the founders of the Frankfurt school. A longstanding critic of Zionism, Fromm wanted to write an article that contrasted "traditional Jews," whom he posited "admire[d] martyrs" with "the Israelis and their American followers [who] admire[d] heroes." Riesman "very much shared" Fromm's views about the bellicosity of supporters of Israel, and he believed Podhoretz was "courageous" enough to print it, even if it evoked negative reactions from the magazine's readership, the AJC, and established Jewry.[161]

Podhoretz declined to pursue the article. While he appreciated Riesman's remarks about his courage, he felt "Fromm's thesis about heroes and martyrs" was "an oversimplification." Podhoretz suspected, based on Fromm's past writings, that he would "use the distinction for the purpose of attacking what I would guess he considers an outburst of Jewish 'chauvinism.'"

Podhoretz, however, did not believe Israel or its supporters behaved chauvinistically during or after the Six-Day War. He was dismayed by what he saw as "a considerable degree of unease and embarrassment among American Jews over the completeness of the Israeli victory." Podhoretz told Riesman, "Jews aren't altogether happy in the role of victor; they are much too accustomed to thinking of themselves as victims, and they tend to be apologetic about their own power to a pathological degree."[162] When Riesman responded a couple months later, he told Podhoretz that he "underestimate[d] the degree of chauvinism aroused in this country during the Arab-Israeli War. Not just protectiveness, which of course I myself felt, along with everyone else, but chauvinism." Riesman thought that American Jews, especially "academics," had not shown so much "embarrassment" as "triumphalism," which Riesman found deeply troubling.[163] The language Podhoretz and Riesman used to describe American Jewish reactions to the 1967 War had gendered undertones: feminine embarrassment versus masculine triumphalism, "traditional" Jews versus Israelis, martyrs versus heroes. Martyrs were "victims," Podhoretz told Riesman. "Jews were martyrs when in their total powerlessness they had to be and to the extent that they could, they made a virtue of martyrdom."[164] Podhoretz was coming to the conclusion that Jews could no longer afford to be martyrs, and that Jewish masculinity could not just be defined by intellectualism.

The October 1967 issue of *Commentary* made clear Podhoretz's new appreciation of Israeli masculinity. The issue included articles by Milton Himmelfarb and Robert Alter, which addressed this topic and the issue raised by Podhoretz's and Riesman's disagreement over Israeli behavior. Before writing his monthly column, Alter wrote to the editors at *Commentary* explaining that he "was toying with the idea of a polemic against all-of-a-sudden Jewish intellectuals of the New Left who are now denouncing Israel in the name of both the higher Jewish morality and the war against American imperialism." A couple weeks later, he developed this train of thought. "In one way or another, what I think I want to deal with is the general question of the modern, Zionist image of the aggressive Jew (Moshe Dayan on the cover of *Time* and *Newsweek* vis a vis the European Jews as seen by [historian Raul] Hilberg and Arendt)."[165]

In his article, Alter admonished the "self-consciously assimilated and militantly 'progressive' segments of the American Jewish intelligentsia." They were finding Israel's victory a "profoundly unsettling experience." Excoriating the American Jewish intellectual, "who knows the truth about the destruction of European Jewry according to the gospel of Raul Hilberg and Hannah Arendt," he criticized their unease about Israeli military actions.

"It escapes me," he wrote, "how any Jew can so smugly accept to have it both ways: on the one hand, to pass judgment on European Jewry for acquiescing in its own destruction; on the other hand, to look askance at Israel for its thorough and efficient use of force when the alternative was annihilation." Some intellectuals, he complained, seemed to think that in fighting back the Israelis were "not behaving as Jews are supposed to behave." That equated to a "flat insistence that Israelis are no longer Jews."[166]

According to Alter, "Israel's stunning victory, whatever its final effect in altering political maps, had knocked askew a whole row of stereotypes of the Jew in his relation to history [and] his location in existence." Previously, "the Jew in the Western mind" was a "demonic, inhuman, or subhuman figure," Alter argued, while Jewish self-perception was also grim: "endless lines of wan, gaunt figures trudging off to the factories of death." Israel's military victory offered "millions, at least in North America and Western Europe, a crash course in corrective reindoctrination."[167]

Milton Himmelfarb concurred. In that same issue he observed that, "while Jews can be pretty good with a fountain pen and briefcase, they can also if necessary be pretty good with a rifle or tank."[168] Like Podhoretz, Himmelfarb was embracing a different model of Jewish masculinity than the New York intellectuals were accustomed to. "Jews have generally had a certain amount of contempt for the military enterprise," he observed. "Our two great cultural heroes, Einstein and Freud, were notably contemptuous." In light of Israel's victory, this perception changed: "Now, for people like us," by which Himmelfarb meant intellectuals, "the Israeli generals are redeeming the military reputation."

Himmelfarb was not only speaking to Jews and about Israel but also to the American public. With the defeats in Vietnam mounting and opposition to the war growing, Himmelfarb remarked that "it has been a long time now . . . that anybody has been able to hear that line of Horace's *dulce et decorum est pro patria mori*—sweet and fitting it is to die for your country—without gagging and giggling. The proper stance has been black humor: *Catch-22*." The Israelis reversed that sense of disillusionment. They showed that "peaceable men can become warriors because of love of country."[169] Himmelfarb implied that America could learn from the Israeli example. Besides upholding the value of militarism, the Israelis had other lessons to impart. "If our respect for fighting and military men has gone up," Himmelfarb wrote, "for talking and diplomats it has gone down." Himmelfarb referred particularly to the failure of the United Nations to avert the crisis and fairly mediate the dispute. The other two lessons of the

Six-Day War for Jews and the American public were "the old truth that you can depend only on yourself" and to "appreciate bourgeois democracy."[170] These lessons would become tenets of neoconservative ideology in the years to come.

———◆———

The emerging neoconservatives looked to Israel as a model of masculinity and as a country that remained both morally and militarily strong in the 1960s. Writing in *Commentary*, Martin Peretz noted that in the months after the Six-Day War, "What became increasingly clear was that many on the Left had swallowed an ill-digested, even a thoughtless pacifism. What had begun as an eminently reasonable nuclear pacifism slowly had been rendered into a pacifism pure and simple—or a pacifism which still allowed for the violence of revolutionaries." Foreshadowing future neoconservative thinking, he continued: "By its horrors, the Vietnam adventure indubitably hastened this process, and only something like the experience of Israel could have made respectable again in certain circles the notion that some countries fight some wars for good and sufficient reason."[171]

Israel also fit within an emerging neoconservative foreign policy agenda that melded anti-communism with a strong military defense. Neoconservatives—a group that included Podhoretz and others who joined the Coalition for a Democratic Majority (CDM), founded in 1972 in reaction to the leftward embrace of the "New Politics" by the Democratic Party, as well as younger hawkish policy wonks clustered around Washington senator Henry "Scoop" Jackson—became some of the most forceful advocates of a tough US foreign policy in the 1970s.[172] Many thought the Vietnam War was misguided—Podhoretz for example, argued that "Vietnam was the wrong war, in the wrong place, at the wrong time." Yet they strongly opposed the notion that the Vietnam War had discredited the use of American military might in future conflicts. "But wrong as the war the United States fought in Vietnam was," Podhoretz wrote in 1976, "it was not wrong in the purposes for which it was fought"—that is, to contain the spread of communism.[173]

While many of the New York intellectuals opposed the Vietnam War by the late 1960s, by the mid-1970s the neocons among them had concluded that defeat in Vietnam had dangerous consequences.[174] In particular, losing the war had stymied America's "will" to wield military force, which the neocons were adamant was necessary for the defense of the free world against communist aggression. Israel in the late 1960s provided them with a model of masculine morality in the realm of foreign policy.

By the 1970s, Israel's critics no longer viewed Israel as the heroic David in the Middle East conflict but as an aggressive Goliath. Accusations of territorial aggression and misconduct toward the Palestinians had been directed at the Israelis since the 1967 Six-Day War, when they conquered territory from Egypt, Jordan, and Syria. These accusations escalated after the October 1973 Yom Kippur War. The neoconservatives defended Israel. They were hawkish on Israel throughout the 1970s but increasingly feared that the United States did not have the strength or the will to protect Israeli interests, which they argued were analogous to American interests in the Middle East. They warned that US policy in the region reflected a "Vietnamization" of Israel, which equated to "an 'honorable' American withdrawal from the area." In a 1976 article titled "The Abandonment of Israel," Podhoretz warned that Vietnam "is not the only ghost hovering over" the Middle East. "The ghost of Munich is also there." As Podhoretz would do repeatedly in the 1970s, he compared the timidity of liberal foreign policy elites in the 1970s to the appeasement of Hitler in the years leading up to World War II.[175]

In a 1983 article that he titled the "State of World Jewry," Podhoretz reflected on the role the Six-Day War played in Jewish consciousness. "Everywhere in the world, spontaneously, without mutual consultation, and all at once Jews affirmed their acceptance of what [Emil] Fackenheim called the commandment of Auschwitz, the 614th commandment, the commandment that negatively forbade the giving of posthumous victories to Hitler, and that positively declared: 'There shall be Jews.'"[176]

For many Jews, fears that the Six-Day War could have been another Holocaust put Jewish survival at the center of their concerns. The Holocaust was "an experience so terrifying, so degrading, so humiliating that it might well have left the survivors," and all Jews around the world, "utterly demoralized and therefore ready to collapse and say Enough," Podhoretz wrote in 1983. "Instead the opposite occurred: a reassertion of the will to live."[177] Midge Decter similarly noted that the war "was a watershed in 20th century Jewish history. For the meaning of that war turns out to have been an unequivocal statement by the Jews—the first, if need be, of a long series—that they are alive, like any other men . . . [and] that they intend in the most basic and primitive way to continue to be so."[178] There were gendered undertones here, too. "The most brilliant institution of a reestablished Jewish sovereignty in the Land of Israel," Podhoretz noted, "would turn out to be not its university or its *yeshivot* but its army. But this is what the will to live dictated," Podhoretz continued, "and this is what the Jews of Israel, against all expectation and against the pacific habits and instincts of the past two thousand years, set about to create."[179] Survival thus meant a strong military and the abandonment of "pacific habits" that included scholarly focus on universities and yeshivot. Survival meant the embrace of a new Jewish masculinity.

Epilogue

I FIRST BEGAN thinking about what became this book during the presidency of George W. Bush. After the September 11, 2001, attacks, Bush launched the War on Terror. The so-called Bush Doctrine proclaimed that the United States had the right to launch preemptive and unilateral war to defend itself against rogue states and terrorists, and that the United States "would work to democratize the greater Middle East as a long-term solution to the terrorist problem." The Bush administration used this justification to expand the War on Terror from Afghanistan to Iraq in fall 2003, arguing that Saddam Hussein had weapons of mass destruction (WMDs) and that his regime provided a haven to Al Qaeda. Both accusations proved false.

Bush's foreign policy pillars were linked to neoconservatives. "More than any other group," Francis Fukuyama wrote in the *New York Times* in 2006, "it was the neoconservatives both inside and outside the Bush Administration who pushed for democratizing Iraq and the broader Middle East." Fukuyama, a political scientist and international relations scholar long tied to neoconservatism, criticized the Bush Doctrine in 2006 for miring the United States in an endless war on terror. "The problem with neoconservatism's agenda lies not in its ends, which are as American as apple pie, but rather in the overmilitarized means by which it sought to accomplish them," Fukuyama wrote. "How did the neoconservatives end up overreaching to such an extent that they risk undermining their own goals?" he asked. "In retrospect," he continued, "things did not have to develop this way. The roots of neoconservatism lie in a remarkable group of largely Jewish intellectuals who attended City College of New York (C.C.N.Y.) in the mid to late 1930s and early 1940s." That sentence brought me to the subject of this book.[1]

The book began with a series of questions about neoconservatism's Jewish roots. Neoconservatism, I soon discovered, was a slippery term whose meaning changed over time. Moreover, many of the New York intellectuals initially tied to neoconservatism had nothing to do with the military initiatives later associated with the term. In 1980, Nathan Glazer defined a neoconservative as "someone who wasn't born that way or didn't start out that way. He stumbled on the principles of conservatism when he became involved in the real world."[2] In the late 1990s, Glazer had parted from neocon orthodoxy when he changed his mind about affirmative action.[3] By the early twenty-first century he barely recognized neoconservatism. In spring 2005, a year after the Bush administration publicly admitted that Saddam Hussein in fact possessed no weapons of mass destruction, and after a well-armed anti-American insurgency had clearly thwarted the administration's plans for a successful regime change, Glazer observed, "there is very little overlap between those who promoted the neoconservatism of the 1970s and those committed to its latter-day manifestation."[4]

When I first read Norman Podhoretz and his account of his conversion from self-identified radical to neoconservative in his 1979 memoir, *Breaking Ranks*, I was struck by the heavily gendered language in it. As this project evolved, however, it became clear that notions of masculinity (Jewish, American, and often an amalgam) were integral to the thinking of other New York intellectuals too, on the left and the right. I saw a new ideology of secular Jewish masculinity emerge, bit by bit, in their published and unpublished words. It became clear that the larger story of the American Jewish experience and American intellectual life and politics in the twentieth century could not be understood without an understanding of that ideology.

The New York intellectuals' ideology of secular Jewish masculinity began as an outsider position in the 1920s and '30s. According to Lionel Abel, the New York intellectuals made "modern politics . . . *a school of rudeness*." They wrote with "polemical ferocity," Irving Howe explained, which was not initially welcomed. Their Jewish *outsiderness*, however, ironically contributed to the remasculinization of American intellectual life in the twentieth century. "Rudeness became a spear with which to break the skin of complacency," Howe explained. He evoked fellow intellectuals' impatience with the "civility" and gentility that had previously defined American letters. "In its early years *Partisan Review* was often rude, sometimes for no reason whatsoever," Howe conceded. He was speaking of the New York intellectuals' aggressively masculine style in general. He hinted at the double meaning that "gentility" so often had for

American Jews. "But rudeness was not only the weapon of the cultural underdog, but also a sign that intellectual Jews had become sufficiently self-assured to stop playing by gentile rules."[5]

In the postwar years, the New York intellectuals brought their combative masculinity to the American mainstream. "As every graduate student in American studies or literature used to know, most of the New York Intellectuals were Jews from working-class backgrounds who abandoned the Marxism of their youth, read widely and fiercely, and gradually became arbiters of the best the nation's culture had to offer," historian Michael Kazin observed in 2007. The New York intellectuals, in no small measure, helped define what it meant to be smart in America in the second half of the twentieth century. "From the 1950s into the 1980s, no one who cared about the ideas swirling through America's politics, writing, or art could avoid their erudite and passionate debate, even though much of it took place in such low-circulation venues as *Commentary* and *The New York Review of Books*."[6] But just as Jews ostensibly became insiders in American life—and the New York intellectuals in many ways epitomized that transformation—this group wrestled over the meaning of their experience as secular Jewish men who were becoming tremendously influential. How much could they integrate into American intellectual and political life without losing their distinctly Jewish, combative, erudite masculine edge?

A masculinity centered on strength, toughness, and virility became the defining feature of neoconservative politics in domestic and foreign affairs in the 1970s. Though several New York intellectuals were tied to neoconservatism—notably Nathan Glazer, Daniel Bell, and Irving Kristol, all of whom cut their teeth in the alcoves of CCNY in the 1930s—only Norman Podhoretz and Midge Decter (neither of whom attended CCNY) remained tied to neoconservatism after its heyday in the Carter–Reagan years.

In the 1990s, after the fall of the Soviet Union, the neoconservatives wandered a bit in the desert. They worked to ensure American military superiority in the post–Cold War era. But their message lay largely dormant for a decade. After the 9/11 attacks, their foreign policy analysis found renewed appeal. Terrorism replaced communism for the next generation of neoconservatives, alongside staunch support for Israel. But the neoconservatives of the Bush White House—Dick Cheney, Donald Rumsfeld, Paul Wolfowitz, Richard Armitage, to name the most prominent—were not "new" to conservatism. Most had always been Republicans. Many had served in the Nixon and Reagan administrations.

These Rumsfeld–Cheney-era neocons, also called "Vulcans," did draw the same lessons from the Vietnam syndrome as Podhoretz drew.[7] In the late 1970s, Podhoretz had railed against Americans' unwillingness to send ground troops into foreign wars in distinctly gendered terms. He blamed homosexuals for what he viewed as America's foreign policy impotency in his 1977 article, "The Culture of Appeasement," for example. After the 9/11 attacks, the Vulcan neocons pushed a hypermasculinized approach to foreign policy, which included unabashed militarism, exporting democracy abroad, and preemptive war. Revealingly, in 2003 Midge Decter wrote a hagiography of Rumsfeld, Bush's secretary of defense, and leading architect of the War on Terror, in which she unambiguously lauded his "manliness." "The key to [Rumsfeld] is that he is a wrestler," Decter told an interviewer. "A wrestler is a lone figure. He battles one on one, and he either wins or loses. There is only one man on the mat at the end of a wrestling match. It is no accident, as the communists used to say, that he wrestled."[8]

Both Podhoretz and Decter had written "conservatively" about gender— or as people said in those days, sex roles—in the late 1950s. That complicates the traditional neoconservative narrative that Podhoretz himself helped to codify. Decter's writings, undergirded by revisionist mid-century neo-Freudianism, with its emphasis on heterosexuality and mature and distinct sex roles, were especially influential. In the 1980s and '90s, Decter played an integral role fusing the neoconservatives into the broader conservative movement, linking their politics to the New Right that emerged in the 1970s and its "family values" agenda. In the 1980s, '90s, and 2000s, she was active in an array of influential conservative think tanks. In addition to the Heritage Foundation, she was the editor of *First Things*, a magazine sponsored by the conservative Catholic Richard John Neuhaus Institute on Religion and Public Life, founded in 1990. Throughout this period she mentored many young movement conservatives.

When Decter died in May 2022, numerous obituaries described her as a matriarch of the conservative movement. She was a "conservative den mother," wrote one of her mentees. "Every boy needs a Jewish mother," wrote another. The editors at *National Review* characterized her as "motherly and grandmotherly to many young people she was not related to at all." Decter was more than the first lady of neoconservatism. According to *National Review*, she was "a force" in the conservative movement writ large.[9]

Significantly, there was a dynastic element to neoconservatism. Podhoretz's and Decter's son, John Podhoretz, a longtime columnist at the *New York Post*, became editor of *Commentary* in 2009. He succeeded Neal Kozodoy, who had joined the staff of *Commentary* in 1966 and had taken over as editor when Norman Podhoretz retired in 1995. His sister, Ruthie Blum, became a conservative writer in Israel, while their older half sister, Rachel Decter, married Elliott Abrams, a veteran Republican foreign policy official who worked in the Reagan administration. The writer and political commentator William Kristol founded the *Weekly Standard* magazine with John Podhoretz in 1994. He is the son of Irving Kristol and Gertrude Himmelfarb.

Several of these sons were at odds with Norman Podhoretz after Donald Trump became president. When Trump campaigned in 2015 his "America First" slogan was seen as a rebuke of the neoconservative foreign policy agenda. It harkened back to an isolationist, nativist, and anti-Semitic group that opposed America's entry into World War II. William Kristol, John Podhoretz, and Elliott Abrams were prominent anti-Trumpers. Abrams, however, served two years in Trump's State Department as a special representative on Iran, hoping to influence the administration when it came to foreign policy. After the January 6 insurrection at the Capitol he told a reporter, "In 2016 I said Donald Trump was not fit, and my view on that never wavered." He lamented that the January 6 attack "taints" the legacy of the administration's work in the Middle East. "It's a great deal harder to remind people of the positive things that were done—for example with respect to the security of Israel."[10] He had in mind especially withdrawing from the Iran nuclear deal.

Norman Podhoretz, in a 2019 interview with the Claremont Institute, a conservative think tank, said that he did not initially like Trump because he sounded too much like a "Buchananite," referring to Pat Buchanan, whom Podhoretz described as "a protectionist, a nativist, and an isolationist." Moreover, "when Trump said that they *lied* us into Iraq, I thought, 'well, to hell with him.'" Yet over the course of Trump's presidency, Podhoretz became increasingly "bothered by the hatred building up against Trump." He gradually became "anti-anti-Trump," playing off Cold War terms (anti-anti-communist). But after Trump appointed John Bolton and Mike Pompeo to his cabinet, Podhoretz became a full-fledged Trump supporter. These appointments "couldn't be better from the point of view of a neoconservative," he said. Most importantly, Podhoretz admired Trump. Trump "fights back. If you hit him, he hits back," he told the interviewer. Harkening back to "My Negro Problem—and Ours," Podhoretz explained: "When I was a kid, you would rather be beaten up than back away from a fight. The worst thing in the world you could be called was a sissy." Trump was no sissy, in Podhoretz's view. His "virtues" are "the virtues of the street kids of Brooklyn. You don't back away from a fight and you fight to win."[11]

In 2009 Podhoretz published a book called *Why Are Jews Liberal?* in which he lamented the continued adherence of Jews to liberalism in the United States. Liberalism had become "the religion of American Jews," Podhoretz complained. Yet the Republican Party, he argued, better represented the interest of Jews, especially when it comes to support of Israel. American Jews were still caught in liberalism's "Tertullian-like grip," Podhoretz wrote. He said that one of the reasons why American Jews stayed with the Democratic Party was because they have an "aversion . . . to the use of military force." In that way, Jews personified "the liberal position" when it came to the military: that "humanitarian considerations are (or were) just about the only justification liberals have come to accept for the use of military force." In Podhoretz's telling, both liberals and American Jews suffered from weakness, timidity, and emasculation.[12]

Podhoretz was right that most Jews remained politically in the center or to the left. Most also rejected the neoconservative vision of virility as a speedy resort to arms in foreign affairs, at least when it came to the United States, and conservative "family values" at home. So did most New York intellectuals. Much more enduring, in many ways, has been Irving Howe and the *Dissent* vision of a scholarly Jewish masculinity, which emphasized a purely verbal combativeness, the individual independence of every writer, and an outsider status.

Though Howe lamented the lack of these traits in the New Left in the 1960s and early 1970s, there was a reconciliation between the New Left and Howe's older socialist movement by the 1980s—though both groups were much smaller by then. The conservative politics of the Reagan era had brought them together. Historian and former New Leftist Todd Gitlin started reading *Dissent* again in 1972, when he "was looking for a way back to rational politics" after the implosion of Students for a Democratic Society (SDS), some of whose most prominent figures had turned to terrorism. President of SDS from 1964–65, he was one of the members of SDS who clashed with the *Dissent* editors at the meeting between the two generations of leftists in 1962. "But by the early eighties I felt very much in harmony with most things [Howe] was saying and thinking about the world," Gitlin later recalled. When Gitlin started writing regularly for *Dissent* in the 1980s, Howe was happy to have him on board, editor Brian Morton later recalled. "Part of what appealed to Irving was the idea of a rapprochement with a prominent member of the 1960s New Left."[13] By the time Gitlin published his 1987 book, *The Sixties: Years of Hope, Days of Rage*, he "felt very much that the *Dissent* group was my crowd. This was basically the world in which I was having my political and cultural arguments."[14] Gitlin soon joined its editorial board.

Michael Kazin, a leader of SDS as an undergraduate at Harvard in the late 1960s, recalled in 1998 that he and his father "began saddling—ever so gradually and seldom without mutual complaint—to the same side of the barricades" after the election of Ronald Reagan in 1980. This was after years of strain between father and son, both personal and political. "The sons were out to get the fathers—especially if the fathers had been 'radicals' during a certain ancient Depression," Alfred Kazin wrote in his 1978 memoir, *New York Jew*. "The sons were attacking the fathers where we lived. They attacked our attachment to libraries; to books uselessly piled on more books, to our fondest belief that violence had nothing proper to do with sex and sex nothing to do with politics."[15] But in the 1980s, their sons began to embrace their fathers' political positions and their intellectually based ideology of secular Jewish masculinity. "I had argued— shouted—my own tune of rebellion in the sixties," Michael Kazin wrote in 1998, shortly after his father died. "I was, like Bazarov, the antihero of Turgenev's *Fathers and Sons*, eager to negate and 'deny everything . . . with indescribable composure.'"[16] But in later years Michael Kazin "felt more like his [father's] peer, almost his comrade." The younger Kazin, too, turned to his pen as a weapon of sorts. "Like many erstwhile New Leftists, I became an academic because I wanted to continue a life of political engagement, albeit with a secure income and the opportunity to spend lots of time in libraries."[17]

In 2007 Michael Kazin argued that the New York intellectuals had no heirs. "All the New York Intellectuals are either dead or in their dotage, and they have no real successors. Filmmakers, creators of innovative TV shows, and edgy contributors to popular magazines, Web sites, and the *Times* op-ed page now rule the cultural dialogue. And they are as likely to live in Los Angeles or Washington, D.C., as on the West Side of Manhattan," Kazin wrote. Here he faintly echoed the argument Russell Jacoby made in *The Last Intellectuals*. Jacoby lamented that the New York intellectuals were the last public intellectuals—the last generalists to write for a broad audience on a range of topics.[18]

Yet the New York intellectuals' ideology of secular Jewish masculinity endures at magazines like *Dissent*. That is because New Leftists like Gitlin and Kazin continued the indispensable voice of the combative critic. It was the voice that their fathers' generation brought to intellectual life. It was so intense and powerful when their fathers were young because Jews *were* still outsiders in American culture, especially within the Ivy League elite of New York publishing houses and literary magazines. Jews had just barely escaped the most serious attempted genocide in their history. The organized intention to industrialize the destruction of Jews was a principal cause of World War II, the deadliest event in human history. In a sexist world where asserting *manhood* seemed the only reliable way to save one's whole people, as well as a sense of responsible and active adulthood, being a man, acting like a man—in postwar times as in wartime—had an irresistible draw for these tremendously energetic and brilliant writers. Writing like a man was the most influential peacetime way to be a man, to shape the leadership and the commitments of the United States, an incontrovertible superpower in the postwar era. But for the *Dissent* crew there remained a responsibility to critique power from the outside.

In 2009 Michael Kazin became coeditor of *Dissent* with Michael Walzer. Walzer joined *Dissent*'s editorial board in the late 1950s, a few years after graduating from Brandeis. Sometime in the 1980s he became coeditor of the magazine with Howe. "But Irving did everything. He did not know how to delegate," Walzer recalled. When Howe died of a stroke in 1993, Walzer "suddenly had to step in. It was a real shock," he later explained, "because I had not been a real co-editor."[19] Later, Walzer's coeditor at *Dissent* was Mitchell Cohen, who had joined the masthead in 1990.[20] But when Cohen stepped down in 2009, Michael Kazin took his place. As Walzer later noted, "I was Irving Howe's and Lew Coser's student at Brandeis, and Michael was my student at Harvard."[21]

When Michael Kazin assumed the editorship of *Dissent*, he reinvigorated the magazine. According to Walzer, Kazin faced several major tasks. Chief among them was finding "that next generation of leftist writers and activists" and then figuring out how to pay them. "For decades, *Dissent* had been parasitic on the American academy; most of our writers were professors with decent salaries," Walzer recalled. "Now more and more of our writers are members of the new academic proletariat or entirely independent of the university world." Michael Kazin succeeded on both counts and in the process made "the magazine livelier than it was, more politically engaged." The 2000s were a "'glum and morbid' time" at *Dissent*, the *Chronicle of Higher Education* reported in 2016. "For one thing, it was getting old."[22] By bringing in a younger generation of intellectual writers, *Dissent* was at the forefront of "an intellectual renaissance" forged by a younger generation of scholars, activists, and writers—"new intellectuals"—many with academic training but forging their own path outside the university. "I always imagined *Dissent* as a magazine for people who worry," Walzer wrote. "Michael is certainly able to worry, but he is perhaps not so trapped in that mental and emotional mode. In any case, the young people he has edited and encouraged seem wonderfully unworried—enthusiastically prepared for battles they can actually imagine winning. Michael isn't quite one of them. He calls himself Mr. In-Between, but they are his legacy."[23]

Many of those young writers also contribute to a slew of "little" magazines founded in the first decades of the twenty-first century, including *n+1*, *Jacobin*, the *Los Angeles Review of Books*, the *New Inquiry*, *Public Books*, and *The Point*. The magazine *n+1* had particularly close ties to *Dissent*. Former *Dissent* writers Keith Gessen, Mark Greif, and Benjamin Kunkel helped found it in 2004. It appeared "a year after *Partisan Review*, the flagship journal of the postwar intellectuals, ceased," as the *Chronicle of Higher Education* noted.[24] While these journals have no direct ties to the Jewishness of the New York intellectuals, their pugnacious vision of combative intellectuals criticizing mainstream institutions lives on in these venues. These new "little" magazines also have just as many women writers and editors.

As for the women New York intellectuals? The men in the group could not be real men in America in the twentieth century without the presence of women. This was not the yeshivas of the shtetls of yore, from which women were barred. Thus for the male New York intellectuals, their own constructions of masculinity were impossible without women, even as they were constantly trying to push the women to the margins.

To be taken seriously, the women New York intellectuals also performed secular Jewish masculinity. Aside from perhaps Arendt, the women were never entirely accepted as intellectual equals. They could just as easily be dismissed as mere "woman writers," or even worse, "lady" writers.

Despite the sexism they encountered, the women New York intellectuals disparaged feminists, whom they dismissed as distinctly "unserious" writers. Feminists wrote like women. Only Diana Trilling emerged as an exception. "Although she wrote important essays during her lifetime," writer Daphne Merkin notes, "she would only fully blossom into authorship after [Lionel's] death in 1975."[25] Around the same time, Diana Trilling also started to come to feminist views that femininity and masculinity were social constructions, distinct from the anatomical categories of male and female. She also started to believe that a woman did not need to write like a man to be intellectually serious. Young feminists in the 1970s challenged and ultimately helped dislodge the New York intellectuals' ideology of secular Jewish masculinity. In key senses, however, they were aided by Diana Trilling, and even by the example of some of the more persistently anti-feminist New York intellectual women, who had risen to prominence in a sexist milieu, despite the militant sexism of their male peers, coworkers, and in many cases husbands.

Daphne Merkin had met Diana Trilling while studying at Columbia University in the 1970s. She became a member of *Partisan Review*'s editorial board in the mid-1970s after meeting William Phillips, one of its editors, at Diana Trilling's home on Martha's Vineyard. At *Partisan Review* board meetings, "the curmudgeonly William Phillips," Merkin later recalled, "would offer impatient comments as we (the board included Steven Marcus and Morris Dickstein) argued about which books were worth reviewing and which critics were good enough to be assigned, say, a new biography of Neville Chamberlain. I was one of only two or three women, depending on who showed up, and felt slightly patronized by the men, as in: 'What does the little lady have to say?' But I also found it sharpened my wits and strengthened my confidence to argue issues with people who thought for a living."

Like Diana had earlier in her career, Merkin went on to contribute to women's magazines, too. In the 1990s Merkin started writing for "*Mirabella, Elle*, and *Allure*," which "were not as limited in their vision as I had imagined them to be and were not to be so lightly dismissed as second-class citizens in the Grand Republic of Letters. There was interesting journalism coming out of these publications, including hardcore reporting, vivid profiles, and introspective personal essays." Writing in women's magazines was not something that Merkin looked down on. The distinction of writing like a woman or a man no longer existed. That owes much to the efforts of second-wave feminism. But also, to the legacy of the women New York intellectuals.[26]

In citing works in the notes, short titles have generally been used. Full citations are found in the bibliography. Archival papers frequently cited have been identified by the following abbreviations:

ACCFP   American Committee for Cultural Freedom Papers

CMP   *Commentary* Magazine Papers

DTP   Diana Trilling Papers

HHP   Henry Hurwitz/Menorah Association Collection

LCP   Lewis Coser Papers

LTP   Lionel Trilling Papers

MMP   Mary McCarthy Papers

NLP   *New Leader* Papers

NMP   Norman Mailer Papers

NPP   Norman Podhoretz Papers

SAFP   Solomon Andhil Fineberg Papers

Introduction

1. Diana Trilling, interview by Joseph Dorman, 1993, transcript, 57, Arguing the World Oral History Collection, 1988–1996, Columbia University Center for Oral History; Jason Epstein, quoted in Laskin, *Partisans*, 18–19.

2. Irving Howe, "The New York Intellectuals: A Chronicle and A Critique," *Commentary* (October 1968): 29–51. Quotes are from pages 40–41, 29.

3. Podhoretz, *Making It*, 83. Podhoretz borrowed the descriptor from journalist Murray Kempton. See Menand, "The Book That Scandalized the New York Intellectuals."

4. Podhoretz, *Making It*, 89, 185, 198.

5. For women and Judaism, see, e.g., Baskin, *Jewish Women in Historical Perspective*; Baskin, "Jewish Traditions about Women and Gender Roles"; and Hyman, *Gender and Assimilation*. For how religious practices began to change in the United States, see, e.g., Goldman, *Beyond the Synagogue*.

6. Daniel Bell, "The Intellectuals in American Society," Daniel Bell Papers, Hebrew Union College, June 18, 1976, box 19, folder 32, Harvard University Archives. Reprinted as "The 'Intelligentsia' in American Society," in *The Winding Passage*, 119–37. Quotes from pages 120, 125, 131, 129.

7. Bell cited Howe and Podhoretz but said they focused on "the characteristic *style* of the group, not of their lives as persons." Bell, "Intelligentsia," 131.

8. Kazin, *New York Jew*; Phillips, *A Partisan View*; Howe, *Margin of Hope*; Barrett, *Truants*; Abel, *Intellectual Follies*; Hook, *Out of Step*; Podhoretz, *Breaking*

Ranks; D. Trilling, *Beginning of the Journey*; McCarthy, *Intellectual Memoirs*; Podhoretz, *Ex-Friends*; and Decter, *Old Wife's Tale*.

9. See, e.g., Bloom, *Prodigal Sons*; Cooney, *Rise of the New York Intellectuals*; Wald, *New York Intellectuals: The Rise and Decline of the Anti-Stalinist Left from the 1930s to the 1980s*; Jumonville, *Critical Crossings*; Wilford, *New York Intellectuals: From Vanguard to Institution*; and Teres, *Renewing the Left*. Teres devotes one chapter to the New York intellectuals who are women.

10. An important exception is Ring, *Political Consequences of Thinking*.

11. See, e.g., Imhoff, *Masculinity and the Making of American Judaism*.

12. I borrow the term "ideology of masculinity" from historian Robert Dean who writes that, "an ideology of masculinity in its *prescriptive* aspect provides the raw material needed to imagine and construct a narrative identity—the internal story that lends coherence to the self. In its *proscriptive* aspect, it rules out certain ways of imagining and acting in the world." Dean, *Imperial Brotherhood*, 5. See also Scott, "Gender: A Useful Category of Historical Analysis"; and Butler, *Gender Trouble*.

13. For neoconservatism, see, e.g., Dorrien, *The Neoconservative Mind*; Gerson, *Neoconservative Vision*; Friedman, *The Neoconservative Revolution*. More recent studies include, e.g., Heilbrunn, *They Knew They Were Right*; Abrams, *Norman Podhoretz and* Commentary *Magazine*; Balint, *Running Commentary*; and Vaïsse, *Neoconservatism*. See also Mann, *Rise of the Vulcans*. For an analysis of neoconservatism and foreign affairs prior to 9/11, see Ehrman, *Rise of the Neoconservatives and Foreign Affairs*.

14. For family values and the New Right, see, e.g., Lassiter, "Inventing Family Values." Self, *All in the Family*; Dowland, *Family Values and the Rise of the Christian Right*; Hartman, *A War for the Soul of America*; and Young, *We Gather Together*.

15. The literature on American Jews and liberalism is extensive. See, e.g., Wenger, *New York Jews and the Great Depression*; Dollinger, *Quest for Inclusion*; and Staub, *Torn at the Roots*.

16. I thank one of my anonymous reviewers for the phrase "tether of masculinity." For intellectual currents in the late twentieth century, see, e.g., Chappell, "Triumph of Conservatism in a Liberal Age"; Livingston, *World Turned Inside Out*; Lassiter, *Silent Majority*; Kruse and Zelizer, *Fault Lines*; and Rodgers, *Age of Fracture*.

17. Lambert, *Literary Mafia*.

18. See, for example, *Annie Hall*, directed by Woody Allen (United Artists, 1977); *Zelig*, directed by Woody Allen (Warner Brothers, 1983); and *Starting Out in the Evening*, directed by Andrew Wagner (Roadside Attractions, 2007).

19. Douglas, *Feminization of American Culture*.

20. See, e.g., Bederman, *Manliness and Civilization*; and Watts, *Rough Rider in the White House*.

21. On immigration, see, e.g., Handlin, *The Uprooted*; Rischin, *Promised City*; Higham, *Send These to Me*. On the Great Migration, see, e.g., Trotter, *Great Migration in Historical Perspective*; Arnesen, *Black Protest and the Great*; Gregory, *Southern Diaspora*; Berlin, *Making of African America*; and Grant, *Great Migration and the Democratic Party*. For Jewish and Black intellectuals navigating this period, see, e.g., Weinfeld, *American Friendship*.

22. See, e.g., Gilman, *Freud, Race, and Gender*; and Mosse, *Image of Man*.

23. Van Wyck Brooks, *America's Coming-of-Age* (New York: B. W. Huebsch, 1915); and Malcolm Cowley, *After the Genteel Tradition: American Writers, 1910–1930* (New York: Norton, 1937). See, e.g., Blake, *Beloved Community*.

24. Bell, "Intelligentsia," 126. For the Southern Agrarians, see, e.g., Conkin, *Southern Agrarians*; and Murphy, *Rebuke of History*.

25. Bell, "Intelligentsia," 125–27.

26. Douglas, *Terrible Honesty*. See also Dumenhill, *Modern Temper*; and Stansell, *American Moderns*.

27. Moore et al., *Jewish New York*; Jay, *Dialectical Imagination*; Krohn, *Intellectuals in Exile*. See also Lederhendler, *New York Jews and the Decline of Urban Ethnicity*.

28. Higham, *Strangers in the Land*; Lee, *At America's Gate*; and Ngai, *Impossible Subjects*.

29. Karabel, *The Chosen*; Bederman, *Manliness and Civilization*; and Hoganson, *Fighting for American Manhood*.

30. Boyarin, *Unheroic Conduct*. See also essays in Boyarin, Itzkovitz, and Pellegrini, *Queer Theory and the Jewish Question*.

31. Howe, "New York Intellectuals," 34.

32. Bell, "Intelligentsia," 134–35.

33. Biale, Galchinsky, and Heschel, *Insider/Outsider*.

34. See, e.g., Goren, "The 'Golden Decade': 1945–55." For a succinct challenge to the narrative of American Jewish exceptionalism, see Michels, "Is America 'Different'? A Critique of American Jewish Exceptionalism."

35. For Jews and whiteness, see, e.g., Goldstein, *The Price of Whiteness*; and Brodkin, *How Jews Became White Folks*.

36. Moore, *At Home in America*. For the ambivalence that came with this transformation, see Berman, "American Jews and the Ambivalence of Middle-Classness," and Kranson, *Ambivalent Embrace*. For Jews and civil liberties, see Svonkin, *Jews Against Prejudice*; and Greenberg, *Troubling the Waters*.

37. Herberg, *Protestant, Catholic, Jew* (1955). See, e.g., Schultz, *Tri-Faith America*. See also Moore, *GI Jews*; Stahl, *Enlisting Faith*.

38. For Jews and radicalism, see, e.g., Michels, *A Fire in Their Hearts*. For Jews and anti-communism, see, e.g., Moore, "Reconsidering the Rosenbergs"; Svonkin, *Jews Against Prejudice*; and Dollinger, *Quest for Inclusion*. For the New York intellectuals, the Cold War, and liberalism, see, e.g., Pells, *Liberal Mind in a Conservative Age*; and Menand, *Free World*.

39. Jacoby, *The Last Intellectuals*.

40. Scholars of American Jewish history have written at length about women's experiences and the construction of female gender roles but American Jewish masculinity is surprisingly understudied. See, e.g., Breines, *Tough Jews*; Wenger, "Constructing Manhood in American Jewish Culture," 352; and Imhoff, *Masculinity and the Making of American Judaism*. Jewish masculinity has been examined more extensively by scholars of European history. See, e.g., Boyarin, *Unheroic Conduct*; Mosse, *Image of Man*; Kaplan and Moore, *Gender and Jewish History*; and Baader, Gillerman, and Lerner, *Jewish Masculinities*. See also Hyman, *Gender and Assimilation in Modern Jewish History*; Prell, *Fighting to Become Americans*.

41. Cuordileone, *Manhood and American Political Culture*; Dean, *Imperial Brotherhood*; and Johnson, *Lavender Scare*.

42. Antler, *Jewish Radical Feminism*.

43. Howe, "New York Intellectuals," 29.

44. Howe, "New York Intellectuals," 31.

45. Michels, "Communalist History and Beyond," 64.

46. Bloom, *Prodigal Sons*.

47. Laskin, *Partisans*; Ring, *Political Consequences of Thinking*; and Abrams, *Mary McCarthy*. An exception is Penner, *Pinks, Pansies, and Punk*. There are biographies about McCarthy, Arendt, Hardwick, and Sontag. See, e.g., Kieran, *Seeing Mary Plain*; Brightman, *Writing Dangerously*; Gelderman, *Mary McCarthy: A Life*; Young-Bruehl, *Hannah Arendt for Love of the World*; Rollyson and Paddock, *Susan Sontag and the Making of an Icon*; Moser, *Sontag: Her Life and Work*; and Curtis, *Life of Elizabeth Hardwick*.

48. Grinberg, "Neither 'Sissy' Boy nor Patrician Man."

49. The term "imagined communities" comes from Anderson, *Imagined Communities*. Kessner, *Other Jewish New York Intellectuals*.

50. Sinkoff, *From Left to Right*, 3; Michels, "Communalist History and Beyond," 64; and Hollinger, "Communalist and Dispersionist Approaches to American Jewish History in an Increasingly Post-Jewish Era," 4.

51. Bell, "Intelligentsia," 130.

52. Brightman, *Between Friends*, 146–49.

53. For *Partisan Review*'s early history, see, e.g., Gilbert, *Writers and Partisans*; and Cooney, *Rise of the New York Intellectuals*.

54. Podhoretz, *Making It*, 87.

55. Podhoretz, *Making It*, 97. For the *Menorah Journal*, see, e.g., Greene, *Jewish Origins of Cultural Pluralism*.

56. Abrams, *Commentary Magazine, 1945-1955*; and Balint, *Running Commentary*.

57. Pells, *Liberal Mind in a Conservative Age*.

58. For *politics*, see Sumner, *Dwight Macdonald and the Politics Circle*; for *Encounter*, see, e.g., Greg Barnhisel, *Cold War Modernists*; and Wilford, *The CIA, the British Left and the Cold War*. For *The New York Review of Books*, see Nobile, *Intellectual Skywriting*.

59. For the Popular Front, see Denning, *Cultural Front*. For a critical view of the Popular Front, see, e.g., Klehr, *Heyday of American Communism*.

60. Howe, "New York Intellectuals," 32–33; and Podhoretz, *Making It*, 86.

61. Podhoretz, *Making It*, 83.

62. Quoted in Wreszin, *Life and Politics of Dwight Macdonald*, 230.

63. Chandler Brossard, "Plaint of a Gentile Intellectual: A New 'Minority Problem'?," *Commentary* (August 1950): 154.

64. Podhoretz, *Making It*, 83–92, 115.

65. Bell, "Intelligentsia," 127–29.

66. Diana Trilling to Norman Mailer, May 7, 1968, box 581, folder 1, Norman Mailer Papers, Harry Ransom Center, University of Texas at Austin. Hereafter, NMP.

67. David A. Bell, interview by author, June 12, 2019, New York City.

68. See, e.g., Halberstam, *Female Masculinity*.

69. Podhoretz, *Making It*, 115.

70. Midge Decter, interview by author, November 21, 2011, New York City.

71. Ann Birstein's books include *Star of Glass* (1950), *The Troublemaker* (1955), *The Sweet Birds of Gorham* (1966), *Summer Situations* (1972), and *Dickie's List* (1973). After her divorce, she continued writing and supported herself doing so while also teaching writing. She published *American Children* (1980), *The Rabbi on Forty-Seventh Street* (1982), *The Last of the True Believers* (1988), and her memoir, as well as short stories, essays, and reviews for the *New Yorker*, *McCall's*, the *New York Times*, and *Vogue*.

72. Birstein, *What I Saw at the Fair*, 182, 145, 133.

73. Bell, "We Gather Together," *New Yorker*, November 26, 1955, 51–56; and David Bell interview, 6.

74. David Bell interview. See Sherry, *Gay Artists in Modern American Culture*.

75. His first two marriages were to Nora Potashnik and Elaine Graham. Matt Schudel, "Daniel Bell," 91; "Sociologist Foresaw the Rise of the Internet," *Washington Post*, January 26, 2011.

76. David Bell interview, 7; and David Bell, "Afterword: A Life of Pearl Kazin Bell," in Towns, *Pearl of Great Price*.

77. John Summers, "Daniel Bell and The End of Ideology," *Dissent* (Spring 2011).

78. David Bell interview; Bell, *End of Ideology* (1960); Bell, *Coming of Post-Industrial Society* (1973); Bell, *Cultural Contradictions of Capitalism* (1976).

79. P. Bell to Mike Kolatch, May 6, 1977, box 228, New Leader Papers, Rare Book and Manuscript Library, Columbia University. Hereafter, NLP.

80. P. Bell to Mike Kolatch, June 1, 1986, box 228, NLP.

81. P. Bell to Stanley Burnshaw, July 3, 1976, box 23, folder 8, Stanley Burnshaw Papers, Harry Ransom Center, University of Texas at Austin.

82. P. Bell to Stanley Burnshaw, November 22, 1982, box 23, folder 8, Stanley Burnshaw Papers.

83. David Bell interview.

84. David Bell interview.

85. In *New York Jew*, Kazin notes that "my sister and I became writers." This is the only mention of his sister in all three of his memoirs. See Kazin, *New York Jew*, 12; Kazin, *A Walker in the City*; Kazin, *Starting Out in the Thirties*.

86. Diana Trilling, interview with Irving Howe, December 19, 1978, box 48, folder 7, 146, Diana Trilling Papers, Rare Book and Manuscript Library, Columbia University. Hereafter, DTP.

87. Berman, *Speaking of Jews*, 108.

88. Tim Lacy, "'Mrs. Hofstadter' and the Myth of the Heroic Lone Scholar," *U.S. Intellectual History Blog, Society for U.S. Intellectual History*, January 18, 2018, https://s-usih.org/2018/01/mrs-hofstadter-heroic-lone-scholar-myth/. Daniel Singal was the emeritus professor who posted his comment on January 22, 2018.

89. Robins, *Untold Journey*; Daphne Merkin, "The Journey of Diana Trilling," *Wall Street Journal*, August 18, 2017. Ann Birstein was perhaps "anonymously involved" in Kazin's writings: see Sandee Brawarsky, "A Literary Life: Remembering Ann Birstein," *NY Jewish Week*, June 2, 2017.

90. While scholars have written at length about Podhoretz and Howe, few have examined them through a gendered lens. Diana Trilling and Midge Decter, meanwhile, have received scant attention. For Diana Trilling, see Robins, *The Untold Journey.* Almost nothing has been written about Decter. Other intellectuals could have easily been case studies. For Norman Mailer and masculinity, see, e.g., Garrett, *Young Lions.*

Chapter One

1. A. L. Shands, "The Cheder on the Hill: Some Notes on C.C.N.Y.," *Menorah Journal* 16, no. 3 (March 1929): 263.

2. Milton Himmelfarb, interview by Suki Sander, July 7, 1981, transcript, pp. 1–3, William E. Wiener Oral History Library of the American Jewish Committee, New York Public Library, the Dorot Jewish Division. Milton Himmelfarb is not usually included among the New York intellectuals, though he wrote for *Commentary.* His sister, the historian Gertrude Himmelfarb, married Irving Kristol and was considered a member of the group.

3. Gorelick, *City College and the Jewish Poor*, 208; and Cohen, *When the Old Left Was Young.* Women were not admitted to the College of Arts and Science at CCNY until 1950. See Van Nort, *City College of New York.*

4. Grinberg, "Neither 'Sissy' Boy nor Patrician Man."

5. Lionel Abel, interview by Joseph Dorman, 1992, p. 1A-4. Arguing the World Oral History Collection, 1988–1996, Columbia University Center for Oral History.

6. Mosse, *Image of Man*; and Imhoff, *Masculinity and the Making of American Judaism.* For quotas, see, e.g., Oren, *Joining the Club.* For Jews and race, see, e.g., Goldstein, *Price of Whiteness.* For anti-Semitism, see, e.g., Higham, *Strangers in the Land*; and Dinnerstein, *Anti-Semitism in America.*

7. Higham, *Send These to Me*; Diner, *A Time for Gathering*; Sorin, *A Time for Building*; Lee, *At America's Gates*; Lee, *America for Americans*; and Ngai, *Impossible Subjects.*

8. Bederman, *Manliness and Civilization*; Hoganson, *Fighting for American Manhood*; and Slotkin, *Gunfighter Nation.*

9. For Victorian manhood, see Carnes, *Secret Ritual and Victorian Manhood in Victorian America.*

10. Dean, *Imperial Brotherhood*; and Karabel, *The Chosen*, 2.

11. Marjorie Garber, "Category Crisis: The Way of the Cross and the Jewish Star," in Boyarin, Itzkovitz, and Pellegrini, *Queer Theory and the Jewish Question*, 32. See also Gilman, *Jews' Body*; Gilman, *Sexuality: An Illustrated History*; Baader, Gillerman, and Lerner, *Jewish Masculinities*; and Hoffman, *Passing Game.*

12. Imhoff, *Masculinity and the Making of American Judaism.*

13. Boyarin, *Unheroic Conduct*, 19, 23.

14. Elizabeth Hardwick, interview by Darryl Pinckney, *Paris Review* 96 (Summer 1985). Draft copy of the interview, box 7, folder 4, Elizabeth Hardwick Papers, Harry Ransom Center, University of Texas at Austin. Also quoted in Laskin, *Partisans*, 189–91.

15. Trilling, *Journey*, 126–27.

16. I thank David A. Bell for this insight.

17. Michels, *A Fire in Their Hearts*, 15.

18. Howe, *World of Our Fathers*, 173.

19. Kristol quoted in Dorman, *Arguing the World*, 29.

20. Howe, *Margin of Hope*, 6–7.

21. Kazin, *Walker in the City*, 12.

22. For the Triangle Shirtwaist fire, see, e.g., Orleck, *Common Sense and a Little Fire*.

23. Alfred Kazin, interview by Joseph Dorman, 1994, Arguing the World Oral History Collection, 1988–1996, Columbia University Center for Oral History, 11.

24. Glazer quoted in Dorman, *Arguing the World*, 31.

25. Glazer interview by Dorman, 1995, Arguing the World Oral History Collection, 5.

26. Hook, *Out of Step*, 8.

27. Lionel Abel, interview by Dorman, 1992, Arguing the World Oral History Collection, 1A-2; "Alter Abelson, Rabbi, 88, Dead: Hebrew Scholar and Poet Served Several Temples," *New York Times*, December 22, 1964; and Abel, *Intellectual Follies*.

28. Phillips, *Partisan View*, 21, 24.

29. Kimmage, *Conservative Turn*, 18–19; Alan Wald, *New York Intellectuals*, 35; Trilling to John Vaughn, December 15, 1972, box 28, Lionel Trilling Papers, Rare Book and Manuscript Library, Columbia University. Hereafter, LTP. Also quoted in Kimmage, *Conservative Turn*, 319–20.

30. Milton Kaplan, "Private Enterprise in the Bronx," *Commentary* (August 1950). Republished in Cohen, *Commentary on the American Scene*, 247.

31. Phillips, *Partisan View*, 21.

32. Kristol, quoted in *Arguing the World*, 29.

33. Alfred Kazin, "The Sweet Nachama," *Present Tense* (September/October 1989): 45.

34. Melosh, "Manly Work: Public Art and Masculinity in Depression America," in *Gender and American History since 1890*.

35. Hapgood, *Spirit of the Ghetto*. See also Anzia Yezierska, *Bread Givers* (Doubleday, 1925).

36. Milton Klonsky, "The Trojans of Brighton Beach," *Commentary* (May 1947). Republished in Cohen, *Commentary on the American Scene*, 184–86.

37. Phillips, *Partisan View*, 21–22, 25.

38. Quoted in Cook, *Alfred Kazin*, 8; Kazin, *New York Jew*, 12; Cook, *Kazin's Journals*, 360.

39. Cook, *Kazin's Journals*, 545.

40. Cook, *Alfred Kazin*, 7.

41. Howe, *World of Our Fathers*, 176. Yet Howe's recollections of his own mother were more affirming. See Howe, *Margin of Hope*, 7. For the history of Jewish mothers, see, e.g., Antler, *You Never Call!*

42. Susan Glenn, *Daughters of the Shtetl*, 10.

43. Howe, *World of Our Fathers*, 173.

44. Wenger, "Constructing Manhood in American Jewish Culture," 360.

45. Cook, *Alfred Kazin*, 9. See also Hertzberg, *Jews in America*.

46. Howe, *World of Our Fathers*, 306.

47. Howe, *World of Our Fathers*, 22.

48. Kazin quoted in Dorman, *Arguing the World*, 36.

49. Cook, *Kazin's Journals*, March 22, 1988, 545.

50. Himmelfarb, interview by Sander, 1–3.

51. Boydston, *Home and Work*; and Douglas, *Feminization of American Culture*.

52. Kazin, *Walker*, 21–22; and Howe, *World of Our Fathers*, 252–54.

53. Howe, *World of Our Fathers*, 173.

54. Bell, "Reflections on Jewish Identity," 315.

55. Kazin, *Walker*, 13–21. Quotes are from pages 19, 21, and 13.

56. Daniel Bell, "Crime as an American Way of Life," *Antioch Review* 13, no. 2 (Summer 1953): 111.

57. Bell, "Crime," 120. See also, Weissman Joselit, *Our Gang*.

58. Nathan Abrams argues it was a "cheap" imitation. "But as hard as Jews try to be like everyone else, it is the very excess of their efforts, their desire to out-perform, that marks them as different." See Abrams, "Muscles, Mimicry, *Menschlikyat*, and Madagascar," 130, 132.

59. Bell, "Crime," 111.

60. Imhoff, *Masculinity and American Judaism*, 213–14, 222.

61. Bell, "Crime," 133.

62. Howe, *World of Our Fathers*, 110; Fried, *Jewish Gangsters*, 36.

63. Howe, *World of Our Fathers*, 258.

64. William Poster, "'Twas a Dark Night in Brownsville," originally published in *Commentary*, May 1950. Republished in Cohen, *Commentary on the American Scene*, 70.

65. Poster, "Dark Night," 60.

66. Phillips, *Partisan View*, 21.

67. Hook, *Out of Step*, 7–8.

68. Fried, *Jewish Gangsters*, 38.

69. Podhoretz, *Making It*, 15.

70. Milton Klonsky, "The Trojans of Brighton Beach," in Cohen, *Commentary on the American Scene*, 180.

71. Reiss, "A Fighting Chance: The Jewish-American Experience, 1890–1940"; and Norwood, "American Jewish Muscle: Forging," 174.

72. Silver, "Boxing in Olde New York," 318.

73. Wenger, "Constructing Manhood in American Jewish Culture," 357.

74. Kazin, interview by Dorman, 1994, Arguing the World Oral History Collection, 13.

75. Gurock, "During the Heyday of Jewish Sports in Gotham," 262, 258.

76. Howe, *World of Our Fathers*, 259.

77. Klonsky, "Trojans," 181.

78. Milton Kaplan, "Private Enterprise in the Bronx," *Commentary* (August 1950). Reprinted in Cohen, *Commentary on the American Scene*, 244.

79. Klonsky, "Trojans," 181.

80. Klonsky, "Trojans," 182.

81. Poster, "Dark Night," 65.

82. Quoted in Howe, *World of Our Fathers*, 182.

83. Abrams, "Muscles, Mimicry, *Menschlikyat*, and Madagascar," 126.

84. Lionel Trilling, "The Mind of Robert Warshow," *Commentary* (June 1961): 505; and Warshow, *Immediate Experience*.

85. Bell quoted in Dorman, *Arguing the World*, 42. Exact numbers of Jewish students are unavailable. Scholars estimate that Jews constituted 20 percent to 40 percent of the student body at Columbia, 35 percent to 50 percent of the student body at NYU, and 80 percent to 90 percent of the student body at CCNY. Steinberg, *Academic Melting Pot*, 9.

86. Shands, "Cheder on the Hill," 263; M. G. Torch, "The Spirit of Morningside: Some Notes on Columbia University," *Menorah Journal* 18 (March 1930): 254; and Felix Morrow, "Higher Learning on Washington Square: Some Notes on New York University," *Menorah Journal* (April 1930): 348.

87. Phillips, *Partisan View*, 27.

88. Torch, "Spirit of Morningside," 254–55.

89. Morris Freedman, "The Jewish College Student, 1951 Model: Is the Old Idealism and Zeal for Learning Gone?," *Commentary* 12 (1951): 306; and Meyer Liben, "CCNY—A Memoir," *Commentary* (September 1965): 70.

90. Morrow, "Higher Learning on Washington Square," 249; Shands, "Cheder on the Hill," 263, 268.

91. Cohen was quoted in a newspaper article, "Football Wrong, says Prof. Cohen" (date, publication, and author unknown). This most likely appeared in *The Campus*, CCNY's school newspaper, folder 4, box 58, Morris Raphael Cohen Papers, 1898–1981, Special Collections Research Center, University of Chicago.

92. Goldstein, *Price of Whiteness*, 127. Goldstein argues that the stereotype of Jews lacking athleticism was exaggerated. For the importance of football, see, e.g., Griswold, "The Flabby American, the Body, and the Cold War." For Cohen, see Cohen Rosenfield, *Portrait of a Philosopher*; Hollinger, *Morris R. Cohen and the Scientific Ideal*; and Konvitz, *Nine Jewish American Thinkers*.

93. Kugelmass, *Jews, Sports and the Rights of Citizenship*.

94. Boyarin, *Unheroic Conduct*, especially chapter 4; Baskin, "Jewish Traditions about Women and Gender Roles"; and Hyman, *Gender and Assimilation*.

95. Shands, "Cheder on the Hill," 269.

96. Freedman, "Jewish College Student," 305; Howe, *Margin of Hope*, 62; Liben, "CCNY—A Memoir," 68; and Howe, *World of Our Fathers*, 284–85.

97. Paul, last name unknown, to Leonora Cohen Rosenfield, April 26, 1959, box 67, folder 14; David Savan to Leonora Cohen Rosenfield, July 16, 1959, box 67, folder 9; Duncan E. Littlefair to Leonora Cohen Rosenfield, 1959, box 67, folder 1; Victor Lowe to Leonora Cohen Rosenfield, June 5, 1959, box 67, folder 2; Arthur F. Smullyan to Leonora Cohen Rosenfield, April 16, 1959, box 67, folder 10; Harold Winkler to Leonora Cohen Rosenfield, July 7, 1961, box 67, folder 14; "The Eternal Light: Chapter Two Hundred and Thirty Seven, 'A Dreamer's Journey,'" radio broadcast transcript, June 12, 1949, box 58, folder 4, 5, the National Broadcasting Company Inc. and the Jewish Theological Seminary, all in the Morris Raphael Cohen Papers, University of Chicago Library.

98. Howe, *World of Our Fathers*, 284–85; Liben, "CCNY—A Memoir," 65; Sidney Hook, "Morris Cohen—Fifty Years Later," *American Scholar* 43 (1976).

99. Irving Kristol, "Memoirs of a Trotskyist," in *Reflections of a Neoconservative: Looking Back, Looking Ahead* (New York: Basic Books, 1983), 6; Liben, "CCNY—A Memoir," 65; and Howe quoted in Bloom, *Prodigal Sons*, 39.

100. Kristol, "Memoirs of a Trotskyist," 7.

101. *The Microcosm*, City College of New York Yearbook, 1936, Morris Raphael Cohen Library, Archives and Special Collections, the City College of New York.

102. Ring, *Political Consequences*, 135.

103. Seymour Martin Lipset, "Out of The Alcoves," *Wilson Quarterly* 23 (1999): 85; and Kristol, "Memoirs of a Trotskyist," 10, 8.

104. *The Menorah Movement for the Study and Advancement of Jewish Culture and Ideals: History, Purpose, Activities*; and Greene, *Jewish Origins of Cultural Pluralism*.

105. Max Handman to Henry Hurwitz, no date, folder 1, box 14, Horace Kallen Papers, Jacob Rader Marcus Center of the American Jewish Archives, Cincinnati, Ohio.

106. Mayer, "From Zero to Hero: Masculinity in Jewish Nationalism," 101. Trilling quoted in Kimmage, *Conservative Turn*, 33. See also Green, *Jewish Origins*, 168–72.

107. Hurwitz remained the magazine's editor until his death in 1961. The *Journal* folded in 1962. See Greene, *Jewish Origins*; Mark Krupnick, "The Menorah Group and the Origins of Modern Jewish-American Radicalism," *Modern Jewish Studies Annual III, Studies in American Jewish Literature* 5 (1979): 56–67; Lauren B. Strauss, "Staying Afloat in the Melting Pot: Constructing an American Jewish Identity in the *Menorah Journal* of the 1920s," *American Jewish History* 84 (1996): 315–31; Jenna Weissman Joselit, "Without Ghettoism: A History of the Intercollegiate Menorah Association, 1906–1930," *American Jewish Archives Publication* 30 (1978): 133–54; Seth Korelitz, "The Menorah Idea: From Religion to Culture, from Race to Ethnicity," *American Jewish History* 85 (1997): 75–100.

108. Robert Alter, "Epitaph for a Jewish Magazine: Notes on the 'Menorah Journal,'" *Commentary* 39 (1965): 52; and Podhoretz, *Making It*, 96.

109. Lionel Trilling, "Young in the Thirties," *Commentary* 41 (1966): 47; and "Elliot E. Cohen, Editor of 'Commentary,' Dead; Funeral Services Held," *Jewish Telegraph Agency*, June 1, 1959.

110. Lionel Trilling to Elliot Cohen, December 2, 1929, box 7, folder 16; and Felix Morrow to Elliot Cohen, undated, box 36, folder 9, Henry Hurwitz Papers/Menorah Association Collection, Jacob Rader Marcus Center of the American Jewish Archives, Cincinnati, Ohio. Hereafter, HHP.

111. Halper, *Good-Bye, Union Square*, 42–43. L. Trilling, "Young in the Thirties," 45; and L. Trilling, "On the Death of a Friend," *Commentary* (February 1960): 94.

112. Lionel Trilling, eulogy for Elliot Cohen, final draft, box 6, folder 1, LTP; L. Trilling, "On the Death of a Friend," 93.

113. Lionel Trilling was arguably an exception. He viewed Cohen as a mentor but increasingly moved away from Jewish concerns. Yet Trilling also associated Jewish intellectuality with masculinity. As Michael Kimmage notes: "By equating Judaism with a culture of intelligence and delight—with a kind of Jewish Hellenism—Trilling paved the way for his own departure from Jewish concerns." See Kimmage, *Conservative Turn*, 32–34.

114. Krupnick, "Menorah Group," 63.

115. Elliot E. Cohen, "The Age of Brass," *Menorah Journal* 11, no. 5 (1925): 427–28, 436; 444–46.

116. Krupnick, "Menorah Group," 63; and Greene, *Jewish Origins*, 143.

117. Cohen, "Age of Brass," 438. Cohen used the term "Israel" as a synonym for the Jewish people, not "Zionism."

118. Elinor Grumet, "Elliot Cohen: The Vocation of a Jewish Mentor," *Studies in the American Jewish Experience* 1 (1981): 16.

119. Lishmoh Committee to Henry Hurwitz, December 12, 1929, box 7, folder 16, HHP. Also in box 6, folder 1, LTP.

120. Morris Dickstein, "Womb versus World," *BookForum* (June/July/September 2006). https://www.bookforum.com/print/1302/womb-versus-world-564.

121. Slesinger, *The Unpossessed*. According to Murray Kempton in *Part of Our Time*, *The Unpossessed* was "almost our only surviving document" of this group. He linked the characters to real-life counterparts. Lionel Trilling, however, countered that "as a document of its time, *The Unpossessed* must be used with caution." L. Trilling, "Young in the Thirties," 48. See also Wald, *New York Intellectuals*, 68.

122. L. Trilling, "Young in the Thirties," 44; Elizabeth Hardwick, Introduction to *The Unpossessed* (New York: New York Review Books Classics, 2002), viii.

123. L. Trilling, "Young in the Thirties," 44; Slesinger, *The Unpossessed*, 301; Dickstein, "Womb versus World." According to Dickstein, Slesinger's short story about abortion, "Missis Flinders," published in *Story* magazine in 1932, was "based on her own experience" and became the final chapter of *The Unpossessed*.

124. Alter, "Epitaph for a Jewish Magazine," 54; Halper, *Good-bye Union Square*, 26–32; Alan M. Wald, "The Menorah Group Moves Left," *Jewish Social Studies* 38 (1976): 297.

125. Elliot Cohen to Henry Hurwitz, September 17, 1931, box 7, folder 7, HHP. See also Herbert Solow to Henry Hurwitz, June 18, June 19, June 22, 1931, box 56, folder 21; and Henry Hurwitz to Elliot Cohen, August 12, 1931, box 7, folder 17, HHP.

126. Alter, "Epitaph," 65. On the financial stresses, see Solow to Hurwitz, July 7, and August 12, 1931; Solow to Board of Governors, Menorah Association, November 18, 1931; Samuel Jaffe, Felix Morrow, Nathan Reich, and Kopel S. Pinson to Solow, November 17, 1931; and Albert Halper to Solow, November 17, 1931; F. F. Greenman to Solow, November 13, 1931, all in box 56, folder 21, HHP; and Lionel Trilling to Henry Hurwitz, September 3, 1932, box 60, folder 1, HHP.

127. Philip Abbott, "Are Three Generations of Radicals Enough? Self-Critique in the Novels of Tess Slesinger, Mary McCarthy, and Marge Piercy," *Review of Politics* 53 (1991): 613; and L. Trilling, "Young in the Thirties," 44, 48.

128. Ring, *Political Consequences*, 135; and Howe, "New York Intellectuals," 33.

129. Howe, "New York Intellectuals," 32.

130. Bell, "Reflections on Jewish Identity," 321.

131. Kristol, "Memoirs of a Trotskyist," 12.

132. William Phillips, "How 'Partisan Review' Began," *Commentary* (December 1976). For *Partisan Review*'s early history, see, e.g., Cooney, *Rise of the New York Intellectuals*.

133. Phillips quoted in Kieran, *Seeing Mary Plain*, 127; Laskin, *Partisans*, 191.

134. *Paris Review* interview with Hardwick, unpublished carbon notes, no date, 12, box 7, folder 4, Elizabeth Hardwick Papers, Harry Ransom Center, University of Texas at Austin.

135. Dickstein, "Womb versus World."

136. Phillips, *Partisan View*, 113.

137. Phillips and Abel quoted in Kieran, *Seeing Mary Plain*, 123.

138. Laskin, *Partisans*, 190.

139. D. Trilling, *Journey*, 307.

140. Phillips, *Partisan View*, 271.

141. Macdonald quoted in Kieran, *Seeing Mary Plain*, 121; McCarthy, *Intellectual Memoirs*, 96. See also Kadish, *Secular Rabbi*.

142. McCarthy, *Intellectual Memoirs*, 65.

143. For McCarthy, see, e.g., Brightman, *Writing Dangerously*; Gelderman, *Mary McCarthy: A Life*.

144. Kadish, *Secular Rabbi*, ix.

145. Mary McCarthy, "Obituary: Philip Rahv (1908–1973)," *Occasional Prose*, 5.

146. Jeffrey Meyers, "The Transformations of Philip Rahv," *Salmagundi* (Spring–Summer 2019); and McCarthy, "Obituary: Rahv," 6.

147. "The Transformation of Philip Rahv"; and Wald, *New York Intellectuals*, 76.

148. Abel and Howe quoted in Kieran, *Seeing Mary Plain*, 128.

149. Macdonald quoted in Kieran, *Seeing Mary Plain*, 146.

150. McCarthy, *Intellectual Memoirs*, 101.

151. McCarthy, *Intellectual Memoirs*, 103; and Fuchs Abrams, *Mary McCarthy*, 30.

152. Diana Trilling interview by Dwight Macdonald, 46–48, March 28, 1979, box 49, folder 3, DTP.

153. McCarthy, *Intellectual Memoirs*, 68–69.

154. Gelderman, *Mary McCarthy*; and John Simon, "Mary McCarthy and the Company She Keeps," *Washington Post*, May 22, 1988.

155. Howe quoted in Frances Kieran's *Seeing Mary Plain*, 131.

156. Barrett, *The Truants*, 4, 67.

157. Mary told her biographer, Carol Brightman, that Hardwick slept with Rahv and if she denied it she was lying. See Brightman, *Writing Dangerously*, 301. Hardwick was adamant that it never happened. See Darryl Pinckney, "The Ethics of Arendt, Hardwick, McCarthy, Sontag," *Threepenny Review* (Fall 2013).

158. Quoted in Laskin, *Partisans*, 190–91.

159. For Hardwick, see Curtis, *Splendid Intelligence*.

160. Podhoretz, *Making It*, 124.

161. Thomas Mallon, "Marriage, Betrayal, and the Letters behind the Dolphin," *New Yorker*, December 9, 2019.

162. Laskin, *Partisans*, 191; Hamilton, *Dolphin Letters*. For the Southern New Critics, see, e.g., Jancovich, *Cultural Politics of the New Criticism*.

163. Barrett, *The Truants*, 48–49.

164. Phillips, *Partisan View*, 113.

165. Young-Bruehl, *Hannah Arendt*, 154–64.

166. Barrett, *The Truants*, 103.

167. Barrett, quoted in Laskin, *Partisans*, 157.

168. Phillips, *Partisan View*, 106.

169. Laskin, *Partisans*, 157.

170. Howe, *Margin of Hope*, 270.

171. Kazin quoted in Cook, *Alfred Kazin: A Biography*, 116.

172. Phillips, *Partisan View*, 106.

173. According to Barrett, Phillips "could only think of [Arendt] as the stern figure of intellectual politics." See Barrett, *The Truants*, 102.

174. D. Trilling, *Journey*, 330–31.

Chapter Two

1. Diana Trilling, interview by Joseph Dorman, 2000, transcript, p. 57, Oral History Research Office (Columbia University, New York); and Dorman, *Arguing the World*, 102.

2. D. Trilling, *Journey*, 331, 148; and Sinkoff, *From Left to Right*, 193.

3. Barrett, *The Truants*, 48.

4. Darryl Pinckney, Introduction to *The Collected Essays of Elizabeth Hardwick*, xiii.

5. Diana Trilling to Norman Mailer, May 7, 1968, box 4, folder 4, DTP; Norman Mailer to Diana Trilling, August 1, 1968, box 4, folder 4, DTP.

6. Laskin, *Partisans*, 191.

7. Gelderman, *Mary McCarthy*; Kieran, *Seeing Mary Plain*; Hamilton, *Dolphin Letters*; and Curtis, *Splendid Intellectual*.

8. All quoted in Laskin, *Partisans*. According to Laskin, Blücher had affairs, and Arendt was "deeply hurt by his betrayals." But "it never occurred to Arendt to divorce Blücher for his adulteries—a practice she found absurdly American." Laskin, *Partisans*, 160, 219.

9. D. Trilling quoted in Laskin, *Partisans*, 26.

10. D. Trilling, *Journey*, 350–51.

11. Barrett, *The Truants*, 162.

12. Sidney Hook, "The Trillings: A Memory in Monologue" (compiled by Ernest Hook), *Commentary* (October 1, 2015).

13. Laskin, *Partisans*, 26.

14. I thank David A. Bell for this insight.

15. Hook, "The Trillings: A Memory in Monologue."

16. Phillips, *Partisan View*, 71.

17. Kazin, *New York*, 45–46. Of Kazin, Diana Trilling once said: "I have never *not* had a disagreement with Alfred Kazin. We have been disagreeing since the day we were born." Patricia Bosworth interview, "Diana Trilling: An Interview," *Paris Review* (Winter 1993): 251.

18. Epstein, *Gossip: The Untrivial Pursuit*, 66.

19. Sabrina Fuchs Abrams, "The Bitch Is Back: A Reappraisal of Mary McCarthy for the 21st Century," *Women's Studies: An Interdisciplinary Journal* 49, no. 4 (July 2020): 347–59. See also Nelson, *Tough Enough*; Dean, *Sharp*.

20. Daphne Merkin, "The Journey of Diana Trilling," *Wall Street Journal*, August 20, 2017, C5.

21. Heilbrun, *When Men Were the Only Models We Had*, 100.

22. Tobi Haslett, "The Feuds of Diana Trilling," *New Yorker*, May 29, 2017.

23. Morris Dickstein, "A Man Nobody Knew: Lionel Trilling Remembered," in *Lionel Trilling and the Critics: Opposing Selves*, xv–xvi; and Phillips, *Partisan View*, 71–72.

24. D. Trilling, *Journey*, 47; and Robins, *Untold Journey*, 1–5.

25. D. Trilling, *Journey*, 47.

26. Gorelick, *City College and the Jewish Poor*. For the strains between "uptown" Jews and "downtown" Eastern European Jews, see Goren, *New York Jews and the Quest for Community*; and Rischin, *Promised City*.

27. D. Trilling, *Journey*, 69.

28. D. Trilling, *Journey*, 77–78; 68.

29. For quotas and anti-Semitism, see, e.g., Karabel, *The Chosen*.

30. D. Trilling, *Journey*, 73.

31. D. Trilling, *Journey*, 98.

32. Their mutual friends were Clifton "Kip" and Polly Fadiman.

33. Robins, *Untold Journey*, xiv.

34. D. Trilling, *Journey*, 32.

35. Kimmage, *Conservative Turn*, 18.

36. Lionel Trilling, *Matthew Arnold*; Dickstein, "The Critic Who Made Us: Lionel Trilling and the Liberal Imagination," *Sewanee Review* 94, no. 2 (Spring 1986). Reprinted in Rodden, *Lionel Trilling and the Critics*, 379.

37. Diana Trilling interview by Stephen Donadio, January 14, 1976, 2, box 51, folder 7, DTP.

38. Barrett, *The Truants*, 161; and Phillips, *Partisan View*, 71.

39. Irving Howe, "On Lionel Trilling: 'Continuous Magical Confrontation,'" in Rodden, *Lionel Trilling and the Critics*, 348. Originally published in the *New Republic*, March 1976.

40. D. Trilling, *Journey*, 87.

41. Robert Alter to Norman Podhoretz, August 20, 1967, box 1: 4, folder 136, *Commentary* Magazine Papers, Harry Ransom Center, University of Texas at Austin. Hereafter, CMP.

42. Dickstein, "The Critic Who Made Us," 379–80.

43. Kazin, *New York Jew*, 47.

44. Lionel Trilling, "Four Decades of American Prose," *New Republic* 155, no. 19 (November 7, 1942): 483–84.

45. Kazin, *New York Jew*, 43, 46.

46. Kazin, *New York Jew*, 43; Dickstein, "The Critic Who Made Us," 380; Dickstein, Foreword to *A Voice Still Heard*, xviii.

47. Dickstein, "A Man Nobody Knew," xxii.

48. Dickstein, "A Man Nobody Knew," xvii.

49. Bloom, *Prodigal Sons*, 26.

50. D. Trilling, *Journey*, 9–10.

51. Quoted in Kimmage, *Conservative Turn*, 18.

52. Kimmage, *Conservative Turn*, 19.

53. D. Trilling, *Journey*, 32.

54. D. Trilling, *Journey*, 32.

55. D. Trilling, *Journey*, 34.

56. From 1906 to 1929, DeWitt Clinton was located on Fifty-Ninth Street and West Tenth Avenue. In 1929, the school moved to the Bedford Park section of the Bronx.

57. Diana Trilling interview by Stephen Donadio, January 14, 1976, box 51, folder 2, DTP.

58. D. Trilling, *Journey*, 82.

59. Kazin, *New York Jew*, 42.

60. Letter from Diana Trilling to Francis Steegmuller, February 27, 1976, box 5, folder 1, DTP.

61. Diana Trilling interview by Stephen Donadio, January 14, 1976, 25–27, box 51, folder 2, DTP; D. Trilling, *Journey*, 268.

62. Diana Trilling interview by Stephen Donadio, 26.

63. D. Trilling, *Journey*, 280.

64. D. Trilling, *Journey*, 268–80; Diana Trilling interview by Stephen Donadio.

65. D. Trilling, *Journey*, 321.

66. See Dickstein, *Why Not Say What Happened*.

67. Dickstein, "A Man Nobody Knew," xvii.

68. Diana Trilling interview by Stephen Donadio, January 14, 1976, 18, 23, box 51, folder 2, DTP.

69. Hook, "The Trillings: A Memory in Monologue," 50.

70. James Trilling, "My Father and the Weak-Eyed Devils," *American Scholar* 68, no. 2 (Spring 1999): 26.

71. D. Trilling, *Journey*, 9, 37–38.

72. D. Trilling, *Journey*, 282–84.

73. D. Trilling, *Journey*, 134.

74. Glenn, *Daughters of the Shtetl*; and Hyman, *Gender and Assimilation in Modern History*.

75. Birstein, *What I Saw at the Fair*, 85. See also Bell, *Winding Passage*, 132.

76. James Trilling, "My Father and the Weak-Eyed Devils," 26.

77. D. Trilling, "Footnote to My Life as a Critic," February 20, 1996, box 31, folder 10, DTP.

78. D. Trilling, *Journey*, 326, 19.

79. D. Trilling, *Journey*, 19–20, 326; James Trilling, "My Father and the Weak-Eyed Devils," 29–30; and Robins, *Untold Journey*, 97–101.

80. Tim Lacy, "'Mrs. Hofstadter' and the Myth of the Heroic Lone Scholar," *U.S. Intellectual History Blog, Society for U.S. Intellectual History*, January 18, 2018, https://s-usih.org/2018/01/mrs-hofstadter-heroic-lone-scholar-myth/; and Berman, *Speaking of Jews*, 108.

81. Moser, *Susan Sontag*, 120–21; 129–30.

82. Subsequent editions of the book saw the acknowledgment removed entirely. Moser, *Susan Sontag*, 122.

83. Quoted in Robins, *Untold Journey*, 85.

84. Diana Trilling interview by Midge Decter, February 21, 1976, 14, Columbia Rare Books and Manuscript Library.

85. Robins, *Untold Journey*, 83.

86. Michael Kimmage, "Journeys without End," *Jewish Review of Books* (Fall 2017).

87. Rodden, *Lionel Trilling and the Critics*, 465.

88. Dickstein, "A Man Nobody Knew," xii.

89. Mark Krupnick, "The Trillings: A Marriage of Two Minds?," *Salmagundi* (Summer 1994): 214–15.

90. Midge Decter, "Inside Story," *Commentary* 97, no. 1 (January 1994): 59–61.

91. James Atlas, "Diana Trilling at 88 Remembers, Rebukes and Ponders Marriage," *New York Times*, October 25, 1993; and see also Vivian Gornick, "Getting Even," *The Nation*, June 2017.

92. D. Trilling, *Journey*, 147.

93. D. Trilling, *Journey*, 147.

94. Patricia Bosworth interview, "Diana Trilling: An Interview," *Paris Review* (Winter 1993): 242.

95. Diana Trilling, "Footnote to My Life as a Critic," February 20, 1996, box 31, folder 10, DTP.

96. D. Trilling, *Journey*, 18–19.

97. D. Trilling, *Journey*, 325, 126. Her first long-form book was *Mrs. Harris: The Death of the Scarsdale Diet Doctor* (1981). Mrs. Harris was not fiction but in the genre of the New Journalism.

98. Kimmage, *Conservative Turn*, 173–74.

99. For the Hiss case, see Jacoby, *Alger Hiss and the Battle for History*; and Tanenhaus, *Whittaker Chambers*.

100. Kimmage, *Conservative Turn*, 200; and Menand, *Free World*, 164–68.

101. Hilton Kramer, "Thinking About Witness," *New Criterion* (March 1988), reprinted in *Alger Hiss, Whittaker Chambers, and the Schism in the American Soul*, 308.

102. Kimmage, *Conservative Turn*, 182; and D. Trilling, *Journey*, 387.

103. Mendelson, *Moral Agents*, quoted in Robins, *Untold Journey*, 129.

104. D. Trilling, *Journey*, 371. See also Epstein, *Gossip*, 65.

105. D. Trilling, "Footnote to My Life as a Critic," 6.

106. D. Trilling, *Journey*, 325; and D. Trilling, "Footnote to My Life as a Critic," 3–4.

107. D. Trilling, "Footnote to My Life as a Critic."

108. D. Trilling, *Journey*, 328.

109. D. Trilling, "Footnote to My Life as a Critic"; and D. Trilling, *Journey*, 330, 336–37.

110. D. Trilling, *Reviewing the Forties*, 237.

111. Bellow quoted in Tobi Haslett, "The Many Feuds of Diana Trilling," *New Yorker*, May 29, 2017. Diana was more laudatory toward Bellow's second novel, *The Victim*. But in her review she harkened back to "the self-pitying literalness which robbed his first [novel] of scale." *Reviewing the Forties*, 227. In her memoir she wrote, "Sometimes I had to write about books by friends; I always found this troublesome. But to fail to write about the book of a friend could make for even worse problems." D. Trilling, *Journey*, 338.

112. Diana was reviewing Christina Stead's, *For Love Alone* (1944). See D. Trilling, *Reviewing the Forties*, 110.

113. Barrett, *The Truants*, 68; and Patricia Bosworth, "Diana Trilling: An Interview," *Paris Review* 35 (Winter 1993): 248.

114. Here she was reviewing Merriam Modell, *The Sound of Years* (1946). D. Trilling, *Reviewing the Forties*, 172.

115. D. Trilling, *Reviewing the Forties*, 126–28.

116. Diana Trilling, "Virginia Woolf, A Special Instance," *Claremont Essays*, 88. First published in the *New York Times Book Review*, March 21, 1948.

117. D. Trilling, *Journey*, 342.

118. Diana Trilling interview by Stephen Donadio, January 14, 1976, box 51, folder 2, 43, DTP; Patricia Bosworth interview, "Diana Trilling: An Interview," *Paris Review*, Winter 1993, 247. See also D. Trilling, *Journey*, 331–33; and Alpern, *Frida Kirchwey*.

119. D. Trilling, *Journey*, 348.

120. Diana Trilling, "A Tentative Outline for a Series of Articles on the American Female," undated, box 30, folder 9, DTP.

121. Kimmage, *Conservative Turn*, 269.

122. "Queenly" is Tobi Haslett's apt description of Trilling. Haslett, "The Feuds of Diana Trilling," *New Yorker*, May 29, 2017.

123. D. Trilling, *Journey*, 182.

124. D. Trilling, *Journey*, 208. For the Scottsboro case, see, e.g., Carter, *Scottsboro: A Tragedy of the American South*; and Goodman, *Stories of Scottsboro*. For a sympathetic treatment of the Communist Party in Alabama, see Kelly, *Hammer and Hoe*.

125. D. Trilling, *Journey*, 181.

126. See, e.g., Pells, *The Liberal Mind in a Conservative Age*.

127. Cuordileone, *Manhood and American Political Culture*, xxi.

128. May, *Homeward Bound*.

129. Cuordileone, *Manhood and American Political Culture*, 2.

130. Kimmage, *Conservative Turn*, 113.

131. Kimmage, *Conservative Turn*, 83.

132. Kimmage, *Conservative Turn*, 80.

133. Epstein quoted in Saunders, *Who Paid the Piper*, 157–58.

134. Kazin, *New York Jew*, 45–46.

135. D. Trilling, *Journey*, 358.

136. Statement read by Diana Trilling to Board of Directors on the occasion of her resignation from the ACCF, January 10, 1961, box 36, folder 9, DTP.

137. Diana Trilling, "A Memorandum on the Hiss Case," *Partisan Review* 17, no. 5 (1950): 484; reprinted in D. Trilling, *Claremont Essays*, 65–86. Quotes from pages 78–81.

138. D. Trilling, "A Memorandum on the Hiss Case," in *Claremont Essays*, 68.

139. D. Trilling, "A Memorandum on the Hiss Case," in *Claremont Essays*, 85.

140. Diana Trilling, "A Communist and His Ideals," *Partisan Review* 18 (July–August 1951): 432.

141. D. Trilling, "A Communist and His Ideals," 433–34.

142. D. Trilling, "A Communist and His Ideals," 439.

143. Diana Trilling, "America through Dark Spectacles," *Twentieth Century* (July 1953): 33–35.

144. D. Trilling, "America through Dark Spectacles," *Twentieth Century* (July 1953): 39.

145. Robins, *Untold Journey*, 167.

146. Hook, *Out of Step*, 421.

147. Sol Stein, "Working for the CIA and Not Knowing It," unpublished manuscript, no date, box 50, folder 23, Sol Stein Papers, Rare Book and Manuscript Library, Columbia University.

148. Scanning the American Committee for Cultural Freedom (ACCF) stationery, which listed the group's membership over the years in the ACCF Papers, I found only a handful of women listed: educational reformer and author Dorothy Canfield Fisher; the harpsichordist Sylvia Marlowe; Austrian-British psychologist Marie Jahoda; and Alice Beal Parsons, a novelist and short story writer. American Committee for Cultural Freedom Papers, the Tamiment Library and Robert F. Wagner Labor Archives, New York University. Hereafter, ACCFP.

149. American Committee for Cultural Freedom stationery, no date, box 50, folder 13, in Sol Stein Papers, Rare Book and Manuscript Library, Columbia University. The other women listed were Eleanor Clark, Dorothy Canfield Fisher, Esther S. Goldfrank, Elinor Rice Hays, Marie Jahoda, Nancy Lenkeith, Katherine Anne Porter, and Alice Beal Parsons. Diana Trilling was then chairman of the Administrative Committee.

150. Diana Trilling told Jason Epstein that she served on the board from 1952 to 1957 in a letter dated April 21, 1967, box 3, folder 4, DTP. But a 1954 letter from Sol Stein suggests she was nominated to the board that year. Perhaps she served earlier, too. Letter from Sol Stein to Diana Trilling, October 29, 1954, DTP.

151. Robins, *Untold Journey*, 167.

152. Kimmage, *Conservative Turn*, 7.

153. Minutes, the first membership meeting of the American Committee for Cultural Freedom, box 7, folder 3, ACCFP; and "Resolution 1," undated, box 7, folder 3, ACCFP.

154. Daniel Bell to Diana Trilling, February 16, 1968, box 36, folder 8, DTP.

155. Diana Trilling to Arnold Beichman, January 23, 1953, box 3, folder 2, DTP.

156. D. Trilling, *Journey*, 346.

157. Diana Trilling, "America through Dark Spectacles," 38.

158. Saunders, *Who Paid the Piper*, 232–33; and Wilford, *Mighty Wurlitzer*, 197.

159. Hook, *Out of Step*, 430; and Phillips, *Partisan View*, 164.

160. Diana Trilling to William Phillips, May 24, 1969, box 4, folder 5, DTP.

161. Diana Trilling to Arnold Beichman, October 19, 1960, box 36, folder 23, DTP.

162. Diana Trilling to William Phillips, May 24, 1969, box 4, folder 5, DTP.

163. Diana Trilling, "The Other Night at Columbia (A report from the Academy)," *Partisan Review* 25, no. 1 (January 1958): 214; and "Statement read by Diana Trilling to Board of Directors," ACCF, January 10, 1961, box 36, folder 9, DTP.

164. D. Trilling resignation and ACCF minutes, December 19, 1960, box 36, folder 23, DTP.

165. "Statement read by Diana Trilling to Board of Directors," ACCF, January 10, 1961, on the occasion of her resignation from the ACCF, box 36, folder 9, DTP.

166. Minutes from ACCF Board meeting, December 19, 1960, box 36, folder 23, DTP.

167. Diana Trilling to Arnold Beichman, November 4, 1960, read on December 19, 1960, ACCF Board meeting, box 36, folder 23, DTP.

168. "Statement read by Diana Trilling to the Board of Directors," ACCF, January 10, 1961, on the occasion of her resignation, DTP, box 36, folder 9.

169. Diana Trilling to Arthur Schlesinger Jr., April 24, 1961, box 5, folder 1, DTP.

170. Diana Trilling interview by Barbara Crenshaw, 27.

171. Diana Trilling to William Phillips, January 2, 1980, box 6, folder 5, DTP.

172. Present at that December 13 or 19, 1960 Executive Board meeting: Arnold Beichman, Daniel Bell, Sidney Hook, [?] Kohn, William Phillips, Mel Pitzele, Norman Podhoretz, Bertram Wolfe, and [?] Williams. Absent were [?] [Hays], Sol Levitas, [?] Ross, and Diana Trilling. See minutes, ACCF Board of Directors, box 36, folder 23, DTP.

173. Diana Trilling to William Phillips, May 5, 1969, box 4, folder 5, DTP.
174. William Phillips to Diana Trilling, May 21, 1969, box 4, folder 5, DTP.
175. Diana Trilling interview by Barbara Crenshaw, 36.
176. Diana Trilling to William Phillips, May 24, 1969, box 4, folder 5, DTP.

Chapter Three

1. Editorial Statement, "Our Country and Our Culture," *Partisan Review* 19, no. 3 (May–June 1952): 282–84.

2. Contributors to the symposium were: Newton Arvin, James Burnham, Allan Dowling, Leslie Fiedler, Norman Mailer, Reinhold Niebuhr, Philip Rahv, David Riesman, Mark Schorer, Lionel Trilling, William Barrett, Jacques Barzun, Joseph Frank, Horace Gregory, Louis Kronenberger, C. Wright Mills, Louis Bogan, Richard Chase, Sidney Hook, Irving Howe, Max Lerner, William Phillips, Arthur Schlesinger Jr., and Delmore Schwartz. See "Our Country and Our Culture," *Partisan Review* 19, no. 3, 4, and 5 (May–June, July–August, and September–October 1952).

3. Leslie A. Fiedler, "Our Country and Our Culture," *Partisan Review* 19, no. 3 (May–June 1952): 294.

4. Newton Arvin, "Our Country and Our Culture," *Partisan Review* 19, no. 3 (May–June 1952): 286–88.

5. May, *Homeward Bound*; Buhle, *Feminism and Its Discontents*; and Herzog, *Cold War Freud*.

6. Ehrenreich, *Hearts of Men*, 17.

7. Reinhold Niebuhr, "Our Country and Our Culture," *Partisan Review* 19, no. 3 (May–June 1952): 301.

8. Pells, *Liberal Mind in a Conservative Age*, 122. See also Chappelle, "Triumph of Conservatives in a Liberal Age," in *A Companion to Post-1945 America*. Examples of this new "maturity" include Richard Crossman, ed., *The God That Failed* (1949); Lionel Trilling, *The Liberal Imagination* (1950); John Kenneth Galbraith, *American Capitalism* (1952); Bell, *End of Ideology* (1960); Richard Hofstadter, *Anti-Intellectualism in American Life* (1963).

9. Nathan Glazer, "*Commentary*: The Early Years," in *Commentary in American Life*, 46–47. See also Abrams, *Commentary: 1945–49*, 66.

10. Sidney Hook, "Our Country and Our Culture," *Partisan Review* 19, no. 5 (September–October 1952): 569–74.

11. Philip Rahv, "Our Country and Our Culture," *Partisan Review* 19, no. 3 (May–June 1952): 304–10.

12. Norman Mailer, "Our Country and Our Culture," *Partisan Review* 19, no. 3 (May–June 1952): 299.

13. Irving Howe, "Our Country and Our Culture," *Partisan Review* 19, no. 5 (September–October 1952): 575.

14. Podhoretz, "The Young Generation," *Doings and Undoings*, 108.

15. Podhoretz, *Making It*, 74. The literary critic Edmund Wilson referred to *Partisan Review* as "Partisansky Review." See Kazin, *New York Jew*, 44.

16. For the strains between "uptown" Jews and "downtown" Eastern European Jews, see, e.g., Goren, *New York Jews and the Quest for Community*; and Rischin, *Promised City*.

17. Diner, *Jews of the United States*, 195, 215; Abrams, *Commentary: 1945–59*; Balint, *Running Commentary*. For a history of the AJC, see Cohen, *Not Free to Desist*. For the AJC, AJC Congress, and ADL and anti-communism, see Svonkin, *Jews Against Prejudice*.

18. Abrams, *Commentary: 1945–59*, 30.

19. Abrams, *Commentary: 1945–59*, 32.

20. Only Lionel Trilling and Arendt had written for the *Record* before. "Under Forty: A Symposium on American Literature and the Younger Generation of American Jews," *Contemporary Jewish Record* 7 (1944): 3–36.

21. Nathan Schachner, *The Price of Liberty: A History of the American Jewish Committee* (New York: The American Jewish Committee, American Books–Stratford Press, 1948), 213, 180.

22. Daniel Bell to AJC, July 1, 1959, box 117, folder 11, CMP.

23. Phillips, *Partisan View*, 162.

24. Abrams, *Commentary: 1945–59*, 23–27.

25. In 1956, Cohen checked himself into the Payne Whitney Psychiatric Clinic on the Upper East Side, leaving Martin Greenberg to edit the magazine. He returned to the magazine in 1958, "shaken and diminished." In May 1959, at age sixty, he killed himself. See Balint, *Running Commentary*, 74–76.

26. Abrams, *Commentary: 1945–59*, 27.

27. 1953 memo defining staff positions, box 117, folder 6, CMP.

28. Bell to AJC, July 1, 1959.

29. Glazer, "*Commentary*: The Early Years," 51.

30. The lack of women is perhaps unsurprising given the climate toward female employment after World War II and the sex-segregated nature of the labor force. Nonetheless, it contributed to *Commentary* functioning as a masculine Jewish space.

31. Abrams, *Commentary: 1945–59*, 45.

32. Hanna F. Dessner and Anne Magnes appeared in a 1946 memo from the editorial department, alongside Nathan Glazer and Clement Greenberg. "Memorandum on Editorial Costs," May 1, 1946, box 117, folder 14, CMP.

33. Sherry Goldman and Lionel Abel married in 1939. They divorced, but when is unclear. Sherry was likely still married to Abel in 1950. "Sherry Goldman Abel, Editor, 88," *New York Times*, June 8, 1992, B4; Abrams, *Podhoretz and Commentary*, 52; Balint, *Running Commentary*, 21, 174.

34. For women and Judaism, see, e.g., Hyman, *Gender and Assimilation*; Goldman, *Beyond the Synagogue Gallery*.

35. Elliot E. Cohen, "An Act of Affirmation," *Commentary* (November 1945): 3.

36. Abrams, *Commentary: 1945–49*, 44.

37. David Bernstein, "Jewish Insecurity and American Realities: A Prescription against Mental Escapism," *Commentary* 5 (1948): 126.

38. Cohen's writings defy the idea that the Holocaust was not discussed until the 1960s. See Novick, *The Holocaust in American Life*. Challenges to that thesis include Fermaglich, *American Dreams and Nazi Nightmares*; and Diner, *We Remember with Reverence and Love*.

39. Cohen, "An Act of Affirmation," 1–2.

40. Abrams, *Commentary: 1945–49*, 57.

41. For *Commentary*'s early views of Zionism, see Abrams, *Commentary: 1945–49*, 72; and Balint, *Running Commentary*, 36. Articles supporting a binational state, proposed by the far-left Zionist Ihud group, did appear in the magazine. See Alterman, *We Are Not One*, 56–57.

42. Cohen, "An Act of Affirmation," 2.

43. Abrams, *Commentary: 1945–49*, 59.

44. See, for example, Irving Howe, "The Lost Young Intellectual," *Commentary* (October 1946); Milton Klonsky, "The Trojans of Brighton Beach," *Commentary* 3 (1947); Charles Reznikoff, "New Haven: The Jewish Community," *Commentary* 4 (1947); Hortense Perell, "The Good Life in Fayetteville," *Commentary* (December 1948); William Poster, "The Day the Bronx Invader Came: A Short Story of the Brownsville Frontier," *Commentary* 19 (1955); and Myer Liben, "Homage to Benny Leonard," *Commentary* 27 (1959).

45. Elliot E. Cohen, Foreword, *Commentary on the American Scene*, xxi–xxii.

46. This line appeared in a slightly different version of Cohen's foreword, published in *Commentary*. See David Riesman and Elliot E. Cohen, "The American Scene in Commentary's Mirror: Introduction to an Anthology from Our Pages," *Commentary* (February 1953): 179.

47. David Riesman, "Introduction," *Commentary on the American Scene*, xii–xiii.

48. Elliot E. Cohen, "Jewish Culture in America: Some Speculations by an Editor," *Commentary* (May 1947): 412–20.

49. Cohen, "The Intellectuals and the Jewish Community: The Hope for Our Heritage," *Commentary* (1949): 20.

50. Cohen, "The Intellectuals and the Jewish Community: The Hope for Our Heritage," 26.

51. Cohen, "The Intellectuals and the Jewish Community," 30, 22, 24.

52. Cohen, "The Intellectuals and the Jewish Community," 28–30. Cohen noted that many esteemed refugees had come to the United States. Together with "fresh intellectual talent" they would transform American Jewish life.

53. Cohen, "The Intellectuals and the Jewish Community," 23–24.

54. Special Aims memo, box 117, folder 3, CMP; "Commentary: Its Aim—and Influence," undated, box 117, folder 3, CMP.

55. Elliot E. Cohen, "Memo from E.E.C for Staff Sub-Committee on Proposal for Public Meetings on 'Czechoslovakian Situation,'" December 1, 1952, revised December 17, 1952, box 12, folder 12, ACCFP.

56. Phillips, *Partisan View*, 162–63.

57. Cohen, "An Act of Affirmation," 2.

58. Arendt would famously do so in 1951 with *The Origins of Totalitarianism*.

59. Acheson quoted in Dudziak, *Cold War Civil Rights*, 80. See also, e.g., Pells, *Liberal Mind*; Hamby, *Beyond the New Deal*; and Horton, *Race and the Making of American Liberalism*.

60. For HUAC, see, e.g., Goodman, *The Committee*; Navasky, *Naming Names*; and Schrecker, *Many Are the Crimes*.

61. Dean, *Imperial Brotherhood*, 205; Cuordileone, *Manhood and American Political Culture*; Johnson, *Lavender Scare*; and Gilbert, *Men in the Middle*.

62. See, e.g., Tanenhaus, *Whittaker Chambers*.

63. Cuordileone, *Manhood and American Political Culture*, 45.

64. Pells, *Liberal Mind in a Conservative Age*; Gillion, *Politics and Vision*; Brinkley, *Liberalism and Its Discontents*; Schrecker, *Many Are the Crimes*; Haynes, *Red Scare or Red Menace?* Bell, *Liberal State*; and Cohen, *Consumer's Republic*.

65. Devine, *Henry Wallace's 1948 Presidential Campaign and the Future of Postwar Liberalism*; and Rossinow, *Visions of Progress*.

66. Elliot E. Cohen, "Citizen's Victory: Defeat of the 'Common Man', the American People and Its Opinion Molders," *Commentary* (December 1948): 513.

67. Cohen, "Citizen's Victory," 519.

68. Leslie Fiedler, "Hiss, Chambers, and the Age of Innocence," *Commentary* (August 1951): 119.

69. Arthur M. Schlesinger Jr., *The Vital Center* (Boston: Houghton Mifflin, 1962).

70. Cuordileone, *Manhood and American Political Culture in the Cold War*, 23, 36.

71. His great-grandfather on his father's side was of Jewish descent. See Harper, *Straddling Worlds*, 99–100.

72. For Schlesinger Jr., see his autobiography, *A Life in the Twentieth Century*. Christopher Lasch, *World of Nations*; and Diggins, *Liberal Persuasion*.

73. Cuordileone, "Cold War Political Culture and a Crisis of Masculinity," 43–49.

74. Breines, *Tough Jews*, 3.

75. For the evolving relationship between anti-Semitism and antiradicalism in nativist ideology, see Higham, *Strangers in the Land*.

76. Diner, *Jews in the United States*, 237, 276–77; Michels, *Fire in Their Hearts*; and Wenger, *New York Jews and the Great Depression*.

77. Moore, *At Home in America*; Svonkin, *Jews Against Prejudice*; and Dollinger, *Quest for Inclusion*.

78. See, e.g., Doherty, *Show Trial*.

79. Leslie Fiedler, "Hiss, Chambers, and the Age of Innocence," *Commentary* (1951): 114.

80. Fiedler, "Hiss, Chambers, and the Age of Innocence," 109–10.

81. David Riesman and Nathan Glazer, "Intellectuals and the Discontented Class: Some Further Reflections," *Partisan Review* (Winter 1955): 58.

82. Quoted in Abrams, *Commentary*, 48.

83. "The Problem of Disassociating Jews and Communism in the Public Mind," report prepared by Elliot Cohen, January 7, 1948, box 1, folder 7, Solomon Andhil Fineberg Papers, the Jacob Rader Marcus Center of the American Jewish Archives at Hebrew Union College–Jewish Institute of Religion. Hereafter SAFP.

84. Podhoretz, *Making It*, 101.

85. The Rosenberg case has long divided scholars and journalists. For accounts that emphasized the couple's guilt, see Radosh and Milton, *Rosenberg File*. For accounts that maintained the couple's innocence, see Meeropol and Meeropol, *We Are Your Sons*; and Schneir, *Invitation to Inquest*. In 1995, disclosures from the Venona project, an American spy operation, revealed that Julius spied for the Soviet Union but Ethel was not implicated. For books since those disclosures, see, e.g., Roberts, *The Brother*; and Sebba, *Ethel Rosenberg*.

86. Moore, "Reconsidering the Rosenbergs," 22, 34.

87. Mrs. Harry Capron to Mr. Roy Cohn, Attorney for Senate Committee, March 24, 1953, box 1, folder 7, SAFP.

88. Edwin L. Lukas to S. Andhil Fineberg, "Re Suggested reply to Mrs. Harry Capron's letter to Mr. Roy Cohn, U.S. Senate," April 9, 1953, SAFP, box 1, folder 7.

89. S. Andhil Fineberg, The American Jewish Committee, Memorandum to all members of the Committee on Communism, SAFP, box 1, folder 7.

90. While all three of the major Jewish Defense organizations—the AJC, the Anti-Defamation League (ADL), and the American Jewish Congress—cooperated with the purging of communists from their rosters, the AJC was the most aggressive in its actions. See Svonkin, *Jews Against Prejudice*.

91. Besides Fineberg and Cohen, the committee included George Hexter, Simon Segal, Morris Fine, Morris Kertzler, Joseph Woolfson, Eliezer Greenberg, Lucy Dawidowicz, and Joseph Gordon. See the American Jewish Committee Memorandum to Members of the Planning Committee (on Communism), from Solomon Andhil Fineberg, March 17, 1952, SAFP, box 1, folder 7.

92. See American Jewish Committee Memorandum, from S. Andhil Fineberg, March 17, 1952, SAFP, box 1, folder 7. In a 1952 internal memo to AJC leaders, Cohen called for an "All-Out effort" to dissociate Jews from communism. "It goes without saying that an all-out effort does not mean that we should blow our top or act extremely or hysterically," Cohen explained. "AJC statesmanship can stand us in good stead by making sure that we adopt measures which, while they give expression to our basic emotions, do not flout the criteria of effectiveness, reasonableness, and American Jewish self-respect."

93. Elliot E. Cohen, "Memo from E.E.C for Staff Sub-Committee on Proposal for Public Meetings on 'Czechoslovakian Situation,'" December 1, 1952, revised December 17, 1952, box 12, folder 12, ACCFP.

94. Lucy Dawidowicz, "'Antisemitism' and the Rosenberg Case," *Commentary* (1952): 41. For Dawidowicz, see Sinkoff, *From Left to Right*.

95. Quoted from David Thorburn, "The Rosenberg Letters," *Boston Review* (February/March 1995); Julius and Ethel Rosenberg, *Death House Letters* (New York: Jero Publishing, 1953).

96. Sol Stein to Daniel Bell, July 5, 1953, box 50, folder 13, Sol Stein Papers, Rare Book and Manuscript Library, Columbia University.

97. Leslie A. Fiedler, "A Postscript to the Rosenberg Case," *Encounter* 1 (October 1953): 17; Robert Warshow, "The Idealism of Julius and Ethel Rosenberg," *Commentary* (November 1953): 417.

98. Warshow, "Idealism of Julius and Ethel Rosenberg," 415.

99. Fiedler, "Postscript to the Rosenberg Case," 19.

100. Warshow, "Idealism of Julius and Ethel Rosenberg," 415.

101. Fiedler, "Postscript to the Rosenberg Case," 19, 16.

102. For Ethel, see Antler, *Journey Home*; Abrams, "More Than One Million Mothers Know It's the Real Thing," Carlston, *Double Agents*; and Sebba, *Ethel Rosenberg*.

103. Fiedler, "Postscript to the Rosenberg Case," 18.

104. Warshow, "Idealism of Julius and Ethel Rosenberg," 415; Kristol, "Memoirs of a Trotskyist," 7 (see chap. 1, n. 101).

105. Schrecker and Deery, *The Age of McCarthyism*, 60–63.

106. Irving Kristol, "'Civil Liberties,' 1952—A Study in Confusion: Do We Defend Our Rights by Protecting Communists?," *Commentary* (March 1952): 229.

107. Elliot Cohen, "The Free American Citizen, 1952: Our Democracy, Two Years after Korea," *Commentary* (September 1952): 229.

108. Nathan Glazer, "The Method of Senator McCarthy: Its Origins, Its Uses, and Its Prospects," *Commentary* (March 1953): 256. See also Glazer's "Civil Liberties and the American People: Tolerance and Anti-Communism," *Commentary* (August 1955).

109. See, e.g., Alan F. Westin, "Our Freedom and the Rights of Communists: A Reply to Irving Kristol," *Commentary* (July 1952); Alan F. Westin, "Winning the Fight against McCarthy: The Need to Struggle on Two Fronts," *Commentary* (July 1954).

110. Daniel Bell, "Interpretations of American Politics—1955," in *The Radical Right*, Daniel Bell, ed., 54. See also Cuordileone, *Manhood and American Political Culture in the Cold War*, vii–vii. An excellent guide to these discussions is David Chappell, "Triumph of Conservatism."

111. Glazer and Riesman, "The Intellectuals and the Discontented Class," 52, 54.

112. On the CCF and the debate over the significance of CIA funding, see, e.g., Coleman, *Liberal Conspiracy*; Saunders, *Who Paid the Piper?*; Wilford, *The CIA, the British Left, and the Cold War*; Wilford, *Mighty Wurlitzer*; and Iber, *Neither Peace Nor Freedom*.

113. Wilford, *Mighty Wurlitzer*, 87.

114. The remaining delegates were Herman J. Muller (University of Indiana); Giuseppe Antonio Borgese (an Italian then at the University of Chicago); Irving Brow (American Federation of Labor); Carl J. Friedrich (Harvard University); Franz Neumann (Columbia University Law School); novelist Carson McCullers; actor Robert Montgomery; author Boris Nicolaevsky; Sterling Stone (New York University); author Grace Zering Stone. See press release, "Cultural Congress opens in Berlin this weekend as last of U.S. delegates depart," June 25, 1950, ACCF; Congress for Cultural Freedom manifesto, unanimously adopted in Berlin, Germany, on June 30, 1950; American Delegates to Congress for Cultural Freedom, all in box 1, folder 2, ACCF Papers.

115. "The Congress for Cultural Freedom," brochure, no date, likely fall 1952, printed in France, box 50, folder 12, Sol Stein Papers, Rare Book and Manuscript Library, Columbia University.

116. Seventy years later, in a 2020 publication on the history of the AJC's work with Germany, the AJC mentioned Cohen's speech as an example of the organization's engagement with Germany. The editor of *Commentary* said Cohen represented the group at the "Society of Christians and Jews in Berlin." There was no mention of the

Congress for Cultural Freedom. The AJC probably did not mention the CCF since the organization folded many years earlier. It was a relic of the Cold War, and few Americans or even American Jews had heard of it. But the choice to omit it also probably reflected the fact that the CCF was funded by the Central Intelligence Agency (CIA). See "AJC and Germany: History in the Making," American Jewish Committee, 2020, 8. Accessed online: www.ajc.org/sites/default/files/pdf/2020-06/AJC%20 GERMANY%20BOOK_6.22.20.pdf.

117. Elliot E. Cohen, "What Do the Germans Propose to Do? An Address to the German People," *Commentary* (September 1950). Accessed online: www.commentary .org/articles/elliotecohen/what-do-the-germans-propose-to-doan-address-to-the -german-people/.

118. For the founding of the ACCF, see, e.g., Coleman, *Liberal Conspiracy*, 159–62; Hook, *Out of Step*, 420–21; and Wilford, *Mighty Wurlitzer*, 70–98.

119. According to the group's by-laws, "To become a member of the organization, an applicant must be sponsored by three members in good standing. Before being accepted, he must receive a two-thirds affirmative vote of the Executive Committee in regular session." But minutes of the ACCF suggest that it was more common for members to be nominated and elected by the ACCF Executive Board. According to the by-laws, one "annual meeting of the membership" would be held each year "in New York," but members were not required to attend. See American Committee for Cultural Freedom, Inc. By-Laws, presented at the October 3, 1951, Executive Committee Meeting, box 7, folder 3, ACCF.

120. Diana Trilling to Jason Epstein, March 6, 1948, box 3, folder 4, DTP.

121. Wilford, *Mighty Wurlitzer*, 73.

122. Hook, *Out of Step*, 248–74, 420–31.

123. François Bondy, "Berlin Congress for Cultural Freedom: A New Resistance in the Making," *Commentary* (October 1950): 245–51.

124. Scholars have long debated the role the USSR played in the American Communist Party. For the traditionalist view, see, e.g., Draper, *Roots of American Communism*; and Klehr and Haynes, *The Secret World of American Communism*, among many other books by them. For the revisionist view, see, e.g., Isserman, *Which Side Were You On?*; Ottanelli, *Communist Party of the United States*; and Naison, *Communist in Harlem during the Depression*. For memoirs on the CPUSA, see, e.g., Jessica Mitford, *A Fine Old Conflict*.

125. Other sponsors of the Waldorf conference included Helen and Robert Lynd, Carey McWilliams, Norman Mailer, F. O. Matthiessen, Arthur Miller, Clifford Odets, Dorothy Parker, Paul Robeson, Budd Schulberg, Artie Shaw, Studs Terkel, Dalton Trumbo, and Henry Wallace.

126. Jumonville, *Critical Crossings*, 1–2; Wilford, *New York Intellectuals: From Vanguard to Institution*, 197. For a firsthand account, see William Barrett, "Cultural Conference at the Waldorf: The Artful Dove," *Commentary* (July 1949).

127. Hook, *Out of Step*, 421.

128. Phillips, *Partisan View*, 150–51.

129. American Committee for Cultural Freedom stationery, no date, box 50, folder 13, Sol Stein Papers, Rare Book and Manuscript Library, Columbia University. The other women were Eleanor Clark, Dorothy Canfield Fisher, Esther S. Goldfrank,

Elinor Rice Hays, Marie Jahoda, Nancy Lenkeith, Katherine Anne Porter, and Alice Beal Parsons. Diana Trilling was then chairman of the Administrative Committee.

130. By 1953 she was no longer active in the ACCF.

131. Wilford, *Mighty Wurlitzer*, 84–85.

132. Hook, *Out of Step*, 421.

133. Present were "Mrs. [Arnold] Beichman, Mrs. [Daniel] Bell, Mrs. [Sidney] Hook, Mrs. [Hans] Kohn, Mrs. [Sol] Levitas, and Mrs. [?] Mazur." Executive Committee Meeting minutes, January 8, 1954, box 7, folder 3, ACCFP.

134. Wilford, *Mighty Wurlitzer*, 73–74.

135. Sidney Hook to Milton Konvitz, no date, box 3, folder 19, ACCFP.

136. Elliot E. Cohen, "Memo from E.E.C for Staff Sub-Committee on Proposal for Public Meetings on 'Czechoslovakian Situation,'" December 1, 1952, revised December 17, 1952, box 12, folder 12, ACCFP.

137. George S. Counts, Chairman of ACCF, to Mr. John Slawson, American Jewish Committee, December 8, 1952, ACCFP, box 4, folder 15. See also Memorandum re Nature of Projected Carnegie Hall Meeting, from David Martin to National Committee for Free Europe, Sunday, March 1, box 12, folder 12, ACCFP.

138. Norman Thomas to Dr. George S. Counts, January 26, 1953, box 12, folder 12, ACCFP.

139. Michael Harrington, "The American Committee for Cultural Freedom," *Dissent*, Spring 1955.

140. Jumonville, *Critical Crossings*, 35.

141. Resignation from James Burnham to Robert Gorham Davis, September 15, 1954, box 3, folder 4, ACCFP.

142. Resignation from George S. Schuyler to Robert Gorham Davis, September 20, 1954, box 4, folder 17, ACCFP.

143. Arthur Schlesinger Jr., to Sol Stein, May 24, 1954, box 4, folder 16, ACCFP. See Dillard Stokes, "How Insure Security in Government Service: Past Failures and Present Realities" [*sic*], *Commentary* 17 (1954).

144. Arthur Schlesinger Jr., to James T. Farrell, March 16, 1955, box 4, folder 16, ACCFP.

145. Arthur Schlesinger Jr. to Sol Stein, May 9, 1955, box 4, folder 16, ACCFP.

146. David Riesman to Norman Thomas, February 7, 1955, box 4, folder 12, ACCFP. Riesman published the reasons for his resignation from the ACCF in the *New Republic*, angering the Executive Board of the ACCF. See Sol Stein to David Riesman, February 24, 1955, box 4, folder 12, ACCFP.

147. R. M. MacIver to Irving Kristol, November 3, 1952, box 4, folder 5, ACCFP.

148. Meyer Schapiro to Irving Kristol, October 22, 1952, box 7, folder 35, ACCFP.

149. Balken, *Harold Rosenberg*, 311.

150. Jason Epstein, "The CIA and the Intellectuals," *New York Review of Books*, April 20, 1967; Diana Trilling to Jason Epstein, March 6, 1968; Irving Kristol to Jason Epstein, February 19, 1968, box 3, folder 4, DTP. Kristol and Trilling were right that Epstein was nominated as a member. See minutes to executive committee of February 1, 1954, box 7, folder 3, ACCFP.

151. Jason Epstein to Diana Trilling, February 26, 1968, and February 29, 1968, box 3, folder 4, DTP. See also Jason Epstein to Irving Kristol, February 12, 1968, box 3,

folder 4, DTP; Irving Kristol to Jason Epstein, February 19, 1968, box 3, folder 4, DTP. Epstein was nominated at Executive Committee meeting of February 1, 1954, box 7, folder 3, ACCFP.

152. Howe, *Margin of Hope*, 217–18.

153. Irving Howe, "A Mind's Turning: Notes on Politics and the Intellectual Life," *Dissent* 7, no. 1 (Winter 1960): 34.

Chapter Four

1. Howe, "New York Intellectuals," 33.

2. For the Popular Front, see, e.g., Denning, *Cultural Front*; Isserman, *Which Side Were You On?*; Draper, *American Communism and Soviet Russia*; and Klehr, *Heyday of American Communism*.

3. Howe, "New York Intellectuals," 33.

4. Irving Kristol and Irving Howe, "Controversy: The New York Intellectuals," *Commentary* (January 1969): 12.

5. "Herd of Independent Minds" comes from an article of the same title by Harold Rosenberg. "A Herd of Independent Minds: Has the Avant-Garde its Own Mass Culture?" *Commentary* (September 1948).

6. Howe, "Controversy: The New York Intellectuals," 16.

7. Editorial Statement, "A Word to Our Readers," *Dissent* (Winter 1954): 3.

8. See Jacobson, "A Ghetto to Look Back To"; and Diner, "Embracing World of Our Fathers," both in *American Jewish History* 88, no. 4 (December 2000). That entire issue of *American Jewish History* was dedicated to a reassessment of Howe's *World of Our Fathers*.

9. Sorin, *Life of Passionate Dissent*, 230. See also Gerald Sorin, "Irving Howe's 'Margin of Hope,'" 475–94, and Michels, "Socialism and the Writing of American Jewish History."

10. Weinberg, "The World of Our Fathers and the World of Our Mothers."

11. Sorin, *Life of Passionate Dissent*, 1; Nina Howe, "Irving Howe: Tenement Talk from May 2015," video, May 27, 2015, the Tenement Museum, accessed online: www .dissentmagazine.org/blog/video-irving-howe-tenement-museum-talk-sarah-leonard -paul-berman; and Alexander, *Irving Howe: Socialist, Critic, Jew*, 48.

12. Howe, *Margin of Hope*, 2, 7.

13. Howe, *Margin of Hope*, 6, 8 and "Range of the New York Intellectuals," in *Creators and Disturbers*, 267–68.

14. Howe, *Margin of Hope*, 8–9; and "Range of the New York Intellectuals," 269.

15. Before 1929, DeWitt Clinton High School had been located on Tenth Avenue and Fifty-Ninth Street. Lionel Trilling attended the school at this Upper West Side location. See www.nycago.org/Organs/Brx/html/DeWittClintonHS.html.

16. Howe, "Range of the New York Intellectuals," 271–72; Howe, *Margin of Hope*, 22–23.

17. Howe, *Margin of Hope*, 13–14.

18. Howe, "Range of the New York Intellectuals," 273.

19. Howe, *Margin of Hope*, 43–45. See, Sorin, *Life of Passionate Dissent*, 30.

20. Sorin, *Life of Passionate Dissent*, 20. See also Isserman, *If I Had a Hammer*.

21. Howe quoted in Dorman, *Arguing the World*, 55.

22. Howe, "Range of the New York Intellectuals," 280; and Sorin, *Life of Passionate Dissent*, 32.

23. Howe wrote a resignation letter to the Independent Socialist League (with Henry Judd) on October 13, 1952, box 26, folder 9, Lewis Coser Papers, John J. Burns Library, Boston College. Hereafter, LCP.

24. Howe, *Margin of Hope*, 83

25. Howe, "Forming Dissent," in *Conflicts and Consensus*, ed. Powell, Robbins, 61.

26. Howe replaced Emanuel Geltman as editor of *Labor Action;* he later worked closely with Geltman at *Dissent*.

27. Howe, *Margin of Hope*, 84–85; and Sorin, *Life of Passionate Dissent*, 32.

28. Howe, *Margin of Hope*, 85; Sorin, *Life of Passionate Dissent*, 34.

29. Moore, *GI Jews*; Stahl, *Enlisting Faith*; Herberg, *Protestant, Catholic, Jew* (1955); and Schultz, *Tri-Faith America*.

30. Moore, *To the Golden Cities*; for Jews and whiteness, see, e.g., Goldstein, *Price of Whiteness*.

31. Dollinger, *Quest for Inclusion*; and Svonkin, *Jews Against Prejudice*. While some scholars have referred to the ten years following World War II as a golden age of American Jewry, others have emphasized continued angst and worry in the postwar era. See Goren, "A Golden Decade for American Jews, 1945–1955." For the anxieties associated with affluence, see, e.g., Berman, "American Jews and the Ambivalence of Middle-Classness"; and Kranson, *Ambivalent Embrace*.

32. Moore, *GI Jews*, 9–10, 35.

33. Moore, *GI Jews*, 9; Diner, *Jews of the United States*, 221; and Sarna, *American Judaism*, 264.

34. Bloom, *Prodigal Sons*, 135; Dorman, *Arguing the World*; Christopher Lehmann-Haupt, "Leslie Fiedler Dies at 85; Provocative Literary Critic," *New York Times*, January 31, 2003.

35. Cook, *Alfred Kazin's Journals*, 31; Cook, *Alfred Kazin: A Biography*, 88.

36. Howe, *Margin of Hope*, 90, 102–3.

37. Bloom, *Prodigal Sons*, 135; Peter Skerry, "Nathan Glazer—Merit before Meritocracy," *American Interest* (April 3, 2019). As far as I know, Glazer never wrote about why he did not serve during World War II. See, for example, Nathan Glazer, "My Life in Sociology," *Annual Review of Sociology* 38 (2012).

38. S. M. Levitas to Draft Board #10, August 26, 1942, box 61, folder 9, NLP.

39. Dr. Monroe Yudell, June 26, 1943, box 61, folder 9 (20857), NLP; Sidney Tarachow, M.D., to Doctor Yudell, March 5, 1942, box 61, folder 9, NLP. That final letter was dated June 26, 1943, just ten days before Bell's scheduled induction on July 6, 1943.

40. S. M. Levitas to Maurice Glinert, July 9, 1943, box 61, folder 9, NLP.

41. Quoted in Garrett, *Young Lions*, 203–4.

42. David A. Bell interview by author, June 12, 2019.

43. Cook, *Alfred Kazin: A Biography*, 86, 99–100.

44. Howe, *Margin of Hope*, 91, 102–3.

45. Howe, *Margin of Hope*, 105; Sorin, *Life of Passionate Dissent*, 51.

46. See Sumner, *Dwight Macdonald and the Politics Circle*.

47. Howe, "Forming Dissent."

48. Sorin, *Life of Passionate Dissent*, 52.

49. Irving Howe to Dwight Macdonald, August 27, 1948, box 23, folder 586, Dwight Macdonald Papers, Yale University.

50. Howe would marry four times. His marriage to Phillies ended in divorce after Howe had an affair with the wife of a colleague at Brandeis, bringing the school its first scandal. In 1964 Howe married Arien Mack, a thirty-two-year-old graduate student in psychology at Yeshiva University. Their marriage lasted a decade. It ended after Mack had an affair. In 1976 Howe married Ilana Weiner, an Israeli. They remained married until Howe's death in 1993.

51. Michael and Judith Walzer interview by author, Princeton, New Jersey, February 3, 2020; Sorin, *Life of Passionate Dissent*, 42–43, 92, 95.

52. For the family wage, see, e.g., Harris, "Postwar Women's History: From the 'Second Wave' to the End of the Family Wage?," *In Pursuit of Equality: Maclean.*

53. Howe to Coser, undated, box 26, folder 9, LCP.

54. Howe, *Margin of Hope*, 127.

55. Howe to Trilling, June 20, 1950, box 3, LTP. Also quoted in Sorin, *Life of Passionate Dissent*, 54.

56. Bell, *Winding Passage*, 132.

57. David A. Bell, "Daniel Bell at 100," *Dissent* (May 9, 2019).

58. Jacoby, *Last Intellectuals*, 73–75.

59. Howe, *Margin of Hope*, 184. For Brandeis, see, e.g., Whitfield, *Learning on the Left: Political Profiles of Brandeis.*

60. Richard Severo, "Max Lerner, Writer, 89, Is Dead: Humanist on Political Barricades," *New York Times*, June 6, 1992; JTA Daily News Bulletin, published by Jewish Telegraph Agency, Vol. 16, no. 90, April 20, 1949—http://pdfs.jta.org/1949/1949-04-20_090.pdf?_ga=2.161532862.362589831.1583172555-1943586463.1562636430; Howe to Coser, no date; Howe to Coser, November 29, 1952, box 26, folder 9, LCP. "In those days there were only schools and divisions, no departments, no sociology," Coser told an interviewer. Douglas Martin, "Lewis Coser, 89, Sociologist Who Focused on Intellectuals," *New York Times*, July 12, 2003; and Bernard Rosenberg, "An Interview with Lewis Coser," in *Conflicts and Consensus*, 41.

61. Howe, "Forming *Dissent*," 61–62.

62. Howe to Coser, undated, box 26, folder 9, LCP.

63. Howe published *The UAW and Walter Reuther* (with B. J. Wildick) in 1949; *Sherwood Anderson*; and *William Faulkner: A Critical Study*. See Roden, Introduction to *The Worlds of Irving Howe*, xviii.

64. Howe to Coser, December 9, 1952, box 26, folder 9, LCP.

65. Sorin, *Life of Passionate Dissent*, 92–95.

66. Howe to Coser, undated, box 26, folder 9, LCP.

67. Howe to Coser, November 29, 1952, box 26, folder 9, LCP.

68. Howe to Coser, January 8, 1953, box 26, folder 9, LCP.

69. Howe, *Margin of Hope*, 183.

70. Howe to Coser, undated letter, box 1, folder 4, LCP.

71. Howe, *Margin of Hope*, 183.

72. Howe to Coser, undated letter, box 26, folder 9, LCP.

73. Walter W. Powell and Richard Robbins, "Lewis Coser: Intellectual and Political Commitments," in *Conflict and Consensus*, 7.

74. Howe to Coser, undated letter, box 27, folder 4, LCP.

75. According to Gerald Sorin, "From 1946 on, Howe's pieces indicate and help illuminate some mildly reawakened stirrings of Jewishness, as well as corresponding gradual disengagement from Marxist orthodoxy." Sorin, *Life of Passionate Dissent*, 60–61.

76. Howe reviewed Isaac Rosenfeld's *Passage from Home.* "The novel, which initially attracted Howe because Rosenfeld had once been a Trotskyist, involved the eternal and universal pattern of conflict between father and son, here made graphic in an immigrant Jewish family." Sorin, *Life of Passionate Dissent*, 61. Howe, "Of Fathers and Sons," *Commentary* 2 (August 1946): 190–92.

77. Howe to Macdonald, August 1, 1946, box 23, folder 586, Dwight Macdonald Papers, Yale University.

78. Irving Howe, "James T. Farrell—The Critic Calcified," *Partisan Review* 14, no. 5 (1947). The essay defended Lionel Trilling from partisan attacks by Farrell and garnered the attention of Trilling, who asked to see Howe's work. See Alexander, *Lionel Trilling and Irving Howe*, 4.

79. Irving Howe, "The Lost Young Intellectual," *Commentary* (October 1946): 362.

80. Howe, "Lost Young Intellectual," 363–64.

81. Howe, "Lost Young Intellectual," 362, 364.

82. Howe, "Lost Young Intellectual," 363, 365.

83. Howe, "Lost Young Intellectual," 367.

84. Howe, "Our Country and Our Culture," 579.

85. Howe, "Our Country and Our Culture," 581.

86. Howe, *Steady Work*, 313.

87. Howe, "This Age of Conformity," *Partisan Review* 21 (January–February 1954): 10–11.

88. Critics who warned of a crisis of masculinity included Arthur Schlesinger Jr., David Riesman, and William H. Whyte, among others. See Gilbert, *Men in the Middle*; and Cuordileone, *Manhood and Cold War Culture*.

89. Howe, "This Age of Conformity," 12, 16. Howe chided Lionel Trilling for his celebration of a moderate and centrist liberalism in his influential book *The Liberal Imagination* (1950).

90. Howe, "This Age of Conformity," 12, 17–19.

91. Irving Howe, "Introduction," *25 Years of Dissent: An American Tradition*, xv.

92. Irving Howe and Henry Judd to Independent Socialist League, October 13, 1952, box 26, folder 9, LCP.

93. Howe, "Forming Dissent," 62; and Rosenberg, "An Interview with Lewis Coser," 42.

94. Interest letter from Coser, June 20, 1952; Letter from Lewis Coser and Irving Howe, November 12, 1952, box 26, folder 9, LCP.

95. Interest letter from Coser, June 20, 1952, box 26, folder 9, LCP.

96. Howe, "Forming Dissent," 62–63.

97. Howe to C. Wright Mills, February 18, 1953, box 26, folder 9, LCP.

98. Progress Report, Committee for an Independent Magazine, May 15, 1953, box 26, folder 9, LCP.

99. The meeting took place at Adelphi Hall in New York over the weekend of December 20–21, 1952. "A New Socialist Magazine," undated, box 26, folder 9, LCP.

100. Bernard Rosenberg, "An Interview with Lewis Coser," *Conflict and Consensus*, 42.

101. Fundraising letter from Meyer Schapiro, box 26, folder 9, LCP.

102. Howe, Coser, Plastrik, and Geltman attended, as did Travers Clement, Bert Hoselitz, Murray Kempton, Norman Mailer, Harold Orlans (Orlansky?), and Murray Wax. Others invited to the meeting included Sidney Lens, Harold Issacs, Frank Maruardt, Melvin Tumin, and C. Wright Mills. "A New Socialist Magazine," undated, box 26, folder 9, LCP.

103. Fromm, Muste, and Shapiro lent their names but were not active in the magazine. Walzers, interview by author, 24–25. Mailer wrote an average of one article a year for *Dissent* in its first decade, including his famous piece, "The White Negro" (Fall 1957). Thanks to Michael Kazin for pointing this out.

104. Howe, *25 Years of Dissent*, xvi.

105. Howe, "A Few Words about Dissent" (from its five-year anniversary), box 27, folder 4, LCP.

106. "Why a new radical magazine," undated, no author, box 26, folder 10.

107. Walzer, interview by author.

108. Irving Howe, "A Mind's Turning: Notes on Politics and the Intellectual Life," *Dissent* 7 (Winter 1960): 34.

109. Walzer, interview by author.

110. C. Rose Laub Coser, "The Cost of Mental Health Care," *Dissent* (Winter 1959); Deborah Meir, "From a Harlem School," *Dissent* (March–April 1968); and Brendan and Patricia Sexton, "Labor's Decade—Maybe," *Dissent* (August 1971).

111. *Dissent* published about twenty articles and book reviews by women in total in the 1950s.

112. Barkan, interview by author.

113. Many editors at *Dissent* did not want to print the sure-to-be-controversial essay. "I don't imagine I'm revealing any state secrets if I say that a good portion of the board was against printing her article to begin with, feeling it was stupid and insensitive and pretentious. I certainly agree with all three of those characterizations, especially the last, but I still think it was worth printing," Howe told a friend. Letter to Kurt [no last name], March 21, 1959, box 27, folder 3, LCP. But Howe knew it would bring attention to the magazine. In a letter to Lewis Coser he wrote, "Hannah Arendt agrees to let us have her piece on integration etc. which you'll remember (did you see it?) from last year. Now this is a big thing, very controversial, will arouse a lot of heat (in a way like Mailer's), & will no doubt stir some kind of people to say we're sabotaging the fight for Negro rights. But it's the kind of boldness we ought to risk." Howe to Coser, September 19, 1958, box 27, folder 2, LCP. For perspective on this controversy, see King, "American Dilemmas, European Experiences."

114. Walzer, interview by author, 34.

115. Walzer, interview by author, 41; and Isserman, "Steady Work: Sixty Years of Dissent." Accessed online: www.dissentmagazine.org/online_articles/steady-work -sixty-years-of-dissent.

116. Brian Morton, "In Memoriam: Edith H. Tarcov, 1919–1990," *Dissent* (Spring 1990): 279.

117. Howe, "Forming Dissent," 67–68.

118. Walzer, interview by author.

119. Isserman, "Steady Work: Sixty Years."

120. Walzer, interview by author, 5, 25.

121. Isserman, "Steady Work: Sixty Years."

122. Howe, "Forming Dissent," 68.

123. Howe to Coser, June 11, 1961, box 3, folder 4, LCP.

124. Bulletin of Information No. 1, *Dissent*, February 1962, box 3, folder 6, LCP.

125. Walter W. Powell and Richard Robbins, "Lewis Coser: Intellectual and Political Commitments," in *Conflict and Consensus*, 7; Cynthia Fuchs Epstein, "In Memoriam: Rose Laub Coser, 1916–1994," *Dissent* (Winter 1995): 107.

126. Howe, "Forming Dissent," 63.

127. Isserman, "Steady Work: Sixty Years."

128. Fuchs Epstein, "In Memoriam: Rose Laub Coser," 107; Walter W. Powell and Richard Robbins, "Lewis Coser: Intellectual and Political Commitments," in *Conflict and Consensus*, 7.

129. Walzer, interview by author, 47; Fuchs Epstein, "In Memoriam: Rose Laub Coser," 108.

130. Walzer, interview by author, 4.

131. Fuchs Epstein, "In Memoriam: Rose Laub Coser," 108. Her interest in women and feminism extended to her scholarship. According to Fuchs Epstein, when Rose Coser died in 1994 she was working on a new book, *World of Our Mothers*, which "sought to identify the qualities and activities of immigrant mothers and the social structures in which they lived that led to differential achievement among a generation of Jews and Italians in America," 107.

132. Barkan, email to author and interview, January 29, 2020.

133. Sorin, *Life of Passionate Dissent*, 250.

134. Walzer, interview by author, 8.

135. Howe, *Margin of Hope*, 334.

136. Sorin, *Life of Passionate Dissent*, 250. In his memoir Howe concluded: "The more grandiose feminist visions may turn out to be blocked by barriers of nature that no cultural transformation is likely to remove. I don't know and neither does anyone else. But this margin of doubt is surely no reason for not moving toward a fundamental change in the status of women. . . . Two cheers, then, for liberation: I say two because no public movement quite merits three." Howe, *Margin of Hope*, 335.

137. Howe, *Margin of Hope*, 324.

138. Walzer, interview by author.

139. Irving Howe, "The Middle-Class Mind of Kate Millett," *Harper's*, December 1970, reprinted as "On Sexual Politics: The Middle-Class Mind of Kate Millett," in Howe, *Critical Points: On Literature and Culture*, 209–11. Page numbers correspond to the book *Critical Points*.

140. Howe, "On Sexual Politics: The Middle-Class Mind of Kate Millett," in *Critical Points: On Literature and Culture*, 231.

141. Millett would soon come out as bisexual, and later as a lesbian, though Howe did not know that when he wrote the essay.

142. Poirot, "Mediating a Movement, Authorizing Discourse," 218–19.

143. Howe, "On Sexual Politics: The Middle-Class Mind of Kate Millett," 215.

144. Howe, "On Sexual Politics: The Middle-Class Mind of Kate Millett," 220; Alice Rossi, "Women—Terms of Liberation," *Dissent*, (November–December 1970), 538; Rossi, "Equality between the Sexes: An Immodest Proposal," in *Life Cycle and Achievement*, ed. Rose Laub Coser (New York: Harper Torchbooks, 1969), 135–96; and Rossi, "Abortion and Social Change," *Dissent*, July–August 1969, 338–46.

145. Walzer, interview by author, 50.

146. Sonya Rudikoff, "Trashing Patriarchy," *Dissent*, February 1971, 50–57.

147. The cover stated: "The Politics of Sex: Kate Millett of Women's Lib." The issue included two positive articles about women's liberation: "Who's Come a Long Way, Baby" and "The Liberation of Kate Millett," *Time*, August 31, 1970, 16–21. Reviews and articles in *Time* were unsigned, as was then the practice of the magazine.

148. "Behavior: Women's Lib: A Second Look," *Time*, December 4, 1970.

149. Midge Decter, "The Liberated Woman," *Commentary* (October 1970): 3–44.

150. Howe, *Twenty-Five Years of Dissent*, 119–37.

151. Howe, *Margin of Hope*, 333–34.

152. Howe, "On Sexual Politics: The Middle-Class Mind of Kate Millett," 204.

153. Michael Kazin, "Two Cheers for Utopia," 43. Originally published as "The Port Huron Statement at Fifty," *Dissent* (Spring 2012).

154. Paul Buhle, "The Jewish Presence among Students for a Democratic Society," *Jewish Currents* (May 2007).

155. Sara M. Evans, "Sons, Daughters, and Patriarchy: Gender and the 1968 Generation," *American Historical Review* 114, no. 2 (April 2009): 335, 332.

156. Hayden quoted in Dorman, *Arguing the World*, 142.

157. Howe and other New York intellectuals did protest in the 1930s and '40s. But the perception of New Leftists was that they did not. Thanks to Eric Alterman for this detail.

158. Thanks to Michael Kazin for this reminder. Many New Leftists also became academics later in life.

159. Gitlin, *The Sixties*, 175. "Pishers" is Yiddish for a nobody or inexperienced person.

160. Newfield, *Prophetic Minority*, 133.

161. Seymour Martin Lipset, "The Activist: A Profile," in *Confrontations: The Student Rebellion and the Universities*, ed. Irving Kristol and Daniel Bell (New York: Basic Books, 1969), 52; Feuer, *Conflict of Generations*, esp. 423–31; Norman Podhoretz, "The Tribe of the Wicked Son," *Commentary* (February 1971). Tom Hayden was Irish Catholic. Doug Rossinow notes that the SDS "old guard" was predominantly Jewish as opposed to its "prairie power" contingent after 1965. Rossinow, *Politics of Authenticity*, 10–11, 159.

162. Kranson, *Ambivalent Embrace*.

163. Howe interview by Stephen Lewis, *A Voice Still Heard*, 376; Howe repeated the story in *Margin of Hope*, 306. Howe's insult also echoed one Trotsky hurled at the Socialist Party around World War I. See Michael Kazin, *War against War*, 158.

164. Howe, *Margin of Hope*, 235; Howe, "Forming Dissent," 63

165. Walzer quoted in *Arguing the World*, 139.

166. "Psychic smog" comes from Howe's essay, "Radical Criticism and the American Intellectuals," in Howe, *Steady Work: Essays*, 21; and Howe, Introduction to *Twenty-Five Years of Dissent*, xiii.

167. Arthur Mitzman, "Campus Radical in 1960," 142–48; and Michael Walzer, "The Young: A Cup of Coffee and a Seat," *Dissent* (Spring 1960).

168. Editors at the magazine hoped Walzer would bring younger activists into the purview of *Dissent*. But Walzer was unable to bridge the divide between these two generations of leftists. As Dennis Wrong presciently observed in a letter to Coser in 1962, "I knew Walzer was in his twenties and a former student of yours. But the 'New Left' isn't a matter entirely of chronological age, and I would still consider him an exponent of the 'Old Left' viewpoint having acquired it from such venerable (?!) figures as yourself and *Dissent*." Dennis Wrong to Lewis Coser, February 16, 1962, box 3, folder 6, LCP.

169. Dissent, "Bulletin of Information," no. 1, February 1962, box 3, folder 6, LCP.

170. Isserman, "Sixty Years of Dissent."

171. "A Word to Our Readers," *Dissent* (Winter 1954): 3–4.

172. Irving Howe and Lewis Coser, "New Styles in Fellow-Travelling," *Dissent* (Fall 1961): 497.

173. Howe and Coser, "New Styles in Fellow-Travelling," 498.

174. Thanks to Michael Kazin for these insights. For the New Left and Cuba, see Van Gosse, *Where the Boys Are*.

175. Howe and Coser, "New Styles in Fellow-Travelling," 498.

176. At the *Dissent*-SDS meeting in 1962 eight or nine of the ten participants were Jewish, and all were men. Accounts vary regarding who represented SDS. Howe identified Paul Potter, Tom Hayden, and Paul Booth. Todd Gitlin claims it was Hayden, Lee Webb, Paul Potter, Steve Max, and himself. Howe, *Margin of Hope*, 292–93; Gitlin, *The Sixties*, 171–72. See also Sorin, *Life of Passionate Dissent*, 203–6.

177. Gitlin, quoted in Dorman, *Arguing the World*, 140.

178. Walzer, interview by author, 75.

179. Howe, *Margin of Hope*, 291–92; Gitlin, *The Sixties*, 171–72. Sorin, *Life of Passionate Dissent*, 203–6.

180. Hayden quoted in Dorman, *Arguing the World*, 142.

181. Isserman, "Sixty Years of Dissent."

182. Howe quoted in Dorman, *Arguing the World*, 142–43. According to Todd Gitlin, "No younger generation likes to feel like it's being lectured to by their parents, ideological parents or biological parents," Gitlin, *The Sixties*, 172.

183. Irving Howe to Michael Harrington, February 12, 1962, box 3, folder 6, LCP.

184. Irving Howe, "New Styles in Leftism," *Dissent* (Summer 1965): 300, 297.

185. Tyson, *Radio Free Dixie*; and Peniel Joseph, *The Sword and the Shield*.

186. Howe, "New Styles in Leftism," 315–18, 307.

187. Howe, "New Styles in Leftism," 309.

188. Marshall Berman, "Irving and the New Left," in *Irving Howe and the Critics*, ed. John Rodden, 58–59.

189. Howe, *Steady Work: Essays*, 39–40. Howe connected this collection of essays, mostly on politics in the 1960s, to Jewishness in his epigraph: "Once in Chelm, the mythical village of the Eastern European Jews, a man was appointed to sit at the village gate and wait for the coming of the Messiah. He complained to the village elders that his pay was too low. 'You are right,' they said to him, 'the pay is low. But consider: the work is steady.'"

190. Dickstein, Foreword to *A Voice Still Heard*, xix.

191. Howe, Introduction to *Beyond the New Left*, 13.

192. Howe, Introduction to *Beyond the New Left*, 13.

193. Howe, *Margin of Hope*, 298.

194. Walzer, "Notes for Whoever's Left," *Dissent* (Spring 1972): 309; and Isserman, "Sixty Years of Dissent."

195. Howe, *Margin of Hope*, 315.

196. Howe, *Margin of Hope*, 314–15.

Chapter Five

1. Diana Trilling, "Female Biology in a Male Culture," in *We Must March My Darlings*, 197.

2. Manso, *Norman Mailer*, 519.

3. Kate Millett, *Sexual Politics* (1970).

4. Manso, *Norman Mailer*, 462, 519; Norman Mailer, "The Prisoner of Sex," *Harper's*, March 1971; and Morris, *New York Days*, 355.

5. Willie Morris at *Harper's* is discussed in more detail in chapter 6. In a press release Morris wrote that, "It all boiled down to the money men and the literary men. And as always, the money men won." Morris's resignation, however, resulted from several simmering tensions over profits and the direction of the magazine. Mailer's article was "not the central issue," Morris later wrote, "only part of it, less at that moment substantive than symbolic." Morris, *New York Days*, 356; Manso, *Norman Mailer*, 519–20. See also Alden Whitman, "Morris Resigns in *Harper's* Dispute," *New York Times*, March 5, 1971.

6. Quoted in Robins, *Untold Journey*, 199.

7. Sabrina Fuchs Abrams, "'The Bitch Is Back,' A Reappraisal of Mary McCarthy for the 21st Century," *Women's Studies: An Interdisciplinary Journal* (July 16, 2020): 347–59.

8. Nelson, *Tough Enough*, 2, 74.

9. Diana Trilling, "Feminism and Women's Liberation: Continuity or Conflict," version two, unpublished speech for Andover Club, box 31, folder 20, DTP.

10. Michiko Kakutani, "Diana Trilling, Pathfinder in Morality," *New York Times*, November 16, 1981. Feminism, like any major ideology, was full of often fierce conflicts over its priorities and basic meaning. See, e.g., Cott, *Grounding of Modern Feminism*; and Stansell, *American Moderns*.

11. Robins, *Untold Journey: The Life of Diana Trilling*, 184.

12. Birstein, *What I Saw at the Fair*, 160.

13. Vivian Gornick, "Getting Even," *The Nation*, June 1, 2017.

14. D. Trilling, "Culture, Biology, and Our Sexual Role," speech at Radcliffe, June 12, 1970, box 31, folder 12, DTP. Reprinted in altered form as "Female Biology in a Male Culture," in *We Must March My Darlings*, 189–98.

15. For Freud and feminism, see M. Buhle, *Feminism and Its Discontents*; and Gerhard, *Desiring Revolution*.

16. Klein, *Dissent, Power, and Confrontation*, xi–xii; and Christopher Lehmann-Hupt, "Ideas Yes, Theater Rarely," *New York Times*, February 24, 1972, 37.

17. Manso, *Norman Mailer*, 521.

18. Mailer, "Theater of Ideas: A Dialogue on Women's Liberation," raw and unedited transcript, I-37, box 104, folder 9, NMP.

19. Millett quoted in Manso, *Mailer*, 524.

20. Original program, "A Dialogue on Women's Liberation," benefit discussion and party, part of the Spring Festival for the Theater of Ideas, April 30, 1971, box 36, folder 21, DTP. See also crossed-out program with cancelled speakers, box 104, folder 9, NMP. In her prepared remarks, Diana noted: "I watched one woman speaker after another drop away from this panel as if under penalty of some special form of female torture, should she submit to the presence of a male moderator, and in particular this male moderator." See "Theater of Ideas" transcript, p. 0–5.

21. Germaine Greer, "My Mailer Problem: Will the Prisoner of Sex Please Rise and Hear the Verdict," *Esquire*, September 1971, 92.

22. Rosalyn Drexler, "Theater for Ideas: A Night of Lib and Let Lib—What Happened to Mozart's Sister," *Village Voice*, May 6, 1971, 28.

23. D. Trilling, quoted in Manso, *Norman Mailer*, 521.

24. Greer, "My Mailer Problem," 214.

25. "The American Sixties: Diana Trilling Talks with Philip French," October 11, 1977, 12, box 30, folder 4, DTP.

26. Frederic Morton, "Sexism—A Better Show Than Sex," *Village Voice*, May 6, 1971, 28.

27. Press release for "Prisoner of Sex," May 6, 1971, Little, Brown and Company, box 609, folder 2, NMP.

28. Greer, "My Mailer Problem," 92.

29. Morton, "Sexism," 28.

30. Greer, "My Mailer Problem," 214.

31. Morton, "Sexism," 70.

32. Drexler, "A Night of Lib and Let Lib," 28.

33. Morton, "Sexism," 70.

34. Israel Shenker, "Norman Mailer vs. Women's Lib," *New York Times*, May 1, 1971, 19.

35. Mailer, "Theater of Ideas," transcript, 0–4.

36. "Theater of Ideas," transcript, 0–16–17.

37. "Theater of Ideas," transcript, 3–94.

38. "Theater of Ideas," transcript, 2–48, 2–52.

39. Greer, "My Mailer Problem," 214.

40. Dearborn, *Mailer: A Biography*, 293.

41. David Hollinger, "Communalist and Dispersionist Approaches to American Jewish History in an Increasingly Post-Jewish Era," 8. See also Diner, *Jews of*

the United States, 350–51; Antler, *Journey Home*, 260; and Antler, *Jewish Radical Feminism*.

42. Mailer, "Theater of Ideas," transcript, 3–96. "Harridans" is old English and means an "unpleasant woman, especially an older one, who is often angry and often tells other people what to do." It likely stems from the French word, *haridelle*, or "old horse," and comes from seventeenth-century slang. While its old English roots suggest a desire to transcend Jewishness, the description also matches the stereotype of the Jewish mother that was established by this time. See Prell, *Fighting to Become Americans*; Antler, *You Never Call!*

43. Ann Birstein to Germaine Greer, May 2, 1971, box 2, folder 8, Ann Birstein Papers, Queens College, New York.

44. Birstein, *What I Saw at the Fair*, 159.

45. Shenker, "Mailer vs. Women's Lib," 19.

46. D. Trilling, "The Prisoner of Sex," *We Must March My Darlings*, 201.

47. Mailer, "Theater of Ideas", transcript, I-34.

48. Mailer, "Theater of Ideas," transcript, I-35–36; D. Trilling, *Beginning of the Journey*, 353–54.

49. Manso, *Mailer*, 524, 520.

50. Mailer, "Theater of Ideas," transcript, 3–86–87.

51. D. Trilling, "Theater of Ideas," transcript, 3–113.

52. Laskin, *Partisans*, 17.

53. Friedan quoted in Kieran, *Seeing Mary Plain*, 711.

54. Ross, "Freud and the Vicissitudes of Modernism," 164–65.

55. Gerhard, *Desiring Revolution*, 29–30.

56. Ross, "Freud and the Vicissitudes of Modernism," 165.

57. Barrett, *The Truants*, 38.

58. Lionel Trilling, "The Legacy of Sigmund Freud, Part 2: Literary and Aesthetic," *Kenyon Review* 2, no. 2 (Spring 1940): 152–73. Reprinted as "Freud and Literature," in *The Liberal Imagination* (1950). See also Lionel Trilling, *Freud and the Crisis of Our Culture* (1955).

59. Ross, "Freud and the Vicissitudes of Modernism," 169.

60. Wilford, *The New York Intellectuals: From Vanguard to Institution*, 71–72; Genter, *Late Modernism: Art, Culture, and Politics in Cold War America*; and Cooney, *Rise of the New York Intellectuals*. On the Frankfurt school in America, see, for e.g., Jay, *Dialogic Imagination*; and Wheatland, *Frankfurt School in Exile*.

61. Sidney Hook, "The Trillings: A Memory in Monologue," *Commentary* (October 2015).

62. D. Trilling, *Journey*, 234.

63. D. Trilling, *Journey*, 234, 225, 227.

64. Diana Trilling, "Culture, Biology, and Our Sexual Role," speech delivered at Radcliffe, June 12, 1970, box 31, folder 12, DTP. Reprinted in altered form as "Female Biology in a Male Culture," in D. Trilling, *We Must March My Darlings*, 189–98.

65. Patricia Bosworth interview, "Diana Trilling: An Interview," *Paris Review*, Winter 1993, 245.

66. Diana Trilling, "A Tentative Outline for a Series of Articles on the American Female," box 30, folder 9, DTP. The outline is undated. Natalie Robins says it was

written in the early 1970s. But references to Margaret Mead and Lundberg-Farnham as examples of "the replacement of the psychological emphasis on Freudianism by the social-science emphasis on our sexual literature" suggests an earlier date. Robins, *Untold Journey*, 263.

67. Friedan, *Feminine Mystique*. For Friedan, see, e.g., Rosen, *World Split Open*; Horowitz, *Betty Friedan and the Making of the Feminine Mystique*.

68. D. Trilling, "A Tentative Outline for a Series of Articles on the American Female."

69. D. Trilling, "A Tentative Outline for a Series of Articles on the American Female."

70. Robins, *Untold Journey*, 138.

71. D. Trilling, *Journey*, 347.

72. *Look* was a biweekly general interest magazine akin to *Life*. Diana Trilling, "The Case for the American Woman," *Look*, March 3, 1959, 50–54; Diana Trilling, "Women and Their Minds," draft article for *Charm*, box 36, folder 20, DTP; and Diana Trilling, "Female-ism: New and Insidious," *Mademoiselle*, June 1950.

73. D. Trilling, "Female-ism: New and Insidious," 97.

74. D. Trilling, "Women and Their Minds," 3.

75. D. Trilling, "Women and Their Minds," 9–10.

76. For this crisis in masculinity, see, e.g., Barbara Ehrenreich's *Hearts of Men*; and Gilbert, *Men in the Middle*.

77. D. Trilling, "Case for the American Woman," 54.

78. D. Trilling, "Case for the American Woman," 51.

79. D. Trilling, "Case for the American Woman," 53.

80. D. Trilling, "Female-ism: New and Insidious," 98.

81. D. Trilling, "Women and Their Minds," draft, 11.

82. D. Trilling, "Case for the American Woman," 54.

83. D. Trilling, "Case for the American Woman," 53.

84. Friedan, *Feminine Mystique*, 103, 106.

85. Buhle, *Feminism and Its Discontent*, 196.

86. Friedan, *Feminine Mystique*, 138, 142.

87. Diana Trilling, "Men, Women, and Sex," in *Claremont Essays*, 54–55. First published in *Partisan Review* (Spring 1950).

88. D. Trilling, "Men, Women and Sex," 51–52.

89. D. Trilling, "Women and Their Minds," draft, 3, 5.

90. D. Trilling, *Journey*, 347.

91. Theodore Solotaroff to Tom Rogers, June 25, 1963, box 18, folder 1, CMP.

92. Gelderman, *Mary McCarthy: A Life*, 253.

93. Mary McCarthy, "Dottie Makes an Honest Woman of Herself," *Partisan Review* 21, no. 1 (1949).

94. Nancy K. Miller, "Women's Secrets and the Novel: Remembering Mary McCarthy's 'The Group,'" *Social Research* 68, no. 1 (Spring 2001): 178.

95. Kieran, *Seeing Mary Plain*, 510.

96. Mary McCarthy, "Polly Andrews, Class of '33," *New Yorker*, June 29, 1963.

97. Arthur Mizener, "The Sense of Life in the Modern Novel," *New York Times Book Review*, 27. Charles Poore, "Mary McCarthy's Lives of the Vassari," *New York Times*, August 29, 1963, 22. See also Kieran, *Seeing Mary Plain*, 518.

98. Podhoretz, *Doings and Undoings*, 87, 93. Originally Norman Podhoretz, "Mary McCarthy and the Leopard's Spots," *Show*, October 1963.

99. Norman Mailer, "The Mary McCarthy Case," *New York Review of Books*, October 17, 1963; Hilton Kramer, "Mary McCarthy's Valentine to Fanny Farmer," Book Word, *Washington Post*, May 1971.

100. Kieran, *Seeing Mary Plain*, 517, 536.

101. Arendt to McCarthy, September 20, 1963, box 181, folder 8, Mary McCarthy Papers, Vassar College. Hereafter MMP.

102. Arendt to McCarthy, September 16, 1963, box 181, folder 8, MMP.

103. Arendt to McCarthy, Fall 1963, box 181, folder 8, MMP.

104. Brightman, *Writing Dangerously: Mary McCarthy and Her World*, 478.

105. "The name alludes to Hester Prynne, the woman whose illegitimate child causes her to wear a badge of shame in Hawthorne's *The Scarlet Letter*, and Xavier Rynne, pseudonym of Francis X. Murphy, who wrote about the Second Vatican Council in *The New Yorker*." See Curtis, *A Splendid Intelligence*, 172.

106. McCarthy to Arendt, October 24, 1963, box 181, folder 8, MMP.

107. Hardwick to McCarthy, August 3, 1963, box 198, folder 1, MMP.

108. Birstein, *What I Saw at the Fair*, 160.

109. Hardwick to McCarthy, November 30, 1963, box 198, folder 1, MMP.

110. McCarthy to Arendt, September 24, 1963, box 181, folder 8, MMP. The Eichmann controversy Arendt's book provoked is discussed in more detail in chapter 7.

111. Mary McCarthy, "The Hue and the Cry," *Partisan Review* (Winter 1964): 82–94.

112. Arendt to McCarthy, September 20, 1963, box 181, folder 8, MMP.

113. Laskin, *Partisans*, 246.

114. Morgan, *Sisterhood Is Powerful: An Anthology of Writings from the Women's Liberation Movement*.

115. Patricia Bosworth, "Diana Trilling: An Interview," *Paris Review* (Winter 1993): 269.

116. D. Trilling, *Journey*, 304.

117. Barrett, *The Truants*, 67–68.

118. D. Trilling to McCarthy, February 7, 1983, box 229, folder 9, MMP.

119. Bosworth, "Diana Trilling: An Interview," 248.

120. McCarthy, *Intellectual Memoirs*, 73–74.

121. Mary McCarthy, "Report from Vietnam I. The Home Program," *New York Review of Books*, April 20, 1967; "Report from Vietnam II: The Problem of Success," *New York Review of Books*, May 4, 1967; "Report on Vietnam III: Intellectuals," *New York Review of Books*, May 18, 1967. McCarthy, *Vietnam* (New York: Harcourt Brace and World, 1967).

122. Diana Trilling, "On Withdrawing from Vietnam: An Exchange," *New York Review of Books*, January 18, 1968.

123. Mary McCarthy, "On Withdrawing from Vietnam: An Exchange," *New York Review of Books*, January 18, 1968. McCarthy published the essays as a book, *Vietnam* (New York: Harcourt Brace and World, 1967).

124. McCarthy to Arendt, January 26, 1968, box 181, folder 11, MMP. For the controversy between the two women, see Diana Trilling and Mary McCarthy, "On

Withdrawing from Vietnam: An Exchange," *New York Review of Books*, January 18, 1968.

125. Joan Dupont, "Mary McCarthy: Portrait of a Lady," *Paris Metro*, February 1978, 15–16, 78. Reprinted in Gelderman, *Conversations with Mary McCarthy*, 166.

126. D. Trilling, *Journey*, 305.

127. Bosworth, "Diana Trilling: An Interview," 250.

128. Hook, "The Trillings: A Memory in Monologue," 49.

129. Sam Roberts, "Ann Birstein, Memoirist and Novelist, Dies at 89," *New York Times*, May 29, 2017; Ann Birstein, *The Rabbi on Forty-Seventh Street* (New York: Dial Press, 1982).

130. Birstein, *What I Saw at the Fair*, 115–16, 131.

131. Arien Mack, interview by James Miller, "Fifty Years of Social Research: Arien Mack reflects on her half-century stewardship of The New School's flagship quarterly journal," March 1, 2020, https://publicseminar.org/essays/fifty-years-of-social -research/.

132. Paula Hyman, "Ruth Gay," in *The Shalvi/Hyman Encyclopedia of Jewish Women*, https://jwa.org/encyclopedia/article/gay-ruth.

133. Birstein, *What I Saw at the Fair*, 155.

134. Birstein, *What I Saw at the Fair*, 133, 135.

135. Birstein, *What I Saw at the Fair*, 159.

136. Pearl K. Bell, "Valley of the Dolls," *New Leader*, December 14, 1970, 5–8.

137. P. Bell, "Valley of the Dolls."

138. Peter Duval Smith, "Mary McCarthy Said: Men Have More Feeling; Women Have More Intelligence," *Vogue* 149, October 1963, reprinted in Gelderman, *Conversations with Mary McCarthy*, 59–60.

139. But McCarthy stated she was "enough of a feminist not to like the kind of praise that says, 'she has the mind of a man.' I always hated that." Dean, *Sharp*, 309–10; and Pinckney, "The Ethics of Admiration," *Threepenny Review*, Fall 2013, 12–16.

140. McCarthy quoted in Kieran, *Seeing Mary Plain*, 710; Mary Ann Seawell, "Frank Talk from Mary McCarthy," *Times Tribune*, May 8, 1985, C1; "The Lively Arts at Stanford Presents an Evening with Mary McCarthy," May 7, 1985, box 185, folder 5, MMP.

141. *Paris Review* interview with Hardwick, unpublished carbon notes, no date, box 7, folder 4, Elizabeth Hardwick Papers, Harry Ransom Center, University of Texas at Austin.

142. "Without God: Elizabeth Hardwick in Maine talks to Athea Disney about Friendship, Marriage and Writing Fiction," *The Observer*, Sunday August 5, 1979, found in box 7, folder 4, Elizabeth Hardwick Papers, Harry Ransom Center, University of Texas at Austin.

143. Elizabeth Hardwick, "The Subjugation of Women," 1955, reprinted in Pinckney, *The Collected Essays of Elizabeth Hardwick*, 28, 31.

144. Hardwick, "Subjugation of Women," 35.

145. Hardwick, *Paris Review* interview, transcript 16, box 7, folder 4, Elizabeth Hardwick Papers, Harry Ransom Center, University of Texas at Austin.

146. Michelle Dean, "The Formidable Friendship of Mary McCarthy and Hannah Arendt," *New Yorker*, June 4, 2013; Dean, *Sharp*, 310–11.

147. "What Remains? The Language Remains? A Conversation with Günter Gaus," October 28, 1964, in Arendt, *Hannah Arendt: The Last Interview and Other Conversations*, 5.

148. Susan Sontag, "Notes on Camp," *Partisan Review* 31, no. 4 (Fall 1964).

149. Susan Sontag, "The Third World of Women," *Partisan Review* 40, no. 2 (Spring 1973). See also Rieff, *Susan Sontag: On Women*.

150. Rollyson and Paddock, *Sontag: The Making of an Icon*, 156–58.

151. Moser, *Sontag: Her Life and Work*, 397–98; Penner, "Gendering Susan Sontag's Criticism in the 1960s."

152. Michiko Kakutani, "Diana Trilling, Pathfinder in Morality," *New York Times*, November 16, 1981, C13.

153. Diana Trilling, "On the Steps of Low Library: Liberalism and the Revolution of the Young," *Commentary* (November 1968). Reprinted in D. Trilling, *We Must March My Darlings*.

154. *Columbia Daily Spectator*, April 30, 1968.

155. Diana Trilling and Robert Lowell, "Liberalism and Activism," an exchange in *Commentary* (April 1969); Dwight Macdonald to Lionel Trilling, May 20, 1968, box 7, folder 4, LTP.

156. D. Trilling, *We Must March My Darlings*, xv, 211; "Women's Lib," draft of speech for Town Hall, 1–11, box 36, folder 21, DTP.

157. D. Trilling, "Women's Lib," 6.

158. D. Trilling, "Feminism and Women's Liberation: Continuity or Conflict," version two, unpublished speech for Andover Club, 14, box 31, folder 20, DTP.

159. D. Trilling, "Feminism and Women's Liberation: Continuity or Conflict."

160. "The American Sixties," Diana Trilling talks to Philip French, interview recorded October 11, 1977, 13, box 30, folder 4, DTP.

161. D. Trilling, "Female Biology in a Male Culture," 190.

162. D. Trilling, "Female Biology in a Male Culture," 191.

163. Harkening back to her 1950 review of Mead's *Male and Female*, Diana noted, "in every society which has ever been studied—so Margaret Mead tells us—whatever is the occupation of men has the greater prestige."

164. D. Trilling, "Female Biology in a Male Culture," 192.

165. D. Trilling, "Women's Lib."

166. D. Trilling, "Feminism and Women's Liberation: Continuity or Conflict."

167. D. Trilling, "The Prisoner of Sex," 202.

168. D. Trilling, "Footnote to My Life as a Critic," unpublished essay, February 26, 1996, box 31, folder 10, DTP.

Chapter Six

1. Judy Klemesrud, "It Was Ladies Day at the Party Meeting," *New York Times*, December 14, 1970, 62.

2. Decter, *An Old Wife's Tale*, 77.

3. Midge Decter, "The Liberated Woman," *Commentary* (October 1970): 33–44.

4. Michael Harrington, "The Welfare State and Neoconservative Critics," *Dissent* (Fall 1973): 435–54.

5. Podhoretz, *Breaking Ranks*. For scholars who have followed Podhoretz's trajectory, see, e.g., Wise, "The Maturing of Commentary and the Jewish Intellectual"; Friedman, *Neoconservative Revolution*. See also Dorrien, *Neoconservative Mind*; and Gerson, *Neoconservative Vision*.

6. For neoconservative opposition to affirmative action, see Nancy MacLean, *Freedom Is Not Enough*.

7. An exception is Hartman, *A War for the Soul of America*. See also Roth, "Neoconservative Backlash against Feminism."

8. For the New Left as a "movement of movements," see Gosse, *Rethinking the New Left*.

9. More recent studies of neoconservatism include Heilbrunn, *They Knew They Were Right*; Abrams, *Norman Podhoretz and* Commentary *Magazine*; Balint, *Running Commentary*; and Vaïsse, *Neoconservatism: The Biography of a Movement*.

10. Sue Wimmershoff-Caplan, Ann J. Lane, Vivian Gornick, and Madelyn Gutwirth, "Letters from Readers: Women's Lib and the Liberated Women," *Commentary* (February 1971): 12–18.

11. For rebuttals to her critics, see Midge Decter's replies in "Letters from Readers: Women's Lib and the Liberated Woman," *Commentary* (February 1971): 32–36.

12. Gerhard, *Desiring Revolution*; and Buhle, *Feminism and Its Discontents*.

13. See, e.g., Zaretsky, *Secrets of the Soul: A Social and Cultural History of Psychoanalysis*; Herzog, *Cold War Freud*; and Buhle, *Feminism and Its Discontents*.

14. Gertrude Himmelfarb, the eminent historian of Victorian Britain was also a neoconservative. Himmelfarb was married to Irving Kristol. Himmelfarb's writings defended Victorian and Western virtues from the assaults of modernity. See, e.g., Gertrude Himmelfarb, *The De-Moralization of Society: From Victorian Virtues to Modern Values* (New York: Alfred A. Knopf, 1995); and Gertrude Himmelfarb, *One Nation, Two Cultures: A Searching Examination of American Society in the Aftermath of Our Cultural Revolution* (New York: Vintage, 2001). See also Hartman, *War for the Soul of America*, 39, 138.

15. Decter, *Liberated Woman and Other Americans*; Decter, *New Chastity and Other Arguments against Women's Liberation*; and Decter, *Liberal Parents, Radical Children*.

16. Laurie Johnston, "'Women Power' Protests 'Male Domination' of Wall St.," *New York Times*, August 24, 1973, 39; Decter quoted in Laurie Johnston, "Women's Liberation Movement Is Seen Leading to 'Self-Hatred,'" *New York Times*, November 30, 1972, 12; and Deirdre Carmody, "A Critic Offers Views on Women's Lib: Everybody Cowed," *New York Times*, March 21, 1973, 47. See also Decter, *An Old Wife's Tale*, 94.

17. Douglas Martin, "Phyllis Schlafly, '1924–2016, First Lady' of a Political March Right, Dies at 92," *New York Times*, September 5, 2016.

18. Critchlow, "Conservatism Reconsidered: Phyllis Schlafly and Grassroots Conservatism," in *Conservative Sixties*, ed. Farber and Roche, 124; Spruill, "Gender and America's Right Turn," in *Rightward Bound*, ed. Schulman and Zelizer, 72.

19. Decter, quoted in Megan Rosenfeld, "Midge Decter and the Crisis of Feminism: Politics, Paradoxes, and Pleas for Manliness," *Washington Post*, July 31, 1979, B1.

20. For Schlafly, see Critchlow, *Phyllis Schlafly and Grassroots Conservatism*. For more on the "family wage" see Gordon, *Pitied But Not Entitled*; Self, *All in the*

Family. For the "family wage" and second-wave feminism, see Nancy MacLean, "Postwar Women's History: The 'Second Wave' or the End of the Family Wage," in Agnew and Rosenzweig, *A Companion to Post-1945 America*, 235–59. For an astute critique of the family wage ideology, see Ehrenreich, *The Hearts of Men*.

21. Midge Decter, interview by author, November 21, 2011 (in author's possession), MP3, transcript notes, 46.

22. See, e.g., McGirr, *Suburban Warriors*; Nickerson, *Mothers of Conservatism*; and Taranto, *Kitchen Table Politics*.

23. For "Family Values," see, e.g., Self, *All in the Family*; Hartman, *War for the Soul of America*; Young, *We Gather Together*; Dowland, *Family Values*. For how "family values" became integral to the Republican Party, see Matthew D. Lassiter, "Inventing Family Values," in Schulman and Zelizer, *Rightward Bound*; and Chappell, "The Triumph of Conservatives in a Liberal Age," in Agnew and Rosenzweig, *A Companion to Post-1945 America*.

24. Decter, *An Old Wife's Tale*, 3, 21–24.

25. Decter, *An Old Wife's Tale*, 3, 20–28. See also Midge Decter, "An Activist Critic on the Upper West Side," in Rosenberg and Goldstein, *Creators and Disturbers: Reminiscences by Jewish Intellectuals of New York*, 351–67.

26. Decter, *An Old Wife's Tale*, 38; Midge Decter, "The Gay Divorcee," in Decter, *Liberated Woman and Other Americans*, 52–53.

27. Decter, *An Old Wife's Tale*, 38–45; and Jeffers, *Norman Podhoretz: A Biography*, 45–48.

28. Midge Decter to Bernard Malamud, April 2, 1957, box 14, folder 6, Bernard Malamud Papers, Rare Book and Manuscript Library, Columbia University.

29. Decter, interview with author.

30. Jeffers, *Norman Podhoretz: A Biography*, 52; and Decter to Malamud, April 2, 1957.

31. Decter, *An Old Wife's Tale*, 40.

32. Decter, *An Old Wife's Tale*, 30.

33. Decter, *An Old Wife's Tale*, 69–70; and Carmody, "A Critic Offers Views on Women's Lib," 47.

34. See, e.g., Hoeveler, *Watch on the Right: Conservative Intellectuals in the Reagan Era*.

35. Horowitz, *Betty Friedan and the Making of The Feminine Mystique*, 8.

36. Horowitz, *Betty Friedan and the Making of The Feminine Mystique*.

37. For debates about women's roles in postwar America, see, e.g., Meyerowitz, *Not June Cleaver*. For Jewish women and the "feminine mystique," see Diner, Kohn, and Kranson, *Jewish Feminine Mystique?*

38. See, e.g., Stansell, *American Moderns*.

39. Gerhard, *Desiring Revolution*, 31.

40. Buhle, *Feminism and Its Discontents*, 76–77. See also Hale, *The Rise and Crisis of Psychoanalysis in the United States*.

41. My discussions of Horney and Deutsch draws largely from Gerhard and Buhle. See Buhle, *Feminism and Its Discontents*, esp. 74–81; Gerhard, *Desiring Revolution*, 31–39. See also Herzog, *Cold War Freud*, 35–37.

42. Buhle, *Feminism and Its Discontents*, 161–62, 178–80, 190–92.

43. Friedan, *Feminine Mystique*, 42, 103, 119–21.

44. Ehrenreich, *Hearts of Men*, 17.

45. Decter, "Marriage as a Way of Life," in *Liberated Woman*, 17–19.

46. Decter, "Marriage as a Way of Life," 19.

47. Decter, "Secrets," in *Liberated Woman*, 22–23.

48. Decter, "Secrets," 23.

49. Decter, *An Old Wife's Tale*, 49.

50. Decter, *An Old Wife's Tale*, 48.

51. Decter, *An Old Wife's Tale*, 51.

52. Kessler Harris, *In Pursuit of Equality*; MacLean, *Freedom Is Not Enough*; and Turk, *Equality on Trial*.

53. Midge Decter, "A Commentary Report: Women at Work," *Commentary* (March 1961). The essay was republished in Decter, *The Liberated Woman and Other Americans*. Quotations are from the book, 25.

54. Decter, "Women at Work," 34, 25.

55. *American Women: Report of the President's Commission on the Status of Women* (Washington, DC: Government Printing Office, 1963), reprinted in Miriam Schneir, ed., *Feminism in Our Time: The Essential Writings, World War II to the Present* (New York: Vintage, 1994), 38–47. For the President's Commission on the Status of Women and its influence on second-wave feminism, see Harrison, *On Account of Sex*; Rosen, *World Split Open*.

56. Decter, "A Commentary Report: Women At Work," 30, 40.

57. Klemesrud, "It Was Ladies Day at the Party Meeting," 62.

58. Critchlow, "Conservatism Reconsidered: Phyllis Schlafly and Grassroots Conservatism," 115.

59. "Decter, Midge," in *Current Biography Yearbook*, vol. 43 (New York: H. W. Wilson, 1982).

60. Correspondence from Decter as acting managing editor is found at CMP; Decter, interview with author, 21; and Decter, *New Chastity*, 133. See also "Decter, Midge," in *Current Biography Yearbook*.

61. Morris, *New York Days*, 100.

62. Podhoretz, *Breaking Ranks*, 151.

63. Morris, *New York Days*, 64, 190.

64. Morris, *New York Days*, 190; and Podhoretz, *Breaking Ranks*, 153.

65. Morris, *New York Days*, 193, 100.

66. Morris, *New York Days*, 105.

67. Morris, *New York Days*, 216–17.

68. Decter quoted in Manso, *Mailer*, 264.

69. Norman Mailer, "The Steps of the Pentagon," *Harper's*, March 1968.

70. Norman Mailer, *The Armies of the Night* (New York: Weidenfeld and Nicolson, 1968).

71. Norman Mailer, "The Prisoner of Sex," *Harper's*, March 1971.

72. Alden Whitman, "Morris Resigns in *Harper's* Dispute," *New York Times*, March 5, 1971. See also Morris, *New York Days*, 356; and Manso, *Mailer*, 519–20.

73. Morris, *New York Days*, 100–101. Decter, "Sex, My Daughters, and Me," *Harper's*, August 1967; and Decter, "Anti-Americanism in America," *Harper's*, April 1968. After

leaving *Harper's*, Decter worked part-time as a literary editor of *World* magazine and later as an editor at *Saturday Review/World* (1972–74), and Basic Books from 1974 until she turned her attention to the Committee for the Free World in 1980. See Midge Decter in *Current Biography Yearbook*; Carmody, "A Critic Offers Views on Women's Lib," 47.

74. Decter, *An Old Wife's Tale*, 26, 50; Decter, interview with author, 27.

75. Norman Podhoretz, "Reflections on Earth Day," *Commentary* 49, no. 6 (June 1970): 26; Dorrien, *Neoconservative Mind*, 164.

76. Decter, "Liberated Woman," 44.

77. Decter, "Liberated Woman," 33.

78. Decter, "Liberated Woman," 35, 35, 36.

79. Decter, "Liberated Woman," 42.

80. Decter, "Liberated Woman," 37–38.

81. Decter, "Liberated Woman," 39.

82. Decter, "Liberated Woman," 39–40.

83. Decter, "Liberated Woman," 41.

84. Decter, "Liberated Woman," 41.

85. Carmody, "A Critic Offers Views on Women's Lib," 47.

86. Decter, *An Old Wife's Tale*, 76.

87. For the Jewish American Princess stereotype, see Riv Ellen Prell, *Fighting to Become Americans*.

88. Decter, "Liberated Woman," 34.

89. Philip Roth, *Goodbye, Columbus, and Five Short Stories* (Boston: Houghton Mifflin, 1959).

90. Macdonald S. Moore, "Letters from Readers: Women's Lib and the Liberated Women," *Commentary* (February 1971): 12; and Jane O'Reilly, "Liberal Parents, Radical Children," *New York Times*, June 22, 1975, 24. For the New Journalism, see, e.g., Polsgrove, *It Wasn't Pretty Folks, but Didn't We Have Fun?*

91. Decter, *Liberal Children, Radical Parents*, 37.

92. Lee Wohlfert-Wihlborg, "Parents Who Are 'Nice Guys' Can Ruin Their Children, Insists Author Midge Decter," *People*, September 22, 1975, https://people.com/archive/parents-who-are-nice-guys-can-ruin-their-children-insists-author-midge-decter-vol-4-no-12/.

93. Rosalind Rosenberg, *Divided Lives*, 151; and Patterson, *Grand Expectations*, 362.

94. Benjamin Spock, "Male Chauvinist Spock Recants," *New York Times Sunday Magazine*, September 12, 1971, 98. Midge Decter, "Letters: Dr. Spock's Recantation," *New York Times*, October 10, 1971; Patti Hagan, "Dr. Spock Tells Why He No Longer Sings in Praise of Himself," *New York Times*, October 13, 1973, 30; and Decter, *An Old Wife's Tale*, 55.

95. Thomas Edwards, "The Liberated Woman and Other Americans," *New York Times*, September 19, 1971, BR31.

96. Barbara Harrison, "For Decter and Friedan," *New York Times*, August 5, 1972, 25.

97. Lehmann-Haupt, "This Body May Have Many Heads," 45.

98. Carmody, "A Critic Offers Views on Women's Lib," 47.

99. Decter, *New Chastity*, 23, 33.

100. Decter, *New Chastity*, 138–39.

101. Decter, *New Chastity*, 124–25.

102. Maclean, *American Women's Movement*, 27–29; Potter, "Not in Conflict but in Coalition: Imagining Lesbians at the Center of the Second Wave," 26; Gerhard, *Desiring Revolution*, esp. chapter three; and Echols, *Daring to Be Bad*. For firsthand accounts, see, e.g., Jill Johnston, *Lesbian Nation: The Feminist Solution* (1973); Deborah Goleman Wolf, *The Lesbian Community* (1979); Cheryl Clarke, "Lesbianism: An Act of Resistance," in *This Bridge Called My Back*, ed. Cherríe Moraga and Gloria Anzaldúa (1981); Adrienne Rich, "Compulsory Heterosexuality and Lesbian Existence," *Signs* 5, no. 4 (Summer 1980): 631–60; Karla Jay, *Tales of the Lavender Menace: A Memoir of Liberation* (New York: Basic Books, 1999).

103. Decter, *New Chastity*, 95. See also Decter, "Secrets," 23.

104. Decter, *New Chastity*, 97, 102–3.

105. Decter, *New Chastity*, 87–89.

106. Midge Decter, "The Boys on the Beach," *Commentary* 70, no. 3 (September 1980): 42, 44.

107. Decter, "Boys on the Beach," 37, 39, 40.

108. Lewis Coser, "Midge Decter and the Boys on the Beach," *Dissent*, Spring 1981, 218.

109. Gore Vidal, "Neo-Con Homophobia: Some Jews and the Gays," *The Nation*, November 14, 1981, 508–17.

110. Johnson, *This Is Our Message*, 39; Frank, "The Civil Rights of Parents."

111. Dowland, *Family Values and The Rise of the Christian Right*, 161, 164.

112. Ernest van den Haag, "Letters from Readers: Women's Lib and the Liberated Woman," *Commentary* (February 1971): 51; and Nash, *Reappraising the Right*, 92–93.

113. Ernest van den Haag and Robert Nisbet, "Letters from Readers: The Boys on the Beach," *Commentary* (December 1980): 6.

114. Decter quoted in Rosenfeld, "Midge Decter and the Crisis of Feminism," B1.

115. Midge Decter, "Liberating Women: Who Benefits," *Commentary* 77, no. 33 (March 1984): 31–36.

116. Decter, interview with author.

117. Norman Podhoretz, "The Culture of Appeasement," *Harper's*, October 1977, 25, 29. In 1975 *Commentary* published a seventy-page symposium with more than thirty participants: "America Now: A Failure of Nerve," *Commentary* 60, no. 1 (July 1975): 16–86.

118. David Greenberg, "Saigon and Saddam: The Use and Abuse of Vietnam Analogies," *Slate*, April 19, 2004. https://slate.com/news-and-politics/2004/04/the-use-and-abuse-of-vietnam-analogies.html.

119. McAlister, *Epic Encounters*, 186–87.

120. Podhoretz, "Culture of Appeasement," 29, 31.

121. Podhoretz, "Culture of Appeasement," 31.

122. Midge Decter et al., *The Trans-Atlantic Crisis: A Conference of the Committee for the Free World* (New York: Orwell Press, 1982), 1–2; Ehrman, *Neoconservatism*, 57.

123. Midge Decter, interviewed by *Human Events* 51, no. 1 (January 13, 1995): 16.

124. See, e.g., Mann, *Rise of the Vulcans*.

125. Nathan Glazer, "Neoconservative from the Start," *Public Interest* 159 (2005): 17. Glazer and Daniel Bell are often classified as neoconservatives because of their initial association with the movement and their inclusion in Steinfels, *The Neoconservatives*.

126. For the Old Right, see Ribuffo, *Old Christian Right*. See also Nash, *Conservative Intellectual Movement since 1945*. For American Jews and liberalism, see, e.g., Svonkin, *Jews against Prejudice*; Dollinger, *Quest for Inclusion*; and Staub, *Torn at the Roots*.

127. Feulner, *March of Freedom*, 240.

128. "What Heritage Foundation Does," *New York Times*, November 18, 1984, 36; Bernard Weintraub, "Heritage Foundation Ten Years Later," *New York Times*, September 30, 1983, A20; and Jason M. Stahl, *Right Moves: The Conservative Think Tank in American Political Culture since 1945* (Chapel Hill: University of North Carolina Press, 2016), 77–83.

129. Midge Decter, "Why American Families Are So Unhinged," in *Always Right: Selected Writings of Midge Decter* (Washington, DC: Heritage Foundation, 2002), 91. The essay was a speech Decter gave at the Heritage Foundation on November 8, 1993, as part of the W. H. Bradley Lecture Series on Defining Conservatism. Decter, interview with author.

130. Feulner, *March of Freedom*, 243.

Chapter Seven

1. Podhoretz, *Breaking Ranks*, 21.

2. Podhoretz, *Breaking Ranks*, 361–65.

3. Nathan Glazer, "Neoconservative From the Start," *Public Interest* (Spring 2005); Steinfels, *The Neoconservatives*; and Dorrien, *Neoconservative Mind*; Vaïsse, *Neoconservatism: The Biography of a Movement*; Ehrman, *Rise of Neoconservatism*.

4. Wilson identified neoconservatism in 1980 as "a mood, not an ideology." "There is no such thing as a neoconservative manifesto, credo, religion, flag, anthem, or secret handshake," he noted. "As a tendency, it is shot through with inner tension." James Q. Wilson, "Neoconservatism: Pro and Con," *Partisan Review* 47, no. 4 (1980): 509.

5. Kristol, "Looking Back: Forty Good Years," *Public Interest* (Spring 2005): 8.

6. Daniel Bell, "Forward: 1978," in *The Cultural Contradictions of Capitalism*, Twentieth Anniversary ed. (New York: Basic Books, 1996 [1976]), xi. See essays in Starr and Zelzer, *Defining the Age: Daniel Bell*.

7. James Traub, "Nathan Glazer Changes His Mind, Again," *New York Times*, June 28, 1998; "Glazer, "Neoconservative from the Start."

8. Quoted Hodgson, *World Turned Right Side Up*, 130.

9. Justin Vaïsse, "Was Irving Kristol a Neoconservative?," *Foreign Policy*, September 23, 2009.

10. Isserman, *If I Had A Hammer*, xv.

11. Podhoretz, *Making It*, 198.

12. Norman Podhoretz, "The Reminiscences of Norman Podhoretz," interview by Joseph Dorman, transcript of tape recording, Oral History Research Office, Butler Library, Columbia University, 11. See also Dorman, *Arguing the World*.

13. Podhoretz, *Making It*, 87–88, 114.

14. Jeffers, *Podhoretz: Biography*, 4–5.

15. Podhoretz, *Making It*, 15.

16. Aronowitz used the derogatory term "spade" to refer to Black Americans. For the trajectory of that word, see Miedler, *Call a Spade a Spade*. In 1970, Podhoretz wrote Aronowitz: "I'm just going off now on a leave of absence to work on a book, and in the process of getting my desk cleaned off, I came across that letter you wrote me ages ago about "My Negro Problem and Ours." I didn't know that I never answered it; something about it probably irritated me at the time." Undated letter from Al Aronowitz to Podhoretz and Podhoretz's response, January 20, 1970, box 18, folder 7, CMP.

17. Podhoretz, *Making It*, 3.

18. Mrs. K was Mrs. Harriet Cashemore Taft, a teacher at Boys High. "The Cashemores were an 'old Brooklyn' WASP family. After an education at Vassar, Harriet had married an elderly, wealthy, well-assimilated German-Jewish businessman." See Jeffers, *Podhoretz: Biography*, 8; Podhoretz, *Making It*, 5–13. Quote from page 7.

19. Podhoretz, *Making It*, 14–15.

20. Podhoretz, *Making It*, 33, 35; and Jeffers, *Podhoretz: Biography*, 5.

21. Podhoretz, *Making It*, 30.

22. Norman Podhoretz to Lionel Trilling, November 23, 1951, box 7, folder 7, LTP.

23. Kimmage, *Conservative Turn*, 99.

24. Podhoretz, *Making It*, 36.

25. Podhoretz, *Making It*, 26. Podhoretz may have had Allen Ginsberg in mind with this reference to homosexuals. See Podhoretz, *Ex-Friends*, 24, 35–37; and Abrams, *Podhoretz and Commentary*, 156–57.

26. Norman Podhoretz to Lionel Trilling, June 6, 1951, box 7, folder 7, LTP; Podhoretz, *Making It*, 60.

27. Lionel Trilling to Elliot Cohen, December 3, 1951, box 1, folder 1, Norman Podhoretz Papers, Library of Congress. Hereafter, NPP.

28. Kristol to Norman Podhoretz, January 31, 1952, box 1, folder 1, NPP.

29. Norman Podhoretz to Lionel Trilling, June 6, 1951; and Norman Podhoretz to Lionel Trilling, April 17, 1955, box 7, folder 7, LTP.

30. Podhoretz, *Ex Friends*, 38.

31. Podhoretz, *Making It*, 124.

32. Podhoretz, *Making It*, 130–31.

33. Norman Podhoretz to Lionel Trilling, February 3, 1955, box 7, folder 7, LTP.

34. Podhoretz, *Making It*, 113.

35. Podhoretz, *Making It*, 79. Norman Podhoretz, interview by Joseph Dorman, 2000, Arguing the World project, Oral History Research Office, Columbia University, 14.

36. Norman Podhoretz to Lionel Trilling, May 20, 1954, box 7, folder 7, LTP.

37. Podhoretz, *Making It*, 135–36.

38. Norman Podhoretz to Lionel Trilling, April 17, 1955, box 7, folder 7, LTP.

39. Podhoretz, *Making It*, 141.

40. Norman Podhoretz to Lionel Trilling, February 3, 1955, box 7, folder 7, LTP.

41. Abrams, *Commentary: 1945–59*, 150.

42. Podhoretz, *Making It*, 148.

43. Quoted in Jeffers, *Podhoretz: Biography*, 51; Podhoretz, *Making It*, 157.

44. Podhoretz, *Making It*, 168–70.

45. Abrams, *Podhoretz and Commentary*; and Balint, *Running Commentary*.

46. Jeffers, *Podhoretz: Biography*, 49–52.

47. Midge Decter, interview by Rosalind S. Mayer, tape recording transcript, March 2 and 31, 1981. New York Public Library, Dorot Division, 2–51–52; and Decter, interview by author, 21.

48. Podhoretz, *Making It*, 179.

49. Podhoretz, "Book Reviewing and Everyone I Know," *Doing and Undoings*, 262; Philip Nobile, *Intellectual Skywriting: Literary Politics and the New York Review of Books* (New York: Charterhouse, 1974).

50. Podhoretz, *Making It*, 184–85.

51. Podhoretz, *Making It*, 176.

52. For Podhoretz's account, see *Ex-Friends*, 22–56.

53. Norman Podhoretz, "A Howl of Protest," *New Republic*, September 16, 1957, 20.

54. Podhoretz, "The Young Generation," in *Doings and Undoings*, 105–11, originally published in *The New Leader*, March 11, 1957.

55. Podhoretz, "Where Is the Beat Generation Going?," *Esquire*, December 1, 1958, 147–50.

56. These lines made it into the final draft.

57. Podhoretz, "The Future of the International Beats," draft, box 6, NPP.

58. Podhoretz, "Where Is the Beat Generation Going?" For juvenile delinquency, see James Gilbert, *A Cycle of Outrage* (Oxford: Oxford University Press, 1988).

59. Podhoretz, "Where Is the Beat Generation Going?"

60. Norman Podhoretz, "The Know-Nothing Bohemians," *Partisan Review* (Spring 1958). Republished in Podhoretz, *Doing and Undoings*.

61. Podhoretz, "The Know-Nothing Bohemians," *Doing and Undoings*. See Ned Polsky, "Reflections on Hipsterism," *Dissent* (Winter 1958): 78. Diana Trilling was also critical of the Beats. See Diana Trilling, "The Other Night at Columbia," *Partisan Review* (Spring 1959); Norman Mailer was the exception. His 1956 essay, "The White Negro," celebrated hipsterism and struck many observers as overlapping with beatnik culture. Mailer, "The White Negro," *Dissent* (Fall 1957).

62. Podhoretz, "The Know-Nothing Bohemians," 152.

63. Podhoretz, "The Know-Nothing Bohemians," 157.

64. Podhoretz, *Breaking Ranks*, 27; and Podhoretz, *Ex-Friends*, 33.

65. Podhoretz, *Breaking Ranks*, 28; Podhoretz, *Ex-Friends*, 42; and Jumonville, *Critical Crossings*, 196.

66. Norman Podhoretz to Philip Rahv, September 23, 1963, box 17, folder 1, NPP.

67. Norman Podhoretz, "Mary McCarthy and the Leopard's Spots," *Show*, October 1963. Republished "John O'Hara and Mary McCarthy," in *Doing and Undoings*. Quotes are from the book, 93, 87.

68. King, *Arendt and America*, 55. See also Ring, *Political Consequences of Thinking*.

69. Norman Podhoretz, "Hannah Arendt on Eichmann: A Study in the Perversity of Brilliance," *Commentary* (September 1963).

70. Norman Podhoretz to Dan Jacobson, December 27, 1963, box 11, folder 10, CMP.

71. "*Newsweek* on Commentary," *Newsweek*, March 16, 1964.

72. Letter from Albert Furth, October 14, 1959, box 117, folder 6, CMP.

73. Daniel Bell to Albert Furth, July 1, 1959, box 11, folder 6, CMP.

74. Leslie Fiedler to Albert Furth, September 3, 1959, box 117, folder 6, CMP.

75. R. Constable to Albert Fuchs, August 12, 1959, box 117, folder 6, CMP.

76. Fiedler also asked for a substantial moving allowance and salary since the job required him to leave a stable academic position. Alan Furth to Albert (Bill) Furth, October 14, 1959; Albert (Bill) Furth to AJC subcommittee, September 16, 1959, box 117, folder 4, CMP.

77. Jeffers, *Podhoretz: Biography*, 63.

78. Bill Fuchs conveying his conversation with Daniel Bell in a memo to Sher, Taub, Tarcher, and Glinert, August 26, 1959, box 117, folder 4, CMP. See also Podhoretz, *Making It*, 137–62.

79. Podhoretz, *Ex-Friends*, 42.

80. Decter, interview by author, 59–60.

81. Diana Trilling to Norman Podhoretz, June 27, 1960, box 1, folder 1, NPP.

82. Solotaroff, "Adventures in Editing: Ted Solotaroff's Editing Days," *The Nation*, January 22, 2009. Thanks to Eric Alterman for this reference.

83. Norman Podhoretz to James Gatsby, March 13, 1962. In a letter dated January 24, 1962, Podhoretz recommended Stoughton Lynd, Michael Maccoby, Philip Green, Nat Hentoff, and Barbara Probst Solomon as possible contributors to a New Left anthology, box 1, folder 1, NPP.

84. Norman Podhoretz to Lewis Coser, May 21, 1962, box 3, folder 7, LCP.

85. Harris Dienstfrey to Tom Hayden, November 27, 1961, box 10, folder 6, CMP.

86. Norman Podhoretz to Tom Hayden, April 16, 1963, box 10, folder 6, CMP.

87. Podhoretz, *Breaking Ranks*, 197–98.

88. In a 1995 interview, Podhoretz claimed that *Commentary* was an "intellectual center for the dissemination" of New Left ideas. See Harry Kreisler, "Conversations with History: Norman Podhoretz," University of California at Berkeley, www.youtube .com/watch?v=kfdeCi8kU8s.

89. Podhoretz, *Making It*, 104–5.

90. Norman Podhoretz to Dan Jacobson, September 26, 1962, box 11, folder 10, CMP.

91. Podhoretz, *Making It*, 244.

92. James Baldwin, "A Letter from the Region of My Mind," *New Yorker*, November 17, 1962.

93. Podhoretz, *Making It*, 254.

94. Norman Podhoretz to James Baldwin, July 14, 1961, box 1, folder 6, CMP.

95. Podhoretz, *Making It*, 252; Podhoretz, "'My Negro Problem—and Ours' at 50," *Commentary* (May 2013). For the controversy, see Buccola, *Fire Is Upon Us*.

96. Podhoretz, *Making It*, 252.

97. Podhoretz, *Breaking Ranks*, 121, 125.

98. Podhoretz, "'My Negro Problem—and Ours' at 50." The term "Crow Jim" long had currency in the Black press. According to Leonard C. Simmons, Crow Jim refers to the animosity, bitterness, and hostility felt by Blacks toward whites and a

predisposition to discriminate against whites. Leonard C. Simmons, "Crow Jim: Implications for Social Work," *Social Work* 8, no. 3 (July 1963): 2.

99. Norman Podhoretz to Dan Jacobson, June 23, 1961, box 11, folder 10, CMP.

100. Dan Jacobson to Norman Podhoretz, June 29, 1961, box 11, folder 10, CMP.

101. Podhoretz to Jacobson, July 18, 1961, box 11, folder 10, CMP.

102. Jacobson to Podhoretz, August 22, 1961, box 11, folder 10, CMP.

103. Podhoretz to Jacobson, July 26, 1961, box 11, folder 10, CMP.

104. Dan Jacobson, "James Baldwin as Spokesman," *Commentary* (December 1961). Reprinted as "James Baldwin and the American Negro" in Jacobson, *Time of Arrival and Other Essays* (New York: Macmillan, 1962).

105. Podhoretz, "My Negro Problem—and Ours," *Commentary* (February 1963): 93–101. The essay has been reprinted numerous times, including in *Doings and Undoings*. Quotes here are from Podhoretz, *The Commentary Reader: Two Decades of Articles and Stories* (New York: Atheneum, 1966), 378.

106. Podhoretz, "My Negro Problem," 382.

107. Podhoretz, "My Negro Problem," 377, 384–85.

108. There is no consensus about whether Podhoretz was really calling for miscegenation. For contrary views, see, e.g., Jumonville, *Critical Crossing*, 197; and Glaser, *Borrowed Voices*, 80.

109. Podhoretz, "My Negro Problem," 386–87.

110. Himmelfarb, "Negroes, Jews, and Muzhiks," *Commentary* (October 1966): 83.

111. Himmelfarb, "Negroes, Jews, and Muzhiks," 83–84.

112. Ralph Ellison, "Letters No Apologies," *Harper's Magazine* 23, no. 5, July 1967, 14, 4, 8.

113. For the Holocaust as lesson in liberal discourse, see Staub, *Torn at the Roots*, 77.

114. Podhoretz, "Hannah Arendt on Eichmann," 201.

115. For the controversy over *Eichmann in Jerusalem*, see Young-Bruehl, *Hannah Arendt*; Novick, *Holocaust in American Life*; Ring, *Political Consequences of Thinking*; King, *Arendt in America*; Ezra, "The Eichmann Polemics."

116. Podhoretz, "Hannah Arendt on Eichmann," *Commentary* (September 1963): 206.

117. Podhoretz, "Hannah Arendt on Eichmann," 205.

118. Norman Podhoretz to Philip Rahv, August 14, 1963, box 17, folder 1, CMP.

119. Philip Rahv to Norman Podhoretz, August 28, 1963, box 17, folder 1, CMP.

120. Howe, *Margin of Hope*, 274.

121. Podhoretz, "Hannah Arendt on Eichmann," 201.

122. Ring, *Political Consequences of Thinking*, 111.

123. Podhoretz, "Hannah Arendt on Eichmann," 201.

124. Philip Rahv to Norman Podhoretz, August 28, 1963, box 17, folder 1, CMP.

125. Podhoretz, *Breaking Ranks*, 220, 223.

126. Norman Podhoretz to Nathan Glazer, October 4, 1967, box 9, folder 2, CMP.

127. Podhoretz quoted in Bloom, *Prodigal Sons*, 359.

128. Friedenberg published sixteen articles in *Commentary* between 1960 and 1966.

129. Quoted in Balint, *Running Commentary*, 82.

130. Mailer, *Existential Errands*, 170–71.

131. Quotes in Dorrien, *Neoconservative Mind*, 159.

132. Mario Puzio, "Big Literary Gun Aims and Misses," *Chicago Tribune*, January 7, 1968, K1.

133. Podhoretz, *Making It*, 262.

134. Robert Kirsch, "Hang-Ups of Podhoretz in Aping Mailer," *Los Angeles Review of Books*, January 14, 1968, D34.

135. Oppenheimer, *Exit Right*, 259; Abrams, *Norman Podhoretz and* Commentary *Magazine*, 81; and Louis Menand, "The Book That Scandalized the New York Intellectuals," *New Yorker*, April 24, 2017.

136. Podhoretz, *Breaking Ranks*, 224, 226.

137. Quoted in Diner, *Jews of the United Sates*, 322.

138. For recent work on the Six-Day War, see, e.g., Laron, *The Six-Day War: The Breaking of the Middle East*.

139. Moore, "From David to Goliath," in Lederhendler, *The Six-Day War and World Jewry*, 69–70.

140. McAlister, *Epic Encounters*, 196.

141. See, e.g., Presner, *Muscular Judaism*; Mosse, "Max Nordau, Liberalism, and the New Jew."

142. Tamar Mayer, "From Zero to Hero," in Mayer, *Israeli Women's Studies: A Reader*, 104.

143. Gartner, *History of the Jews*, 392–95.

144. Lederhendler, *The Six-Day War and World Jewry*, 3.

145. Alterman, *We Are Not One*; Rachel Fish, "Bi-Nationalist Visions."

146. Abrams, *Commentary: 1945–59*, 69–72.

147. "How *Commentary* Furthers the AJC Program," 1958, box 117, folder 4, CMP.

148. Nathan Glazer joined the left-wing Zionist group Avuka at City College, "which opposed a Jewish state, which was then on the program of the Official Zionist movement. Our socialism led us to call for a binational workers' state, if any state at all." See Glazer, "*Commentary*: The Early Years," in Friedman, *Commentary in American Life*, 40.

149. Abrams, *Commentary: 1945–59*, 72.

150. Norman Podhoretz to Lionel Trilling, November 23, 1951, box 7, folder 7, LTP.

151. Leon Uris, *Exodus* (New York: Doubleday, 1958). For *Exodus* and American Jewry, see, Moore, "From David to Goliath," 73; Mart, *Eye on Israel*; Weissbroad, "*Exodus* as Zionist Melodrama."

152. Quoted in Breines, *Tough Jews*, 54; and McAlister, *Epic Encounters*, 164.

153. Joel Blocker, "Books in Review: Fantasy of Israel," *Commentary* (June 1959): 539.

154. Robert Alter, "Israel and the Intellectuals," *Commentary* (October 1967): 46.

155. For the increasing role Israel played in American Jewish life, see, e.g., Kaufman, "From Philanthropy to Commitment." For a more tempered view, see Chaim I. Waxman, "The Limited Impact of the Six-Day War on America's Jews," in Lederhendler, *The Six-Day War and World Jewry*, 99–115. See also Berman, *American Jewish Philanthropic Complex*.

156. Abrams, *Podhoretz and* Commentary, 151.

157. Draper, "Israel and Word Politics"; Walter Laqueur, "Israel and the Arabs"; Herzberg, "Israel and American Jewry"; and Elon, "Israel: Letter from the Sinai Front," *Commentary* (August 1967). See Dorrien, *Neoconservative Mind*, 186.

158. Diner, *Jews of the United States*, 334–35.

159. Hall, "On the Tail of the Panther."

160. Herzberg, "Israel and American Jewry," 72.

161. David Riesman to Norman Podhoretz, July 27, 1967, box 17, folder 19, CMP.

162. Podhoretz to Riesman, August 9, 1967, box 17, folder 19, CMP.

163. Riesman to Podhoretz, October 25, 1967, box 17, folder 19, CMP.

164. Podhoretz to Riesman, August 9, 1967, box 17, folder 19, CMP.

165. Robert Alter to Neal Kozodoy, July 20, 1967, box 1, folder 4, CMP.

166. Alter, "Israel and the Intellectuals," 47.

167. Alter, "Israel and the Intellectuals," 46.

168. Milton Himmelfarb, "In Light of Israel's Victory," *Commentary* (October 1967): 59.

169. Himmelfarb, "In Light of Israel's Victory," 56.

170. Himmelfarb, "In Light of Israel's Victory," 57–58.

171. Martin Peretz, "American Left and Israel," *Commentary* (November 1967): 29–30.

172. They included: Richard Perle, Paul Wolfowitz, Ben Wattenberg, Elliot Abrams, Penn Kemble, Joshua Muravchik, and Jeanne Kirkpatrick among others. See, e.g., Ehrman, *Rise of Neoconservatism*, 60–64.

173. Norman Podhoretz, "Making the World Safe for Communism," *Commentary* (April 1976): 31.

174. For examples of calls for withdrawal, see Nathan Glazer, "Vietnam: The Case for Immediate Withdrawal," *Commentary* (May 1971); and Norman Podhoretz, "Issues: A Note on Vietnamization," *Commentary* (May 1971).

175. Norman Podhoretz, "The Abandonment of Israel," *Commentary* 63, no. 1 (July 1976): 25, 30.

176. Norman Podhoretz, "The State of World Jewry," *Commentary* 76, no. 6 (December 1983): 39.

177. Podhoretz, "State of World Jewry," 39.

178. Midge Decter, "A Look at Israel," *Commentary* 51, no. 5 (March 1971): 42.

179. Podhoretz, "State of World Jewry," 39.

Epilogue

1. Francis Fukuyama, "After Neoconservatism," *New York Times*, February 19, 2006.

2. Nathan Glazer, "Neoconservatism: Pro and Con," *Partisan Review* 47, no. 8 (Fall 1980): 501. For the neocons and affirmative action, see MacLean, *Freedom Is Not Enough*.

3. James Traub, "Nathan Glazer Changes His Mind Again," *New York Times*, June 28, 1998.

4. Nathan Glazer, "Neoconservative from the Start," *Public Interest* 159 (Spring 2005): 15.

5. Howe, *Margin of Hope*, 139–40. The new Jewish intellectual masculinity of the 1930s–1970s fed on post–World War I reactions against Victorian gentility. See George Santayana, *The Genteel Tradition in American Philosophy* (1911); Van Wyck Brooks, *America's Coming of Age* (1916); F. Scott Fitzgerald, *The Crack-Up*, ed.

Edmund Wilson (1936); and Malcolm Cowley, "The Revolt against Gentility" in *After the Genteel Tradition*, ed. Cowley (1937). Helpful secondary accounts include May, *End of American Innocence*; Singal, *The War Within*; Rubin, "The Genteel Tradition at Large"; and Douglas, *The Feminization of American Culture* and *Terrible Honesty*.

6. Michael Kazin, "Confronting a Father's Legacy," *Chronicle of Higher Education* 54, no. 17 (December 2007).

7. Mann, *Rise of the Vulcans*.

8. Midge Decter, *Rumsfeld: A Personal Portrait* (New York: Harper Collins, 2003); Larissa MacFarquhar, "Midge's Mash Note," *New Yorker*, November 3, 2003.

9. Robert George, "Midge Decter: Our Jewish Mother," *Washington Examiner*, May 19, 2022; "Midge Decter, R.I.P.," *National Review*, May 10, 2022; Joseph Bottum, "RIP Midge Decter, Conservative Den Mother and Witty Force of Nature," *New York Post*, May 10, 2022; and Edwin J. Feulner, ed., *The March of Freedom: Modern Classics in Conservative Thought* (Dallas: Spence Pub, 1998), 240–43.

10. Elliott Abrams described the January 6, 2020, attack as "a horrifying and criminal attack on our constitution and our Congress." Jacob Kornbluh, "After Serving in His Administration, Elliott Abrams Hasn't Changed His (Negative) View about Trump," *The Forward*, January 27, 2021.

11. Podhoretz said, "That's one of the things the Americans who love him, love him for—that he's willing to fight, not willing to but eager to fight." Charles R. Klesner, "An Interview with Norman Podhoretz: The CRB Interviews Norman Podhoretz," *Claremont Review of Books*, April 16, 2019, digital exclusive. https://claremontreviewofbooks.com/digital/an-interview-with-norman-podhoretz/.

12. Norman Podhoretz, *Why Are Jews Liberal?* (New York: Doubleday, 2009), 253, 267.

13. Brian Morton, "Todd Gitlin, 1943–2022," *Dissent*, February 7, 2022.

14. Gitlin quoted in *Arguing the World*, 176; Gitlin, *Years of Hope, Days of Rage*.

15. Alfred Kazin, *New York Jew*, 259.

16. Michael Kazin, "Fathers and Sons," *Dissent*, Fall 1998, 102.

17. Michael Kazin, "Confronting a Father's Legacy," *Chronicle of Higher Education* 54, no. 17 (December 2007).

18. Jacoby, *Last Intellectuals*.

19. Michael Walzer, interview with author.

20. Maurice Isserman, "Steady Work: Sixty Years of Dissent," *Dissent*, January 23, 2014.

21. Michael Walzer, "Tributes to Michael Kazin," *Dissent*, October 6, 2020.

22. Evan Goldstein, "The New Intellectuals," *Chronicle of Higher Education* (November 13, 2016).

23. Walzer, "Tributes to Michael Kazin."

24. Goldstein, "New Intellectuals."

25. Daphne Merkin, "The Journey of Diana Trilling," *Wall Street Journal*, April 18, 2017.

26. Daphne Merkin, "'Closing Time': My Lost Literary World," *New York Review of Books*, November 1, 2019; Daphne Merkin, "The Golden Age of Glossies," *New York Review of Books*, January 23, 2023.

BIBLIOGRAPHY

Archives Consulted

THE JACOB RADER MARCUS CENTER OF THE AMERICAN JEWISH ARCHIVES AT HEBREW UNION COLLEGE–JEWISH INSTITUTE OF RELIGION

Henry Hurwitz Papers
Horace Kallen Papers
Solomon Andhil Fineberg Papers

BOSTON COLLEGE LIBRARIES

Lewis Coser Papers

COLUMBIA UNIVERSITY RARE BOOKS AND MANUSCRIPT LIBRARY

Arguing the World Oral History Collection, 1988–1996
Bernard Malamud Papers
Diana Trilling Papers
Lionel Trilling Papers
Meyer Schapiro Papers
New Leader Papers
Sol Stein Papers

HARRY RANSOM CENTER, UNIVERSITY OF TEXAS AT AUSTIN

Commentary Magazine Papers
Elizabeth Hardwick Papers
Norman Mailer Papers
Stanley Burnshaw Papers

HARVARD UNIVERSITY ARCHIVES

Daniel Bell Papers

LIBRARY OF CONGRESS, WASHINGTON, DC

Hannah Arendt Papers
Norman Podhoretz Papers

NEW YORK PUBLIC LIBRARY ARCHIVES AND MANUSCRIPTS

Alfred Kazin Papers
Morris Dickstein Papers

THE TAMIMENT LIBRARY AND ROBERT WAGNER
LABOR ARCHIVES NEW YORK UNIVERSITY

American Committee for Cultural Freedom Papers (ACCF)

QUEENS COLLEGE

Ann Birstein Papers

UNIVERSITY OF CHICAGO LIBRARY

Morris Cohen Papers

VASSAR COLLEGE LIBRARIES

Mary McCarthy Papers

YALE UNIVERSITY LIBRARY

Dwight Macdonald Papers

Interviews

Joanne Barkan
David A. Bell
Midge Decter
Jo-Ann Mort
Maxine Phillips (email correspondence)
Judith Walzer
Michael Walzer

Secondary Sources

Abbott, Philip. "Are Three Generations of Radicals Enough? Self-Critique in the Novels of Tess Slesinger, Mary McCarthy, and Marge Piercy." *Review of Politics* 53, no. 4 (1991): 602–6.

Abrams, Nathan. *Commentary Magazine, 1945–1955: "A Journal of Significant Thought and Opinion."* New York: Vallentine Mitchell, 2007.

———. "Muscles, Mimicry, Menschlikyat, and Madagascar: Jews, Sport, and Nature in US Cinema." In *Muscling In on New Worlds*, edited by Raanan Rein and David Shenin. London: Brill, 2015

——. *Norman Podhoretz and* Commentary *Magazine: The Rise and Fall of the Neocons*. New York: Continuum, 2010.

Alexander, Edward. *Irving Howe: Socialist, Critic, Jew*. Bloomington: Indian University Press, 1998.

——. *Lionel Trilling and Irving Howe: And Other Stories of Literary Friendship*. New Brunswick, NJ: Transaction Press, 2009.

Alpern, Sara. *Freda Kirchwey: A Woman of The Nation*. Cambridge, MA: Harvard University Press. 1987.

Alterman, Eric. *We Are Not One: A History over America's Fight over Israel*. New York: Basic Books, 2022.

Anderson, Benedict. *Imagined Communities: Reflections on the Origin and Spread of Nationalism*. New York: Verso, 1983.

Antler, Joyce. *Jewish Radical Feminism: Voices from the Women's Liberation Movement*. New York: New York University Press, 2018.

——. *The Journey Home: How Jewish Women Shaped Modern America*. New York: Schocken Books, 1998.

——. *You Never Call! You Never Write!: A History of the Jewish Mother*. New York: Oxford University Press, 2007.

Arnesen, Eric. *Black Protest and the Great Migration*. Boston: Bedford/St. Martin's, 2002.

Baader, Benjamin Maria, Sharon Gillerman, and Paul Lerner, eds. *Jewish Masculinities: German Jews, Gender, and History*. Bloomington: Indiana University Press, 2012.

Balint, Benjamin. *Running Commentary: The Contentious Magazine That Transformed the Jewish Left into the Neoconservative Right*. New York: Public Affairs, 2010.

Barnhisel, Greg. *Cold War Modernists: Art, Literature, and American Cultural Diplomacy*. New York: Columbia University Press, 2015.

Baskin, Judith R. "Jewish Traditions about Women and Gender Roles: From Rabbinic Teachings to Medieval Practice." In *The Oxford Handbook of Women and Gender in Medieval Europe*, edited by Judith M. Bennett and Ruth Marzo Karras. New York and Oxford: Oxford University Press, 2013.

Baskin, Judith, ed. *Jewish Women in Historical Perspective*. 2nd ed. Detroit: Wayne State Press, 1998.

Bederman, Gail. *Manliness and Civilization: A Cultural History of Gender and Race in the United States, 1890–1917*. Chicago: University of Chicago Press, 1996.

Bell, Jonathan. *The Liberal State on Trial: The Cold War and American Politics in the Truman Years*. New York: Columbia University Press, 2004.

Berlin, Ira. *Making of African America: The Four Great Migrations*. New York: Viking, 2010.

Berman, Lila Corwin. *The American Jewish Philanthropic Complex: The History of a Multibillion-Dollar Institution*. Princeton, NJ: Princeton University Press, 2020.

——. "American Jews and the Ambivalence of Middle-Classness." *American Jewish History* 93, no. 4 (December 2007).

——. *Speaking of Jews: Rabbis, Intellectuals, and the Creation of an American Public*. Berkeley: University of California Press, 2009.

Biale, David, Michael Galchinsky, and Susannah Heschel, eds. *Insider/Outsider: American Jews and Multiculturalism*. Berkeley: University of California Press, 1998.

Bicker Balken, Deborah. *Harold Rosenberg: A Critic's Life*. Chicago: University of Chicago, 2021.

Blake, Casey Nelson. *Beloved Community: The Cultural Criticism of Randolph Bourne, Van Wyck Brooks, Waldo Frank, and Lewis Mumford*. Chapel Hill: University of North Carolina Press, 1990.

Bloom, Alexander. *Prodigal Sons: The New York Intellectuals and Their World*. New York: Oxford University Press, 1986.

Boyarin, Daniel. *Unheroic Conduct: The Rise of Heterosexuality and the Invention of the Jewish Man*. Berkeley: University of California Press, 1997.

Boyarin, Daniel, Daniel Itzkovitz, and Ann Pellegrini, eds. *Queer Theory and the Jewish Question*. New York: Columbia University Press, 2003.

Boydston, Jeanne. *Home and Work: Housework, Wages, and the Ideology of Labor in the Early Republic*. New York: Oxford University Press, 1993.

Breines, Paul. *Tough Jews: Political Fantasies and the Moral Dilemma of American Jewry*. New York: Basic Books, 1990.

Brightman, Carol. *Writing Dangerously: Mary McCarthy and Her World*. San Diego: Harcourt Brace, 1992.

Brightman, Carol, ed. *Between Friends: The Correspondence of Hannah Arendt and Mary McCarthy, 1949–1975*. San Diego: Harcourt Brace, 1995.

Brinkley, Alan. *Liberalism and Its Discontents*. Cambridge, MA: Harvard University Press, 2000.

Brodkin, Karen. *How Jews Became White Folks and What That Says about Race in America*. New Brunswick, NJ: Rutgers University Press, 1998.

Buccola, Nicholas. *The Fire Is upon Us: James Baldwin, William F. Buckley Jr., and the Debate over Race in America*. Princeton, NJ: Princeton University Press, 2019.

Buhle, Mari Jo. *Feminism and Its Discontents: A Century of Psychoanalysis*. Cambridge, MA: Harvard University Press, 1998.

Buhle, Paul. "The Jewish Presence among Students for a Democratic Society." *Jewish Currents* (May 2007).

Butler, Judith. *Gender Trouble: Feminism and the Subversion of Identity*, rev. ed. (New York: Routledge, 1999).

Carlston, Erin G. *Double Agents: Espionage, Literature, and Liminal Citizens*. New York: Columbia University Press, 2013.

Carnes, Mark C. *Secret Ritual and Victorian Manhood in Victorian America*. New Haven, CT: Yale University Press, 1991.

Carter, Dan T. *Scottsboro: A Tragedy of the American South*, rev. ed. Baton Rouge: Louisiana State University Press, 2007.

Chappell, David, *A Stone of Hope: Prophetic Religion and the Death of Jim Crow*. Chapel Hill: University of North Carolina Press, 2004.

———. "The Triumph of Conservatives in a Liberal Age." In *The Roots to Post-1945 America*, edited by Jean-Christophe Agnew and Richard Rosenzweig. New York: Wiley-Blackwell, 2006.

Cohen, Lizabeth. *A Consumer's Republic: The Politics of Mass Consumption in Postwar America*. New York: Vintage, 2003.

Cohen, Naomi. *Not Free to Desist: The American Jewish Committee, 1906–1966*. Philadelphia: Jewish Publication Society of America, 1977.

Cohen, Robert. *When the Old Left Was Young: Student Radicals and America's First Mass Movement, 1929–1941*. New York: Oxford University Press, 1993.

Conkin, Paul K. *The Southern Agrarians*. Knoxville: University of Tennessee Press, 1988.

Cook, Richard M. *Alfred Kazin: A Biography*. New Haven, CT: Yale University Press, 2008.

Cook, Richard M., ed. *Alfred Kazin's Journals*. New Haven, CT: Yale University Press, 2011.

Cooney, Terry A. *The Rise of the New York Intellectuals: Partisan Review and Its Circle, 1934–1945*. Madison: University of Wisconsin Press, 1986.

Cott, Nancy. *Grounding of Modern Feminism*. New Haven, CT: Yale University Press, 1989.

Critchlow, Donald. "Conservatism Reconsidered: Phyllis Schlafly and Grassroots Conservatism." In *The Conservative Sixties*, edited by David Farber and Jeff Roche. New York: Peter Lang, 2003.

———. *Phyllis Schlafly and Grassroots Conservatism: A Woman's Crusade*. Princeton, NJ: Princeton University Press, 2008.

Cuordileone, K. A. "Cold War Political Culture and a Crisis of Masculinity." *Journal of American History* 87, no. 2 (September 2000): 515–45.

———. *Manhood and American Political Culture in Cold War America*. New York: Routledge, 2005.

Curtis, Cathy. *A Splendid Intelligence: The Life of Elizabeth Hardwick*. New York: Norton, 2021.

Cushner, Ari N. "Cold War Comrades: Left-Liberal Anticommunism and American Empire, 1941–1968." PhD diss., University of California, Santa Cruz, 2017.

Dean, Michelle. *Sharp: The Women Who Made an Art of Having an Opinion*. New York: Grove Press, 2018.

Dean, Robert D. *Imperial Brotherhood: Gender and the Making of Cold War Foreign Policy*. Amherst: University of Massachusetts Press, 2001.

Denning Michael. *The Cultural Front: The Laboring of American Culture in the Twentieth Century*. New York: Verso, 1997.

Devine, Thomas. *Henry Wallace's 1948 Presidential Campaign and the Future of Postwar Liberalism*. Chapel Hill: University of North Carolina Press, 2015.

Dickstein, Morris. "The Critic Who Made Us: Lionel Trilling and The Liberal Imagination." *Sewanee Review* 94, no. 2 (Spring 1986). Reprinted in *Lionel Trilling and the Critics*.

———. *Gates of Eden: American Culture in the Sixties*, rev. ed. Cambridge, MA: Harvard University Press, 1997.

———. "A Man Nobody Knew: Lionel Trilling Remembered." In *Lionel Trilling and the Critics: Opposing Selves*, edited by John Rodden. Lincoln: University of Nebraska Press, 1999.

———. "Womb versus World." *BookForum* (June/July/September 2006).

Diggins, John Patrick, ed. *The Liberal Persuasion: Arthur Schlesinger Jr. and the Challenge of the American Past*. Princeton, NJ: Princeton University Press, 1997.

Diner, Hasia. "Embracing *World of Our Fathers*: The Context of Reception." *American Jewish History* 88, no. 4 (December 2000).

——. *The Jews of the United States, 1954–2000*. Berkeley: University of California Press, 2004.

——. *A Time for Gathering: The Second Migration, 1820–1880*. Baltimore: Johns Hopkins University Press, 1995.

——. *We Remember with Reverence and Love: American Jews and the Myth of Silence after the Holocaust, 1945–1962*. New York: New York University Press, 2010.

Diner, Hasia, Shira Kohn, and Rachel Kranson, eds. *A Jewish Feminine Mystique? Jewish Women in Postwar America*. New Brunswick, NJ: Rutgers University Press, 2010.

Dinnerstein, Leonard. *Anti-Semitism in America*. New York: Oxford University Press, 1994.

Doherty, Thomas. *Show Trial: Hollywood, HUAC, and the Birth of the Blacklist*. New York: Columbia University Press, 2018.

Dollinger, Marc. *Quest for Inclusion: Jews and Liberalism in Modern America*. Princeton, NJ: Princeton University Press, 2000.

Dorman, Joseph. *Arguing the World: The New York Intellectuals in Their Own Words*. New York: Free Press, 2000.

Dorrien, Gary. *The Neoconservative Mind: Politics, Culture, and the War of Ideology*. Philadelphia: Temple University Press, 1993.

Douglas, Ann. *The Feminization of American Culture*. New York: Farrar, Straus and Giroux, 1997.

——. *Terrible Honesty: Mongrel Manhattan in the 1920s*. New York: Farrar, Straus and Giroux, 1995.

Dowland, Seth. *Family Values and the Rise of the Christian Right*. Philadelphia: University of Pennsylvania Press, 2015.

Draper, Theodore. *The Roots of American Communism*. New York. Viking, 1958.

Dudziak, Mary. *Cold War Civil Rights: Race and the Image of American Democracy*. Princeton, NJ: Princeton University Press, 2011.

Echols, Alice. *Daring to Be Bad: Radical Feminism in America, 1967–1975*. Minneapolis: University of Minnesota Press, 1990.

Ehrenreich, Barbara. *The Hearts of Men: American Dreams and the Flight from Commitment*. New York: Anchor Books, 1983.

Ehrman, John. *Neoconservatism: Intellectuals and Foreign Affairs*. New Haven, CT: Yale University Press, 1995.

Epstein, Joseph. *Gossip: The Untrivial Pursuit*. Boston: Houghton Mifflin Harcourt, 2011.

Ezra, Michael. "The Eichmann Polemics: Hannah Arendt and Her Critics." *Democratiya* 9 (Summer 2007).

Fermaglich, Kristin. *American Dreams and Nazi Nightmares: Early Holocaust Consciousness and Liberal America, 1957–1975*. Waltham, MA: Brandeis University Press, 2007.

Fish, Rachel. "Bi-Nationalist Visions for the Construction and Dissolution of the State of Israel." *Israel Studies* 19, no. 2 (Summer 2014).

Flacks, Richard, and Nelson Lichtenstein, eds. *Port Huron Statement: Sources and Legacies*. Philadelphia: University of Pennsylvania Press, 2015.

Frank, Gillian. "The Civil Rights of Parents: Race and Conservative Politics in Anita Bryant's Campaign against Gay Rights in 1970s Florida." *Journal of the History of Sexuality* 22 (January 2013): 126–60.

Fried, Albert. *The Rise and Fall of Jewish Gangsters*. New York: Columbia University Press, 1994.

Friedman, Murray. *The Neoconservative Revolution: Jewish Intellectuals and the Shaping of Public Policy*. New York: Cambridge University Press, 2005.

Friedman, Murray, ed. *Commentary in American Life*. Philadelphia: Temple University Press, 2005.

Fuchs Abrams, Sabrina. "The Bitch Is Back: A Reappraisal of Mary McCarthy for the 21st Century." *Women's Studies: An Interdisciplinary Journal* 49, no. 4 (July 2020): 347–59.

———. *Mary McCarthy: Gender, Politics, and the Postwar Intellectual*. New York: Peter Lang, 2004.

Garrett, Leah. *Young Lions: How Jewish Authors Reinvented the American War Novel*. Evanston, IL: Northwestern University Press, 2015.

Gartner, Lloyd P. *History of the Jews in Modern Times*. New York: Oxford University Press. 2001.

Gelderman, Carol. *Mary McCarthy: A Life*. New York: St. Martin's Press, 1988.

Gelderman, Carol, ed. *Conversations with Mary McCarthy*. Jackson: University Press of Mississippi, 2011.

Genter, Robert. *Late Modernism: Art, Culture, and Politics in Cold War America*. Philadelphia: University of Pennsylvania Press, 2010.

Gerhard, Jane. *Desiring Revolution: Second-Wave Feminism and the Rewriting of American Sexual Thought, 1920 to 1982*. New York: Columbia University Press, 2001.

Gerson, Mark. *The Neoconservative Vision: From the Cold War to the Culture Wars*. London: Madison Books, 1997.

Gilbert, James. *Men in the Middle: Searching for Masculinity in the 1950s*. Chicago: University of Chicago Press, 2005.

———. *Writers and Partisans: A History of Literary Radicalism*. New York: John Wiley and Sons, 1968.

Gillion, Steven M. *Politics and Vision: The ADA and American Liberalism, 1947–1985*. New York: Oxford University Press, 1987.

Gilman, Sander L. *Freud, Race, and Gender*. Princeton, NJ: Princeton University Press, 1994.

———. *The Jews' Body*. New York: Routledge, 1991.

———. *Sexuality: An Illustrated History*. New York: John Wiley and Sons, 1989.

Gitlin, Todd. *The Sixties: Years of Hope, Days of Rage*, rev. ed. New York: Bantam, 1995.

Glaser, Jennifer. *Borrowed Voices: Writing and Racial Ventriloquism in the Jewish American Imagination*. New Brunswick, NJ: Rutgers University Press, 2016.

Glenn, Susan. *Daughters of the Shtetl: Life and Labor in the Immigrant Generation*. Ithaca, NY: Cornell University Press, 1991.

Goldman, Karla. *Beyond the Synagogue: Finding a Place for Women in American Judaism*. Cambridge, MA: Harvard University Press, 2001.

Goldstein, Eric. *The Price of Whiteness: Jews, Race, and American Identity.* Princeton, NJ: Princeton University Press, 2008.

Goodman, James. *Stories of Scottsboro.* New York: Vintage, 1995.

Goodman, Walter. *The Committee: The Extraordinary Career of the House Committee on Un-American Activities.* New York: Farrar, Straus and Giroux, 1968.

Gordon, Linda. *Pitied but Not Entitled: Single Mothers and the History of Welfare, 1890–1935.* Cambridge, MA: Harvard University Press, 1998.

Gorelick, Sherry. *City College and the Jewish Poor: Education in New York, 1880–1924.* New Brunswick, NJ: Rutgers University Press, 1981.

Goren, Arthur A. "The 'Golden Decade': 1945–55." In *The Politics and Public Culture of American Jews.* Bloomington: Indiana University Press, 1999.

——. *New York Jews and the Quest for Community.* New York: Columbia University Press, 1979.

Gosse, Van. *Rethinking the New Left: An Interpretative History.* London: Palgrave Macmillan, 2005.

——. *Where the Boys Are: Cuba, the Cold War, and the Making of a New Left.* New York: Verso, 1993.

Grant, Keneshia. *Great Migration and the Democratic Party.* Philadelphia: Temple University Press, 2020.

Greenberg, Cheryl. *Troubling the Waters: Black-Jewish Relations in the 20th Century.* Princeton, NJ: Princeton University Press, 2006.

Greene, Daniel. *The Jewish Origins of Cultural Pluralism: The Menorah Association and American Diversity.* Bloomington: Indiana University Press, 2001.

Gregory, James N. *Southern Diaspora: How the Great Migrations of Black and White Southerners Transformed America.* Chapel Hill: University of North Carolina Press, 2005.

Grinberg, Ronnie. "Neither 'Sissy' Boy nor Patrician Man: New York Intellectuals and the Construction of American Jewish Masculinity." *American Jewish History* 98, no. 3 (Summer 2014): 127–51.

Griswold, Robert L. "The Flabby American, the Body, and the Cold War." In *A Shared Experience: Men, Women, and the History of Gender,* edited by Laura McCall and Donald Yacovone. New York: New York University Press, 1998.

Grumet, Elinor. "Elliot Cohen: The Vocation of a Jewish Mentor." *Studies in the American Jewish Experience* 1 (1981).

Gurock, Jeffrey. "During the Heyday of Jewish Sports in Gotham." In *New York Sports: Glamour and Grit in the Empire City,* edited by Stephen Norwood. Fayetteville: University of Arkansas Press, 2018.

Halberstam, Judith. *Female Masculinity.* Durham, NC: Duke University Press, 1998.

Hale, Nathan. *The Rise and Crisis of Psychoanalysis in the United States.* Oxford: Oxford University Press, 1995.

Hall, Simon. "*On the Tail of the Panther*: Black Power and the 1967 Convention of the National Conference for New Politics." *Journal of American Studies* 37 (2003).

Hamby, Alfonzo L. *Beyond the New Deal: Harry S. Truman and American Liberalism.* New York: Columbia University Press, 1976.

Handlin, Oscar. *The Uprooted,* rev. ed. Philadelphia: University of Pennsylvania Press, 2002. Originally published by Little Brown in 1952.

Harper, Steven J. *Straddling Worlds: The Jewish-American Journey of Professor Richard W. Leopold*. Evanston, IL: Northwestern University Press, 2008.

Harris, Alice Kessler. *In Pursuit of Equality: Women, Men, and the Pursuit of Economic Citizenship in 20th Century America*. New York: Oxford University Press, 2001.

Harrison, Cynthia. *On Account of Sex: The Politics of Women's Issues*. Berkeley: University of California Press, 1988.

Hartman, Andrew. *A War for the Soul of America: A History of the Culture Wars*. Chicago: University of Chicago Press, 2015.

Haynes, John Earl. *Red Scare or Red Menace? American Communists and Anti-Communism in the Cold War Era*. Chicago: Ivan R. Dee, 1996.

Heilbrun, Carolyn G. *When Men Were the Only Models We Had: My Teachers Fadiman, Barzun, Trilling*. Philadelphia: University of Pennsylvania Press, 2015.

Heilbrunn, Jacob. *They Knew They Were Right: The Rise of the Neocons*. New York: Anchor, 2009.

Hertzberg, Arthur. *The Jews in America: Four Centuries of an Uneasy Encounter*. New York: Simon and Schuster, 1989.

Herzog, Dagmar. *Cold War Freud: Psychoanalysis in an Age of Catastrophes*. New York: Cambridge University Press, 2017.

Higham, John. *Send These to Me: Immigrants in Urban America*, rev. ed. Baltimore: Johns Hopkins University Press, 1975.

———. *Strangers in the Land: Patterns of Nativism, 1860–1925*, rev. ed. New Brunswick, NJ: Rutgers University Press, 2002.

Hilton, Saskia, ed. *The Dolphin Letters, 1970–1979: Elizabeth Hardwick, Robert Lowell, and Their Circle*. New York: Farrar Strauss and Giroux, 2019.

Hodgson, Godfrey. *The World Turned Right Side Up*. Boston: Houghton Mifflin, 1996.

Hoeveler, David, Jr. *Watch on the Right: Conservative Intellectuals in the Reagan Era*. Madison: University of Wisconsin Press, 1991.

Hoffman, Warren. *The Passing Game: Queering American Jewish Culture*. Syracuse, NY: Syracuse University Press, 2009.

Hoganson, Kristin. *Fighting for American Manhood*. New Haven, CT: Yale University Press, 2000.

Hollinger, David. "Communalist and Dispersionist Approaches to American Jewish History in an Increasingly Post-Jewish Era." *American Jewish History* 95, no. 1 (March 2009): 1–32.

———. *Morris R. Cohen and the Scientific Ideal*. Cambridge, MA: MIT Press, 1975.

Horowitz, Daniel. *Betty Friedan and the Making of The Feminine Mystique: The American Left, the Cold War, and Modern Feminism*. Amherst: University of Massachusetts Press, 1998.

Horton, Carol. *Race and the Making of American Liberalism*. New York: Oxford University Press, 2005.

Hyman, Paul E. *Gender and Assimilation in Modern History: The Roles and Representations of Women*. Seattle: University of Washington Press, 1995.

Hyman, Paula. "Ruth Gay." In *The Shalvi/Hyman Encyclopedia of Jewish Women*, edited by Jennifer Sartori and Jewish Women's Archive, https://jwa.org/encyclopedia/article/gay-ruth.

Iber, Patrick. *Neither Peace nor Freedom: The Cultural Cold War in Latin America.* Cambridge, MA: Harvard University Press, 2015.

Imhoff, Sarah. *Masculinity and the Making of American Judaism.* Bloomington: Indiana University Press, 2017.

Isserman, Maurice. *If I Had a Hammer: The Death of the Old Left and the Birth of the New.* Urbana: University of Illinois Press, 1993.

——. "Steady Work: Sixty Years of Dissent; A History of *Dissent* Magazine." *Dissent*, January 23, 2014.

——. *Which Side Were You On? The American Communist Party during the Second World War.* Middletown, CT: Wesleyan University Press, 1982.

Jacobson, Mathew Frye. "A Ghetto to Look Back To: World of Our Fathers, Ethnic Rival, and the Arc of Multiculturalism." *American Jewish History* 88, no. 4 (December 2000).

Jacoby, Russell. *The Last Intellectuals: American Culture in the Age of Academe.* New York: Basic Books, 2000.

Jacoby, Susan. *Alger Hiss and the Battle for History.* New Haven, CT: Yale University Press, 2009.

Jancovich, Mark. *The Cultural Politics of the New Criticism*, rev. ed. New York: Cambridge University Press 2006.

Jay, Martin. *The Dialogic Imagination: A History of the Frankfurt School and the Institute of Social Research, 1923–1950.* Berkeley: University of California Press, 1996.

Jeffers, Thomas L. *Norman Podhoretz: A Biography.* New York Cambridge University Press, 2010.

Johnson, David K. *The Lavender Scare: The Cold War Persecution of Gays and Lesbians in the Federal Government.* Chicago: University of Chicago Press, 2004.

Johnson, Emily Suzanne. *This Is Our Message: Women's Leadership in the New Christian Right.* New York: Oxford University Press, 2019.

Joselit, Jenna Weissman. *Our Gang: Crime and the New York Jewish Community.* Bloomington: Indiana University Press, 1983.

——. "Without Ghettoism: A History of the Intercollegiate Menorah Association, 1906–1930." *American Jewish Archives Publication* 30, no. 1 (1978): 133–54.

Joseph, Peniel. *The Sword and the Shield: The Revolutionary Lives of Malcolm X and Martin Luther King Jr.* New York: Basic Books, 2020.

Jumonville, Neil. *Critical Crossings: The New York Intellectuals in Postwar America.* Berkeley: University of California Press, 1991.

Kadish, Doris. *The Secular Rabbi: Philip Rahv and Partisan Review.* Liverpool: Liverpool University Press, 2021.

Kaplan, Marion, and Deborah Dash Moore, eds. *Gender and Jewish History.* Bloomington: Indiana University Press, 2010.

Karabel, Jerome. *The Chosen: The Hidden History of Admission at Harvard, Yale, and Princeton.* Boston: Houghton Mifflin Harcourt, 2005.

Kaufman, Menahem. "From Philanthropy to Commitment: The Six-Day War and the United Jewish Appeal." *Journal of Israeli Studies* (Summer 1994).

Kazin, Michael. *American Dreamers: How the Left Changed a Nation.* New York: Vintage, 2012.

——. "Two Cheers for Utopia." In *The Port Huron Statement: Sources and Legacies of the New Left's Founding Manifesto.* Philadelphia: University of Pennsylvania

Press, 2015. Originally published as "The Port Huron Statement at Fifty." *Dissent* (Spring 2012).

——. *War against War: The American Fight for Peace, 1914–1918*. New York: Simon and Schuster, 2017.

Kelley, Robin D. G. *Hammer and Hoe: Alabama Communists during the Great Depression*. Chapel Hill: University of North Carolina Press, 1990.

Kessner, Carol S. *The Other Jewish New York Intellectuals*. New York: New York University Press, 1993.

Kieran, Frances. *Seeing Mary Plain: A Life of Mary McCarthy*. New York: W. W. Norton, 2000.

Kimmage, Michael. *The Conservative Turn: Lionel Trilling, Whittaker Chambers, and the Lessons of Anti-Communism*. Cambridge, MA: Harvard University Press, 2009.

King, Richard H. "American Dilemma: European Experiences." *Arkansas Historical Quarterly* 56, no. 3 (1997): 314–33.

——. *Arendt and America*. Chicago: University of Chicago Press, 2015.

Klehr, Harvey. *Heyday of American Communism: The Depression Decade*. New York: Basic Books, 1984.

Klehr, Harvey, and John Earl Haynes. *The Secret World of American Communism*. New Haven, CT: Yale University Press, 1996.

Konvitz, Milton. *Nine American Jewish Thinkers*. New York: Routledge, 2000.

Korelitz, Seth. "The Menorah Idea: From Religion to Culture, from Race to Ethnicity." *American Jewish History* 85 (1997): 75–100.

Kranson, Rachel. *Ambivalent Embrace: Jewish Upward Mobility in Postwar America*. Chapel Hill: University of North Carolina Press, 2017.

Krupnick, Mark. "The Menorah Group and the Origins of Modern Jewish-American Radicalism." *Modern Jewish Studies Annual III, Studies in American Jewish Literature* 5 (1979): 56–67.

Kruse, Kevin, and Julian Zelizer. *Fault Lines: A History of America since 1974*. New York: Norton, 2019.

Kugelmass, Jack. *Jews, Sports, and the Rights of Citizenship*. Urbana: University of Illinois Press, 2007.

Lambert, Josh. *The Literary Mafia: Jews, Publishing, and Postwar American Literature*. New Haven, CT: Yale University Press, 2022.

Laron, Guy. *The Six-Day War: The Breaking of the Middle East*. New Haven, CT: Yale University Press, 2017.

Lasch, Christopher. *The Agony of the American Left*. New York: Knopf, 1969.

——. *The World of Nations: Reflections on American History, Politics, and Culture*. New York. Vintage 1974.

Laskin, David. *Partisans: Marriage, Politics, and Betrayal among the New York Intellectuals*. New York: Simon and Shuster, 2000.

Lassiter, Matthew D. "Inventing Family Values." In *Rightward Bound: Making American Conservative in the 1970s*, edited by Bruce J. Schulman and Julian E. Zelizer. Cambridge, MA: Harvard University Press, 2008.

——. *The Silent Majority: Suburban Politics in the Sunbelt South*. Princeton, NJ: Princeton University Press, 2007.

Lederhendler, Eli. *New York Jews and the Decline of Urban Ethnicity, 1950–1970*. Syracuse, NY: Syracuse University Press, 2001.

Lederhendler, Eli, ed. *The Six-Day War and World Jewry.* Bethesda: University of Maryland Press, 2000.

Lee, Erika. *At America's Gates: Chinese Immigration during the Exclusion Era, 1882–1943.* Chapel Hill: University of North Carolina Press, 2003.

MacLean, Nancy. *The American Women's Movement, 1945–2000.* Boston: Bedford/ St. Martin's, 2009.

——. *Freedom Is Not Enough: The Opening of the American Workplace.* Cambridge, MA: Harvard University Press, 2008.

——. "Postwar Women's History: From the 'Second Wave' to the End of the Family Wage?" In *A Companion to Post-1945 America,* edited by Roy Rosenzweig and Jean-Christophe Agnew. New York: Wiley-Blackwell, 2006.

Mann, James. *Rise of the Vulcans: The History of Bush's War Cabinet.* New York: Viking, 2004.

Manso, Peter. *Norman Mailer: His Life and Times.* New York: Simon and Shuster, 1985.

Mart, Michelle. *Eye on Israel: How America Came to View Israel as an Ally.* Albany: State University of New York Press, 2006.

May, Elaine Tyler. *Homeward Bound: American Families in the Cold War Era.* New York: Basic Books, 1988.

May, Henry. *End of American Innocence: A Study of First Years of Our Own Time, 1912–1917,* rev. ed. New York: Columbia University Press, 1994.

Mayer, Tamar. "From Zero to Hero." In *Israeli Women's Studies: A Reader,* edited by Ester Fuchs. New Brunswick, NJ: Rutgers University Press, 2007.

McAlister, Melani. *Epic Encounters: Culture, Media, and U.S. Interests in the Middle East since 1945,* updated ed. Berkeley: University of California Press, 2005.

McGirr, Lisa. *Suburban Warriors: The Origins of the American New Right.* Princeton, NJ: Princeton University Press, 2001.

Meerople, Robert. *We Are Your Sons: The Legacy of Ethel and Julius Rosenberg.* Boston: Houghton Mifflin, 1975.

Melosh, Barbara. "Manly Work: Public Art and Masculinity in Depression America." In *Gender and American History since 1890,* edited by Barbara Melosh. New York: Routledge, 1993.

Menand, Louis. "The Book That Scandalized the New York Intellectuals." *New Yorker,* April 24, 2017.

——. *The Free World: Art and Thought in the Cold War.* New York: Picador, 2022.

Mendelson, Edward. *Moral Agents: Eight Twentieth-Century American Writers.* New York: New York Review of Books, 2015.

Meyerowitz, Joanne, ed. *Not June Cleaver: Women and Gender in Postwar America, 1945–1960.* Philadelphia: Temple University Press, 1994.

Meyers, Jeffrey. "The Transformations of Philip Rahv." *Salmagundi* (Spring–Summer 2019).

Michels, Tony. "Communalist History and Beyond: What Is the Potential of American Jewish History?" *American Jewish History,* 95, no. 1 (March 2009).

Michels, Tony. *A Fire in Their Hearts: Yiddish Socialists in New York.* Cambridge: Harvard University Press, 2009.

——. "Is America 'Different'? A Critique of American Jewish Exceptionalism." *American Jewish History* 96, no. 3 (September 2010): 201–24.

————. "Socialism and the Writing of American Jewish History: *World of Our Fathers Revisited.*" *American Jewish History* 88, no. 4 (December 2000).

Miedler, Wolfgang. *Call a Spade a Spade: From Classical Phrase to Racial Slur.* New York: Peter Lang, 2002.

Miller, Nancy K. "Women's Secrets and the Novel: Remembering Mary McCarthy's *The Group,*" *Social Research* 68, no. 1 (Spring 2001).

Moore, Deborah Dash. *At Home in America: Second Generation New York Jews.* New York: Columbia University Press, 1981.

————. "From David to Goliath." In *The Six-Day War and World Jewry,* edited by Eli Lederhendler. Bethesda: University of Maryland Press, 2000.

————. *GI Jews: How World War II Changed a Generation.* Cambridge, MA: Belknap Press of Harvard University Press, 2004.

————. "Reconsidering the Rosenbergs: Symbol and Substance in Second Generation Jewish Consciousness." *Journal of American Ethnic History* 8, no. 1 (Fall 1988).

————. *To the Golden Cities: Pursuing the American Jewish Dream in Miami and L.A.* Cambridge, MA: Harvard University Press, 1996.

Moore, Deborah Dash. "When Jews were GIs: How World War II Changed a Generation and Remade American Jewry." David W. Belin Lecture, The Jean and Samuel Frankel Center for Judaic Studies, University of Michigan, March 1994.

Moore, Deborah Dash, et al. *Jewish New York: The Remarkable Story of a City and People.* New York: New York University Press, 2017.

Moser, Benjamin. *Sontag: Her Life and Work.* New York: Ecco, 2019.

Mosse, George L. *The Image of Man: The Creation of Modern Masculinity.* New York: Oxford University Press, 1996.

————. "Max Nordau, Liberalism, and the New Jew." *Journal of Contemporary History* (October 1992): 556–81.

Murphy, Paul V. *The Rebuke of History.* Chapel Hill: University of North Carolina Press, 2003.

Naison, Mark. *Communists in Harlem during the Depression: The Origins and Impact of America's Black Left.* Urbana: University of Illinois Press, 2005.

Nash, George H. *The Conservative Intellectual Movement since 1945.* Wilmington, DE: Intercollegiate Studies Institute, 1996.

————. *Reappraising the Right: The Past and Future of American Conservatism.* Wilmington, DE: Intercollegiate Studies Institute, 2009.

Navasky, Victor. *Naming Names.* New York: Viking, 1980.

Nelson, Deborah. *Tough Enough: Arbus, Arendt, Didion, McCarthy, Sontag, Weil.* Chicago: University of Chicago Press, 2017.

Ngai, Mae M. *Impossible Subjects: Aliens and the Making of Modern America.* Princeton, NJ: Princeton University Press, 2003.

Nickerson, Michelle. *Mothers of Conservatism: Women and the Postwar Right.* Princeton, NJ: Princeton University Press, 2014.

Nobile, Philip. *Intellectual Skywriting: Literary Politics and the* New York Review of Books. New York: Charterhouse, 1974.

Norwood, Stephen. "American Jewish Muscle: Forging a New Masculinity in the Street and in the Ring, 1880–1940." *Modern Judaism* 29, no. 2 (May, 2009).

Novick, Peter. *The Holocaust in American Life.* Boston: Houghton Mifflin, 1999.

Oren, Dan A. *Joining the Club: A History of Jews and Yale*. New Haven, CT: Yale University Press, 2001.

Orleck, Annelise. *Common Sense and a Little Fire: Women and Working-Class Politics in the United States*. Chapel Hill: University of North Carolina Press, 1995.

Ottanelli, Fraser M. *The Communist Party of the United States from the Depression to World War II*. New Brunswick, NJ: Rutgers University Press, 1991.

Patterson, James T. *Grand Expectations: The United Sates, 1945–1974*. New York: Oxford University Press, 1996.

Pells, Richard. *The Liberal Mind in a Conservative Age: American Intellectuals in the 1940s and 1950s*. New York: Harper and Row, 1985.

Penner, James. "Gendering Susan Sontag's Criticism in the 1960s: The New York Intellectuals, the Counterculture, and the Kulturkamp over 'The New Sensibility.'" *Women's Studies* (November 2008).

———. *Pinks, Pansies, and Punk: The Rhetoric of Masculinity in American Literary Culture*. Bloomington: Indiana University Press, 2011.

Pinckney, Darryl. "The Ethics of Admiration: Arendt, McCarthy, Hardwick, Sontag." *Threepenny Review* (Fall 2013).

———. Introduction to *The Collected Essays of Elizabeth Hardwick*. New York: New York Review Books, 2017.

Poirot, Kristin. "Mediating a Movement, Authorizing Discourse: Kate Millett, *Sexual Politics*, and Feminism's Second Wave." *Women's Studies in Communication* 27, no. 2 (2004).

Polsgrove, Carol. *It Wasn't Pretty Folks, but Didn't We Have Fun?: Esquire in the Sixties*. New York: Norton, 1995.

Potter, Claire Bond. "Not in Conflict but in Coalition: Imagining Lesbians at the Center of the Second Wave." In *The Legacy of Second-Wave Feminism in American Politics*, edited by Angie Maxwell and Todd Shields. London: Palgrave Macmillan, 2018.

Prell, Riv Ellen. "Constituting a Jewish Modernity: The Jewish Theological Seminary, Columbia University, and the Rise of a Jewish Counterculture in 1968." In *Between Jewish Tradition and Modernity: Rethinking An Old Opposition*, edited by Michael A. Meyers and David N. Myers. Detroit: Wayne State University Press, 2014.

———. *Fighting to Become Americans: Jews, Gender, and the Anxiety of Assimilation*. Boston: Beacon Press, 1999.

Presner, Todd Samuel. *Muscular Judaism: The Jewish Body and the Politics of Regeneration*. London: Routledge, 2007.

Radosh, Ronald, and Joyce Milton. *The Rosenberg File: A Search for Truth*. New York: Holt, Rinehart and Winston, 1983.

Reiss, Steven A. "A Fighting Chance: The Jewish-American Experience, 1890–1940." *American Jewish History* (March 1985).

Ribuffo, Leo P. *The Old Christian Right: The Protestant Far Right from the Great Depression to the Cold War*. Philadelphia: Temple University Press, 1983.

Ring, Jennifer. *The Political Consequences of Thinking: Gender and Judaism in the Work of Hannah Arendt*. Albany: State University of New York, 1998.

Rischin, Moses. *Promised City: New York's Jews, 1870–1914*, rev. ed. Cambridge, MA: Harvard University Press, 1977.

Robins, Natalie. *The Untold Journey: The Life of Diana Trilling*. New York: Columbia University Press, 2017.

Roberts, Sam. *The Brothers: The Untold Story of the Rosenberg Case*. New York. Simon and Schuster, 2014.

Rodden, John, ed. *Irving Howe and the Critics: Celebrations and Attacks*. Lincoln: University of Nebraska Press, 2008.

———. *Lionel Trilling and the Critics: Opposing Selves*. Lincoln: University of Nebraska Press, 1999.

———. *Worlds of Irving Howe: The Critical Legacy*. New York: Routledge, 2005.

Rodgers, Daniel T. *The Age of Fracture*. Cambridge, MA: Harvard University Press, 2012.

Rollyson, Carl, and Lisa Paddock. *Susan Sontag: The Making of an Icon*, rev. ed. Jacksonville: University Press of Mississippi, 2016.

Rosen, Ruth. *The World Split Open: How the Modern Women's Movement Changed America*. New York: Viking, 2000.

Rosenberg, Rosalind. *Divided Lives: American Women in the Twentieth Century*. New York: Hill and Wang, 1992.

Ross, Dorothy. "Freud and the Vicissitudes of Modernism in the United States." In *After Freud Left: A Century of Psychoanalysis in the United States*, edited by John Burnham. Chicago: University of Chicago Press, 2012.

Rossinow, Doug. *The Politics of Authenticity: Liberalism, Christianity, and the New Left in America*. New York: Columbia University Press, 1998.

———. *Visions of Progress: The Left Liberal Tradition in America*. Philadelphia: University of Pennsylvania Press, 2007.

Roth, Nina. "The Neoconservative Backlash against Feminism in the 1970s and 1980s: The Case of *Commentary*." In *Consumption and American Culture*, edited by David E. Nye and Carl Pedersen. Amsterdam: VU University Press, 1990.

Rubin, Joan Shelley. "The Genteel Tradition at Large." *Raritan* 25, no. 3 (Winter 2006).

Sarna, Jonathan. *American Judaism: A History*. New Haven, CT: Yale University Press, 2004.

Saunders, Francis Stonor. *Who Paid the Piper?: CIA and the Cultural Cold War*. London: Granta Books, 1999.

Schneir, Walter, and Miriam Schneir. *Invitation to an Inquest*. New York: Pantheon Books, 1983.

Schultz, Kevin. *Buckley and Mailer: The Difficult Friendship That Shaped the Sixties*. New York: Norton, 2015.

———. *Tri-Faith America: How Catholics and Jews Held Postwar America to Its Protestant Promise*. New York: Oxford University Press, 2011.

Schrecker, Ellen. *The Age of McCarthyism: A Brief History with Documents*. 2nd ed. Boston: Bedford/St. Martin's, 2002.

———. *Many Are the Crimes: McCarthyism in America*. Princeton, NJ: Princeton University Press, 1999.

Scott, Joan. "Gender: A Useful Category of Historical Analysis." *American Historical Review* 91, no. 5 (December 1986): 1053–75.

Sebba, Anne. *Ethel Rosenberg: An American Tragedy*. New York: St. Martin's Press, 2021.

Self, Robert. *All in the Family: The Realignment of American Democracy since the 1960s*. New York: Hill and Wang, 2012.

———. *All in the Family: Single Mothers and the History of the Family*. Cambridge, MA: Harvard University Press, 1998.

Sherry, Michael. *Gay Artists in Modern American Culture: An Imagined Conspiracy*. Chapel Hill: University of North Carolina Press, 2007.

Silver, Mike. "Boxing in Olde New York." In *New York Sports: Glamour and Grit in the Empire City*, edited by Stephen Norwood. Fayetteville: University of Arkansas Press, 2018.

Singal, Daniel. *The War Within: Victorian to Modernist Culture in the South*. Chapel Hill: University of North Carolina Press, 1982.

Sinkoff, Nancy. *From Left to Right: Lucy S. Dawidowicz, the New York Intellectuals, and the Politics of Jewish History*. Detroit: Wayne State University Press, 2020.

Slotkin, Richard. *Gunfighter Nation: Myth of the Frontier in the Twentieth Century*. Norman: University of Oklahoma Press, 1998.

Sorin, Gerald. *Irving Howe: A Life of Passionate Dissent*. New York: New York University Press, 2003.

———. "Irving Howe's 'Margin of Hope.'" *American Jewish History* 88, no. 4 (December 2000): 475–94.

———. *A Time for Building: The Third Migration, 1880–1920*. Baltimore: Johns Hopkins University Press, 1992.

Spruill, Marjorie J. "Gender and America's Right Turn." In *Rightward Bound: Making America Conservative in the 1970s*, edited by Bruce J. Schulman and Julian E. Zelizer. Cambridge, MA: Harvard University Press, 2008.

Stahl, Jason. *Right Moves: The Conservative Think Tank in American Political Culture since 1945*. Chapel Hill: University of North Carolina Press, 2016.

Stahl, Ronit. *Enlisting Faith: How the Military Chaplaincy Shaped Religion and State in Modern America*. Cambridge, MA: Harvard University Press, 2017.

Stansell, Christine. *American Moderns: Bohemian New York and the Creation of a New Century*, rev. ed. Princeton, NJ: Princeton University Press, 2009.

Starr, Paul, and Julian Zelzer, eds. *Defining the Age: Daniel Bell, His Times and Ours*. New York: Columbia University Press, 2022.

Staub, Michael E. *Torn at the Roots: The Crisis of Jewish Liberalism in Postwar America*. New York: Columbia University Press, 2004.

Steinberg, Stephen. *The Academic Melting Pot: Catholics and Jews in American Higher Education*. New Brunswick, NJ: Transaction Books, 1977.

Steinfels, Peter. *The Neoconservatives: The Men Who Are Changing American Politics*. New York: Simon and Schuster, 1979.

Strauss, Lauren B. "Staying Afloat in the Melting Pot: Constructing an American Jewish Identity in the *Menorah Journal* of the 1920s." *American Jewish History* 84 (1996): 315–31.

Sumner, Gregory D. *Dwight Macdonald and the Politics Circle: The Challenge of Cosmopolitan Democracy*. Ithaca, NY: Cornell University Press, 1996.

Svonkin, Stuart. *Jews against Prejudice: American Jews and the Fight for Civil Liberties*. New York: Columbia University Press, 1999.

Swan, Patrick, ed. *Hiss, Whittaker, Chambers, and the American Soul.* Wilmington, DE: Intercollegiate Studies Institute, 2003.

Tanenhaus, Sam. *Whittaker Chambers: A Biography.* New York: Modern Library, 1998.

Taranto, Stacie. *Kitchen Table Politics: Conservative Women and Family Values in New York.* Philadelphia: University of Pennsylvania Press, 2017.

Teres, Harvey. *Renewing the Left: Politics, Imagination, and the New York Intellectuals.* New York: Oxford University Press, 1996.

Trotter, Joe William, Jr., ed. *The Great Migration in Historical Perspective.* Bloomington: Indiana University Press, 1991.

Turk, Katherine. *Equality on Trial: Gender and Rights in the Modern Workplace.* Philadelphia: University of Pennsylvania Press, 2016.

Tyson, Tim. *Radio Free Dixie: Robert F. Williams and the Roots of Black Power.* Chapel Hill: University of North Carolina Press, 2000.

Vaïsse, Justin. *Neoconservatism: The Biography of a Movement.* Cambridge, MA: Belknap Press of Harvard University Press, 2010.

Van Nort, Sydney C. *The City College of New York.* Dover, NH: Arcadia, 2007.

Velasco, Jesus. *Neoconservatives in U.S. Foreign Policy under Ronald Reagan and George W. Bush.* Baltimore: Johns Hopkins University Press, 2010.

Wald, Alan M. *The New York Intellectuals: The Rise and Decline of the Anti-Stalinist Left from the 1930s to the 1980s.* Chapel Hill: University of North Carolina Press, 1987.

Weinberg, Sidney Stahl. "The World of Our Fathers and the World of Our Mothers." *American Jewish History* 88, no. 4 (December 2000): 547–56.

Weinfeld, David. *An American Friendship: Horace Kallen, Alain Locke, and the Development of Cultural Pluralism.* Ithaca, NY: Cornell University Press, 2022.

Wenger, Beth. "Constructing Manhood in American Jewish Culture." In *Gender and Jewish History*, edited by Marion A. Kaplan and Deborah Dash Moore. Bloomington: Indiana University Press, 2011.

———. *New York Jews and the Great Depression: Uncertain Promise.* New Haven, CT: Yale University Press, 1996.

Weissbroad, Rachel. "*Exodus* as Zionist Melodrama." *Israeli Studies* 4, no. 1 (Spring 1999).

Wheatland, Thomas. *The Frankfurt School in Exile.* Minneapolis: University of Minnesota Press, 2009.

Whitfield, Stephen J. *The Culture of the Cold War*, rev. ed. Baltimore: Johns Hopkins University Press, 1996.

———. *Learning on the Left: Political Profiles of Brandeis.* Waltham, MA: Brandeis University Press, 2002.

———. *Voices of Jacob, Hands of Esau: Jews in American Life and Thought.* Hamden, CT: Archon Books, 1984.

Wilford, Hugh. *The CIA, the British Left, and the Cold War: Calling the Tune?* London: Routledge, 2003.

———. *The Mighty Wurlitzer: How the CIA Played America.* Cambridge, MA: Harvard University Press, 2008.

———. *The New York Intellectuals: From Vanguard to Institution.* Manchester: Manchester University Press, 1995.

Wise, Ruth R. "The Maturing of Commentary and of the Jewish Intellectual." *Jewish Social Studies* 3 (Winter 1997): 29–41.

Wreszin, Michael. *The Life and Politics of Dwight Macdonald.* New York: Basic Books, 1994.

Wreszin, Michael, ed. *A Moral Temper: The Letters of Dwight Macdonald.* Chicago: Ivan R. Dee, 2001.

Young, Neil J. *We Gather Together: The Religious Right and the Problem of Interfaith Politics.* New York: Oxford University Press, 2016.

Young-Bruehl, Elisabeth. *Hannah Arendt: For Love of the World.* New Haven, CT: Yale University Press, 1982.

Zaretsky, Eli. *Secrets of the Soul: A Social and Cultural History of Psychoanalysis.* New York: Vintage, 2005.

Selected Memoirs and Primary Source Collections

Abel, Lionel. *The Intellectual Follies: A Memoir of the Literary Venture in New York and Paris.* New York: Norton, 1984.

Arendt, Hannah. *Hannah Arendt: The Last Interview and Other Conversations.* Brooklyn: Melville, 2013.

Barrett, William. *The Truants: Adventures among the Intellectuals.* Garden City, NY: Anchor Books, 1983.

Bell, Daniel. *The Winding Passage: Sociological Essays and Journeys.* Rev. ed. New Brunswick, NJ: Transaction, 1991.

Bell, Daniel, ed. *The Radical Right: The New American Right, Expanded and Updated.* Garden City, NY: Doubleday, 1963.

Birstein, Ann. *What I Saw at the Fair: An Autobiography.* New York: Open Road Distribution, 2003.

Cohen, Elliot E., ed. *Commentary on the American Scene.* New York: Knopf, 1953.

Decter, Midge. *Liberal Children, Radical Parents.* New York: Coward McCann Geoghegan, 1975.

———. *The Liberated Woman and Other Americans.* New York: Coward, McCann Geoghegan, 1971.

———. *New Chastity and Other Arguments against Women's Liberation.* New York: Coward McCann Geoghegan, 1971.

———. *An Old Wife's Tale: My Seven Decades in Love and War.* New York: Reagan Books, 2001.

Dickstein, Morris. *Why Not Say What Happened: A Sentimental Education.* New York: Liveright, 2015.

Feuer, Lewis S. *The Conflict of Generations: The Character and Significance of Student Movements.* New York: Basic Books, 1969.

Friedan, Betty. *The Feminine Mystique,* rev. ed. New York: W. W. Norton, 1997.

Halper, Albert. *Good-Bye, Union Square: A Writer's Memoir of the Thirties.* Chicago: Quadrangle Books, 1970.

Hook, Sidney. *Out of Step: An Unequal Life in the 20th Century.* Cambridge: Harper and Row, 1987.

Howe, Irving. *The Critical Points: On Literature and Culture*. New York: Horizon, 1973.

———. *A Margin of Hope: An Intellectual Biography*. San Diego: Harcourt, 1983.

———. "The New York Intellectuals: A Chronicle and a Critique." *Commentary* 45, no. 4 (October 1968).

———. "Range of the New York Intellectuals." In *Creators and Disturbers: Reminiscences by Jewish New Intellectuals of New York*, edited by Bernard Rosenberg and Ernest Goldstein. New York: Columbia University Press, 1982.

———. *Steady Work: Essays in the Politics of Democratic Radicalism, 1963–1986*. New York: Harcourt, Brace and World, 1967.

———. *World of Our Fathers*. New York: Harcourt Brace Jovanovich, 1976.

Howe, Irving, ed. *Beyond the New Left*. New York: McCall Publishing, 1970.

———. *25 Years of Dissent: An American Tradition*. New York: Methuen, 1979.

Howe, Nina, ed. *A Voice Still Heard: Selected Essays of Irving Howe*. New Haven, CT: Yale University Press, 2014.

Kazin, Alfred. *New York Jew*. New York: Knopf, 1978.

———. *Starting Out in the Thirties*. New York: Little Brown, 1965.

———. *A Walker in the City*. New York: Harcourt and Brace, 1951.

Kempton, Murray. *Part of Our Time: Some Ruins and Monuments of the Thirties*, rev. ed. New York: Modern Library, 1998.

Klein, Alexander, ed. *Dissent, Power, and Confrontation: Theater for Ideas/Discussion 1*. New York: McGraw Hill, 1971.

Kristol, Irving. "Memoirs of Trotskyist." In *Reflections of a Neoconservative: Looking Back, Looking Ahead*. New York: Basic Books, 1983.

———. *Neoconservatism: The Autobiography of an Idea*. Chicago: Ivan R. Dee, 1995.

McCarthy, Mary. *Intellectual Memoirs: New York, 1936–1938*. New York: Mariner, 1993.

Morris, Willie. *New York Days*. Boston: Little, Brown, 1993.

Newfield, Jack. *The Prophetic Minority*. New York: Signet Books, 1966.

Phillips, William. *A Partisan View: Five Decades of the Literary Life*. New York: Stein and Day, 1983.

Podhoretz, Norman. *Breaking Ranks: A Political Memoir*. New York: Harper and Row, 1979.

———. *Doing and Undoings: The Fifties and After in American Writing*. New York: Farrar, Straus, 1964.

———. *Ex-Friends: Falling Out with Allen Ginsburg, Lionel and Diana Trilling, Lillian Hellman, Hannah Arendt, and Norman Mailer*. New York: Free Press, 1999.

———. *Making It*, rev. ed. New York: Harper Collins, 1980.

Powell, Walter W., and Richard Robbins, eds. *Conflicts and Consensus: A Festschrift in Honor of Lewis Coser*. New York: Free Press, 1984.

Rieff, David, ed. *Susan Sontag: On Women*. New York: Picador, 2023.

Rosenberg, Bernard, and Ernest Goldstein, eds. *Creators and Disturbers: Reminiscences by Jewish Intellectuals of New York*. New York: Columbia University Press, 1982.

Rosenfield, Leonora Cohen. *Portrait of a Philosopher: Morris R. Cohen in Life and Letters*. San Diego: Harcourt, Brace, and World, 1962.

Schlesinger, Arthur, Jr. *A Life in the Twentieth Century: Innocent Beginnings, 1917–1950*. Boston: Houghton Mifflin, 2000.

Slesinger, Tess. *The Unpossessed*, rev. ed. New York: New York Review of Books, Classics, 2002.

Towns, Jeff, ed. *A Pearl of Great Price: The Love Letters of Dylan Thomas to Pearl Kazin Bell*. Cardigan: Parthian, 2014.

Trilling, Diana. *The Beginning of the Journey: The Marriage of Diana and Lionel Trilling*. San Diego: Harcourt Brace, 1993.

——. *Claremont Essays*. New York: Harcourt, Brace, and World, 1964.

——. *Mrs. Harris: Death of a Scarsdale Diet Doctor*. New York: Harcourt Brace Jovanovich, 1981.

——. *We Must March My Darlings*. New York: Harcourt Brace Jovanovich 1977.

Warshow, Robert. *The Immediate Experience*, rev. ed. Cambridge, MA: Harvard University Press, 2002.

INDEX

Abel, Lionel, 11, 12, 23, 98, 254; on Mary McCarthy, 52; middle-class childhood of, 27; *Partisan Review* and, 54

Abel, Sherry, 98, 183–84, 238

abortion, 207

Abrams, Elliott, 273

Abrams, Nathan, 98, 99, 257, 260

Acheson, Dean, 104, 107

Adventures of Augie March, The (Beller), 236

Advertisements of Myself (Mailer), 165

Afghanistan, 269

African Americans, 232, 233, 234, 249–53

Allen, Woody, 8

Allure, 279

Al Qaeda, 269

Alter, Robert, 68, 264–65

America Day by Day (Beauvoir), 86, 88

American Committee for Cultural Freedom (ACCF), 103, 112; anti-communism and, 115–22; Diana Trilling and, 81–91, 118; first meeting of, 117–18; resignations from, 121

American Communist Party: A Critical History, The (L. Coser and Howe), 154

American exceptionalism, 24

American Hebrew, 33

American Jewish Committee (AJC), 94, 109, 110–11, 130, 238–39, 246, 260

American Marriage (Cavan), 207

American Psychiatric Association, 223

Americans for Democratic Action (ADA), 115

Annie Hall (Allen), 8

anti-communism, 10–11, 81–82; American Committee for Cultural Freedom (ACCF) and, 86–91, 115–22; *Commentary* and, 94–95, 103–15; Diana Trilling and, 81–82, 84–86, 91; Elliot Cohen and, 103; Jewish masculinity and, 109–15; Joseph McCarthy and, 84–85, 87–88, 107, 109, 114–15, 122; New Left and, 153–54; replaced by War on Terror, 271; Rosenberg case and, 42, 108–14. *See also* Cold War era

Anti-Defamation League (ADL), 95

anti-Semitism, 23–24, 25, 46–47, 64, 95, 107–8, 129; in the academy, 134; communism and, 110–11; of the Old Right, 228

anti-Stalinism, 11, 41–42, 50, 82, 123; American Committee for Cultural Freedom (ACCF) and, 86–87, 118–19; of *Partisan Review*, 51, 83

Arendt, Hannah, 12, 15, 16, 56–57, 59, 189; Diana Trilling and, 183; *Dissent* and, 144–45; *Eichmann in Jerusalem*, 180, 244, 245, 253–55; embodiment of secular Jewish masculinity by, 25; feminism and, 167, 177; on *The Group*, 179–80; on Israel, 264; Norman Podhoretz on, 244–45; "Under Forty: A Symposium on American Literature and the Younger Generation of American Jews" and, 96

Armies of the Night, The (Mailer), 212

Armitage, Richard, 271

Arnold, Matthew, 67

Aronowitz, Al, 234

Ashkenazi Jews, 4, 138–39, 259

Atkinson, Ti-Grace, 163

Atlantic, 256

Auden, W. H., 87

Austen, Jane, 4

Balanchine, George, 87

Baldwin, James, 12, 167, 227; American Committee for Cultural Freedom (ACCF) and, 87; Norman Podhoretz and, 249–51

Barkan, Joanne, 144, 147

Barrett, William, 12, 55, 56–57, 59, 169, 181

baseball, 36

basketball, 35–36

Bazelon, David, 12; "Under Forty: A Symposium on American Literature and the Younger Generation of American Jews" and, 96

Beats, 240–43